EUROPE'S GLOBAL ROLE

Europe's Global Role
External Policies of the European Union

Edited by

JAN ORBIE
Ghent University, Belgium

ASHGATE

Published by
Ashgate Publishing Limited
Gower House
Croft Road
Aldershot
Hampshire GU11 3HR
England

Ashgate Publishing Company
Suite 420
101 Cherry Street
Burlington, VT 05401-4405
USA

Ashgate website: http://www.ashgate.com

British Library Cataloguing in Publication Data
Europe's global role : external policies of the European
  Union
  1. European Union - Foreign relations 2. European Union -
  Foreign economic relations
  I. Orbie, Jan, 1978-
  327.4

Library of Congress Cataloging-in-Publication Data
Europe's global role : external policies of the European Union / [edited by] Jan Orbie.
    p. cm.
  Includes index.
  ISBN: 978-0-7546-7220-3
  1. Europe--Foreign relations. 2. European Union. I. Orbie, Jan, 1978-
  JZ1570.E934 2008
  341.242'2--dc22

2007031219

ISBN: 978-0-7546-7220-3

Printed and bound in Great Britain by MPG Books Ltd, Bodmin, Cornwall.

Contents

List of Boxes, Figures and Tables

Boxes

Figures

Tables

List of Contributors

Andrei V. Belyi is a Research Fellow at the Centre for Energy Studies at the Institute of World Economy and International Relations (IMEMO, Moscow) and specialises in the political and legal aspects of the international energy trade. He is an associate professor and vice chair of the forum on political issues of international energy at the Faculty of World Economy and International Relations of the State University – Higher School of Economics.

Eline De Ridder is Research Assistant of the Fund for Scientific Research – Flanders (Ghent University, Belgium), focusing on Europeanisation and democratic consolidation in the Czech and Slovak Republics.

Viktoriya Khasson holds a Masters degree in Interdisciplinary European Studies from the College of Europe (Natolin, Poland) and has worked at the Centre for European Policy Studies (CEPS). Her research areas are European neighbourhood policy, countries of the post-Soviet space and regional cooperation.

Tonia Novitz is a Reader at the University of Bristol (UK). In 1998 she completed her doctorate on 'International Protection of the Right to Strike' at Balliol College, Oxford. She was a visiting fellow at the International Institute for Labour Studies in 1999, attached to the ILO (Geneva) and during 2001/02 she was a Jean Monnet Fellow and a Marie Curie Fellow at the EUI (Florence). She has written on international labour standards and on the external role of the EU in this domain.

Jan Orbie is a Professor at the Centre for EU Studies (Ghent University, Belgium). He is co-editor of a book entitled *EU Trade Politics and Development: Everything but Arms Unravelled* (Routledge, 2007). His research focuses on EU trade and development politics and on Europe's role in the social dimension of globalisation.

An Schrijvers is a post-doctoral researcher at the Centre for EU Studies (Ghent University, Belgium). Her research deals with the EU accession process of Poland with special attention on the Europeanisation effects on the Polish polity and politics.

Steven Sterkx obtained his PhD from the Department of Politics of the University of Antwerp (Belgium), examining the external aspects of EU asylum and migration policy from a discourse-analytical perspective. He also worked as a Teaching Fellow in the European Master's Programme on Human Rights and Democratisation (Venice, Italy).

Edith Vanden Brande is Assistant at the Centre for EU Studies (Ghent University, Belgium). Her research focuses on the EU as a leader in international environmental politics.

Syuzanna Vasilyan researches the political dynamics behind the EU's policy of regional cooperation towards the South Caucasus at the Centre for EU Studies (Ghent University, Belgium). She gained practical experience on EU external relations at the Armenian Embassy in Washington, DC, the Committee of Ministers of the Council of Europe in Strasbourg, a Brussels-based consultancy called The Centre and the European Parliament.

Helen Versluys is a researcher at the Centre for EU Studies (Ghent University, Belgium), focusing on the EU's humanitarian aid policies. During her internship at the European Parliament she closely followed the work of the EP Foreign Affairs Committee.

Hendrik Vos is a Professor at the Department of Political Science and Director of the Centre for EU Studies (Ghent University, Belgium).

Angela Wigger is Assistant Professor International Relations at the Radboud University in Nijmegen (The Netherlands). Her research area covers the recent transformation of competition rules and practices at the EU, with particular attention on Europe's international conduct in the domain of competition.

List of Abbreviations

AA	Association Agreement
ACP	Africa Caribbean and Pacific Group
AFSJ	Area of Freedom, Security and Justice
CAMLR	Convention on Artic Marine Living Resources
CAP	common agricultural policy
CC	candidate country
CCP	Common Commercial Policy
CDM	Clean Development Mechanism
CEACR	ILO Committee of Experts on the Application of Conventions and Recommendations
CEE	Central and Eastern Europe
CEECs	Central and Eastern European Countries
CFA	ILO Governing Body Committee on Freedom of Association
CFI	Court of First Instance
CFSP	Common Foreign and Security Policy
CITES	Convention on International Trade in Endangered Species of Wild Fauna and Flora
CLS	Core labour standards
COP	Conference of the Parties
CPE	Civilian Power Europe
CPM	Civil Protection Mechanism
CSP	Country Strategy Paper
CU	Customs Union
DAC	Development Assistance Committee
DCI	Development Cooperation Instrument
DG	Directorates-General
DoJ	Department of Justice
DSM	Dispute Settlement Mechanism
EAP	Environmental Action Programme
EBA	Everything But Arms
EBRD	European Bank for Reconstruction and Development
EC	European Community
ECN	European Competition Network
ECO	European Coal Organisation
ECJ	European Court of Justice
EDF	European Development Fund
EEC	European Economic Community
EES	European Employment Strategy
ENP	European Neighbourhood Policy
EP	European Parliament

ERT	European Round Table of Industrialists
ESDP	European Security and Defence Policy
ETUC	European Trade Union Confederation
EUETS	European Union Emissions Trading Scheme
FPA	Foreign Policy Analysis
FSU	Former Soviet Union
FTC	Federal Trade Commission
GAC	General Affairs Council
GATT	General Agreement on Tariffs and Trade
GCC	Gulf Cooperation Council
GHD	Good Humanitarian Donorship
GHG	Greenhouse gases
GSP	Generalised System of Preferences
HLWG	High-Level Working Group on Asylum and Migration
ICN	International Competition Network
ILC	International Labour Conference
ILO	International Labour Organisation
IMF	International Monetary Fund
JHA	Justice and home affairs
LDC	Least developed country
LIC	Low-income country
LRRD	Linkage between relief, rehabilitation and development
M&As	Mergers and Acquisitions
MCA	Millennium Challenge Account
MCC	Millennium Challenge Corporation
MDGs	Millennium Development Goals
MIC	Medium-income country
MFN	Most-Favoured Nations
MRA	Mutual Recognition Agreement
NAMA	Non-agricultural market access
NATO	North Atlantic Treaty Organisation
NCAs	National competition authorities
OECD	Organisation for Economic Cooperation and Development
OSCE	Organisation for Security and Cooperation in Europe
PCA	Partnership and Cooperation Agreement
PCD	Policy Coherence for Development
QMV	Qualified Majority Voting
REACH	Regulation on the registration, evaluation, and authorisation of chemicals
REIO	Regional Economic Integration Organisation
RRF	Rapid Reaction Force
RRM	Rapid Reaction Mechanism
SAICM	Strategic Approach on International Chemicals Management
SCM	Subsidies and Countervailing Measures
SEA	Single European Act
TABD	Transatlantic Business Dialogue

TAC	Total allowable catch
TCN	Third-country national
TNCs	Transnational Companies
TEC	Treaty Establishing the European Community
TEU	Treaty of the European Union
TNC	Transnationally operating companies
ToA	Treaty of Amsterdam
UN	United Nations
UNEP	United Nations Environment Programme
UNHCR	United Nations High Commissioner for Refugees
UNICE	Union of Industrial and Employers' Confederation of Europe
WEU	Western European Union
WTO	World Trade Organisation

Preface

Interest in Europe's global role has increased sharply in recent years, both among policy-makers and academics. This book aims to contribute to the debate and the literature, focusing on those external policies where the European Union is potentially and prima facie a powerful actor. More specifically, the contributions examine the Union's international role in 'first pillar' domains such as trade, development, humanitarian aid, environment, energy, competition, social issues, and asylum and migration. Europe's influence in the 'near abroad' by means of its enlargement and neighbourhood policies is also considered.

The EU is arguably an important international actor in these 'civilian' domains. But the extent of the Union's power in these areas, as well as Europe's successfulness as regards reaching the objectives that are pursued through these external policies, remain to be examined. This book aims to take a step in this direction by systematically analysing the EU's means of power as well as its pursued goals. This should also enable a critical and well-founded evaluation of the Union's role on the international scene.

Another objective of the book at hand is to present a comprehensive overview of the EU's external relations, paying particular attention to those areas that are often overlooked in textbooks on EU foreign policy, but which nevertheless form vital dimensions of the Union's putative 'civilian power' image. From this perspective, the means-end distinction throughout the chapters creates a pragmatic toolkit with which to structure an increasingly complex area of research. Hopefully, the publication will thus prove useful reading for all students and scholars who are interested in Europe's global role.

The idea behind this book originated from the Centre for EU Studies, which was established within the Department of Political Science at Ghent University (Belgium) in 2005.

One main area of research at the Centre is the 'soft' dimension of Europe's international policies. This publication, which also involves scholars from other universities, is one of the first outcomes of this new line of research. A special note of thanks goes to Prof. Hendrik Vos, Director of the Centre for EU Studies, for his encouragement during this research project.

I also owe special thanks to an external reviewer commissioned by Ashgate, and to Kirstin Howgate, Margaret Younger and Pauline Beavers for their support and efficient handling of the manuscript. In addition, I would like to thank Cecilia Fitch for the careful language editing and the students on my Master's degree in European External Policies course for their critical and constructive comments. Above all, I am very grateful to the contributors for their diligence in meeting the tough deadlines and, more importantly, for their motivating enthusiasm for this project. I am confident that this book has laid the foundations for further political science research on Europe's global role at the Centre for EU Studies in the years to come.

Jan Orbie
Ghent University, Belgium

Chapter 1

A Civilian Power in the World? Instruments and Objectives in European Union External Policies

Jan Orbie

'What is Europe's role in this changed world?' Since the European Council asked this question in the 2001 Laeken Declaration, the topic of Europe's global role has become more and more relevant. Policy-makers as well as academics have engaged extensively in debates on the potential and/or desirable contribution of the European Union (EU)[1] to new international challenges that have arisen since September 11 and the new security agenda, the increased salience of climate change and energy dependency, the changing power relations on the international trade front, the enduring development problems in the poorest countries, and the adverse consequence of globalisation in general.[2] Apparently, the widespread malaise in intra-EU politics which has emerged since the referenda on the Constitutional Treaty in France and the Netherlands in 2005, has only served to increase the interest in the Union's international activities.

The contributions to this book analyse Europe's global role, with a particular focus on its various 'first pillar'[3] external policies such as trade, development, humanitarian aid, environment, energy, competition, social issues, and asylum and migration. It also looks at Europe's role in the 'near abroad' through enlargement and neighbourhood policies. The EU is arguably an important international actor in these 'low politics' or 'civilian' domains. But the degree of the Union's power in these areas, as well as Europe's successfulness in reaching the objectives that

---

1   Throughout the book the terms 'European Union' (EU), 'Union' or 'Europe' are used interchangeably, whereas 'European Community' (EC) is only used when referring specifically to the historical (pre-Maastricht era) or legal (first pillar) dimensions.

2   For excellent recent overviews of the EU's international policies, see Bretherton and Vogler (2006), Elgström and Smith (2006), Lucarelli and Manners (2006), Mayer and Vogt (2006), Hill and Smith (2005), and Marsh and Mackenstein (2005).

3   Since the Maastricht Treaty (Treaty on European Union, signed in 1992) the basic structure of the EU is divided in three 'pillars'. The first pillar can be seen as the successor of the economic community, where the 'Community method' prevails (initiative by Commission, qualified majority voting in the Council, approval by the European Parliament) notwithstanding several exceptions.

are pursued through these external policies, remain to be examined. This book aims to take a step in this direction.

The introductory chapter raises some conceptual issues that will reappear throughout the book, using the concept of the EU as a 'civilian power' in world politics as a leitmotiv. On the basis of the 'civilian power Europe' (CPE) literature, an analytical framework is suggested that will serve as the basis for the study of Europe's external policies in the subsequent chapters.[4] The main argument is that critical studies of Europe's world role should simultaneously consider its power resources and policy objectives. Finally, we will summarise the findings of each chapter and draw some general conclusions. But first, the question arises: why study the EU's global role?

Relevance of European Role Concepts

In the past decade, several role concepts for the EU have been advanced. Each of them suggests that the Union is, and has, a particular kind of power in the world. The idea of Europe as a civilian power underwent a renaissance (Whitman 2002; Telò 2006) but it was joined with other scenarios and ideal types such as a 'magnetic force' (Rosecrance 1998), a 'gentle power' (Padoa-Schioppa 2001), a 'normative power Europe' (Manners 2002), a 'European superpower' (McCormick 2007), a 'quiet superpower' (Moravcsik 2003), a 'Kantian paradise (Venus)' (Kagan 2004), a 'post-modern state' (Cooper 2003), a 'middle power' (Laatikainen 2006), a 'neo-medieval empire' (Zielonka 2006), and a 'responsible Europe' (Mayer and Vogt 2006).[5]

Studying EU role concepts is relevant for both descriptive and explanatory purposes. Most obviously, they constitute a pragmatic and convenient way to come to grips with the Union's international activities. A specific role concept can be assigned to Europe on the basis of the different features in its external relations. This exercise is especially relevant in the case of the EU which is widely considered as a novel and distinctive actor on the world scene. Role concepts have been elaborated for 'traditional' states (e.g. Le Prestre 1997), but classifying the Union's international position is all the more challenging, given its unique institutional nature. Typologies of roles shed light on its international distinctiveness as an 'unidentified political object'.

Besides this classification function, international roles have a broader relevance. As argued by constructivist scholars, the presence of role concepts in the minds of policy-makers may both affect and constrain their definition of interests, and thus shape their policy choices. Within a densely institutionalised environment like

---

4   An earlier and shorter version was published in Orbie (2006a).

5   See also Hill's (1993) earlier account of the 'capability-expectations gap', where existing and possible future European external roles (for example, managing world trade, principal voice in relations with the South, second western voice in international diplomacy, regional pacifier, bridge between rich and poor, mediator of conflicts) are also described.

the EU, such ideational dynamics may be all the more relevant (cf. Goldstein and Keohane 1995, 23–4). In line with the 'logic of appropriateness', the embeddedness of an 'appropriate' role concept indeed influences how the Union behaves in the world (cf. Harnisch and Maull 2001, 138, 150; Elgström and Smith 2006, 5).

The impact of role conceptions does not only stem from the Union's inter-subjective structure. Agency is also important, more specifically in the form of 'role entrepreneurs'. For example, actors may successfully argue that the EU should pursue ethical foreign policies, appealing to Europe's self-image as an actor which is built on principles of democracy and human rights. Such legitimisation in terms of EU role conceptions could influence external policy decisions, even if this runs counter to Europe's material interests.

Roles can also be used instrumentally to advance self-interested objectives. Schimmelfennig's (2003) notion of 'rhetorical action' – the strategic use of norm-based arguments – clarifies the interplay between constructivist and rationalist logics in explaining the relevance of roles. Questioning why the EU decided to expand to Central and Eastern Europe (CEE), he argues that Europe found itself 'rhetorically trapped' by those CEE and EU actors who could justify their interests on the grounds of the Union's self-image as a democratic and liberal community (see also Chapter 11). Sedelmeier (2006) has further elaborated on the relationship between Eastern enlargement and Europe's global role. He shows that EU 'enlargement policy practice' – for example, through political conditionality, discursive acts, and Treaty amendments – stimulated the formation of the Union's role as an international promoter of democracy and human rights.

Analysing the construction and interpretation of EU roles is also interesting because, in a sense, they reflect political preferences and power relations. For example, diverse readings of what exactly the civilian power idea means also reflect a discursive struggle about the desirability of military integration at the EU level. Larsen's (2002) discourse analysis points to both a majority and a minority vision among policy-makers on the interpretation of Europe's 'civilian' behaviour in world politics. As explained below, similar divisions characterise the scholarly work on CPE. The adoption of security and defence competences has not led to a role conflict within the EU, using instead a more flexible interpretation of the civilian power idea. Diez (2005, 614) also draws attention to the political relevance of role concepts in his second-order analysis of the power inherent in the representation of the EU as a normative power. This constructs a particular and non-reflexive self of the Union, against an image of others in the outside word. Again, this suggests a concurrence of academic and political agendas: depiction of the EU as a 'force for the good', in contrast with the US, is nearly consensual among European politicians.

This book pays great attention to discourses constructed by EU policy-makers as regards the Union's civilian or normative global role – for example, the EU as a force for the harnessing of globalisation (Chapter 2), as the most generous development donor (Chapter 3), as a leader in global environmental (Chapter 7) and competition issues (Chapter 8), as an exporter of the European social model (Chapter 6), and as the supporter of a comprehensive approach to asylum and migration (Chapter 5).

In this chapter we expand on the CPE concept. The primary reason for this focus is that the civilian power idea has been central in the political and academic debate about Europe's global role since it was launched by Duchêne in the 1970s. As stated by Nicolaïdis and Howse (2003, 344), it constitutes 'one of the main conceptual anchors for debate over the sources of EU influence in the world'. Second, CPE accounts emphasise Europe's comparative advantage in the 'low politics' dimensions of external relations. Duchêne's concept is often mentioned – but rarely elaborated on and applied – in the context of EU external economic relations (e.g. Holland 2002, 112; Schirm 1998, 76–7; Tsoukalis 2003, 192). Therefore, this book links the EU role literature with research on its international activities under first pillar policies. In the economic domain the Union's 'presence' on the international scene is most tangible and unified (Allen and Smith 1990). In short, we look at Europe's global role in those areas where it is potentially and *prima facie* a powerful actor.

Obviously, it is impossible to make a clear distinction from other aspects of Europe's international policies, including the Common Foreign and Security Policy (CFSP) and European Security and Defence Policy (ESDP). Issues on the coherence between the Union's external policies – and their possible securitisation since the development of a more fully-fledged foreign policy – will emerge in several chapters. The demarcation used in this book is rather pragmatic, focusing on those external areas that are usually not considered as 'high politics' in a country's international affairs, and that are understudied in the EU role literature, but that are nevertheless crucially important for Europe's global role.

Delving into the EU role literature, the next section will clarify the meaning of the CPE concept. Although the analysis shows that the civilian power perspective has strongly normative connotations, we will argue that that stimulates a critical analysis of Europe's global role. Not only does the civilian power debate involve a useful reconsideration of the implications of military integration in the EU, but the proposed CPE framework also allows for an examination of the Union's commitment to reach normative (or other) external policy goals.

Civilian Power Europe – After All

Duchêne among the Founding Fathers

Today, the early observation that it is difficult to find out what exactly the supporters of a civilian power have in mind (Everts 1974, 11) still applies. The CPE concept allows much flexibility (Hill 1990), it has 'multiple meanings' (Telò 2001, 250–51) and it 'is inherently complex and multidimensional, bundling several specific and distinctive role concept elements into a whole' (Harnisch and Maull 2001, 139). Although references to Duchêne's articles are pervasive in the literature on EU external relations, these only offer a short and descriptive account of Europe's possible role in the world. 'Duchêne never developed his vision into a detailed and comprehensive scheme' (Zielonka 1998, 226) and his CPE concept 'is most striking for the unsystematic manner in which it was advanced' (Whitman

1998, 11). Even the term 'civilian power Europe' is remarkably absent in the (sub) titles of his book chapters.[6] And notwithstanding the 'CPE renaissance' since the 1990s, Duchêne's most recent book[7] and commentaries[8] did not explicitly mention it.

One reason behind this apparent paradox is that the vagueness of the CPE scenario opens the door for different interpretations by policy-makers and academics. The enduring resonance of the CPE role is thus *because of*, rather than in spite of, the imprecise description by its founding father. Moreover, much detailed analytical work on this concept deals with the role of (West) Germany and hardly makes any reference to the EU (e.g. Harnisch and Maull 2001). In order to clarify the CPE ideal type, we first sketch its position vis-à-vis other foreign policy role concepts that have been applied to Europe since the 1970s. At the same time, the CPE concept is situated within its theoretical and historical context. In the next section, we elaborate on alternative role concepts that could be categorised *within* the pluralist school, which leads to a more precise outlining of the CPE ideal type.

Duchêne (1973; 1972) introduced the term civilian power to characterise (Western) Europe's position in the world.

> Europe would be the first major area of the Old World where the age-old process of war and indirect violence could be translated into something more in tune with the 20th-century citizen's notion of civilised politics. In such a context, Western Europe could in a sense be the first of the world's civilian centres of power. (Duchêne 1972, 43)

Although the 'founding father' of the CPE idea rejected any naïve notion of European superiority, he states that a united and 'civilian' Europe may be well placed to play a stabilising role on the world scene. Europeans are 'one of the most resolutely amilitary populations in the world' and the ongoing European integration process is in itself an example of how cooperation in low politics may have a stabilising influence. Europe does not need to become a military superpower, on the contrary: in an interdependent world the civilian means of power and influence are gaining currency. 'Lacking military power is not longer the handicap it once was' (1972, 47). 'The world is experiencing a 'sea change in the sources of power': the security policy of a state (including the superpowers) is oriented decreasingly towards security *sensu stricto*, and increasingly towards the promotion of a more favourable international environment. Duchêne (1973, 20) also states that Europe should promote social values that belong to its 'inner

---

6   The titles are respectively 'Europe's Role in World Peace' (Duchêne 1972) and 'The European Community and the Uncertainties of Interdependence' (Duchêne 1973). The 1973 article's subtitles are 'The Ambivalence of Europe', 'A European Super-power?', 'A neutral Community' and 'Europe as a process'. Only this last part describes the CPE idea.

7   Even the chapter on 'Europe in the World 1958–1979' (Duchêne 1994) makes no reference to the CPE concept.

8   E.g. 'Mars, Vénus et l'Olympe' (Commentaire, 100, 2003) and 'Quelle place pour l'Europe dans la politique mondiale?' (Commentaire, 95, 2001).

characteristics' ('equality, justice and tolerance' and an 'interest for the poor abroad').

This line of thinking broadly corresponds with the vision of Jean Monnet and the neo-functionalists on the merits of the European integration project. In fact, Duchêne collaborated closely with Jean Monnet in the 1950s and wrote the biography of 'the first statesman of interdependence'. Since the debacle of the European Defence Community in 1954, most European policy-makers had abandoned the idea of a strong politico-military dimension to the integration project. However, French President De Gaulle did advocate a *Europe puissance*, urging a strong and autonomous military capacity for the EC as a third power between the US and the Soviet Union. Duchêne's articles can be seen as a reaction to De Gaulle's view on Europe's world role. Mirroring the neo-functionalist critique on the federalist view that Europe should acquire state-like features in the political and military domain, Duchêne (1973, 13) warned against a 'collective nationalism ... which aims at a European super state', influenced by 'nostalgia and instinctive ambitions'. He stressed that the EC is about a different kind of power: it 'may be one of the five major powers of the 1970s, but if so 'major power' must not be identified with 'superpower' and Europe's leverage cannot be exerted along traditional lines'.

In the same period, Galtung (1973) also challenged the traditional view that conceptualises the EU as a state under construction. Although the EC may become a military superpower, he considered this as a hypothetical evolution that is actually beside the point. More importantly, he underlines the structural power of Europe through non-military means, especially in Eastern Europe and in the Third World. The European 'Common Market' is more than just a market; it is a 'superpower in the making'. Galtung saw European integration essentially as an international struggle for power, an attempt to restore the *'atimia'* (loss of status of the European continent) and to establish a Euro-centric world and a uni-centric Europe.

Europe derives its structural power, which is far more important than relational power, from its position in the structure of the world system, perpetuating an asymmetrical division of power between the 'centre' and the 'periphery'. European structural power includes three aspects: exploitation (unequal gains following interaction), fragmentation (a *divide et impera* policy of the centre towards the periphery), and penetration (the influence of the centre on the periphery's elite). Galtung applied these aspects of structural power to Europe's external policy and concludes that, in essence, the EC pursues 'old policies with new means' (a neo-colonial policy) towards the Third World. Former colonial powers are engaging in 'an effort to turn history backwards' on a European level. Europe's relationship with the US and other Western countries is characterised by equality and interdependence, as emphasised in Duchêne's work, but Galtung stresses that Europe maintains a strong dependency relationship with the South.

Unique to the EC as a superpower in the making is its 'non-military formula for empire-building'. Galtung considers the ever-expanding and deepening Community as a wolf in sheep's clothing. Precisely thanks to its non-military means, it manages not to be perceived as a classical superpower, which is to its advantage.

Box 1.1   A short period of high ambitions

The beginning of the 1970s proves to be a fascinating time for analysing Europe's international role. This turbulent period – as Duchêne (1973, 1) stated, 'the whole world system appears to be in flux' – coincides with growing scholarly attention and policy initiatives as regards the EC's global role. Both Duchêne and Galtung elaborate their visions on Europe's global role in 1972–73, providing alternative lines of thought to the realist and federalist viewpoints.

In December 1973 – also the year of US President Kissinger's 'Year of Europe' initiative – the nine European Ministers of Foreign Affairs formulated the 'Declaration on European Identity'. The new EPC mechanism had already been introduced in 1970, following The Hague Summit in 1969. The increased Europeanisation of foreign policies under the EPC, although still very modest, became clear in the EC activities within the CSCE conference that was launched in 1973. At the same time, the first enlargement with the United Kingdom (together with Ireland and Denmark) raised the Community's international profile. The first generation of cooperation agreements with the Southern and Eastern Mediterranean countries, signed in the 1970s, strengthened its clout towards the near neighbourhood. The 1973-75 negotiations on the Lomé Agreement, as well as the establishment of the first Generalised System of Preferences (GSP) in 1971, illustrate Europe's more global and ambitious approach to the international trade and development nexus (cf. Chapter 2). Europe's relations with the developing South were also extended from an exclusive focus on former African colonies to Asia and Latin America. The same period also showed increased European activities in international environmental policies (cf. Chapter 7 on the Paris Declaration).

The changing international climate sheds light on this European proactiveness: increased international interdependency, the oil crisis, growing assertiveness from the Third World, the first signs of declining US hegemonic power, and the détente. Internally, the EC had just finished the Treaty of Rome's main objective – the customs union. However, between the second Cold War and the completion of the internal market Europe's global ambitions faded away.

The civilian power idea lost its attractiveness in the 1980s, during the second Cold War, when 'high politics' received more attention, and realist conceptions à la *Europe puissance* became dominant. This decade saw the breaking of the security taboo and the abandonment of Europe's civilian power posture (Lodge 1993, 227, 231; Tsakaloyannis 1989, 242). Although the European Political

Cooperation (EPC) had started in the 1970s, the pursuits of a bigger political role for Europe in the world became more concrete.[9] In the academic field, the role of Europe in the world was increasingly evaluated through a Gaullist lens. Alternative conceptions, such as civilian power, were fiercely criticised, and the dominant way to analyse (read: criticise) European foreign policy was through the prism of a superstate after the example of the US.

In this context, the authoritative article by Bull (1982; see also Moïsi 1982), who argued that Duchêne's civilian power Europe is in fact a *contradictio in terminis*, is often cited. To the extent that the EC can be a civilian power, is thanks to the military protection of the US – an actor over whom the EC has no power. '"Europe" [that is, the nation states of Western Europe] is not an actor on the international scene, and does not seem likely to become one.' Bull neither urges for Atlanticism, nor for neutrality, but for an autonomous European defence, according to a European strategic vision, based on European interests and values. Such an evolution would be desirable, since Europe has different interests than the US, there is the continuous threat from the Soviet Union, and military independence could restore the European 'self respect'. Just like De Gaulle, he wanted Europe to be a third power, on a par with the US and the Soviet Union.

Such 'realist' opinions on European foreign policy as a failure with a dressing of rhetoric[10] – Hill states the 'Emperor has no clothes school' (Hill 1990, 49) – have become widely held since the 1980s. Bull's critique that it may be fine to be an economic giant, but nevertheless an autonomous European military capacity is indispensable, was 'uncritically accepted' and set the tone for a realist 'security paradigm' (Tsakaloyannis 1989, 245). But by the end of the 1990s the civilian power approach become dominant again, although the focus shifted from civilian means to normative ends.

Between a Scandinavian Europe and a European Trading State

These three early conceptualisations of Europe's world role reflect the classical schools in International Relations theory, pluralism, realism and structuralism respectively (cf. Whitman 1997). Until today, they represent the major visions on the EU's international role.

• For example, Duchêne's argument that the EU is a new kind of superpower – because its distinctive post-national and value-based political system which fits in well with the new situation of international interdependence – basically corresponds to the argument of Leonard (2005) and McCormick (2007). In

---

9   E.g. the 1981 London Report and the Genscher-Colombo initiative, and the 1986 incorporation of EPC in the Single European Act. The debate on a European Security and Defence Identity was stimulated and the 1985 Rome Declaration reactivated the 'sleeping' Western European Union (WEU).

10   See also Pijpers' (1988) realist account of the limits of a civilian power 'in an uncivil world'.

a sense, constructivist contributions and the normative power Europe school (NPE; see below) can be positioned in this tradition.

- Bull's critique on Europe's putative civilian power posture, through the lens of the *Europe puissance* ideal type, resonates through Kagan's characterisation of Europe as a 'post-modern paradise'. Kagan (2004) forcefully argues that the EU's military weakness explains why it holds a Kantian vision on international politics – in contrast with the US' Hobbesian position. Tensions between idealistic and self-serving motives remain a central theme in work on Europe's external relations (see e.g. Hyde-Price's (2006) neo-realist critique on NPE; and Chapter 9 on energy security).

- Galtung's analysis of the EU as a capitalist superpower largely reflects the view of critical scholars in international political economy who have emphasised the continuing dependency relationship between the EU and the Third World (for example, the neo-Gramscian perspective of Hurt 2003). For example, it might be applied to Europe's new trade agreements with developing countries (cf. Chapter 2) and to its global competition policies (cf. Chapter 8). Critique from historical materialists that constructivist analyses risk reproducing the pitfalls of idealism (cf. Van Apeldoorn et al. 2003, 30–32) echoes Galtung's vision on the positive representation of Europe as a civilian power.

Beyond this basic division, several new role concepts have been advanced since the 1990s. This section gives a short description of some pluralist role concepts, which also clarifies the contours of the CPE idea around the 'means' and 'ends' dimensions.

Scandinavian Europe: nice ideas, but no power   Looking at a world map using the Peters projection, Europe is only 'a small far-northern periphery', very much like the Nordic countries on a standard European map. Leaving aside this geographical metaphor, Therborn (2001, 1997) argues that Europe may (or should), in its quest for a role on the world scene, find some inspiration with the Scandinavian countries. He argues that although such an actor exercises no considerable power, it has some influence in the world. More specifically, a Scandinavian Europe would play an active role within international fora, promoting norms and values such as democracy, human rights, and sustainable development. Just like Duchêne, the author describes how Europe's internal experiences with social norms and supranational organisation may be a model for the rest of the world. Therborn (2002, 243) concludes that 'the best Europeans can hope for is to constitute a nice, decent periphery of the world, with little power but with some good ideas', but is uncertain whether the EU is going in this direction:

> There is a basis, in Europe's centrality in current global economic flows and in its long experience of trans-national normativity, for a European role as a 'power seeking to set globalization within a moral framework', as the Laeken Declaration put it. To what extent this basis, which is economic, normative, and institutional rather than political and military, will be actually used is an open question.

This scenario does not entirely correspond to what Duchêne envisaged: he argued that Europe should not become a 'neutral community', referring to the Scandinavian countries. According to Duchêne (1973, 14, 20), neutrality is only an option for smaller countries, but a larger group of countries such as the EC – a *'force'* for the international diffusion of civilian objectives – cannot stand aloof from bigger conflicts.

A great Switzerland scenario: rich and selfish   An additional distinction can be made between the 'idealistic' neutrality of the Scandinavian countries and the 'indifference' of a 'great Switzerland scenario' (Telò 2002). Moïsi (*De Standaard* 20 November 2002) fears that European politicians, contrary to their rhetoric, do not promote 'European values such as pluralism, reconciliation, humanism and tolerance' in the world, but rather 'dream of a continent such as a great Switzerland: rich, selfish, boring and essentially trivial'. Equally, Baker mentions the scenario of a 'Swissified Europe' in his *Financial Times* (17 October 2002) column. Referring to the German government's role in the Iraq debate, he argues that the EU may well become 'a neutral continent prosperous, peaceful, united – and utterly irrelevant to what is going in the world outside'. This scenario bears resemblance to the idea of a Fortress Europe as regards its external migration and asylum policies (Chapter 5).

Europe's magnetic force   Richard Rosecrance's (1998) characterisation of the EU as a 'magnetic force' resembles Therborn's Scandinavian scenario. Both conceptualisations are also complementary in that they stress the normative character of a European non-military foreign policy. But whilst Therborn is looking for this normative influence in the politico-diplomatic sphere, Rosecrance underlines the economic aspects of European foreign policy. Just like his previous work (cf. below), Rosecrance assumes that the economic power of an international actor – in this case the EU – renders a military policy redundant. What is more, by developing a European military capacity, other non-European actors are confronted with the security dilemma. They would increase their defence budgets to preserve the balance of power, which could initiate a military race.

An economic power such as the EU, however, reverses this logic. The Union functions as a magnetic force and the 'web of economic and political associations' that constitutes the Union attracts other countries. Thanks to the quasi-absence of a European foreign security policy, the security dilemma has been avoided. Rosecrance (1998, 20) stresses that the EU, as an 'exclusive club' with 'admission requirements', lays down norms to countries that feel attracted to the Union. 'It is perhaps a paradox that the continent which once ruled the world through the physical impositions of imperialism is now coming to set world standards in normative terms. There is perhaps a new form of European symbolic and institutional dominance even though the political form has entirely vanished.'

Recent EU enlargements, with neighbouring countries accepting the *acquis communautaire* as a condition to become a member of the 'EU club', seem to illustrate the bandwagon effect of the Union. From the perspective of the English School, Whitman (2002, 4) suggests that even countries without any prospect of membership are incorporating the EU's *acquis*. He talks about the 'structural power effect' of the Union over a group of non-Member States, including non-candidate countries which, nevertheless, 'self-identify with the common interests, and common values of the EU and accept common sets of rules in the relations with other members of the society'. But the question arises as to what extent Europe's Neighbourhood Policy will be effective in this respect (see Chapter 10).

A continental European trading state   The starting point of Rosecrance's description of 'trading states' is that the acquisition of territory has decreased in importance, while industrial countries increase their welfare through trade and investment. West Germany and Japan are obvious illustrations: after their military defeat they became trading states (Rosecrance 1986). Trading states are not only characterised by their very limited military power, but also by a strongly competitive economy. They are not a protectionist bloc (cf. Chapter 2 on the myth of a protectionist Fortress Europe), but have an open commercial policy in an interdependent world. In the 'trading world', relationships between countries imply a positive-sum game; the 'territorial world' leads to a zero-sum game between nations. Rosecrance admits that his dichotomy between the 'politico-military world' and the 'trading world' is simplifying: from a historical perspective, countries mainly find themselves in-between both sides, albeit they are usually closer to the first ideal type.[11] This implies that trading states also have some military capabilities, although this is undesirable. As for the external objectives, as described by Duchêne (1994, 388), in trading states 'economic interests are in the driving seat'.

Although Rosecrance states that not only West Germany and Japan, but also several other West European countries can be considered as trading states, he makes no explicit reference to the European Community *an sich* in his original work.[12] Telò describes a trading state scenario applied to the EU. Eastern enlargement may imply such an evolution, interrupting the 'traditional positive trade-off between widening and deepening'. This could lead to a 'continental trading state Europe', similar to the first decades of European integration and confirming the EU's image of an economic giant and political dwarf (Telò 2001, 256). More recently, Telò (2007, 214–18) has called this a 'neo-Atlantic, neo-liberal scenario', which is favoured by the Bush Administration in the US, technocratic groups, and transnational interest coalitions. For example, tension between trade-

---

11   Mid-nineteenth-century Great Britain (until the economic depression) came closest to the trading state ideal type.

12   Rosecrance attaches greater importance to the normative aspects of economic power in his 1998 'magnetic force' article than in his 1986 book on trading states, which partly reflects the evolution in FPA (see below). A similar observation goes for Maull's work: in 1990, he makes clear that a civilian power corresponds to a trading state (referring to Rosecrance's book and writing about 'the trading states Germany and Japan'), albeit with a less economic orientation, whereas a 1999 article explicitly differentiates between both concepts (Maul 1991; Maul 1999, 29).

related and normative objectives arises in Europe's external commercial, social and environmental policies (see Chapters 2, 6 and 7).

Good ideas and a powerful actor   This ideal typical overview shows considerable differences between pluralist EU role conceptions. Whereas the trading state emphasises economic power and hardly pays attention to a normative foreign policy, a Scandinavian Europe would concentrate on 'good ideas' and diplomatic initiatives. With a magnetic Europe, the normative aspect is embedded in the economic attraction of the European 'club'. Although the great Switzerland scenario differs from the two latter ideal types in that it has no normative aspirations, equally it has no considerable power on the world stage.

To summarise, two variables can be distinguished (Figure 1.1): whether or not the EU disposes of considerable power on the international scene, and whether normative objectives are prominent in the conduct of external relations. Although such ideal typical depictions may be oversimplifying,[13] this matrix sheds light on two key elements of the CPE concept. Such a depiction also makes clear that a non-military power Europe is not necessarily a civilian power Europe.

	Normative goals	**Interest-based goals**
Power –	Scandinavian Europe (political) European magnetic force (economic)	Great Switzerland
Power +	Civilian power Europe	Continental trading state

Figure 1.1   Means and ends: pluralist conceptions of Europe's world role

The CPE concept can indeed be seen as combining the normative dimension of the Scandinavian ideal type with the politico-economic power of the trading state. The subsequent sections develop the 'civilian means' (forms and sources of power) and 'civilian ends' ('external policy goals') dimensions of the civilian power ideal type.

CPE and Military Integration: A Contradiction in Terms?

Clearly, a European civilian power distinguishes itself in its vast arsenal of non-military policies, such as external trade relations, development and humanitarian aid, and international initiatives in the environmental and social areas. Europe's effectiveness through non-traditional external instruments is often stressed in relation to its neighbouring regions –in particular via enlargement processes – although the EU is arguably a civilian power on the world stage. Apart from the

---

13   It is, for example, difficult to imagine that Scandinavian countries would not use their economic power to conduct a foreign policy, or that West Germany's foreign policy has no normative dimension.

question whether Europe relies on these civilian external policy instruments out of necessity or stemming from a genuine attempt to transform traditional foreign policies – civilian power 'by default' or 'by design' (Stavridis 2001a) – there is a consensus that they constitute the main features of the CPE ideal type.

Although the influence of civilian means of power is less tangible than traditional foreign policy measures, and generally underestimated in the realist Foreign Policy Analysis (FPA) research (Keukeleire 2002), they are increasingly relevant for the EU's international influence. Moravcsik (*Newsweek* 17 June 2002) questions the Union's need for a 'hard' security policy, and castigates the common description of the EU as an 'economic giant but a political dwarf':

> This is misleading. Europeans already wield effective power over peace and war as great as that of the United States, but they do so quietly, through 'civilian power'. That does not lie in the deployment of battalions or bombers, but rather in the quiet promotion of democracy and development through trade, foreign aid and peacekeeping.

In addition to these 'soft' means of power, a CPE also distinguishes itself in the way that its international power is exerted. Although a civilian power does make use of the 'stick', for instance through economic or diplomatic sanctions, it generally favours using the 'carrot' (cf. Hill 1990, 44–5; Larsen 2002, 289). This implies a preference for incentives through development aid, market access, political dialogue, and persuasion in international affairs. Karen Smith's (2003, 199) research indicates that the distinctiveness of an EU identity is much stronger in terms of *the way* it pursues its objectives – relying on persuasion and positive incentives rather than coercion – than in these objectives themselves.

> What it does is less unique than how it does it. And [this] stems, to a great extent, from the special nature of the EU itself, namely the replacement of power politics with the rule of law between states, and a reconceptualisation of the practice of state sovereignty. The EU's foreign policy reflects the view that the imperatives of cooperation, and of compliance with international law and norms, limit the freedom of states to do whatever they wish domestically and externally.

The contributions to this book examine the nature and extent of the EU's power in these civilian external policies. But first we focus on the most controversial element of Europe's assumed civilian power status: the question of military integration. Is the Union's availability of military capabilities compatible with a civilian power role? If yes; what are the conditions under which European defence schemes can uphold a civilian role; if no, does military integration at the EU level necessarily lead to a *Europe puissance* scenario? What about the Petersberg Tasks[14] and military operations under a mandate of the United Nations (UN)?

---

14   These tasks were adopted at the Ministerial Council of the WEU in June 1992. They are an integral part of the ESDP and cover humanitarian and rescue tasks (cf. Chapter 4), peacekeeping tasks, and tasks of combat forces in crisis management, including peacemaking.

The debate can be divided into a majority and a minority view. The former suggests that military means are necessary, but emphasises that two conditions have to be fulfilled: (1) they can only be used as a last resort, when all other 'civilian instruments' have been deployed; and (2) they should be used to uphold 'civilian values' such as democracy and human rights, rather than serving geopolitical and economic interests (see e.g. Stavridis 2001a; Keukeleire 2002, 20; Telò 2007, 57; Schirm 1998; Lagendijk and Wiersma 2004, 96–110).[15] Some (e.g. Hill 1990, 42) also point out that Duchêne himself did not oppose European defence policy integration. Others emphasise that coercive military action by the EU fits in with the CPE role, as a last resort, provided that there is an explicit mandate from the UN Security Council (cf. Biscop 2003, 28–31).

The idea that military means can be embedded in a civilian power context is also dominant among EU policy-makers. Larsen's discourse analysis, based on Council documents and speeches, shows that the prevailing discourse continues to construct the EU as a civilian power. For example, the Union's High Representative Solana declared the following about the Petersberg tasks:

> We are not talking about collective defence. Nor are we talking about building a European army or 'militarising' the EU. But we cannot continue to publicly espouse values and principles while calling on others to defend them ... In the final analysis, as a last resort, after all possible instruments had been tried, the Union has to have the capacity to back up its policies by the use of military means. (Larsen 2002, 291)

A minority view among academics and policy-makers, however, suggests that European military integration repudiates Europe's (potential) identity as a civilian power – even if the emphasis remains on diplomatic and economic instruments. It would weaken the Union's credibility and capacity on the international scene and it might even entail a *Europe puissance*. Smith proposes a clear definition and argues that the mere possession of military instruments – even forces for peacekeeping and humanitarian missions, which are frequently considered 'civilian' instruments – precludes a civilian power label. They are still troops who are *also* trained to kill; and the Somalia case shows that they may turn into a war-fighting mission. Therefore, she concludes that 'civilian power EU is definitively dead', and that the EU has discredited its alternative and postmodern vision of international relations (2005, 76–7). In an earlier contribution (Smith 2000, 28) to the debate she had also ventured that:[16]

---

15   For a similar argument applied to West Germany, see Maull (1990). After Germany's participation in the Kosovo war in 1999 – *nota bene* without UN mandate – Germany was still considered as a civilian power because it used force in order to safeguard solidarity and the promotion of human rights (Maull 1999; Harnisch and Maull 2001).

16   Smith argued that European states could possibly cooperate on the subject of defence, but not in the EU connection. Alternative options are a complete separation of the EU and the West European Union, or the direct participation of EU members in UN missions.

the stated intention of enhancing the EU's military resources carries a price: it sends a signal that military force is still useful and necessary, and that it should be used to further the EU's interests. It would close off the path of fully embracing civilian power. And this means giving up far too much for far too little.

This civilian power debate has raised several arguments that warrant a critical perspective on the creation of defence instruments for the EU. First, military integration could entail a security dilemma – and thus an arms race with other countries. It would undo the Union's magnetic force – as described by Rosecrance – and restore the traditional balance of power logic between the EU and neighbouring regions. Even if EU policy-makers state that military means will only be used in the last resort and in function of normative objectives, European defence integration may arouse suspicion from non-EU countries. Ultimately, then, the question is to what extent the EU's commitment to play a civilian power role will be *perceived* as credible.

Second, it is argued that European defence schemes distract Europe's attention from its true comparative advantage in the economic and diplomatic domain (cf. Moravcsik in the *Financial Times* 3 April 2003; Zielonka 1998, 195–6, 226–9; Tsoukalis 2003, 199–200; Treacher 2004; Manners 2004, 17–20). The EU would forbear using its assets in the non-military sphere. In addition, the mere availability of defence capacities could increase the temptation for the EU to resort to military force – and to discard more sustainable possibilities.

The securitisation of EU external policies (see also Chapters 3, 4 and 5) would lead to a more reactive role, instead of pre-emptive and structural measures. A civilian power role is arguably based on desecuritisation: avoiding an issue becoming a security problem, rather than solving security problems (cf. Keukeleire 2002, referring to Ole Waever and the Copenhagen School). An often-heard metaphor of this logic is that 'if the only instrument you have is a hammer, all your problems start looking like nails'.

The creation of a military-industrial interest group at the EU level might be functional in this evolution. Ian Manners (2006, 191) refers to the 'military industrial simplex' to describe the coalition between the military-armaments lobby and the technology-industrial lobby at the EU level. He also points out that 'the limited equipment needs of the Rapid Reaction Force have been quickly expanded into a quantitatively different arms dynamic by the activism of a Brussels-based transnational policy network'.

Third, there is the argument of democracy, in relation to decisions about military action at the EU level. There are good reasons to delegate competences in areas such as external trade: even if input legitimacy proves to be more difficult, the EU is usually a more effective actor to deal with collective action problems and complex regulatory issues at the international level (cf. Chapter 2 on trade). But does output legitimacy also justify delegation in the military realm? Defence integration may well be a bridge too far from the perspective of democracy and national sovereignty.

Such considerations are all the more relevant because democratic input in foreign policy is sometimes seen as an essential characteristic of the civilian power role (cf. Smith 2005, 68). Wagner (2006) makes the point that the Europeanisation of defence leads to a democratic deficit because it weakens national parliaments' capacity to control executive decisions to use military force, and because neither the European Parliament nor the former assembly of the WEU are able to compensate this loss of parliamentary control. But he also adds that other dimensions of democracy besides parliamentary control of deployment decisions, such as transparency and openness of decision-making, may benefit from an EU defence policy.

Indeed, a look at the institutional structure of Europe's foreign and security policy somewhat qualifies the argument of a democratic deficit. Member States are clearly in the driving seat and have at their disposal a veto in important decisions. Given Europe's relatively open decision-making system – at least 27 national governments have to be involved, besides other actors – 'groupthink' is less likely to occur in EU foreign policy compared with more hierarchical decision-making systems. Similarly, Hazel Smith (2002, 271) suggests that 'the particular and unique nature of European Union foreign policy' – in particular, the visibility of its decision-making system – makes it difficult to 'engage in the worst types of foreign policy realpolitik'.

> Such actions require secrecy and activity by small groups of people who are protected from public scrutiny – often through claims that such clandestinity is in the national interest. In addition, the necessity for the Union to be accountable to and maintain support from 15 sets of public opinion and 15 governments and Parliaments and 15 sets of national media precludes any foreign policy activity that is not underpinned by a very broad level of public consensus. It is in the end the pressure of public opinion that tends to keep European Union foreign policy activity at least relatively 'clean'.

Thus, the EU's institutional features are linked with the influence of public opinion. This brings us to the final point, namely that the European public opinion would be 'one of the most resolutely amilitary populations in the world' (Duchêne 1972, 19). The argument is that Europeans are pacifistic because of their relatively recent experiences with two world wars. Moreover, the European integration project itself constitutes a reaction to the devastation of war-making.

Hopefully, the debate on the implications of Europe's defence capacities for its international role will continue in the coming years. The role of the CPE, and its divergent interpretations, induce us to reflect on the merits of military integration. Through its fuzziness and the inevitable definition discussions, it stimulates thinking on the added value of the EU as a state writ large. But besides theoretical arguments interlarded with anecdotal evidence, a more systematic study of EU discourse and policies would be useful. In his reconsideration of Europe's 'normative power' role, Manners (2006) gives an interesting impetus.

He argues that European military tasks may be consistent with a post-national normative power posture (cf. below) – under a UN mandate as part of a wider peace-building solution, and in a critically reflexive context. But his analysis shows that, instead, the EU has engaged in an 'unreflexive militarisation' since the 2003 European Security Strategy. Stimulated by a Brussels-based transnational policy network – what he calls the European military-industrial simplex – the Union's 'drive towards martial potency' has 'passed beyond the crossroads'. Looking at the short-term operation Artemis (Bunia, Democratic Republic of Congo) and the long-term operation EUFOR Althea (Bosnia and Herzegovina), Manners describes the EU's institutional prioritisation of short-term military responses over long-term civilian objectives of structural conflict prevention. In line with the concerns that were raised by Monnet and Duchêne, he warns that the seduction to become a great nineteenth-century power through militarisation will only replicate the problems of interstate politics. At the same time, this undermines the diffusion of Europe's normative objectives in the world.[17]

This book looks at Europe's global civilian power role from a different perspective. Although questions of securitisation and cross-pillarisation emerge in several chapters, we mainly focus on the EU's international activities under first-pillar domains. Derived from the civilian power literature, our analysis of the Union's world role is structured around the means-and-ends dimensions.

Linking Means and Ends: CPE as an Analytical Framework

More specifically, this approach simultaneously considers the Union's external policy instruments and its pursued objectives. Thereby we attempt to add to the existing literature on Europe's global role. On the one hand, the civilian power debate has mostly focused on the EU's power instruments, and more specifically on the question of military integration. Research then resolves around Europe's civilian and post-national versus state-like and defence instruments, as sketched above. Although (normative) objectives such as conflict prevention and sustainable development are included, these 'milieu goals'[18] are scarcely addressed and problematised in the civilian power literature. Stavridis (2001a) makes a similar point when he states that the 'normative' dimension of civilian power analyses has been overshadowed by the 'descriptive' dimension (see also Holden 2003). He quotes Duchêne's above-mentioned remarks that Europe 'must be a force for the international diffusion of civilian and democratic standards', promoting values that belong to its 'inner characteristics'. Stavridis' (2001b, 97–8, emphasis added) case study on the EU's putative civilian power approach policy towards Cyprus and Turkey illustrates the importance of civilian goals:

---

17   See also Diez's (2005) analysis on the tension between military and normative power – referring to the evolution of the US and potentially the EU, too.

18   The normative objectives of a CPE correspond to what Wolfers (1962) called 'milieu goals' – as against 'possession goals'. States pursuing milieu goals 'are out not to defend or increase possessions they hold to the exclusion of others, but aim instead at shaping conditions beyond their national boundaries'. This does not exclude an 'element of national self-interest, however far-sighted, that leads nations to improve the milieu by rendering services to others'.

Even without the defence dimension ... the discrepancy between the EU's rhetoric and reality is such that it does not deserve the label of a civilian power. In particular, the de facto continued support or a non-democratic regime and its military occupation of a third country (which is a democracy) by many EU member states confirms that the EU, despite the many civilian means at its disposal, is not promoting civilian values. The fact that this is happening in an 'ideal' case scenario, because of the many civilian means at the EU's disposal, including a legal enforcement regime (within the EU thanks to the ECJ and outside it thanks to the Council of Europe), renders this analysis all the more important.

This volume also takes up the last remark on the 'ideal' case study, given its demarcation to external domains where the EU is *prima facie* a powerful actor.

Partly in reaction to the overemphasis on civilian instruments, Ian Manners (2002) pioneered the concept of Normative Power Europe (NPE) in his case study on the EU's international pursuit of the abolition of the death penalty. This role encompasses three characteristics, each of them suggesting that the EU is normatively different and that material interests alone cannot adequately account for Europe's external action: (1) the EU itself is a normatively constructed polity; (2) this predisposes it to act in a normative way in world politics; and (3) a NPE diffuses these norms internationally without resorting primarily resorting to coercion and military means, but by the ability to shape conceptions of 'normal' in international relations. Manners makes a distinction between Europe's 'core norms' such as liberty, democracy, respects for human rights and fundamental freedoms, and rule of law; and 'minor norms', such as social solidarity, non-discrimination, sustainable development and good governance (2002, 242–3). EU norm diffusion is shaped by six factors – contagion, informational diffusion, procedural diffusion, transference, overt diffusion and the cultural filter. Given the relative absence of physical force and the importance of cultural diffusion, the author argues that 'the most important factor shaping the international role of the EU is not what it does or what it says, but what it is' (cf. Manners 2006, 184).

In recent years the notion of a NPE has come to dominate scholarly discussions about Europe's global role. It has provoked several specific applications on cases in EU external policies (e.g. Lightfood and Burchell 2005; Szymanski and Smith 2005). This increased emphasis on the ideational factor reflects a broader evolution in political science and FPA since the 1990s. As pointed out by Manners and Whitman, more and more academics are distancing themselves from the 'hegemonic US discourses' that have dominated FPA, to develop a 'distinctive European FPA'. They observe a third FPA 'category', after the rational actor-model and decision-making models, concerning a whole spectrum of recent studies that take account with the 'less tangible', 'societal' aspects of foreign policy, such as ideology, role conceptions, ethical considerations, and public opinion (Manners and Whitman 2000, 4, 6; see also Carlsnaes 2002, 343; Goldstein and Keohane 1995).

But today the scales may be tilting towards the other extreme. While the EU's normative and value-driven aspirations are ubiquitous in the literature, the power instruments (if any) underpinning these international goals are often less clear-cut.

As underlined in Youngs' (2004, 415) literature review, many scholars 'have come to posit a pre-eminence of ideational dynamics as key to the EU's distinctiveness as an international actor'. Although the new NPE literature pays much attention to the ideational ends component of EU external action, it somehow neglects the linkage with Europe's instruments for achieving these objectives.

This book proposes a more explicit and systematic linkage between the Union's power and goals on the international scene. Rather than examining the famous 'capability-expectations gap' (Hill 1993), it studies the relation between Europe's international capabilities and objectives. Starting from the widespread suggestion that the EU is a 'force for the good', each contribution explores both the 'force' *and* the 'good'. The question then raises to what extent the EU make use of its available means of power *with a view to* achieving a CPE's objectives; or shortly, what about Europe's *commitment* to these normative goals? Equally, it should allow us to draw conclusions on the distinctiveness of the EU on the world scene – both in terms of instruments and objectives.

Role Concepts
Application to external policy domains
(trade, competition, development, humanitarian aid, environment,
social, energy, asylum and migration, enlargement, neighbourhood)
Securitisation?

Means of Power (Instruments)   **External Policy Objectives**

- EU budgets?   - (Which) normative goals?
- EU competences?   - Other goals?
- Decision-making   - Effectiveness and coherence?
- Other actors?   - EU discourse?
- ...   - ...

LINKING means and ends
COMMITMENT to normative objectives?
DISTINCTIVENESS of Europe's action in the world?

Figure 1.2   The EU's role in the world: analytical framework

By deliberately demarcating this research to the external dimension of first pillar – and thus supposedly the most important areas of the EU's global role – we also attempt to meet the criticism that the empirical grounding of the civilian/ normative power literature is insufficient (cf. Sjursen 2006, 177). Rather than elaborating on Europe's role at an abstract level, the contributions can provide an added value at the empirical level. This approach is in line with Smith's (2005) call that we should no longer focus on what the EU *is*, but on what it does; it also tries to combine the normative focus of the NPE literature with the empirical bias of the CPE approach (cf. Manners 2005).

The discussion of the EU's external powerful resources (see Figure 1.2) typically includes an analysis of the institutional dimension. Here questions in relation to the EU's competences and decision-making procedures are raised. To a large extent this dimension focuses on the relative power between the EC and the Member States in a particular external policy domain. The budget constitutes another important means of power: how relevant is the EU's power of the purse? Finally, the contributors to this volume look at Europe's relative power compared with other international actors such as the United States, the near abroad, and the countries in the developing world.

Then the EU's external policy goals are discussed, with particular attention to the normative aspects. The latter are identified in EU discourse and critically considered in relation to their coherence with other objectives – 'milieu goals' as well as 'possession goals'. In doing so, the chapters do not only analyse Europe's declared intentions, but they also turn to the Union's policy practice and the level of implementation. For each particular external policy domain, the question raises whether, how, and to what extent the Union's power instruments (for example, disposal of budgetary resources, or large competences) help of hinder the achievement of normative objectives.

Ultimately, this linkage between means and ends allows us to make an assessment of the EU's international relations, including policy-makers' discourse on Europe's world role. A main objective of this volume is to provide a critical and profound evaluation of Europe's external policies, with particular attention to those areas (for example, humanitarian aid, social policies, competition, and development aid *sensu stricto*) that are often overlooked in political science, but that form vital dimensions of Europe's global role. Another objective is to present a comprehensive overview of the Union's first pillar external activities. From this perspective, the means-end distinction forms a pragmatic toolkit to structure an increasingly complex are of research. It is hoped that the volume will be useful reading for students and scholars who are interested in the EU's role on the international scene.

Book Structure and Summary

The first chapter after this introduction examines Europe's most powerful external policy domain: trade policy. It starts with an examination of the power resources of Europe's common commercial policy, addressing the relevance of EC competences, decision-making procedures, and the level of technicality/ politicisation, Europe's trade relations with third actors, and its ability to project the internal market model to the international trade scene. Although in general the EU's power and the Commission's autonomy in this area are substantial, this section concludes that any evaluation should also look at Europe's successfulness in achieving trade policy objectives.

The next section then proceeds to analyse these goals, as summarised in the 'harnessing globalisation' motto since the second half of the 1990s. At one level, trade politics are obviously driven by (offensive and defensive) economic interests. These generally translate into the debate between Northern free traders and the Southern 'Club Med', and the question whether European protectionism has led to a Fortress Europe. It is argued that a Fortress Europe has not materialised, but also, that another goals-related dimension of trade politics has surfaced in the past decade. The growing emphasis on pursuing normative objectives through trade constitutes an analytically distinct political cleavage which cannot simply be translated into the protectionist-free trade dichotomy. After presenting some theoretical reflections on the relevance of normative objectives such as human rights, democracy, environment, social standards and development in EU trade policy, the chapter raises the questions to what extent these are effectively pursued. Then, Europe's stance in some recent multilateral, bilateral and unilateral trade issues is evaluated through an analysis of two case studies related to 'economic development of the South' and 'core labour standards'.

The chapter concludes that the EU's commitment to realise these objectives through trade is subordinated to the pursuit of market enhancing initiatives, where the Union has been more successful. It is argued that this stems not only from ideological factors, but also from the hybrid institutional setting (community competences and budgetary powers) of Europe's trade architecture. Whereas the EU has become a multilateral and liberal actor in world trade, the asymmetrical state of European integration constrains its capacity to advance ambitious normative objectives through trade.

The next chapter also analyses the Union's relations with developing countries, but not through the lens of trade politics. In contrast with trade, development policy *sensu stricto* is only a recent and a shared competence of the EU. In terms of budget, on the other hand, the Union seems to have more clout in the domain of development policy. The first section of this chapter pays particular attention to this power resource, focusing on the evolution of the Union's development aid budgets and on the role of the Commission in this regard. Jan Orbie and Helen Versluys draw two remarkable conclusions from this analysis: the EC's development assistance has systematically increased in accordance with a concrete schedule, and the Commission played a catalysing role in this 'soft' coordination process.

After elaborating on explanations for this trend, the question is raised whether 'more aid' and 'more Europe' also implies 'more development'. The section on the objectives of Europe's development policy first lists the official goals – in particular poverty reduction – and then makes an assessment of Europe's commitment to these aims by analysing the way in which its aid budgets are actually spent. The analysis makes clear that increased expenditures largely stem from debt relief initiatives – although this applies to Member State rather than Community funding. In addition, it appears that Europe, and in particular the EC, spends a relatively small part of its aid budget on the poorest countries. Financial resources have been (re)allocated to regions that are important for Europe's foreign and security policies.

This is indicative of a more general securitisation trend in the EU's relations with the South. Whereas coherence with non-development policies such as trade, agriculture and fisheries continues to be problematic, Europe's aid policy is more and more linked to broader foreign policy considerations. This also increases the EU's international profile – arguably a main objective of European development policy.

Although these trends have not yet crystallised, the final section of this chapter outlines a number of future scenarios. The main conclusion reads that the Union's first role – providing aid according to its assumed comparative advantage – is becoming less relevant; whereas it is increasingly involved in its second role – coordinating Member State development policies. Therefore the authors argue that the EC is moving towards an 'OECD scenario'. The EU used to be a norm-taker in development, but more recently it is evolving towards a norm-setter in its own right (for example on aid effectiveness, on untying of aid, on conditionality for international loans). This is in line with Europe's nature as a 'regulatory state' – also in development.

In Chapter 4 Helen Versluys examines a distinctive aspect of Europe's action towards the developing South: humanitarian aid policy. Here too the Union's competences are shared, relatively recent, and backed with substantial financial resources. Given the visibility of humanitarian interventions in third countries affected by disaster or conflict, the legitimizing function of this external policy domain may even be greater than in traditional development assistance. But in contrast with the previous chapter, the Community's autonomy is relatively large and insulated from Member State influence. The specialised agency 'ECHO' enjoys a larger degree if autonomy than its development counterpart 'EuropeAid'. The Union's Humanitarian Office forms an administrative structure exclusively dedicated to the management of humanitarian assistance – although its influence is constrained by the presence of competing donors and by its lack of implementation capacity. Another difference with development aid relates to the objectives dimension: the pursued goals are explicitly non-political and non-economic, in accordance with the 'humanitarian imperative' endorsed by the EU.

The question is then raised as to whether European discourse on needs-based and apolitical humanitarian aid is actually being adhered to. The analysis addresses the possible 'securitisation' and 'developmentalisation' of Europe's humanitarian aid activities, which refer to the interlinking with respectively crisis management and sustainable development goals. Until the end of the 1990s, ECHO sometimes engaged in activities which, strictly speaking, went beyond humanitarian assistance and were more oriented towards conflict resolution or development. But from 1999/2000 onwards, and in contrast with the findings in the previous chapter on development, a move away from both the securitisation and developmentalisation can be noted. This relates to the establishment of other European instruments in the security realm – which has allowed ECHO to focus on core humanitarian tasks and on forgotten crises; but also to the institutional autonomy of ECHO and to the preferences of the (large) Member States. To some extent ECHO has managed to use the power of the purse to push implementing partners in the direction of the impartial humanitarian aid philosophy. Equally, the introduction of the LRRD (linkage between relief, rehabilitation and development) concept has prevented the developmentalisation of humanitarian aid – although the Commission's commitment to engage in the development side of protracted crises remains unclear.

Questions of coherence in EU relations with developing countries are also central in Chapter 5, written by Steven Sterkx, on the EU's so-called 'comprehensive approach' to asylum and migration. The external dimension of this policy has become increasingly important since asylum and migration was transferred to the first pillar under the Treaty of Amsterdam (1997). As in development policy, the author points to problems of vertical (between the Member States and the EC level) and horizontal coherence (within the Council and the Commission). In addition, the trend of securitisation also emerges in this area, and the author concludes that migration is increasingly seen as a significant security threat by the Member States.

The chapter starts with an overview of the range of instruments that the Union has at its disposal to address migratory issues in its relations with third countries. These include the Action Plans of the High-Level Working Group on Asylum and Migration, clauses on migration management and dialogue in Europe's bilateral and inter-regional agreements, cooperation in the context of enlargement and neighbourhood policies, and assistance for capacity- and institution-building in third countries. Interestingly, the EU also gradually acquired budgetary means in this domain, with the creation of a new budget line in 2001 and a more extensive multi-annual financial framework in 2004. This provides the Union with considerable leverage in external negotiations on migratory issues. However, the debate on budgetary priorities is indicative of diverging views on the interpretation of a 'comprehensive approach' to asylum and migration. In this context the chapter describes the struggle for ownership between, on the one hand, the Member States and DG Justice and Home Affairs, and DG External Relations and DG Development, on the other. The former want to make use of development and external relations budgets, whereas the latter insist on a separation between these external policy fields.

Although the Union's discourse envisages a balance between internal and external policies, and between proactive and repressive measures, the critical policy analysis shows that in practice these objectives became 'off-balanced'. Broader questions regarding the so-called root causes of migration and the development of countries of origin have been subordinated to measures aimed at controlling and preventing migration into the EU territory. In the area of migration, priority is given to readmission, return and the fight against illegal immigration; in the field of asylum, the main priority is increased reception in the region of origin. Budget allocations illustrate these trends. Migration goals are also increasingly incorporated in the Union's cooperation and development programmes. Sterkx concludes that Europe's 'strategy of externalisation', involving capacity building, remote control, and remote protection, is functional for strengthening Europe's internal area for freedom, security and justice. It shifts responsibility to countries of origin and transit, and can hardly be seen as a normative external project. Thus,

Fortress Europe is expanding: access is not only being restricted on the Union's territory and borders, but also through external action.

The linkage between the internal integration project and the external projection of Europe's putative model is also central in the three subsequent chapters on the EU's global role in social, environmental, and competition policies. In Chapter 6, Tonia Novitz questions whether the Union can be seen as a normative actor in international social affairs. Although the European Commission's capacity to act in the International Labour Organisation (ILO) is limited – the EU's internal role in the ratification and coordination of ILO Conventions is also confined – the author notes that the EU has pursued social objectives through its external trade and development objectives. As for the objectives, the chapter focuses on the international promotion of the Core Labour Standards (CLS) – which are widely considered to be human rights.

The central question reads whether the Union is seeking to export an 'EU social model', or whether it wants to promote the ILO agenda of 'Decent Work'. European discourse seems to suggest the latter option, given the EU's emphasis on the partnership with the ILO and on the promotion of CLS as part of the Decent Work idea. Two case studies in distinctive areas of social policy are examined: collective labour law (cf. ILO Conventions 87 and 98) and gender equality (cf. ILO Conventions 100 and 111). Each time the relevant ILO Conventions are part of Europe's aid and especially trade conditionality. In her analysis of the first case, Novitz points to the failure of the Member States to comply with the relevant obligations, the lack of EU internal competences in collective labour law, and the potential for European law to undermine national systems of industrial relations. Although at first sight this seems incompatible with the EU's trade conditionality, this might not be the case. On the one hand, violators of these ILO norms have been rewarded; on the other, the trade sanctions against Belarus are consistent with a liberal view of freedom of association which values 'freedom' of individual choice rather than the strength of collective voice. The second case elaborates on the Union's extensive legislation in the area of gender, and then notes that gender considerations have not played a role in trade conditionality, but that the Union has pursued a soft developmental agenda in this area. But here too the consistency between Europe's internal and external approach is larger than it seems: internally the Union's gender equality policies are driven by a desire to build productive labour markets and enhance economic activity, whereas the EU has less incentive to enforce this labour standard abroad.

In other words, both case studies indicate that the EU is promoting externally social policy norms tied more closely to ILO standards than its own, but which are certainly not inconsistent with its own market-led agenda. However, in conclusion, the author casts doubt on the new partnership between the EU and the ILO. For one thing, it belies the limited competences of the Union as regards the role it can play in the ILO. Moreover, Novitz points to the incompatibility between the Union's market-driven and the ILO's social mandates, and to the dominant position of the EU in this relationship, potentially influencing the content and relevance of international social standards.

Tensions between Member State and Community competences on the one hand, and between market-oriented and value-related objectives on the other, also emerge in the next section on environmental policies. The chapter starts with a historical overview of the Union's internal power resources and policy goals in this area, arguing that today EU environmental policy is at a new crossroads: either it will become a 'normal' policy domain alongside other areas, or sustainable development will be the next 'big idea' (Lenschow 2004, 140). Then Edith Vanden Brande looks more closely at the Union's international power in this area, focusing on the power base of Europe's vast internal market, the complex institutional setting of competences and decision-making, the changing international context, and the relationship with the EU and developing countries. Cases on chemicals regulation and climate change show that a strong connection between internal and external power aspects enhances the Union's clout in environmental issues.

Subsequently, the chapter scrutinises the EU's international goals in this area – a dimension that is overlooked in the dominant actorness/presence framework. It appears that there is a growing conflict between the different faces of civilian power Europe, where free trade often receives a higher ranking than environmental protection. Although sustainable development should avoid the tension between economic and environmental goals, the author suggests that Europe's commitment to this objective is often undermined by a more market-oriented approach. The EU also pursues global leadership ambitions through environmental policy, but when it comes to implementation, the results are far behind the rhetoric. Moreover, the securitisation of the climate change debate may hinder a European leadership role. Despite these critical observations, Vanden Brande concludes that the legitimising function of the EU's image as a global green civilian power may become a self-fulfilling prophecy. In fact, recent evolutions seem to confirm this hypothesis.

Angela Wigger's contribution on competition policy also starts with a historical analysis of the EU's actorness. Here too the Commission's power has expanded since the Treaty of Rome, with the single market project as a hinge point. After describing the growing role of competition in the EU's internal 'globalisation', the author turns to Europe's international influence. Since the 1990s the Union has successfully pursued the convergence of its competition laws and practices through enlargements and through bilateral agreements. At the same time the EU has advocated global competition rules in the World Trade Organisation (WTO). However, as in international environmental regulation, opposition from the developing world and from the United States has hindered the realisation of Europe's global ambitions.

Then the chapter addresses the Union's objectives pursued through competition policy, Interestingly, the shift within competition policy from a solely intra-Community towards an extra-Community dimension parallels the evolution in ideological thinking from 'ordoliberalism' to neoliberalism. Whereas the Commission was not too intrusive in competition matters during the 1960s and 1970s, and even supported neo-mercantilist initiatives such as the creation of 'Eurochampions', since the end of the 1980s the EU has enthusiastically embraced a neoliberal competition enforcement philosophy, both internally and

at the global level. This section also elaborates on explanations for this shift and
for Europe's insistence on a worldwide competition regime in the WTO. More
specifically, Wigger emphasises the role of the Commission, the influence of the
transnational business community, and the catalysing effect of the single market
project.

Following the downfall of the EU's multilateral competition project, the
alternative route came to be labelled with the catchword 'convergence'. EU and
US competition officials alike were captivated by the convergence discourse, which
led to the establishment of the International Competition Network in 2001. This
network offers a perfect means for the diffusion of norms and regulatory converge
in competition matters, formulated by a duopoly of the two major protagonists,
the EU and the US.

The external effects of market liberalisation in the EU are also a central theme
in the subsequent chapter on energy. Although energy issues were at the origin of
the European integration project, paradoxically, the Union's role is still relatively
limited. Emphasising the uneven integration pattern between geopolitical goals
on the one hand, and energy market liberalisation on the other, Andrei Belyi
first elaborates on the Union's power and objectives in this area. Turning to the
EU's international role, he states that Europe's stance is not always supported
by the political values of liberal democracy. The EU's success in exporting its
(unfinished) model of energy markets in the neighbourhood is also highlighted,
for instance through the Barcelona process and the Energy Community Treaty of
South-eastern Europe. By contrast, the Union's influence in energy issues within
the WTO framework and the Energy Charter Treaty has been limited, which
partly stems from the particular status of the EU regime in the international
legal regimes of energy trade.

The conclusions link the complex and hybrid nature of European integration,
on the one hand, and the EU's external energy policies, on the other. Realist
and intergovernmental logics still apply in the area of energy security – despite
Commission attempts to coordinate this; functionalist and integration dynamics
emerge in the economic realm – although regulatory harmonisation is still
embryonic because of Member State sensitivities; and the Union's normative
influence as a postmodern empire has appeared – although values of liberal
democracy have not always taken priority to security of supply.

Energy is also a prominent topic in the chapter on the European
Neighbourhood Policy (ENP). In their description of this new external policy area
– the EU's self-declared priority since the 2004 enlargement – Viktoriya Khasson,
Syuzanna Vasilyan, and Hendrik Vos emphasise the ENP's comprehensiveness
and ambiguity. Starting with the Union's pursued goals, the authors elaborate
on the role of market integration, political values, and regionalism, as well as
(new) security issues and energy supply. The ambiguity about priorities among
these objectives also gives the Union some room of manoeuvre in dealing with
its neighbours. The analysis of the instruments that the EU is employing in this
relatively new external policy area does not bring much more clarity: here too much
will depend on the actual implementation. It is clear, however, that the Union has
a considerable power in the hub-and-spoke pattern of the ENP. Political dialogue,

the internal market carrot, financial assistance, and conditionality in general, all contribute to the Union's influence in the 'near abroad'.

The authors conclude state that EU priorities through ENP are inspired largely by soft security considerations, such as migration and energy issues, rather than topics such as the free movement of persons and trade in agricultural products. The importance of security and geopolitical considerations may also compel the Union to engage in Realpolitik rather than normative aspirations. Finally, the authors reflect on some future scenarios. The ENP might become void yielding to emergence of a multiplicity of bilateral cooperations. Even the accession of new Member States cannot be excluded, given the Union's ambivalence around the 'hidden objective' of avoiding further enlargement.

Of course, the 'golden carrot' of membership constitutes the main difference with the Union's enlargement policies. Therefore, it may be expected that the EU's relations with candidate countries constitutes a civilian power policy *par excellence*. However, in the final chapter, Eline De Ridder, An Schrijvers and Hendrik Vos argue that the accession procedure has brought unexpected effects on democracy in the new Member States – at least in the short run.

This chapter starts with the rationale behind enlargement with CEE, describing rationalist and constructivist perspectives. Then the instruments that the Union has at its disposal are sketched: besides the general impact of the EU's magnetic force and the membership carrot, the authors look more closely at the role of conditionality and financial assistance. Finally, an assessment is made of the Union's impact through enlargement policies, which puts the distinct EU factor into perspective. The authors emphasise the relevance of the international as well as the domestic context in explaining recent reforms in CEE. Moreover, they point to unanticipated consequences that have accompanied the EU's shifting approach from '*acquis* conditionality' to 'democratic conditionality'. The Polish case illustrates that Europeanisation may have potentially perverse consequences for democracy in acceding countries. One lesson from this is that, in the future, the Union might have to adopt a development agency role, rather than the regulatory role it took on during the accession process.

From Regulatory State to Civilian Power Europe?

In general, the book shows the diversity of the EU's 'first pillar' external policies, both in terms of instruments and objectives. The division of the Union's international relations into two pillars is often, and justifiably, criticised for being artificial. The contributions to this publication make clear that *within* the so-called 'soft' areas of the Union's first pillar, too, the strength and nature of the Union's international activities vary significantly. Europe's vast internal market constitutes a power resource in all the external policy domains that have been discussed. Hence the importance of the single market project for the EU's increased proactivity in international politics since the 1990s – a trend that has been confirmed in most chapters.

But besides this general economic basis of Europe's international 'presence', great diversity in the Union's power resources for external relations can be discerned throughout the contributions. Whereas the EU has at its disposal extensive (yet not undisputed) legal competences in areas such as trade and competition, its capacity to act internationally is usually more constrained. In development and humanitarian aid policies, the Union has a shared competence with the Member States which hold the majority of the budgets. The distribution of competences is more complex and patchy in social and environmental matters. In international energy policies, the Member States are clearly in the driving seat – despite the Commission's attempts to play a larger role in this area. But although issues of coordination and complementarity between the EC and the Member States, as well as intra-EU divergences on the contents of external policies, arise in all the chapters, the Union usually acts in a concerted way on the international scene.

The budgetary dimension of Europe's external relations proved important for determining the Union's power in the world, and for assessing the normativity of its international activities. The disposition of finances varies considerably, from extensive (albeit decreasing) budgets in development affairs, to purely regulatory functions in trade, competition and environment. In contrast, Europe's policies towards the neighbourhood and candidate countries have included large financial aid programmes, linked with political and economic conditionality, although the suggestion has been made that the EU should behave more like a 'developmental state' and less like a 'regulatory state' in this area. The Union's international activities in social and environmental issues are hardly buttressed by European budgets, even though the EU aims to mainstream these issues in its development programmes. In recent years, the Union's budget for external asylum and migration policies has been growing – which has given rise to conflicts within the Commission about the allocation of money.

More fundamentally, bureaucratic competition also reveals divergent visions on Europe's global role. Over the past decade, policy-makers have converged around the idea that the EU should play a normative role in the world, in the sense of promoting 'milieu goals' or 'far-sighted self-interests'. Even external policies which are traditionally seen as favouring European interests, such as trade and competition, have been involved in Europe's normative discourse. Development of the Third World figures high on the Union's external policy agenda, alongside other objectives such as human rights, democracy, and sustainable development. The dominant vision of the EU's global role as a 'force for the good' successfully surpasses the 'pillarisation' and institutional complexities of Europe's international policies.

However, concerns have been expressed that increased coherence as regards the Union's global orientation – both at the discursive and at the institutional level – has, in fact, entailed the subordination of external policies to Europe's broader ambitions in the foreign policy and security realm. Then, the normativity of Europe's international role can be questioned, in line with the civilian-military power discussion sketched at the beginning of this chapter. For example, the chapters on development aid and on the external dimension of asylum and migration advocate that the importance of security considerations is growing in the post 9/11 climate, to the detriment of a more far-sighted and normative role. The ENP contribution also hinted at the priority of geopolitical and security considerations in the near neighbourhood. On the other hand, the development of fully-fledged security capabilities might facilitate the pursuit of an apolitical humanitarian aid policy. Since the importance of geopolitical and security considerations will probably increase – in the chapter on energy, it is stated that Europe's (limited) role in providing energy security already takes precedence over normative goals – one main challenge for the Union will be to generate coherent *and* normative external policies. Both aspects do not always go together.

Our analysis of the Union's external objective is not only concerned with the civilian 'versus' security debate. The military dimension apart, several chapters highlight the difficulties to pinpoint the so-called 'civilian' or 'normative' goals, and the need for explicit standards to evaluate Europe's normative objectives (cf. Sjursen 2006, 173). More specifically, this book illustrates that ideological factors quickly arise when examining the normative content of first-pillar external policies. To a large extent, the discussion on *the way that* normative objectives such as human rights and sustainable development can be promoted through EU external relations, boils down to the ideological left-right cleavage. For example, the chapters on trade and competition policies suggest a correspondence between normative power Europe and the promotion of 'embedded liberalism' or 'ordoliberalism'. Similarly, the chapters on the Union's international social and environmental activities point to Europe's market-oriented approach, questioning whether this is sufficient to act as a real civilian or normative power.

Ultimately, this links to the EU's nature as a regulatory state. Community competence tends to be greater in the area of regulatory policies – the costs of which are borne by those who have to comply with the regulatory rules (individuals, firms, and so on) – than with regard to distributive policies – the costs of which are borne by Member State governments themselves via their obligatory contributions to the budget. Regulatory policies are usually market-enhancing, aiming to correct market failures that accompany liberalisation (cf. Majone 1994). The Union's external activities basically reflect this focus on regulatory tasks. Even in the area of development policy, the EU's own budgets are becoming less extensive, whereas the Commission is playing an increasingly important role in standard-setting.

Much of the current criticism against the European integration project can be ascribed to the EU's regulatory state image: its activities are seen as overly technical and too market-oriented. Interestingly, several chapters (development, humanitarian aid, and environment) make a link between the Union's internal legitimacy problems and its global role. It is suggested that the EU's ambition to play a more global and normative role on the world stage could enhance its internal credibility. It is, however, questionable whether the Union's equipment as a regulatory state (the means dimension) will be sufficient to act as a real civilian or normative power (the external goals) on the international scene. Building on these observations, further research could elaborate on this more systematically, with specific attention to the budgetary resources of the Union's external policies and the ideological dimension of its international activities. Both aspects are insufficiently studied in the existing literature, although vital in evaluating Europe's global role.

References

Allen, D. and Smith, M. (1990), 'Western Europe's Presence in the Contemporary International Arena', *Review of International Studies* 16, 19–37.

Biscop, S. (2005), *The European Security Strategy – A Global Agenda for Positive Power*, (Aldershot: Ashgate).

Bull, H. (1982), 'Civilian Power Europe: A Contradiction in Terms?', *Journal of Common Market Studies* 12:2, 149–64.

Carlsnaes, W. (2002), 'Foreign Policy', in W. Carlsnaes, T. Risse and B.A. Simmons (eds), *Handbook of International Relations* (London: Sage).

Cooper, R. (2003), *The Breaking of Nations: Order and Chaos in the Twenty-First Century* (London: Atlantic Books).

Diez, T. (2005), 'Constructing the Self and Changing Others: Reconsidering "Normative Power Europe"', *Millennium* 33:3, 613–36.

Duchêne, F. (1973), 'The European Community and the Uncertainties of Interdependence', in M. Kohnstamm and W. Hager (eds), *A Nation Writ Large? Foreign-Policy Problems before the EC* (London: Macmillan).

—— (1972), 'Europe's Role in World Peace', in R. Mayne (ed.), *Europe Tomorrow: Sixteen Europeans Look Ahead* (London: Fontana).

Elgström, O. and Smith, M. (2006) (eds), *The EU's Roles in International Politics* (New York: Routledge).

Everts, P. (1974), 'Het "Civiele Europa". Een Fraaie Conceptie onder het Mes', *Transaktie* 3:6, 10–13.

Freres, C. (2000), 'The European Union as a Global "Civilian Power": Development Cooperation in EU-Latin American Relations', *Journal of Interamerican Studies and World Affairs* 42:2, 63ff.

Galtung, J. (1973), *The European Community: A Superpower in the Making* (Oslo: Universitetsforlaget).

Goldstein, J. and Keohane, R.O. (1995), *Ideas and Foreign Policy: An Analytical Framework* (USA: Cornell University Press).

Harnisch, S. and Maull, H.W. (2001), *Germany as a Civilian Power?* (Manchester: Manchester University Press).

Hill, C. (1990), 'European Foreign Policy: Power Bloc, Civilian Model – or Flop?', in R. Rummel (ed.), *The Evolution of an International Actor. Western Europe's New Assertiveness* (Boulder, CO: Westview Press).

—— (1993), 'The Capability-Expectations Gap, or Conceptualising Europe's International Role', *Journal of Common Market Studies* 31:3, 305–27.

Holden, P. (2003), 'The European Community's MEDA Aid Programme: A Strategic Instrument of Civilian Power?', *European Foreign Affairs Review* 8, 347–63.

Holland, M. (2002), *The EU and the Third World* (Houndmills: Palgrave).

Hurt, S.R. (2003), 'Cooperation and Coercion? The Cotonou Agreement between the EU and ACP States and the End of the Lomé Convention', *Third World Quarterly* 24:1, 161–76.

Hyde-Price, A. (2006), '"Normative" Power Europe: A Realist Critique', *Journal of European Public Policy* 13:2, 217–34.

Kagan, R (2004), *Of Paradise and Power: America and Europe in the New World Order* (New York: Vintage Books).

Keukeleire, S. (2002), 'Reconceptualizing (European) Foreign Policy: Structural Foreign Policy', draft paper presented at the ECPR First Pan-European Conference on EU Politics, Bordeaux, 26–28 September.

Laatikainen, K.V. (2006), 'Pushing Soft Power: Middle Power Diplomacy at the UN', in K.V. Laatikainen and K.E. Smith (eds), *The EU at the UN: Intersecting Multilateralism* (Houndmills: Palgrave Macmillan).

Larsen, H. (2002), 'The EU: A Global Military Actor?', *Cooperation and Conflict* 37:3, 283–302.

Leonard, M. (2005), *Why Europe will Run the 21st Century* (London and New York: Fourth Estate).

Le Prestre, P.G. (1997), *Role Quests in the Post-Cold War Era: Foreign Policies in Transition* (Montreal: McGill-Queen's University Press).

Lightfoot, S. and Burchell, J. (2005), 'The EU and the World Summit on Sustainable Development: Normative Power Europe in Action?', *Journal of Common Market Studies* 43:1, 75–95.

Lodge, J. (1993), 'From Civilian Power to Speaking with a Common Voice: The Transition to a CFSP', in J. Lodge (ed.), *The EC and the Challenge of the Future* (London: Pinter Publishers).

Majone, G. (1994), 'The Rise of the Regulatory State in Europe', *West European Politics* 17:3, 77–101.

Manners, I. (2002), 'Normative Power Europe: A Contradiction in Terms?', *Journal of Common Market Studies* 40:2, 235–58.

—— (2006), 'Normative Power Europe Reconsidered: Beyond the Crossroads', *Journal of European Public Policy* 13:2, 182–99.

—— and Whitman, R.G. (2000) (eds), *The Foreign Policy of EU Member States* (Manchester: Manchester University Press).

Marsh, S. and Mackenstein, H. (2005), *International Relations of the EU* (Harlow: Pearson Longman).

Maull, H.W. (1991), 'Germany and Japan: The New Civilian Powers', *Foreign Affairs* 69:5, 91–116.

—— (1999), *Germany and the Use of Force: Still a Civilian Power?* (Washington DC: The Brookings Institution).

McCormick, J. (2007), *The European Superpower* (New York: Palgrave Macmillan).

Moïsi, D. (1982), 'Civilian Power Europe. Comment', *Journal of Common Market Studies* 21:1-2, 166–70.

—— (2002), 'Het "Gedwongen" Huwelijk van Amerika met Europa', *De Standaard*, 20 November.

Moravcsik, A. (2003), 'Striking a New Transatlantic Bargain', *Foreign Affairs* 82:4, 74–89.

Nicolaïdis, K. and Howse, R. (2003), '"This is my EUtopia …": Narrative as Power', in J.H.H. Weiler, I. Begg and J. Peterson (eds), *Integration in an Expanding EU* (Oxford: Blackwell).

Orbie, J. (2006), 'Civilian Power Europe. Review of the Original and Current Debates', *Cooperation and Conflict* 41:1, 123–8.

Pijpers, A. (1988), 'The Twelve Out-of-Area: A Civilian Power in an Uncivil World?', in A. Pijpers, E. Regelsberger and W. Wessels (eds), *European Political Cooperation in* the 1980s: a Common Foreign Policy for Western Europe? (The Netherlands: Martinus Nijhoff).

Rosecrance, R. (1986), *The Rise of the Trading State* (New York: Basic Books).

—— (1998), 'The EU: A New Type of International Actor', in J. Zielonka (ed.), *Paradoxes of European Foreign Policy* (London: Kluwer Law International).

Schimmelfennig, F. (2003), 'The Community Trap: Liberal Norms, Rhetorical Action, and the Eastern Enlargement of the EU', *International Organization* 55:1, 47–80.

Schirm, S.A. (1998), 'Europe's Common Foreign and Security Policy: The Politics of Necessity, Viability, and Adequacy', in C. Rhodes (ed.), *The EU in the World Community* (Boulder: Lynne Rienner).

Sedelmeier, U. (2006), 'The EU's Role as a Promoter of Human Rights and Democracy: Enlargement Policy and Role Formation', in O. Elgström and M. Smith (eds), *The EU's Roles in International Politics* (New York: Routledge).

Sjursen, H. (2006), 'What Kind of Power?', *Journal of European Public Policy* 13:2, 169–81.

Smith, K.E. (2000), 'The End of Civilian Power EU: A Welcome Demise or Cause for Concern?', *The International Spectator* 35:2, 11–28.

—— (2003), *EU Foreign Policy in a Changing World* (Cambridge: Polity).

—— (2005), 'Beyond the Civilian Power EU Debate', *Politique Européenne* 17, 63–82.

Stavridis, S. (2001a), '"Militarising" the EU: The Concept of Civilian Power Europe Revisited', *The International Spectator* 41:4, 43–50.

—— (2001b), 'Failing to Act like a "Civilian Power": The EU's Policy towards Cyprus and Turkey', *Studia Diplomatica* 54:3, 75–102.

Szymanski, M. and Smith, M.E. (2005), 'Coherence and Conditionality in European Foreign Policy: Negotiating the EU-Mexico Global Agreement', *Journal of Common Market Studies* 43:1, 171–92.

Telò, M. (ed.) (2001), *EU and New Regionalism. Regional Actors and Global Governance in a post-hegemonic era* (Aldershot: Ashgate).

Therborn, G. (1997), 'Europe in the Twenty-first Century: The World's Scandinavia?', in P. Gowan and P. Anderson (eds), *The Question of Europe* (London: Verso).

—— (2002), 'Europe: The World's Trader, World's Lawyer', excerpt from speech, Conference of Europeanists, 15 March.

Treacher, A. (2004), 'From Civilian Power to Military Actor: The EU's Resistible Transformation', *European Foreign Affairs Review* 9, 49–66.

Tsakaloyannis, P. (1989), 'The EC: From Civilian Power to Military Integration', in J. Lodge (ed.), *The EC and the Challenge of the Future* (London: Pinter Publishers).

Tsoukalis, L. (2003), *What Kind of Europe?* (Delhi: Oxford University Press).

Van Apeldoorn, B., Overbeek, H. and Ryner, M. (2003), 'Theories of European Integration: A Critique', in A.W. Cafruny and M. Ryner (eds), *A Ruined Fortress? Neoliberal Hegemony and Transformation in Europe* (Lanham, MD: Rowman and Littlefield Publishers).

Wagner, W. (2006), 'The Democratic Control of Military Power Europe', *Journal of European Public Policy* 13:2, 200–16.

Whitman, R.G. (1997), 'The International Identity of the EU: Instruments as Identity', in A. Landau and R.G. Whitman (eds), *Rethinking the EU: Institutions, Interests and Identities* (Basingstoke: Macmillan).

—— (1998), *From Civilian Power to superpower? The International Identity of the EU* (Basingstoke: Macmillan).

—— (2002), 'The Fall and Rise of Civilian Power Europe', <http://hdl.handle.net/1885/41589>, accessed 20 June 2007.

Youngs, R. (2004), 'Normative Dynamics and Strategic Interests in the EU's External Identity', *Journal of Common Market Studies* 42:2, 415–35.

Zielonka, J. (1998), *Explaining Euro-Paralysis. Why Europe is Unable to Act in International Politics* (Basingstoke: Macmillan).

—— (2006), *Europe as Empire: The Nature of the Enlarged EU* (Oxford: Oxford University Press).

Chapter 2

The European Union's Role in World Trade: Harnessing Globalisation?

Jan Orbie

Trade is the European Union's most powerful external policy domain. Taking this statement as a starting point, rather than a conclusion, this chapter addresses several questions relating to Europe's power in its common commercial policy. First, what exactly are the EU's internal and external power resources in this domain? What factors contribute to – or qualify – Europe's capacities to exert power in trade? Second, what about the objectives that are pursued through trade, and Europe's effectiveness in achieving them? The discussion of the latter will pay particular attention to normative aims. Besides arguing that the EU follows a middle course between old-fashioned protectionism and unbridled free trade, Europe's 'harnessing globalisation' discourse has indeed emphasised that its trade policy promotes development of the South, as well as environmental and social goals. Based on two case studies, the concluding discussion links Europe's commitment to these objectives with the institutional setting of EU trade policy-making. It suggests that, whereas the EU has become a multilateral and liberal actor in world trade, the hybrid state of European integration constrains its capacity to advance ambitious normative objectives through trade.

Trading Power

Few would dispute the EU's considerable power in external economic relations, particularly in external trade policy. But although political science literature has elaborated extensively on the institutional setting of EU trade policy, it scarcely delves into the general question of Europe's 'trading power' (notable exceptions are Smith and Woolcock 1999; Meunier and Nicolaïdis 2005). This section gives a general overview and analysis of Europe's trade power instruments. It starts with the economic underpinnings of EU power and then discusses the division of competences and decision-making process, pointing to the challenges that are raised by the increased politicisation of EU trade policy. Finally, we look at Europe's 'trading power' vis-à-vis other international actors and within the international trade regime.

Europe's Economic Weight: The Internal Market's Magnetic Force

A glance at the statistics reveals that the EU is on a par with the US as regards import and export figures. Both make up about 20 per cent of the trade in goods and services. If intra-EU trade is included, Europe's trade in goods amounts to 40 per cent of world trade. The Union's share of services imports and exports – the backbone of the European economy and a booming dimension of international commerce – is slightly larger than that of the US. The EU and the US are also undisputed leaders in international investment flows. Since the 2004/2007 enlargements, the Gross Domestic Product (GDP) of the EU-25 has exceeded that of the US. These figures confirm the common image of the EU as an 'economic giant'. Although this observation is often contrasted with Europe's international posture as a 'political dwarf', this chapter raises the question whether and how this economic strength translates into EU trade power. What is the relevance of import and export statistics as regards Europe's capacity to act in trade?

From a political economy point of view, two avenues for EU influence can be detected. First, the presence of a large market – which has only increased through subsequent enlargements – provides an attractive carrot for EU trade negotiators. As Smith and Woolcock (2001, 451) stated, 'perhaps the most powerful instrument available to the EC for the implementation of commercial policy is market access, or the granting, conditioning or denial of access to the European Single Market, one of the most prosperous markets in the world'. The possibility to decide on the level and the conditions of access for particular countries/sectors to the world's largest market constitutes a considerable source of power for the Union's trade policy. The EU has much to offer its negotiating partners, and the latter pay dearly for European concessions in sensitive domains such as textiles and agriculture. This allows the EU to 'trade' market opening to third countries in exchange for better export opportunities in NAMA (non-agricultural market access) and services.[1]

This power resource corresponds to the traditional definition of external trade politics: negotiating levels of market access. In contrast, the second consideration stems from the deepening of Europe's customs union into a single market, and the concomitant shift from 'at-the-border' to 'behind-the-border' issues. This has given rise to the so-called 'new trade politics' (Young and Peterson 2006). Europe's internal experience in dealing with a 'deep' trade agenda may well enhance its clout in the World Trade Organisation (WTO) and in bilateral trade negotiations, where regulatory issues are increasingly important. Arguably, EU negotiators are well endowed with the management of economic interdependence. Europe's *acquis* in internal market regulations also creates a 'first-mover advantage' (see also Chapter 7 on environment and Chapter 8 on competition) when similar arrangements have to be developed on the world trade scene. Even when several regulatory options are on the table, existing EU approaches are often used as a

---

[1]   The EU has even more discretion in 'unilateral' trade policies, such as anti-dumping measures and the establishment of the Generalised System of Preferences (GSP), since no negotiations with third countries are involved.

starting point in WTO negotiations (Elgström and Strömvik 2003, 13; Smith and Woolcock 1999, 444; Smith 1999, 339). This also explains the Union's ambition to develop a regulatory framework on competition, investment, government procurement, and trade facilitation – the so-called 'Singapore' issues – within the WTO. As argued by Young and Peterson (2006, 796, 804–5), the EU has been the 'most aggressive and persistent' advocate of a 'deep' international trade agenda because of its own experience of market integration, and not simply because of corporate lobbying (compare Chapter 8 on competition).

Besides the EU's deliberate attempts to export its 'model', non-EU countries have incentives to conform their regulations with Union rules in order to facilitate exports to Europe's large internal market. Brenton (2000, 24) speaks of a process of 'hegemonic harmonisation'. Companies that are interested in this market will pressurise their governments to align their legislation with EU standards. For example, the Mutual Recognition Agreements (MRA) between the Union and other industrial countries leads to a de facto harmonisation which is often to the benefit of the EU. As Shaffer (2002, 48–9) points out: 'Consciously or unconsciously, the EC is steadily exporting its system globally.

The following section will analyse how this economic power, which confirms Europe's magnetic force vis-à-vis its trading partners (see Chapter 2), translates into the political conduct of EU trade policy. Looking at Europe's trade objectives, this chapter will also examine the 'Fortress Europe' hypothesis. After all, the EU may well have a strong and attractive market, but does this not confirm the image of a prosperous but protectionist island in the world economy?

The Institutional Setting

In Pollack's overview of community competences, external trade negotiations is the only issue among 28 policy domains with the highest level of integration (Pollack 2000, 522). Tsoukalis (2003, 68) is similarly enthusiastic, stating that 'in trade, the EU has a common policy that operates along federal lines, with a single representation ensuring that its negotiating power is commensurate with its collective weight'. Nevertheless, some trade-related issues have not been delegated to the EU level, whereas decision-making in traditional trade issues has sometimes been challenging. Peterson (2001, 51) pointedly describes the EU as a 'schizophrenic hegemon' in trade. During the Uruguay Round (1986–93) at times it was more difficult to reach an internal European agreement than to negotiate with third countries (Paemen and Bensch 1995, 95). This section summarises the institutional setting of Europe's common commercial policy, aiming to identify the implications for EU trade power.

Member State vs. Community competences: an Echternach Procession   Europe's exclusive competence in trade is undisputed. This is a textbook case of a functional spill-over as described by neo-functionalists: the customs union requires a common external tariff which in turn, necessitates a common commercial policy. The question is not so much whether the Community disposes of an exclusive competence – for that matter, the European Court of Justice (ECJ) left no doubt in its *Opinion 1/75* – but the European debate concerns the *scope* of trade policy. The Treaty Provisions (Article 113/133) give no definition of 'common commercial policy', but limit themselves to a non-exhaustive list of trade issues: 'changes in tariff rates, the conclusion of tariff and trade agreements, the achievement of uniformity in measures of liberalisation, export policy and measures to protect trade such as those to be taken in the event of dumping or subsidies' (Devuyst 2003, 118).

The Commission typically pleads for a broad interpretation of 'trade policy', while most Member States hold a narrower view. The 1970s saw the emergence of several conflicts around this topic. The negotiations on the International Rubber Agreement gave rise to an intense and scholastic dispute before the ECJ, which eventually led to the Court's *Opinion 1/78*. In line with neo-functionalist thinking, the Court largely supported the Commission's integrationist view. They successfully argued for an 'objective/instrumental approach' (the commercial policy's instruments can be used for broader purposes) instead of the Council's 'subjective/purposive approach' (Eeckhout 2004, 11–25). In 1971, the Court had already established the 'AETR Doctrine' on implicit external competences (see also Chapter 6). Simply stated, the Commission can act externally when it has an exclusive competence within the Community, and if this is necessary for reaching its objectives. *Opinion 1/76* confirmed that this is also the case in the absence of prior internal legislation.

Following the conclusion of the Marrakesh Agreements, including the establishment of the WTO, another important dispute emerged. The Commission stood by its plea for broad competences, including the so-called 'new' or 'trade-related' subjects such as services, investment, and intellectual property rights. It basically argued that Community competences in the field of trade had to keep pace with the evolving nature of international trade relations, as became clear during the Uruguay Round trade negotiations. Once again, most Member States challenged this broad definition of EU trade policy before the Court of Justice. But this time the Court's judgement confirmed intergovernmental theorising: in 1994, it largely followed the reasoning of the Member States.

At each renegotiation of the Treaty the question of trade-related competences resurfaces. Without elaborating on the complex legal entanglements, we can summarise it by saying that from an integration perspective Europe follows the pattern of the 'procession of Echternach': three steps forward, and then two steps back. The smaller Member States usually side with the Commission, whereas larger countries, such as France, Spain and the UK, are reluctant to cede competences in trade-related affairs (Meunier and Nicolaïdis 1998, 10–12; Young 2004, 206). The restrictive tenor of *Opinion 1/94* was largely adopted in the Amsterdam Treaty, according to Meunier and Nicolaïdis (1998, 10–12) more because of some Member States' profound distrust of the transfer of sovereignty than rational economic interests. The Treaty of Nice brought the fundamental reform of the provisions on trade policy, extending Community competences to some services and trade-related aspects of intellectual property rights. However, since other issues such as investment and transport remained a national competence, and in some cases unanimity was established instead of qualified majority voting (QMV), Krenzler and Pitschas (2001, 312) consider Nice to have been but a small step forward. Again, the Constitution, as drafted by the European Convention, increased EU competences, much to the pleasure of the Commission (Lamy 2002). And again, the subsequent intergovernmental conference partly turned back this evolution: although most 'new trade issues' remain Community competences, in several cases the QMV has been replaced by unanimity (see Article 188C of the Reform Treaty of Lisbon).

It should be noted that the EU sometimes manages to assert itself as a unitary actor on the international trade front – in spite of limited competences. From a historical-institutionalist angle, Young (2002) convincingly shows that EU cooperation can be successful in new trade issues where the Community has no legal competence. For instance, the Union played a leading role in the WTO negotiations on telecommunication services, even though its competences were unclear and subject of debate. In the TRIPS issue (trade-related intellectual property rights) the EU also managed to speak with one voice (Young 2004, 212). In fact, as explained in the next section, EU trade controversies often relate to decision-making on 'traditional' trade topics such as agriculture.

Decision-making in trade: the Commission versus the Council   Indeed, the issue of control over trade negotiations is much more contentious than the competence issue (cf. Woolcock 2002, 384, 395). Even when Community competences remain unquestioned, considerable disagreements between (and within) the Commission and the Council may emerge, weakening Europe's international negotiating power. One famous example is the informal Blair House Agreement (1992) on agriculture between the Commission and the US negotiators during the Uruguay Round. The Council subsequently blew the whistle on the Commission, which led to a deadlock in the trade negotiations and a long-lasting crisis of confidence in Europe's trade policy decision-making system.

How powerful is the EU – in particular the Commission – in trade negotiations? Or conversely, how effective is the Council's control over the Commission? The question of interinstitutional divergences is all the more relevant because, under the Nice Treaty and the Treaty of Lisbon, many new trade-related competences are subject to unanimity voting in the Council instead of QMV. The increased unanimity requirements may well impede the establishment of a common position and thus hurt Europe's negotiation position in international trade (Krenzler and Pitschas 2001, 313).

In analysing the complex relationship between the Commission and the Council, three phases in trade policy-making can be distinguished. The Council preponderates over the Commission in the first phase, when a negotiation mandate has to be approved (indeed, on the proposal of the Commission) authorising the Commission to start negotiations; and in the third phase, when the negotiated agreement has to be approved by the Council. Typically, the means of a principal to control its agent also apply, for example, nominating Commissioners, limiting budgets, and changing Treaties. For example, the Blair House trauma may well explain the Council's reluctance to cede trade competences during the Amsterdam, Nice, and Constitution/Reform Treaty discussions. Since trade policy is a case of 'iterated delegation', each specific trade negotiation requires a different mandate which strengthens the principal's possibilities to discipline an agent which behaved too autonomously during previous acts of delegation (Kerremans 2004, 370).

During the second phase – the actual trade negotiations on the basis of the Council mandate – the Council keeps a close eye on the Commission through the 'Article 133 committee'. This committee of Member State representatives, named after the relevant Treaty article, should monitor the Commission negotiators. But various considerations suggest a relatively significant power of the Commission during this negotiation stage. First, EU trade experts tend to be socialised as an 'epistemic community'. Commission trade officials and Article 133 members hold shared values and ideas (Mortensen 1998, 221–2). Bretherton and Vogler (2006, 69) also emphasise the 'informal' and 'club-like atmosphere'. They consider the Article 133 committee as a 'policy collaborator' rather than a body supervising the Commission. A former British representative in this committee speaks of 'a highly pragmatic body in which most of the time individuals who recognise each other as experts can settle trade issues in a familiar setting' (Johnson 1998, 37). The committee avoids politicisation of trade issues and involvement of the COREPER (Smith and Woolcock 1999, 446).

Second, the Commission disposes of a spectrum of strategies which are inherent to its position as the negotiator on behalf of the EU. A vast volume of literature has theorised on the relative independence of the Commission in trade negotiations, either from a principal-agent perspective (Meunier and Nicolaïdis 2000, 327–8; Pollack and Shaffer 2001; Kerremans 2004) or by means of the two/three-level game model (Meunier 1998; Young 2002; Van den Hoven 2007). These not only conceptualise the constraints which the Commission experiences in the middle of complex trade negotiations, but also the opportunities that are offered to the Commission to push through its own preferences. Principal-agent perspectives talk about 'agency losses'; multi-level-game approaches situate the negotiator's autonomy within the EU's 'win-set'. Because of its central role as a negotiator, the Commission disposes of unique advantages in terms of expertise and information. For example, the Commission may confront the Council members with a *fait accompli* and present a take-it-or-leave-it package deal. Larsen's (2006, 17) account of the EU-South Africa trade negotiations gives a concrete example of 'synergistic issue-linkage' as a Commission strategy:

> ... some Member States in the South, i.e. Spain, Italy and Portugal, were unwilling to offer South Africa concessions on oranges, as it was felt it would cause competition to their domestic production. The Commission then offered South Africa a concession on apples and pears, something which South Africa had not asked for. Yet the Commission insisted that South Africa accepted the offer, as apples and pears mainly grow in the northern Member States, i.e. Germany, the Netherlands and Denmark. Once the offer had been accepted by South Africa the Commission could go back to the Council and request a concession on oranges and on apples and pears, and thus maintain the regional balance among the Member States in the Council.

Yet trade negotiations touch upon various policy domains and the Commission cannot be seen as a unitary actor. Larsen (2006) minimises the role of the Council/Member States, but she emphasises the game that is being played inside the Commission between the different DGs (DG Development, DG Trade, DG Enterprise and DG Agriculture). Van den Hoven (2007) argues that the main cleavage in EU trade policy-making is not between the Council and the Commission, but rather between trade and agricultural constituencies. His 'competing two-level game' model underlines the linkages between the General Affairs and External Relations Council (GAERC) and the Trade Commissioner, on the one hand, and the Agricultural Council and Commissioner on the other. The latter should indeed be involved, both at the Council and at the Commission level, when negotiations deal with trade in agriculture. Starting from this observation, Mortensen (1998, 218–20) explains the institutionalised influence of agricultural interests, which have a de facto veto-power at the Council and Commission levels. 'Whereas the DG VI [Agriculture] can defend its institutional interest among like-minded agricultural ministers, the DG I [Trade] has to defend its position on all other areas of international trade in front of the EU foreign ministers who have several other – and perhaps more immediate – issues on their agenda.'

But then again the autonomy of the Commission is further enhanced by the 'technocratic style' of EU trade policy-making where 'neither the legislatures (national or European) nor interest groups (business and other lobbies) have any real power or ability to participate in negotiations' (Smith and Woolcock 2001, 449; see also Wolf 1997, 134; Winham 1986, 449; Woolcock 1990, 8). Because of Europe's nature as a multi-level polity and the delegation to trade policy experts within the Commission, EU trade policy-making has long been insulated from politicians and lobbies –compared with the US. Yet in recent years this has changed; below we elaborate on the implications of an increasingly politicised EU trade policy.

Moreover, the Commission is relatively powerful in what could be called the 'fourth phase' of EU trade policy-making: the day-to-day implementation. Based on interviews, Bretherton and Vogler (1999, 65) point to the influence and limited accountability of DG Trade officials in technical but sometimes far-reaching trade decisions. One main reason is the 'the absence of clear lines of accountability' compared with administrations in the Member States. The Commission also has significant clout in unilateral trade policies: it plays a major role in the investigation and implementation of alleged anti-dumping practices, as well as in the decision-making process on GSP regulations.

There is one caveat to the common-sense assumption that unanimity/consensus requirements and cumbersome internal decision-making processes impair Europe's international power. For example, divergences within the Council, and between the Council and the Commission, may indeed be used as a negotiation leverage by the Commission vis-à-vis third countries. The 'tied-hands strategy' (Mortensen 1998, 221; Meunier 2000, 64) could be particularly effective for the EU. Given the technocratic trade policy-making style in the Union, third parties experience difficulties in verifying the Commission's statements about allegedly recalcitrant constituencies (cf. Bretherton and Vogler 1999, 65-6). Meunier's research has compellingly shown that the EU's power in trade partly stems from 'the incomplete integration of European trade policy, leaving room for involvement by the Member States, and from the constant political battles over trade competence between national and supranational actors'. Several variables (voting rules, distribution of preferences, specifics of the issue) influence whether divergent European positions become a vice or a virtue in international trade negotiations. For example, unanimity voting strengthens the EU negotiators to resist demands for policy changes (conservative position) but it weakens their ability to advocate policy changes (reformist attitude) (Meunier 2006, 2–3).

This links up with the general point that Europe's power in trade cannot be fully understood without looking at the objectives that it wants to achieve. In Meunier's model, the power of the EU is not only dependent on the institutional setting (QMV versus unanimity, shared versus exclusive competences) but also on the preferred trade policy options (conservative versus reformist attitude). The second part of this chapter will focus on the latter dimension, namely the EU trade policy objectives, arguing that analyses of Europe's goals in world trade should go beyond the conventional protectionist/free trade cleavage.

Politicisation of EU trade policies: challenges and opportunities   Despite its traditionally technocratic policy style, EU trade policy has become increasingly politicised since the 1990s. The above-mentioned conflicts concerning Community competences (cf. ECJ *Opinion 1/94*) and the autonomy of the Commission (cf. Blair House) illustrate that policy-makers are becoming more and more involved in this domain. Although the formal role of the European Parliament (EP) remains limited, it makes its voice heard through hearings, reports, resolutions and parliamentary questions, and at times it manages to be involved by the Commission. Under the Treaty of Lisbon, the EP's role increases: trade legislation follows the co-decision procedure and the EP should be kept informed by the Commission during trade negotiations. EU trade policy is also increasingly scrutinised by non-governmental actors such as environmental groups, human rights activists and trade unions, as well as 'traditional' lobby groups in the industry and services business. Although the influence of industry associations (Gerlach 2006; Young and Peterson 2006, 806) and broader civil society groups (Dür and De Bièvre) is as yet limited, Europe's common commercial policy is certainly no longer shielded from pressure.

This contestation of trade politics reflects a worldwide trend since the 'battle of Seattle' in 1999. This, in turn, mirrors the degree of trade globalisation and the shift to more sensitive and intrusive behind-the-border issues, such as food safety, environmental protection and health. But the augmented politicisation of trade is particularly salient in the EU, and also poses a number of new challenges for Europe's international power in trade. On the one hand, the conduct of trade policy negotiations becomes more complicated. One example is the leaking of confidential documents on the EU position in services negotiations in 2003 – followed by demonstrations blaming the Union for being too secretive, too friendly towards European businesses, and harming developing country interests. On the other hand, the politicisation of trade offers opportunities for the Commission to enhance its negotiation leverage vis-à-vis the Council as well as non-EU partners.

Pressure from policy-makers and NGOs can make the Commission's tied-hands strategies more effective. For example, examining transatlantic trade relations, Peterson (2004, 44) suggests that the Commission's relative insulation from lobbying activities may weaken its power: this makes it more difficult to convince the Member States, which claim to be supported by their industries. Therefore, the Commission's initiatives to consult with civil society groups – it created a Civil Society Dialogue in 1998 and a Contact Group in 2000 – and its stimulation of European lobbies such as the European Services Forum, are not just defensive responses to mounting criticism. They also form a Commission strategy to forge allies and gather information at the EU level. Similarly, the increased involvement of the EP could strengthen its negotiating position. As former Trade Commissioner Sir Leon Brittan argued:[2]

> If Mr Kantor [the US negotiator] is able to say that he must do this because Senator X and Representative Y insist on it, I do not see why I should not be able to do the same and say I must have this because Mr So-and-So and Mr So-and-So of this committee and that committee are pressing me and I cannot possibly resist them. So it is of practical benefit as well as constitutional importance to have the active involvement of Parliament.

The politicisation of EU trade also points to a more fundamental challenge. Apart from the implications for negotiation strategies, it raises the question of the legitimacy of EU trade politics. The growing contestation of governmental and non-governmental actors may undermine Europe's power in international trade negotiations. This relates the 'soft power' of the EU through trade (see Chapter 2): to what extent is Europe's approach considered to be legitimate by the parliaments, by civil society and by the public at large?

This topic is of utmost importance given Europe's current legitimacy crisis, but has only recently been addressed in the literature. Simply summarised, Meunier (2003) uses Fritz Scharpf's distinction to argue that EU trade politics are characterised by outcome-legitimacy ('government for the people') rather than process-legitimacy ('government by the people'). Demands for greater participation in the formulation and conduct of European trade policy fail to realise that the public interest is best guaranteed by a relatively large and autonomous role for the European Commission – facilitated by QMV and exclusive competences. The underlying rationale seems to be that a relatively technocratic policy-making environment helps to solve the collective action problem in trade – namely specific costs and the diffuse benefits of liberalisation. Limited politicisation facilitates the pursuit of free trade which, in turn, enhances general welfare. In contrast, the involvement of more actors inevitably leads to the insertion of protectionist tendencies in trade policies.

---

2   Debates of the EP, 14 December 1994, 4-455-123.

Rather than transcending the efficiency-legitimacy dilemma, this analysis somehow takes sides in the ideological debate on the preferred direction of EU trade policies. The idea that a less politicised policy-making style benefits consumers and harms specific interests may not always come true – for example, under these circumstances policy-makers may not look adequately at diffuse benefits resulting from the environmental implications of trade policies. Increased influence from governmental and non-governmental actors may lead to so-called 'protectionist' trade measures which are nevertheless favourable for the public interest – as suggested in Pascal Lamy's stillborn call for a debate on 'collective preferences' in 2004. Therefore, critics of trade globalisation cannot simply be dismissed as old-fashioned protectionists defending specific interests to the detriment of consumers. Once again, the debate on the objectives of Europe's trade policy arises. Europe's legitimacy in trade is not only based on procedural arguments, but is firmly bound up with the normative debate on trade policy objectives.

The External Context

External factors also influence EU power in trade. First, as suggested above, the general nature of the current world trade regime may be particularly beneficial for the Union – both in terms of procedures (global governance, instead of hierarchical decision-making) and contents (behind-the-border instead of tariff measures). EU negotiators are experienced in dealing with the consequences of 'deep' integration without simply harmonising trade-related regulations of national countries. Elgström and Strömvik (2003, 11–12) explicitly link the EU's multi-level governance system with the global governance situation on the world stage.

> The Union thereby has an unusually large pool of experienced and skilled negotiators, used to an everyday environment that can most aptly be described as an extreme version of the emerging global situation. By constantly participating in the 'multilateral inter-bureaucratic negotiation marathon' that the EU constitutes, they are for instance no strangers to the creative use of informal strategies to avoid dead-locks in complicated negotiations. The EU can thus be seen as an international actor already quite adjusted to the changing global conditions.

This partly explains why the EU argues for a broad international trade agenda negotiated under the multilateral WTO, including provisions on investment, competition, government procurement, as well as environment and social issues. Such an external projection of the 'EU model' – this is indeed how European policy-makers justify the broad and multilateral agenda – would obviously be advantageous for the Union.

A more straightforward argument is that the EU benefits from the international trade system because, together with the US, it has heavily impacted on the design of the WTO system. This is most clearly illustrated by the complex provisions on agriculture which, to some extent, allow for the continuation of EU subsidies. The

WTO dispute settlement body is also advantageous for the EU, even though its jurisprudence sometimes limits Europe's capacity to act – for example, the WTO panels on bananas, sugar, and genetically modified organisms. The EU has actively used the WTO dispute settlement mechanism, mostly as the plaintiff and against the US, which has strengthened the Union's overall power in the multilateral trade arena (Meunier and Nicolaïdis 2005, 261–2). Generally, the dispute mechanism also guarantees that other states will not lapse into protectionism and regionalism. This is important because, in parallel with the EU's larger market size since the 1990s, its interest in a stable and multilateral trade regime has also increased. This is what Kerremans (2000, 140–41) called the 'bloc size effect'.

Second, Europe's power as a trading bloc can be evaluated through comparisons with other trade negotiators. The US is the most obvious point of reference. Arguably, the US and the EU are equally powerful in trade politics. Their numerous trade conflicts reflect the deep mutual interdependence between both economic giants – rather than unbridgeable transatlantic gaps in their approaches to trade politics. Following the New Transatlantic Agenda (1995) and urged on by the Transatlantic Business Dialogue, the EU and the US have engaged in regulatory cooperation, including a series of MRAs on various issues such as pharmaceuticals and telecoms (Meunier and Nicolaïdis 2005, 264). During the Doha Round, Union and US positions on agriculture even converged. Even though considerable divergences continue to exist, the main challenge for EU (as well as US) trade power seems to come from the emerging developing country markets grouped in the G-20 (such as Brazil, Argentina, China, India, Thailand and Indonesia).

Whereas EU-US trade is characterised by mutual interdependence, Europe's trade relations with developing countries have traditionally mirrored North-South dependence.[3] During the past five decades, a patchwork of bilateral trade agreements has been created with developing countries, basically resulting in a 'hub and spoke' pattern which benefits Europe's import and export interests (Bretherton en Vogler 1999, 64). Because of its central place in the myriad of preferential trade agreements, the EU disposes of a 'structural power' vis-à-vis the South. The economic dependence of Europe's former colonies in Africa, the Caribbean and the Pacific (ACP) is widely illustrated in the literature. In his authoritative account of the EU-ACP Lomé regime, Ravenhill (1985) talks about 'collective clientelism' between the ACP group and the 'patron' EC. Although Lomé I (1975) was hailed as a progressive model for development, it gradually became clear that it perpetuated unequal power relations between both parties. The decreased power of the ACP is also reflected in the trade provisions in the EU-ACP Cotonou Agreement, signed in 2000. Despite reluctance from the ACP, the EU successfully insisted on establishing reciprocal trade liberalisation with six separate ACP regions. These Economic Partnership Agreements (EPAs), which should be implemented from 2008 onwards, seem to confirm Europe's 'divide

---

3   The same is true for Europe's trade relations with its close neighbours. Many of its neighbouring countries have first concluded a Free Trade Agreement with the EU, and most have become Member States.

and rule' policies vis-à-vis developing countries (cf. Elgström 2000, 192; Holland 2003, 170). The much-quoted 'Everything But Arms' initiative – which continues to grant non-reciprocal market access for the least-developed countries (LDCs) – also proved to be functional for the break-up of the ACP group and the shift to reciprocal free trade (Orbie 2007a). This gloomy picture resembles the scenario outlined by Galtung in the 1970s (see Chapter 1).

In contrast with ACP and LDC developing countries, the G-20 poses a considerable challenge for EU power in trade politics. Europe's defensive sectors are particularly vulnerable towards these competitive export economies. Competition from India and China has already led to a major restructuring in textiles and clothing, and agricultural exports from countries such as Brazil and South Africa are increasingly affecting European farmers. Yet the emergence of these relatively prosperous developing countries also offers opportunities for EU trade policy-makers. In contrast to the ACP and LDC groups, the G-20 countries do have a clear stake in (multilateral or bilateral) trade negotiations. Given their increasing domestic purchasing power, they could also satisfy Europe's offensive export interests, for example in telecommunications and financial services. At the same time, negotiations with Mercosur and South Africa, for example, offer opportunities for those European actors which favour the liberalisation of agriculture.

Thus looking from the outside, it seems that the bipolarity in trade is gradually shifting towards a multi-polar trade regime. Whereas trade relations with the ACP and the LDC groups (essentially the G-90 in the WTO) continue to illustrate EU dominance in trade, the Union is now faced with the more assertive G-20 trading partners (basically a 'non-ACP' group). This facilitates the further deepening of Europe's international trade relations although, on the other hand, it also increases competitive pressures on its defensive sectors. The question arises as to whether this evolution incites protectionist tendencies within the EU, hindering the pursuit of an open and multilateral trading system.

Trading Objectives: Harnessing Globalisation?

The previous section showed that Europe's decision-making machinery in trade is far from unitary, but also that this institutional complexity is not necessarily disadvantageous. In fact, the EU's distinctive multi-level governance system may even be fruitful in international trade negotiations – together with its experience in dealing with deep integration. The Union is certainly a powerful actor in trade, but the extent to which this is the case depends on various variables. In this section, one of these will be explicitly highlighted: the objectives that are pursued through EU trade policy. Indeed, any evaluation of Europe's power in trade ultimately depends on an analysis of the aims that the EU wants to achieve. For example, does Europe use its economic weight as leverage for fostering the international trade regime, or does it rather aim for a continental Fortress Europe; how does the increased politicisation of EU trade policy relate to the objectives pursued; and how does the institutional setting of EU trade policy influence these policy choices?

Studies on Europe's trade policy goals usually focus on economic interests. The major 'possession goal' (cf. Chapter 2) of the common commercial policy is to promote Europe's economic sectors, both in a defensive way (such as tariff barriers and anti-dumping measures) and offensively (for example, opening of third-country markets through negotiations or WTO disputes). Trade policy can be conducted on a multilateral (for example, WTO), bilateral (such as EU-Mercosur) and unilateral (such as the GSP) level. The extent to which defensive or offensive economic objectives predominate translates into the familiar protectionism versus liberalisation dichotomy, and the concomitant debate on whether the EU should be seen as a protectionist fortress in trade, or a liberalising force in the world economy. After addressing this question, we look at Europe's pursuit of 'milieu goals' such as development of the South and core labour standards (CLS). These normative objectives have become increasingly salient in EU trade policy discourse since 1995. What about Europe's commitment to achieving these aims through trade, and how does this feed back to the power resources of EU trade policy?

Europe's 'harnessing globalisation' discourse (*'maîtriser la mondialisation'*, *'gerechtere Globalisierung'*) summarises nicely both categories of trade objectives. Besides arguing that the EU follows a middle course between old-fashioned protectionism and unbridled free trade, it emphasises that trade policy advances development of the South, as well as environmental and social concerns.

The Myth of a Fortress Europe: Institutions, Ideas and Interests

> The question raised by the trade policy of the European Union is the one once raised by Sherlock Holmes: why did the dog fail to bark? Why, in this case, has the European Union – with its high unemployment, belief in the need to harmonise policies toward the environment and the labour market, its concentration on its internal development and, to a lesser degree, on its relations with its 'near abroad' – not become more protectionist? (Wolf 1997, 125)

Until the 1990s, Europe reluctantly supported multilateral trade negotiations under the various rounds of the GATT (General Agreement of Tariffs and Trade). In fact, the European integration project *as such* has always been a major exception to GATT's Most-Favoured Nations (MFN) principle, and subsequent enlargements made this regionalist exception all the more important. Externally, the EC used to prefer bilateral trade agreements with developing countries (especially the ACP group) and with the 'near abroad' (such as the Southern Mediterranean countries). Various exceptions to the MFN principles[4] resulted

---

4   These exceptions are legitimised by GATT/WTO rules. First, Article XXIV allows for (reciprocal) free trade areas beyond the level of MFN tariffs, provided that 'substantially all' trade is liberalised within a 'reasonable length of time', and that the overall outcome is not more protectionist. Applications of this rule are the creation of the EC, its subsequent enlargements, Europe's recent free trade agreements with Chile, Mexico, and South Africa, and future agreements including EPAs. Second, the GSP, established under the GATT Enabling Clause, allows for a more favourable *and* non-reciprocal treatment

in what Bhagwati (2002, 112–14) called the European 'spaghetti bowl': a complex web of discriminatory trade relations. The European 'preferential pyramid' summarises this myriad of trade relations (see Orbie 2007c).

This situation has always provoked fears for a Fortress Europe in trade. Historically, this concern refers to the protectionism and regionalism of the 1930s; economically, it stems from the consideration that regional and bilateral trade agreements bring more trade diversion than trade creation. The debate on Europe's international posture as a protectionist regional bloc became particularly acute during the second half of the 1980s. On the one hand, this period saw the establishment of the internal market (without similar external commitments to liberalisation), while on the other hand the European market was extended with Spain and Portugal (which traditionally hold a rather protectionist position). At the same time, the Uruguay Round was muddling on.

Yet, Fortress Europe did not materialise. The ratio between intra-European trade and external trade has remained relatively stable over the past 30 years (Tsoukalis 2003, 68). Over the past 15 years, many tariff and non-tariff barriers have been removed.

Of course, this statement should be qualified. For one thing, there have always been internal disagreements between southern Member States (the 'Club Med') favouring a more protectionist and regionalist trade policy, and the northern 'free traders' with a more liberal and global orientation. Originally, both camps were represented by France and Germany respectively, but each enlargement shifted the balance somewhat. Within the Commission, DG Trade has generally sided with the northern group, whereas DG Agriculture rather defends the protectionist interests of the southern countries. Secondly, there are notable exceptions to Europe's fairly liberal trade orientation. Considerable tariff barriers and trade-distorting subsidies remain in agriculture. Despite the increased exposure of European farmers to world markets under the 2003 agricultural reforms, further reduction of export subsidies and tariffs are needed (WTO 2007). In addition, non-tariff barriers, such as restrictive rules of origin and food safety requirements, as well as anti-dumping measures and other trade defence instruments, continue to restrict trade (see, for example, Messerlin 2001). Nonetheless, there is a consensus in the literature that the EU has not become a protectionist fortress – quite the contrary (e.g. Tsoukalis 2003, 70).

Several reasons have been advanced to explain why 'the dog failed to bark' – as Wolf (1997) described the non-appearance of a Fortress Europe. Hanson (1998) provided one of the first and most sophisticated accounts. From a historical-

---

of developing country imports. This has long been the major export opportunity for Asian and Latin American countries to Europe. The 'Everything But Arms' initiative for LDCs is the most radical application of this provision. The third exception also enables non-reciprocity, namely the negotiation of a GATT/WTO waiver. This makes it possible to grant preferential market access to a geographically defined group of countries. The most famous example is the Lomé trade regime, where waivers allowed for non-reciprocal access of the ACP group to the European market. Since the 1990s, it became more difficult to negotiate such a waiver in the WTO.

institutionalist point of view, he argues that the EU's remarkably liberal *external* policy is an unanticipated consequence of the construction of Europe's *internal* market. The establishment of the single market programme was primarily an internal project – without much attention for the world outside. However, when EU Member States decided to eliminate barriers at their internal borders, the question arose as to what extent these would be re-established at the Union's external borders. The decision-making system proves to be crucial. Given the QMV rule, northern Member States always disposed of a veto when restrictive barriers at the EU level were on the Council's negotiating table. In short, Hanson illustrates how EU decision-making rules entailed a systematic liberalisation bias, at least with regard to non-tariff barriers.[5]

Other new-institutionalist arguments have also been advanced. For example, Wolf (1997) emphasises the large bureaucratic power of the Commission compared with the Council, and the limited influence of lobbies and the EP.[6] Given its role as an 'agent' in EU trade policy, the Commission can indeed be expected to be more liberal than its 'principals'. This is a major reason why trade policy has often been delegated to the executive level (e.g. Meunier 2006, 8).

The institutional set-up is thus closely related to the ideological dimension of trade politics. What about the role of ideas in the stillborn Fortress Europe? Hanson (1998) argues that the construction of the internal market entailed a more liberal external posture, *in spite of* protectionist tendencies with main European actors. Therefore, he speaks of an 'unintended' consequence: the European Commission (Trade Commissioner De Clercq: 'We are not building a single market in order to turn it over to hungry foreigners'), the Member States (especially France) and European business (such as the European Round Table of Industrialists) all envisaged a protectionist Europe in the second half of the 1980s. However, it should be noticed that some European actors did favour a shift to worldwide free trade (for example, the neoliberal strand of the ERT, and the UK government). Furthermore, whereas Hanson explains why the Fortress Europe failed to materialise despite the single market architects' protectionist sentiments, he does not make clear why the EU evolved from a protectionist and regionalist actor to become the most outspoken proponent of an ambitious round of multilateral trade negotiations from 1995 onwards.

The 1997 'multilateralism first strategy' (Lamy 2002, 1412) underlined EU policy-makers' commitment to more and deeper liberalisation under the umbrella

---

5   Young's analysis somewhat contradicts Hanson's findings: Young concludes that the dynamics of EU decision-making on the internal market – pushing for approximation at the level of the most stringent national rules – have produced regulatory peaks vis-à-vis third countries. This explains why the EU has been a respondent in a number of high-profile trade disputes, and has had problems complying with WTO judgments. Young considers these 'tendencies towards being an incidental fortress' as an exception to Europe's liberal and multi-lateralist trade policy.

6   Again, agriculture is the exception that proves the rule: agricultural lobbies traditionally have a large influence on EU policies, and are institutionally embedded in the Council as well as the Commission.

of the WTO. Nevertheless, the EU negotiated several bilateral trade agreements during this period, for example with Mexico (1997), South Africa (1999), Chile (2002), and ongoing negotiations with Mercosur, the Gulf Cooperation Council (GCC), the Southern Mediterranean countries, and the ACP. Moreover, in 2007 Europe started WTO-plus negotiations with India, Korea and ASEAN. Although the WTO (2007, xii) warns that these negotiations 'could further complicate its trade regime, and divert interest from the multilateral trading system', the EU emphasises its compatibility with the WTO system. It seems that Europe's new bilateral agreements are a 'building block' for pursuing an international free trade agenda, rather than a 'stumbling block' obstructing progress in the WTO. They also tend to pressurise the WTO negotiating partners in a dynamic of 'competitive liberalisation'.

Ideological factors clearly played a role in this shifting EU trade posture. This paradigmatic shift becomes evident in Europe's negotiations at the WTO, and even more clearly in its trade relations with developing countries. WTO compatibility and reciprocal trade liberalisation has indeed become the 'new catechism', an 'indisputable dogma' (cf. Holland 2003, 162–4; Elgström 2000, 184) in EU trade policies vis-à-vis the South. This evolution is influenced by the 1995 enlargement with Sweden, Finland and Austria, which changed the ideological composition of the Council. More generally, and from a neo-Gramscian viewpoint, Hurt (2003, 164; 2004, 164) points to the ideological hegemony of neoliberalism with European elites since the end of the Cold War. European trade policy discourse tends to present the WTO as an external and predetermined factor, compelling the EU to follow a neoliberal course. However, WTO compatibility is often used strategically by European policy-makers who have increasingly favoured a neoliberal agenda.

Recently, the EU's belief in the virtues of free trade for development has been softened, or at least complemented with a greater emphasis on flanking measures, transition periods, asymmetric commitments, and 'Aid for Trade' funding. This changing attitude reflects the 'post-Washington Consensus' which puts more emphasis on aid and the Millennium Development Goals. But this has not heralded a fundamental change of course so far (Orbie 2007b). Because Europe's economic significance has grown since the completion of the internal market – both in manufacturing *and* in services – it has an interest in a neoliberal trade regime embodied in the WTO (cf. the bloc-size effect above). Looking at specific sectors, it seems that the EU is gradually trading concessions in agriculture in exchange for market access to third-country goods and services markets, as well as regulatory issues reflecting the EU model. This partly explains Europe's preference for a broad trade round – so that inevitable concessions in agriculture can be compensated with gains in other domains – although it also illustrates Europe's offensive interests in NAMA. It should also be noticed that the existence of an extensive social safety net in most European countries decreases the likelihood of an anti-globalist backlash by the 'losers of globalisation' in the EU.

Thus, notwithstanding agricultural resistance against reform and protectionist pressure from textile lobbies, Europe's free trade stance is here to stay. In fact, some segments of Europe's assumed 'defensive' sectors – such as food processors and clothing distributors – have argued for more far-reaching trade openness. As explained above, the assertiveness of the G-20 also offers opportunities for EU trade interests. Europe's willingness to engage in trade relations with these countries reveals itself in its pursuit of ambitious WTO negotiations and of comprehensive bilateral trade arrangements. Although these will inevitably hurt Europe's sensitive sectors, the EU seems to be convinced that free trade relations with these countries will bring more substantial economic benefits.

This cocktail of institutions, ideas and interests explains Europe's increasing proactivity in advocating global and liberal trade relations, rather than hiding behind a continental tariff wall. The European Commission – especially DG Trade, but increasingly also DG Development and DG Agriculture (cf. Van den Hoven 2007; Petiteville 2001) – plays a crucial role in these dynamics. But this is only one part of the story. In parallel with the victory of free trade over protectionist objectives since 1995, the EU started to highlight the normative dimension of its trade policies. Is the pursuit of non-trade objectives such as democracy, human rights and sustainable development merely a normative dressing over a free trade menu, or does it witness a new form of hidden protectionism?

The Rise of Values in Trade: A Contradiction in Terms?

> The Europeans have values as well as goods and services they would like to export. These values include a developed sensitivity for the environment, the rights of workers, and distributional justice. They form part of the European model, if there is to be one. (Tsoukalis 2003, 193)

Meunier and Nicolaïdis (2005) distinguish between the EU's power *in* trade (cf. the power resources in the first part of this chapter) and *through* trade, including the normative dimension. However, the second dimension mainly focuses on the objective of multilateralism, rather than explicitly looking at the promotion of objectives such as human rights and sustainable development through trade. Does it make sense to look at normative objectives in a policy domain like trade? Academic work on Europe's international role seems to assume that the objectives in this area are restricted to the pursuit of 'selfish' or 'self-interested' economic motives. Although many recent writings have discussed Europe's 'normative power' on the world scene, these accounts scarcely focus on trade policy. It is characteristic that the comprehensive review by Youngs (2004, 416–19) of the expanding normative power Europe literature does not mention one single study explicitly looking at EU trade.[7] There are nevertheless compelling reasons why the relevance of such objectives in Union trade policy cannot *a priori* be excluded. In

---

7   Van den Hoven (2004; 2006) and Szymanski and Smith (2005) are exceptions. Van den Hoven (2004) applies Schimmelfennig's 'rhetorical trap' to EU trade policy. Similarly, Szymanski and Smith (2005) argue that the Commission applied a form of 'rhetorical action' in negotiating the democracy and human rights provisions of the EU-Mexico agreement.

this section we sketch a number of considerations, ranging from a rationalistic viewpoint to more constructivist-oriented lines of approach.

Starting with the rationalist view that politics are driven by a calculation of costs and benefits, one can point to long-term advantages of normative achievements (cf. 'milieu goals' in Chapter 1). For example, the EU may have a long-term interest in a more prosperous South, since this enlarges the scope for exports and investments, and might also diminish migratory pressure on the EU. The post-war international economic architecture characterised by 'embedded liberalism' and the first Lomé Convention in the 1970s were based on such far-sighted interests. On the other hand, normative arguments can also be rationally used as a veil over protectionist measures – hidden 'possession goals' which explain developing countries' reluctance to social and environmental clauses in trade.

The second point stems from the political economy of trade politics. Trade policy-makers are confronted with a typical collective action problem. Although most observers agree that free trade is generally welfare-increasing – at least in northern economies – policy-makers experience difficulties in realising free trade because this brings diffuse benefits (e.g. for consumers) and specific costs (e.g. for farmers). One way to solve this puzzle involves delegation to an agent within the executive. Principal-agent analyses of trade policy have indeed illustrated that an agent (such as the Commission negotiator) is generally more in favour of free trade than its principals (such as the Member States in the Council). But Van den Hoven (2006, 186–7) suggests another strategy to facilitate the case for free trade: using normative arguments. When normative considerations converge with free trade objectives, their consideration in the political debate may tip the balance toward the latter. When the pursuit of free trade is framed as pursuing broader value-related objectives, this may legitimise the case for trade liberalisation. For example, pledges for more market opening are often presented as a moral imperative in favour of the South; and some argue that integrating ecological and social considerations in trade rules is necessary to prevent a popular backlash against the global free trade regime. However, these examples also make clear that the argument can be turned upside down. Normative considerations can also be used as a seemingly legitimate veil over protectionist intentions. Either way – free trade or protectionist – normative objectives have become an important element of the trade policy debate.

This relates to another political economy consideration, namely the evolution from 'at-the-border' to 'behind-the-border' regulations. Giving its growing intrusiveness, trade policy increasingly touches upon politically sensitive and value-related issues. These new trade policy issues (for example, genetically modified organisms, beef hormones, intellectual property rights, geographical indications, audio-visual and health services) often reflect preferences that originated in specific national contexts – which also sheds light on the politicisation of trade. Given the changing nature of trade politics, normative considerations have acquired a permanent place in trade policy-making, and are here to stay.

Normative arguments are even more relevant in dense institutional environments such as the EU, as argued in sociological-institutionalist theorising (see Chapter 1). Explaining that ideas may play an autonomous role in the long run, even when their instrumental (rationalist) significance has faded away, Goldstein and Keohane (1995) refer to the EU, where the large degree of legalisation and institutionalisation brings about more incentives to make policies consistent with norms. This increases the potential influence of ideas (including normative considerations) in foreign policy making. The initially pragmatic use of normative arguments could, in time, lead to a 'rhetorical entrapment' of EU policy choices. Thus, without positing a pre-eminence of ideational factors, it is clear that the external promotion of normative objectives and strategic power dynamics intermesh in a complex way (Youngs 2004). 'Norm entrepreneurs' in the EP, the Council and the Commission can play an important role in this respect. The increased involvement of the EP and civil society (see above) in EU trade politics also enhances the scope for sociological-institutionalist dynamics. This analysis goes a long way towards constructivist approaches to EU external policy, which *inter alia* examine the impact of Europe's discourse and self-image. As explained in Chapter 1, the pervasive representation of the EU as a 'normative power' cannot simply be dismissed as empty rhetoric.

From this perspective, the normative trade policy objectives in Europe's legal texts and political discourse may be helpful. A first glance at the EU/EC Treaties is not very impressive. Normative goals are barely mentioned in the context of Europe's common commercial policy. In general, the EC Treaty shows a bias in the direction of further liberalisation (Brenton 2000, 5). Article 131 speaks of the 'aim to contribute, in the common interest, to the harmonious development of world trade, the progressive abolition of restrictions on international trade and the lowering of customs barriers'.[8] However, the EU Treaty (Article 3) also established the principle of consistency: the EU 'shall in particular ensure the consistency of its external activities as a whole in the context of its external relations, security, economic and development policies' – which includes the foreign policy objectives under the second pillar, such as 'democracy and the rule of law, and respect for human rights and fundamental freedoms' (Article 11, EU Treaty).

The Treaty of Lisbon strengthens the consistency requirement in two ways. On the one hand, it explicitly adds to the trade policy provisions that Europe's common commercial policy 'shall be conducted in the context of the principles and objectives of the Union's external action' (Article 188C). On the other hand, and in contrast with the present EU Treaty, the Constitution's general articles on Europe's international objectives explicitly refer to trade policy; Article 2(5) speaks of 'fair trade' besides 'free trade'. Although it is unclear what the fair trade stipulation actually means, it is certainly not a veiled reference to protectionism.

---

8   As for *internal* trade objectives, we can also point to Article 2 of the EC Treaty, which underlines the general aims of the common policies, namely 'to promote throughout the Community a harmonious, balanced and sustainable development of economic activities, a high level of employment and of social protection, equality between men and women, sustainable and non-inflationary growth, a high degree of competitiveness and convergence of economic performance, a high level of protection and improvement of the quality of the environment, the raising of the standard of living and quality of life, and economic and social cohesion and solidarity among Member States'.

It rather reflects the general normative tenor of this article, which also mentions the goals of peace, sustainable development, solidarity, eradication of poverty, and human rights (Eeckhout 2004, 53).

These changes in the Treaty illustrate the blurred boundaries between 'first pillar' and 'second pillar' policies, and the concomitant diffusion of the normative objectives of 'traditional' foreign policy into the realm of trade policy. This legal evolution had already become clear in EU trade policy practice. For example, since 1992, all EU trade and cooperation agreements have contained a clause on human rights; since 1995, trade preferences under Europe's GSP have included labour conditionality. Given the absence of a full-fledged foreign policy apparatus, trade policy instruments are all the more relevant for Europe's international action. Trade policy serves partly as a substitute for a 'real' EU foreign policy.

This evolution illustrates the Union's growing consensus on the role of normative objectives in trade.[9] Since 1996, EU trade policy discourse has devoted much attention to the promotion of objectives such as development of the South, human rights and sustainable development (Van den Hoven 2006, 188). Beforehand, Europe's trade objectives were basically translated into economic interests. Trade policy was the 'core business' of EU external policy – in both senses of the word. By the end of the 1990s, the EU, instigated by DG Trade and northern Member States, deliberately put 'sustainable development' and 'social solidarity' at the heart of EU trade policy discourse. The following citation by former Trade Commissioner Pascal Lamy illustrates the new trade discourse:

> It is no longer only economic interests that are in question, but also values, the concept of society, of what is desirable and of what is risky. Health, environment, the quality of life, culture are henceforth stakes that must be reconciled with open and competitive markets. Regarding development, human rights, social and environmental standards, the European Union brings with it values that have the aim of becoming universal. (Agence Europe, 10 November 1999)

This pursuit of normative objectives is at the centre of the overarching trade objective of 'harnessing globalisation' – Lamy's favourite motto.[10]

Since 1999, DG Trade has used trade sustainability impact assessments (Trade SIAs) to analyse the economic, environmental, and social impact of trade agreements, both in Europe and among its trading partners. For example, SIA studies were commissioned on the impact of EU agreements with Chile, Mercosur, the GCC, the ACP, and of the Doha negotiations. Although a considerable amount of financial and staff resources were devoted to these studies, their impact

---

9   It also reflects a compromise among European actors. For example, some British members of the Convention wanted to scrap general references to normative foreign policy objectives in the trade articles, whereas others wanted to explicitly add 'sustainable development' and 'poverty reduction' (see CONV 850/03, 18 July 2003).

10   Trade Commissioner Peter Mandelson (since 2004) has basically adopted this discourse. But as the WTO Round muddles on, the Commission has complemented this approach with an emphasis on Europe's 'main trade interests', to be achieved through multilateral *and* bilateral negotiations (European Commission 2006, 9).

has been limited. According to Raza (2007, 80), Trade SIAs remain 'an academic exercise' which serves to legitimise EU trade policies, but without substantial impact upon the actual conduct of the negotiations.

Obviously, there are always normative dimensions to political constructs – also to economic relations and to trade policies. The question is thus not whether trade policy has value-related aspects, but rather: what values are we talking about, how are they promoted through trade, and what about Europe's commitment to achieve them? This analysis concerned values such as development, social solidarity and environmental sustainability. It made clear that their relevance in trade policy cannot *a priori* be neglected. In fact, some arguments suggest that a normative trade policy is all the more plausible for the European Union – compared with other actors – given its dense institutional environment, the recent politicisation of trade policy in Europe, the absence of a traditional foreign policy, and the EU profile as a normative power in the world.

An extensive body of research (see Chapter 1) has discussed the distinctiveness of the EU as a 'civilian' or 'normative' power on the international scene. In order to evaluate this vision, we postulate that trade is the place to look. Trade has indeed been the most powerful and most integrated area of EU external relations, and European policy-makers have deliberately highlighted the normative aspirations pursued through trade. This brings us to the next question about Europe's commitment to these objectives.

Examining Europe's Commitment

The question of Europe's commitment to promote values through trade quickly encounters sensitive controversies about the merits of trade liberalisation. Inevitably, the question presents itself whether and how free trade may contribute to normative objectives. It may be assumed that free trade as such cannot guarantee 'milieu goals', and that some forms of economic protection or interventionism may be legitimate when they contribute to the realisation of normative external policy objectives without jeopardising the international trading regime. This broad assumption draws from the notion of 'embedded liberalism', which was coined by John Gerard Ruggie in 1982 and reverts to the ideas outlined in Polanyi's *The Great Transformation* (1944). In short, this approach shows that reliance on the forces of the free market cannot guarantee goals such as development of the South and social progress, and that social values should be embedded in the economic system. It roughly corresponds to EU discourse on 'harnessing globalisation' – although on reflection it is unclear how this phrase translates into concrete trade policy measures.

Below two cases have been briefly sketched. The first one deals with the intention to promote 'economic development of the South' through trade, while the second concerns the inclusion of CLS in Europe's trade relations. Both cases have occupied an important place on Europe's normative trade agenda since the second half of the 1990s, each time we consider the multilateral, bilateral and unilateral trade dimension. Europe's unilateral trade policy through its GSP system proves to be particularly interesting because here the EU disposes of a considerable leeway to push through its preferences. Therefore, we focus on the GSP's role in promoting economic development (the 'Everything But Arms' initiative) and CLS (through positive and negative conditionality). In contrast, it proves to be more difficult to dissect the 'EU factor' in decisions at the multilateral trade level.

Economic Development of the South: EPA and EBA

On the multilateral trade scene, the EU has been at the forefront of advocating a 'Development Round' of WTO negotiations. Applying Schimmelfennig's rhetorical trap (see Chapters 1 and 11) to EU trade policy, Van den Hoven (2004) examined how DG Trade's new 'development discourse' in the run-up to the Doha Conference was instrumental for convincing actors within and outside Europe to launch a new WTO trade round. For example, it helped to forge a more development-friendly stance within the EU vis-à-vis agricultural interests (putting DG Agriculture on the defensive) and business interests (as in the TRIPS debate on AIDS medicines). In the Doha negotiations, which were launched in 2001, the EU continually emphasised the development dimension of all the issues on the negotiating table. Several months after the debacle of the Cancún summit in 2003, the EU also stated that the poorest countries would 'get the round for free', implying that no concessions from the 50 LDCs were expected. In Hong Kong (2005), the EU successfully insisted on the 'globalisation' of 'Everything but Arms' in the WTO framework.

But with the trade round still unfinished, it remains difficult to evaluate Europe's development-friendliness in the WTO. Observers from developing countries and NGOs have been critical of the achievements to date. Following Cancún, the EU has eventually agreed to eliminate its exports subsidies in agriculture by 2013, although the timetable still needs to be negotiated. On agricultural tariffs and domestic subsidies, the 'blame game' between the EU and the US has resurfaced, with developing countries on the sidelines. The EU argues that its tariff barriers for agricultural imports will only be decreased in exchange for concessions in NAMA and services trade by the G-20. Europe's negotiating stance on services, and especially on the Singapore issues, has also been controversial from a development perspective. Developing countries prefered to discuss the implementation of previous commitments, made during the Uruguay Round, rather than engaging in new negotiations on trade-related issues. Yet the EU has shown itself to be the most offensive proponent of discussions on competition, investment, and government procurement, despite strong resistance from most developing countries. It only abandoned its insistence on these regulatory issues in July 2004, as part of a package deal where developing countries (except the poorest) pledged to further increase their NAMA, for example for manufacturing products from the EU.

The bilateral EU-ACP relationship remains the most important venue for Europe's activities in the trade and development nexus. The Lomé trade regime has been overhauled by the Cotonou Agreement, which foresees free trade agreements between 2008 and 2020. Although the EU has emphasised the development dimension of these agreements and the asymmetrical liberalisation schemes, the move to reciprocity has been criticised for meeting export interests of European firms and implementing neoliberal preferences of EU policy-makers. The necessity of WTO compatibility should be qualified: the Union was (and is) scarcely committed to negotiate a new waiver for the continuation of Lomé-style preferences. This would be costly for the EU, especially as regards the increasingly important trading partners of the G-20.

The ACP group fears that increased market openings will hurt their less competitive sectors, and that their incomes from import duties will fall. These concerns have provoked demands for 'light EPAs'. First of all, these imply limited liberalisation commitments over long transition periods for the ACP, and generous market openings on the part of the EU. Europe has already committed to grant 100 per cent duty-free access under EPAs, except for rice and sugar, which is a *de facto* extension of EBA. A second and crucial component of light EPAs is financial support for the building of regional markets and regional supply capacities. But the Commission claims that it is unable to grant aid additional to the European Development Fund (EDF), because this is largely a Member State competence (see Chapter 3), and is not foreseen either in the Cotonou Agreement or in the Council's mandate. The GAERC ultimately agreed that Member States will provide bilateral funds on top of the EDF, but it remains to be seen how the trade negotiations and the different bilateral aid disbursements will be coordinated. Divisions between DG Trade and DG Development – since 1999, the latter is no longer involved in trade negotiations with the ACP – also hamper the realisation of a coherent 'Aid for Trade' dimension to the EPAs.

Together with the abolition of the STABEX and SYSMIN aid mechanisms for stabilisation of export earnings (replaced by the more modest FLEX scheme), and with the gradual erosion of the commodity protocols (providing stable and higher prices for bananas and sugar, for example), the move to reciprocity illustrates the neoliberal inspiration of the Cotonou Agreement. The interventionist spirit of the Lomé regime – which had been hailed as a model for North-South cooperation in the 1970s – has evaporated and given way to a market-oriented approach to trade and development. In this context, Arts and Dickson (2004, 11–12) argue that Europe's development policy has evolved 'from model to symbol': 'Whereas in 1975 the EU was prepared to challenge the prevailing liberal consensus and sign an innovative chapter with the ACP, by the 1990s this was no longer the case.'

Besides WTO requirements, EU preferences and interests have played a crucial role in this evolution. As explained above, Europe's external trade policies have witnessed a fruitful combination of ideological beliefs and economic interests.

Furthermore, the Union wants the EPAs to be so-called 'WTO-plus' agreements. The new EU-ACP trade regime would include trade in services, as well as clauses on competition, investment, trade facilitation and government procurement. Since 9/11, the EU has also attempted to introduce clauses on cooperation against weapons of mass destruction, combating terrorism and supporting the International Criminal Court in the EPAs. It is still unclear to what extent security concerns will overshadow trade agreements (see also Chapters 1, 3, 4 and 5 on securitisation), and might affect the EU's neoliberal orientation.

Europe emphasises that EPAs will stimulate the regional integration schemes among ACP economies. The Union has always insisted on the simultaneous creation of South-South and North-South trade agreements. But critics argue that Europe's policies – including its 'Aid For Trade' agenda – should give priority to regional integration in the South, before considering reciprocal liberalisation with the EU. Some scholars have even questioned the merits for regional integration: the negotiation of EPAs may in fact 'throw in disarray long-standing regional integration plans and initiatives' in Africa, rather than stimulating regionalisation (Goodison 2006, 173; see also Stevens 2006).

At first sight, one much-discussed trade initiative contradicts these critical observations: 'Everything But Arms' (cf. Orbie 2007a). Since 2001, this unilateral GSP regulation has granted completely free market access for all LDC products on the European market – with transition periods for rice, bananas and sugar. EU trade policy discourse has continually emphasised the relevance of EBA as a sign of Europe's development-friendliness through trade. Nevertheless, Europe's rules of origin are remarkably restrictive, implying that only about half of the LDC products that are theoretically eligible for duty-free access actually receive this treatment. Moreover, African LDCs ultimately feel obliged to participate in reciprocal EPAs. And most importantly, EBA proved to be instrumental in the reform of Lomé. It facilitated the break-up of the ACP group, radically establishing the distinction between LDC ACPs and non-LDC ACPs, and it played a catalysing role in reforming the sugar protocol. In recent years, EBA beneficiaries have even called for an amendment of the EBA. Most LDCs prefer to continue to benefit from relatively fixed and high prices, rather than enjoying free access to the European market at world prices. Yet this proposal runs counter to the spirit of EBA, which turns out to be the most symbolic part of Europe's free trade agenda towards the South, rather than constituting a major breakthrough for development through trade. This also puts the regionalisation (in the EPAs) and globalisation (in the WTO) of EBA into perspective.

Social Dimension of Globalisation: Core Labour Standards

Although the EU is often described as the champion of a social clause,[11] its position in the WTO has long been ambiguous. When this issue came to occupy centre stage at the international trade debate during the last months of the Uruguay Round (1993), EU Member States were divided. France and Belgium showed themselves to be enthusiastic supporters of a social clause, whereas Germany and the United Kingdom were reluctant. These divergences continued for about five years. Even during the crucial Singapore conference in 1996, where the fate of labour standards in the WTO was to be decided after months of heated debate, the EU lacked a common position. The Council Presidency statement

---

11   A social clause is defined as the inclusion of core labour standards in trade relations. It concerns the ILO core labour standards (see enumeration in Chapter 6).

at the conference did not even mention the issue, whereas each Member State defended its own position.

In the run-up to Singapore, it had become clear that some countries feared that a proactive EU stance would create a 'boomerang effect' on their national competences in social affairs. Indeed, the ratification, coordination, control and implementation of core labour standards (CLS), as defined by the International Labour Organisation, are only partly EU competences (Novitz 2002/2007). The Member States' reluctance to grant the Commission a larger role in the external promotion of these objectives was clearly linked to Europe's hybrid internal situation. Their lack of enthusiasm is also in line with two ECJ cases about EU competences in trade-related issues (see above, *Opinion 1/94*) and about the EU role in the ILO (*Opinion 2/91*) (see also Chapter 6).

But ideological factors also played a role. This explains why the EU finally found a common position, after social democratic parties came to power in the United Kingdom and in Germany. At the WTO summit in Seattle (1999), the EU prudently argued for a joint ILO-WTO forum on labour standards. Yet, US President Clinton's statements about possible trade sanctions following labour standards violations infuriated developing country delegations and formed part of the explosive cocktail that led to the failure of Seattle. When the WTO members gathered again in Doha two years later, another opportunity arose. However, three months before the conference, it became clear that the EU would not forcefully argue to place labour standards on the agenda of the new trade round. In the run-up to Doha, the EU had cautiously reviewed its Seattle positions, including the issue of labour standards, which were henceforth referred to the ILO. From 2002, the EU played a proactive role in the ILO's World Commission on the Social Dimension of Globalisation, but any possible linkage with trade relations was ruled out (cf. Orbie et al. 2005).

Europe's weakened position on a social clause is partly related to suspicion from developing countries and the reluctance of the US. However, this explanation is not sufficient to evaluate Europe's commitment (cf. Orbie 2006). First, the EU continued to insist on including competition and investment in the Doha agenda until 2004, although these issues also faced hostility in the South and reluctance in the US. Second, if we look at Europe's bilateral and unilateral trade policies – where the EU disposes of considerably more power to push its preferences through – labour standards are again subordinated to other trade objectives.

In Europe's newly established bilateral trade agreements, ILO labour standards are only marginally referred to. Also, in his extensive enumeration of the 'rule-making' and 'deep integration' contents of the WTO-plus agreements that Europe intends to conclude, the then Trade Commissioner Lamy (2002, 1408–10) elaborates on trade-related issues, such as standards and technical regulations, intellectual property rights, services, investment, competition, government procurement, rules of origin, and trade defence instruments, but he does not mention a single word about labour/social issues. Article 50 of the Cotonou Agreement is most explicit on labour standards, but in connection with development cooperation rather than trade issues; and cooperation under these articles has not taken place. In fact, EU bilateral agreements focus on trade liberalisation, general human rights, development cooperation and political dialogue, rather than on specific and enforceable labour rights provisions; and there is 'no evidence of significant progress' in promoting labour rights by means of Europe's trade agreements (Greven 2005, 43–4).

For some time, Europe's GSP has included a punitive (since 1995) and incentive (since 1998) social clause. Based on the GSP regulations, the EU could reward countries complying with CLS by unilaterally increasing its market access for their imports, or conversely, GSP trade preferences could be withdrawn in cases of serious violations of these standards. But this social GSP clause never got off the ground. Despite subsequent revisions, the punitive clause was used only once (Burma/Myanmar, 1997) and the incentive regime only twice (Sri Lanka, Moldova).

Again, EU preferences rather than external factors seem to be decisive. In fact, some countries (such as India) did not apply for the incentive clause because of ideological resistance to the idea of a social clause. But Europe's limited generosity under this social incentive regime was probably more important. This does not simply witness Europe's protectionist inclinations. In fact, the EU *did* grant substantial GSP tariff reductions, but for reasons other than the GSP incentive regime. These other trade preferences where granted simultaneously with the establishment of the social GSP clause, and basically made it redundant. For example, LDCs were granted more favourable tariffs in 1998, and duty-free market access under EBA in 2001, which removed any incentive to apply for additional preferences under the social GSP regime. Another example relates to the so-called drugs GSP preferences: Latin-American countries fighting drugs production and trafficking could benefit from extra GSP preferences. In 1998, this system was extended to include a number of Central American countries, implying that these could henceforth benefit from generous export opportunities to the European market, *without* having to comply with the newly established social GSP clause. The beneficiaries of the GSP drugs system included putative violators of CLS such as Colombia.

After Pakistan had been included in the GSP drugs regime in November 2001, Europe's GSP was challenged by India and declared illegal by a WTO judgment. The reformed 'GSP-plus' regime on sustainable development and good governance (since 2006) still includes the eight ILO core labour standards, besides a number of other international norms. It remains to be seen whether this new system will be more successful, but for the time being it seems that not much has changed. The new system may have spurred on countries such as El Salvador to ratify all the fundamental ILO Conventions. However, several beneficiaries have been criticised by the ILO for not *implementing* the relevant conventions. It appears that the EU looks mainly at the ratification record, rather than the *implementation* of CLS. The result is that former drugs beneficiaries continue to benefit from the special GSP preferences, in spite of alleged violations of CLS. Moreover, the application of the new system is henceforth limited to vulnerable countries. Therefore, the EU parts with its potential leverage vis-à-vis more important developing countries, which are often in the process of negotiating bilateral trade agreements with the EU.[12]

The Paradox of Normative Power Through Trade

Since the 1990s, Europe's common commercial policy has been confronted with serious challenges. Following the completion of the internal market project and several waves of enlargement, the question was raised as to whether a European trade fortress would be erected. The competencies of the European Community vis-à-vis the Member States in trade-related areas have been challenged (cf. Court of Justice *Opinion 1/94*) and the Commission's negotiating autonomy vis-à-vis the Council has been criticised (cf. the Blair House dispute). Parliaments and civil society groups have increasingly pressurised the relatively technocratic EU trade policy-making process. On the international front, the new WTO trade regime, the shift to behind-the-border issues, and the emergence of the G-20 all created a new situation for European trade policy-makers.

Nevertheless, during the past decade the EU has showed itself to be a powerful and assertive international actor in trade relations. Rather than continuing its regionalist and protectionist posture, the Union became the most enthusiastic supporter of the liberal and multilateral trading regime. Its bilateral trade policies are being reformed and made WTO compatible. The EU is willing to further liberalise its market, even in agriculture, provided that this goes hand-in-hand with substantial economic benefits. This position reflects some of the power resources that were discussed at the beginning of this chapter: Europe's economic interests as a large power in manufacturing and services (the bloc-size effect), the hegemony of neoliberal ideas in the international political economy, the relatively large clout of the European Commission, and Europe's (especially the Commission's) eagerness to export its 'model' of deep integration.

At the same time, normative objectives became a priority on the EU trade agenda. Indeed, the shift from an interest-based to a value-based trade discourse also took place in the second half of the 1990s. Both categories of trade goals have been addressed separately in the second part of this chapter. How are they interrelated? Has the EU been looking for alternative forms of 'hidden protectionism', do normative trade objectives such as sustainable development and human rights hide a neoliberal trade agenda, or can we speak of a genuine commitment to a normative trade policy?

Examination of two cases confirms that protectionist sentiments have not had a dominant influence on the normative trade policy agenda. Europe's policy in the trade and development nexus is characterised by an increasingly neoliberal outlook. The EU has not pressed very hard to include labour standards in the WTO and the punitive social GSP clause has been scarcely used. The regulatory

---

12   As for the punitive clause: in 2007 Belarus' preferences were withdrawn because of the violation of freedom of association. In Chapter 6 Tonia Novitz elaborates on this case.

issues that the EU attempts to introduce in multilateral and bilateral trade – such as competition and investment clauses – are market-enhancing rather than protectionist.

The cases even suggest that Europe's trade policy has primarily been driven by a free trade agenda, rather than normative objectives as such. In other words, the advancement of economic and social development through trade has largely been subordinate to the pursuit of free trade goals. This policy is in line with neoliberal logic that normative results should be seen as a side effect of the realisation of free trade – rather than the 'embedded liberalism' assumption that both objectives should be complementary and that some forms of interventionism in the political economy may be required to achieve normative objectives.

As stated above, the accuracy of this latter assumption, and thus also the consequent conclusion about Europe's normative trade commitments, may be contested. Yet the fundamental point remains that the conduct of EU trade policy is prioritising a free trade agenda. The chapter has made clear that European interests and ideas provide part of the explanation, but also that the institutional set-up of Union trade policy plays a crucial role. It appears that the EU trade policy-machinery is geared to the pursuit of market-enhancing aims, given the delegation to the Commission in regulatory (non-interventionist) issues, and the relatively large discretion exercised by other actors such as the parliaments. Institutionally, the EU is less well equipped to aim at normative objectives through trade, since this requires interventionist and/or distributive policies. For example, the Community's ability to engage in ambitious 'trade and aid' policies is constrained by its limited competencies in development budgets. Equally, the Community's resistance in advancing core labour standards through trade relates to its incomplete role in the internal coordination of the very same social standards.

Thus, on top of ideological convictions and interest motivations, the institutional dimension of EU trade policies further impedes the realisation of a normative external trade agenda. The rise of value-based objectives in Europe's trade policy profile appears to be a normative dressing over a free trade agenda, in response to the increased politicisation of Union trade policy, rather than a genuine commitment to reach these objectives. In line with its 'harnessing globalisation' discourse, over the past ten years the EU has been a force for multilateralism in trade. However, it has proven to be much more difficult to act as a 'force for the good' through trade, pursuing normative objectives such as economic development and core labour standards.

This chapter suggests that the limited capacity of the EU to engage in a normative external trade agenda basically relates to its raison d'être: the Union is institutionally designed to promote negative integration and market-enhancing policies (indeed, through multilateralism) rather than positive integration and redistribution. Hence, in external trade the EU reproduces its internal role as a regulatory state (see Chapter 1); although 'negative' integration (liberalisation) is accompanied with 'positive' integration (for example, competition, investment rules) the Union's regulatory aims are essentially market-enhancing. Although the EU is particularly well endowed to promote a deep international trade agenda because of its internal market experience, this still falls short of a more ambitious and interventionist approach in line with the idea of 'embedded liberalism'.

In brief, despite Europe's aspirations to become a 'civilian' or 'normative' power through trade, it rather confirms the image of a large trading state (see Chapter 1), pursuing liberalising policies via multilateral means. Further, theoretical and empirical research should qualify and falsify these findings. Meanwhile, we conclude with the paradox that, although trade is the EU's most integrated external policy domain, the hybrid state of European integration implies that the Union is very much constrained to engaging in ambitious normative policies.

References

Arts, K. and Dickson, A.K. (eds) (2004), *EU Development Cooperation: From Model to Symbol?* (Manchester: Manchester University Press).

Bhagwati, J.N. (2002), *Free Trade Today* (Princeton, NJ: Princeton University Press).

Brenton, P. (2000), 'The Changing Nature and Determinants of EU Trade Policies', CEPS Working Document 150.

Bretherton, C. and Vogler, J. (1999), *The EU as a Global Actor* (London and New York: Routledge).

Brown, W. (2000), 'Restructuring North-South Relations', *Review of African Political Economy* 27:85, 367–83.

Devuyst, Y. (1995), *The EU at the Crossroads* (Brussels: Presses Interuniversitaires Européennes).

Dür, A. and De Bièvre, D. (2007), 'Inclusion Without Influence? NGOs in European Trade Policy', *Journal of Public Policy* 27:1, 79–101.

Eeckhout, P. (2004), *External Relations of the EU* (Oxford: Oxford University Press).

Elgström, O. (2000), 'Lomé and Post-Lomé: Asymmetric Negotiations and the Impact of Norms', *European Foreign Affairs Review* 5, 175–95.

—— and Strömvik, M. (2003), 'The EU as an International Negotiator', Paper presented at the Eight Biennial Conference of the EUSA, Nashville, 27–29 March.

European Commission (2006), 'Global Europe: Competing in the World: A Contribution to the EU's Growth and Jobs Strategy', COM(2006)567.

Gerlach, C. (2006), 'Does Business Really Run EU Trade Policy? Observations about EU Trade Policy Lobbying', *Politics*, 26:3, 176–83.

Gibb, R. (2000), 'Post-Lomé: the EU and the South', *Third World Quarterly* 21:3, 457–81.

Goldstein, J. and Keohane, R.O. (1995), *Ideas and Foreign Policy* (Ithaca, NY: Cornell University Press).

Goodison, P. (2006), 'New Start or Old Spin?', *Review of African Political Economy*, 32:103, 167–76.

Greven, T. (2005), 'Social Standards in Bilateral and Regional Trade and Investment Agreements', Occasional Paper 16, Geneva: Friedrich-Ebert-Stiftung.

Hanson, B. (1998), 'What Happened to Fortress Europe? External Trade Policy Liberalization in the EU', *International Organization* 52:1, 55–85.

Holland, M. (2003), '20/20 vision? The EU's Cotonou Partnership Agreement', *The Brown Journal of World Affairs* IX:2, 161–75.

Hurt, S.R. (2003), 'Cooperation and Coercion? The Cotonou Agreement between the EU and ACP States and the End of the Lomé Convention', *Third World Quarterly* 24:1, 161–76.

—— (2004), 'The EU's External Relations with Africa after the Cold War', in I. Taylor and P. Williams (eds), *Africa in International Politics* (London: Routledge).

Johnson, M. (1998), *European Community Trade Policy and the 113 Committee* (London: Royal Institute of International Affairs).

Kerremans, B. (2000), 'The Links between Domestic Political Forces, Inter-bloc Dynamics and the Multilateral Trading System', in B. Kerremans and B. Switky (eds), *The Political Importance of Trading Blocs* (Aldershot: Ashgate).

—— (2004), 'What Went Wrong in Cancun? A Principal-Agent View on the EU's Rationale towards the Doha Development Round', *European Foreign Affairs Review* 9:3, 363–93.

Krenzler, H.G. and Pitschas, C. (2001), 'The Common Commercial Policy after Nice', *European Foreign Affairs Review* 6, 291–313.

Lamy, P. (2002), 'Stepping Stones or Stumbling Blocks?', *The World Economy* 25:10, 1399–413.

Larsen, M.F. (2006), 'The EU as an International Trade Negotiator – A Case-Study of Negotiations between the EU and South Africa', paper prepared for the EUSA workshop: EU Foreign/Security/Defence Policy, 3 April.

Lucarelli, S. and Manners, I. (eds) (2006), *Values and Principles in EU Foreign Policy* (London and New York: Routledge).

Messerlin, P.A. (2001), *Measuring the Costs of Protection in Europe: European Commercial Policy in the 2000s* (Washington DC: Institute for International Economics).

Meunier, S. (2003), 'Trade Policy and Political Legitimacy in the EU', *Comparative European Politics* 1, 67–90.

—— and Nicolaïdis, K. (2005), 'The EU as a Trade Power', in C. Hill and M. Smith (eds), *International Relations and the EU* (Oxford: Oxford University Press).

Mortensen, J.L. (1998), 'The Institutional Challenges and Paradoxes of EU Governance in External Trade: Coping with the Post-Hegemonic Trading System and the Global Economy', in A. Cafruny and P. Peters (eds), *The Union and the World: The Political Economy of a Common European Foreign Policy* (The Hague: Kluwer Law International).

Novitz, T. (2002), 'Promoting Core Labour Standards and Improving Global Social Governance: An Assessment of EU Competence to Implement Commission Proposals', *EUI Working Papers* 59.

—— (2007), 'The Exercise of Internal and External Competence by the EU in the Social Policy Field', in L. Tortell, C. Pimenta and J. Orbie (eds), *The EU and the Social Dimension of Globalisation: Minutes of Proceedings* (Lisbon: ISCTE).

Orbie, J. (2006), 'GSP Labour Conditionality: Normative Power Europe through Trade?' Paper prepared for the Third Pan-European Conference, ECPR Standing Group on EU Politics, Bilgi University, Istanbul, 21–23 September.

—— (2007a), 'The Development of EBA', in G. Faber and J. Orbie (eds), *EU Trade Politics and Developing Countries: Everything But Arms Unravelled* (London and New York: Routledge).

—— (2007b), 'The EU and the Commodity Debate: From Trade to Aid', *Review of African Political Economy* 34:112, 297–311.

—— (2007c), 'EU Trade and Development Policy: On Pyramids and Spaghetti Bowls', *Studia Diplomatica*, LX:2, 109–18.

——, Vos, H. and Taverniers, L. (2005), 'EU Trade Policy and a Social Clause', *Politique Européenne* 17, 159–87.

Paemen, H. and Bensch, A. (1995), *Du Gatt à l'OMC. La Communauté Européenne dans l'Uruguay Round* (Leuven: Leuven University Press).

Peterson, J. (2001), 'Get away from me closer, you're near me too far: Europe and America after the Uruguay Round', in M. Pollack and G.C. Shaffer (eds), *Transatlantic Governance in the Global Economy* (Lanham, MD: Rowman and Littlefield Publishers).

Petiteville, F. (2001), 'La Coopération Économique de l'Union Européenne entre Globalisation et Politisation', *Revue Française de Science Politique* 51:3, 431–58.

Pollack, M. (2000), 'The End of Creeping Competence? EU Policy-Making since Maastricht', *Journal of Common Market Studies* 38:3, 519–38.

Ravenhill, J. (1985), *Collective Clientelism: The Lomé Conventions and North-South Relations* (New York: Columbia University Press).

Raza, W. (2007), 'EU Trade Politics: Pursuit of Neo-Mercantilism in Different Fora?', in W. Blaas and J. Becker (eds), *Strategic Arena Switching in International Trade Negotiations* (Aldershot: Ashgate).

Shaffer, G. (2002), 'Managing US-EU Trade Relations through Mutual Recognition and Safe Harbor Agreements: "New" and "Global" Approaches to Transatlantic Economic Governance', draft, 15 July.

Smith, M. (1999), 'Negotiating Globalization: The Foreign Economic Policy of the EU', in R. Stubbs and G. Underhill (eds), *Political Economy and the Changing Global Order* (Oxford: Oxford University Press).

—— and Woolcock, S. (1999), 'European Commercial Policy', *European Foreign Affairs Review* 4, 439–62.

Stevens, C. (2006), 'The EU, Africa and Economic Partnership Agreements', *Journal of Modern African Studies* 44:3, 1–18.

Szymanski, M. and Smith, M.E. (2005), 'Coherence and Conditionality in European Foreign Policy: Negotiating the EU-Mexico Global Agreement', *Journal of Common Market Studies* 43:1, 171–92.

Tsoukalis, L. (2003), *What Kind of Europe?* (Delhi: Oxford University Press).

Van den Hoven, A. (2004), 'Assuming Leadership in Multilateral Economic Institutions', *West European Politics* 27:2, 256–83.

—— (2006), 'EU Regulatory Capitalism and Multilateral Trade Negotiations', in S. Lucarelli and I. Manners (eds), *Values and Principles in EU Foreign Policy* (London: Routledge).

Van den Hoven, A. (2007), 'Bureaucratic Competition in EU Trade Policy: EBA as a Case of Competing Two-Level Games?', in G. Faber and J. Orbie (eds), *EU Trade Politics and Development: Everything But Arms Unravelled* (London: Routledge).

Winham, G.R. (1986), *International Trade and the Tokyo Round Negotiation* (Princeton, NJ: Princeton University Press).

Wolf, M. (1997), 'The Dog that Failed to Bark: Climate for Trade Policy in the EU', in J.J. Schott (ed.) *The World Trading System: Challenges Ahead* (Washington DC: Institute for International Economics).

Woolcock, S. (1990), *The Uruguay Round: Issues for the EC and the US* (London: Royal Institute of International Affairs).

—— (2000), 'European Trade Policy: Global Pressures and Domestic Constraints', in H. Wallace and W. Wallace (eds), *Policy Making in the EU* (Oxford: Oxford University Press).

WTO (2007), 'Trade Policy Review: European Communities', Report by the Secretariat, WT/TPR/S/177, 22 January.

Young, A.R. (2002), *Extending European Cooperation. The EU and the 'New' International Trade Agenda* (Manchester: Manchester University Press).

Young, A.R. (2004), 'The EU and World Trade: Doha and Beyond', in M. Green Cowles and D. Dinan (eds), *Developments in the EU 2* (Basingstoke: Palgrave Macmillan).

—— and Peterson, J. (2006), 'The EU and the New Trade Politics', *Journal of European Public Policy* 13:6, 795–814.

Youngs, R. (2004), 'Normative Dynamics and Strategic Interests in the EU's External Identity', *Journal of Common Market Studies* 42:2, 415–35.

Chapter 3

The European Union's International Development Policy: Leading and Benevolent?

Jan Orbie and Helen Versluys

The European Union is often portrayed as a development-friendly actor towards the South. The following quote from the 'European Consensus on Development' is illustrative: 'The EU provides over half of the world's aid and has committed to increase this assistance, together with its quality and effectiveness' (EU 2005, 4). Although such statements have been scrutinised by NGOs, Europe's role in international development has barely been studied in political science (notable exceptions are Lister 1998; Holland 2002; Arts and Dickson 2004; Carbone 2007). Academic research mainly focuses on Europe's development policies through *trade* (see Chapter 2), or on the EU's relations with specific *regions*, such as Asia, Latin America and, in particular, the former ACP colonies (Africa, Caribbean and Pacific).

This chapter examines the EU's development policy *sensu stricto*. After outlining the Union's double role in development, we elaborate successively on Europe's power resources and on the objectives that it pursues in this domain. Looking at the 'means', it appears that the EU has only recently acquired competences in the area of development policy. Because this is a shared competence, Europe's international influence is sometimes jeopardised by the parallel existence of 28 European development policies. Furthermore, this chapter examines the EU's budgetary power in the development sector. Here the Union seems relatively powerful, having substantial resources at its disposal through the European Development Fund (EDF) and the regular Community budget. Moreover, the EU is also playing a coordinating role in monitoring national aid targets.

Next we deal with the objectives of EU development policy: the Millennium Development Goals (MDGs) and, in particular, poverty reduction. In order to assess Europe's commitment to these stated aims, the allocation of European aid resources is scrutinised. The analysis illustrates the lack of clarity surrounding the definition of 'official development assistance' (ODA). It also makes clear that the EU spends a relatively small part of its aid budget on the least-developed countries (LDCs), and that financial resources have been reallocated to other regions that are strategically more important. In this context, the 'securitisation' trend in European development policy is also analysed, as reflected in European budgetary expenditures, discourse, and institutional arrangements. Although it remains to be seen whether Europe's development agenda will be considered subordinate to broader foreign policy and security concerns, attempts to increase the coherence of EU external action may, in fact, entail such an evolution.

One conclusion is that the availability of EU financial resources does not necessarily translate into a more normative external policy practice. It is also argued that Europe's fragmented structure in this area explains the Union's difficulties to act as a norm-setter and to focus its development objectives clearly. However, outlining a number of possible future scenarios based on existing political cleavages in EU development, we argue that the Union may be moving towards an 'OECD scenario'. Whereas its own budgets are becoming less extensive, it is playing an increasingly important role in standard setting in development. This illustrates a broader evolution in EU development policy. The Union used to be a norm-taker in development, absorbing international norms from the Member States, the OECD, the G7 and the Bretton Woods institutions. More recently, it seems to be evolving into a norm-setter in its own right (for example on aid effectiveness, on the untying of aid, on conditionality for international loans), despite the fact that it has decreasing aid resources at its disposal. This is in line with Europe's nature as a 'regulatory state' – possibly also in development.

Struggling with Two Roles: A Policy Under Continuous Reform

The EU fulfils a double role in the area of development cooperation (cf. European Commission 2005c, 22–3). It acts both as an implementer of its own development policy *and* as a coordinator of Member State initiatives in this area. Each of these roles raises a number of questions that dominate the ongoing debate on the vices and virtues of European development cooperation.

First, the EC (represented by the European Commission) is a development actor in its own right. The fact that the Union formulates and implements such a policy is in itself rather remarkable, since it is first and foremost a 'regulatory state'. Community competence tends to be greater in the area of regulatory policies than with regard to distributive policies (see Chapter 1). The question emerges as to what the EC's comparative advantage is in the field of development cooperation. What justifies the existence of a separate policy at the EU level? What can the Union do better than the Member States in the area of development?

The fact that parallel initiatives are taken by 27 + 1 European development donors might very well lead to a duplication of effort. Therefore, the need arises for the second role exercised by the EU, namely that of coordinating Member State policies in order to reach a common 'European' development policy (27 + 1 = 1). The Commission encourages coordination and complementarity between its own programmes and those of the Member States. The EC also attempts to play a central role in administrative harmonisation among European donors, and in disseminating best practices. However, as explained below, the Commission has struggled to coordinate national development policies. Member States' sensitivities and historical ties to developing countries create an obstacle to establishing a streamlined European approach to development.

How does the EU attempt to coordinate the different European development policies and how successful has it been so far? Again, the question arises of its distinctiveness: how do Union efforts relate to 'other' international organisations that also play a role in the coordination of development practices, such as the Organisation for Economic Coordination and Development (OECD), the United Nations (UN) and its agencies, the World Bank, and the G7?

Both roles and the concomitant questions will be addressed in this chapter. However, before doing so, we give a short overview of the key moments and evolutions in EU development policy, demonstrating that Europe's double role has been difficult to carry out. In fact, EU development has been in constant development, it has been reformed continuously. Three periods can be distinguished since the introduction of EU competences in this area, corresponding to the three subsequent Commissions. The period 1995–99 was a problematic one during which the Commission faced serious difficulties in successfully exercising its role as autonomous implementer of development assistance. The next Commission (1999–2004) undertook efforts at the institutional level to enhance the EC's performance as development provider. The most recent Commission has concentrated more on its second role of trying to coordinate EC and national development aid initiatives.

Under the Santer Commission, the administrative responsibility for development issues was based on a regional division. DG VIII (Development) dealt with ACP countries under the authority of Commissioner João de Deus Pinheiro. DGIA was responsible for Common Foreign and Security Policy (CFSP) as well as for relations with the Central and Eastern European Countries, Turkey, Cyprus, Malta, and countries belonging to the former Soviet Union. DGIB focused on the Middle and Far East, the Mediterranean, and Latin America. During this period, the Commission faced severe staffing problems, with too few staff members responsible for too large a budget. The volume of EC aid increased 2.8 times between 1989 and 1999, yet staff levels only increased by 1.8 times. A comparison with other international aid donors is illustrative. Whereas Member States or the World Bank had between four and nine officials to manage every €10 million, the Commission had just 2.9 (EuropeAid 2004).

Development funds remained unspent and implementation was slow. The average delay in the disbursement of committed funds stood at four and a half years by the end of 1999, and the backlog of aid commitments amounted to €20 billion (Holland 2002, 97). The fragmented and overstretched administration in Brussels was not able to ensure effective monitoring or evaluation of EC aid programmes.

Attempting to reverse these negative trends, the Prodi Commission engaged in far-reaching institutional reforms in the EU's development aid architecture. First and foremost, responsibilities within the Commission were shuffled in order to guarantee more coherence. This reorganisation provoked the criticism that the new Commissioner for Development – the Danish Poul Nielson – became 'an emperor without clothes', 'undressed' by both the Relex and Trade Commissioners (e.g. Stocker 2000, 14).

On the one hand, ACP trade-related issues were transferred from DG Development to DG Trade. For example, the latter is in charge of trade negotiations with the ACP (see Chapter 2 on the Economic Partnership Agreements). The portfolio of DG External Relations was expanded to cover all countries other than the ACP, which remained the competence of DG VIII. DG External Relations also plays first fiddle in the implementation of EU development policies – both in ACP and non-ACP countries – given the hierarchy within EuropeAid (see below).[1] As Holland (2002, 91) points out, the Commissioner for External Relations is now in a position to employ development aid in the pursuit of EU foreign policy objectives. Concerns have been expressed that these reforms weaken the role of DG Development, and thus compromise the objective of poverty reduction.

Three further important institutional changes were introduced as part of the 2000 reform agenda, namely the establishment of EuropeAid, the introduction of Country Strategy Papers (CSPs), and the devolution of responsibility to EC Delegations in third countries. Operating under the control of a board comprising the Commissioners with external portfolios, EuropeAid oversees the implementation of external aid programmes in *all* third countries.[2] As such, the coherence of EC policies vis-à-vis developing countries has increased and its geographical fragmentation (that is the traditional 'Africa and the rest' approach) has been mitigated. However, DG External Relations and DG Development continue to have the responsibility for programming the aid operations EuropeAid implements, respectively in non-ACP and ACP countries.

Many see the continuing policy split between DG Development and DG External Relations as a reflection of 'the unresolved issue of the relationship between a poverty-reduction-oriented development policy and the wider concerns of EU external relations' (Dearden 2007, 34 – see below). Moreover, while the creation of EuropeAid might help to address the horizontal split in development cooperation (between different geographical policies and the corresponding DGs), it simultaneously creates a new vertical dichotomy between policy formulation and implementation (EuropeAid versus planning by DG Relex and Development), possibly disrupting project-cycle management (OECD-DAC 2002, 73). Figure 3.1 provides a schematic representation of the Commission's current aid architecture.

Since 2001, the programming of EC aid has been centred on the CSP mechanism. CSPs set a strategic framework for the central priorities in a given country or region, covering both development assistance and other EC activities ('the policy mix'). Each strategy paper contains a National Indicative Programme

---

1   The Commissioner for External Relations is Chair of the EuropeAid Board, while the Development Commissioner is Chief Executive.

2   Three exceptions remained. DG Enlargement continues to manage all pre-accession aid (Chapter 11), ECHO remains responsible for emergency humanitarian aid (Chapter 4), and DG Economic and Financial Affairs stays in charge of macro-financial assistance (e.g. debt relief).

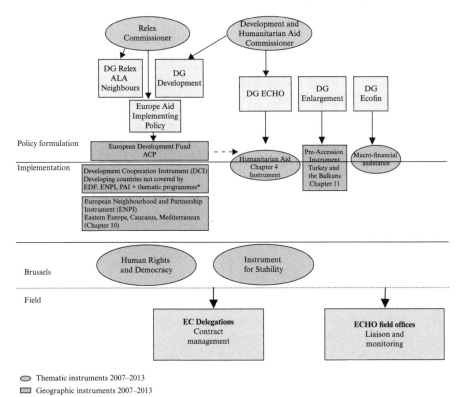

Thematic instruments 2007–2013
Geographic instruments 2007–2013

* The following thematic programmes are included in the DCI (legal basis is Regulation EC 1905/2006; different from the thematic instruments which have a specific legal basis): migration and asylum (Chapter 5), investing in people, environment and sustainable management of natural resources including energy, food security, and non-state actors and local authorities in development.

Figure 3.1   EU development aid architecture

(NIP) which indicates the focal areas where EC resources will be spent. CSPs allow for the multi-annual programming of EC aid to particular developing countries. All relevant Commission DGs participate in the drafting of CSPs. In addition, CSPs and NIPs are developed in collaboration with national governments, Member States, other donors and, wherever possible, with representatives of the recipient country's civil society. A new Inter-service Quality Support Group, situated in DG Development but reporting directly to all Commissioners dealing with external relations, was also set up to contribute to improvements in development aid programming, and to ensure quality control and policy coherence in the preparation of the CSPs. In 2007, the second generation of CSPs came into force.

Staff in Commission Delegations often possess the most accurate knowledge on conditions and needs in developing countries. Nevertheless, prior to the 2000 reform, authority was concentrated in Brussels. In order to make aid programmes more responsive to local needs and to speed up implementation, the Commission decided to devolve responsibility for the management of external aid to the 80 Commission Delegations present in 148 third countries. The transfer of responsibility to the Delegations has now been completed, with 70 per cent of EC development funds being managed locally (European Commission 2005b).

While the emphasis was on institutional adaptations, the Prodi Commission also made some efforts at the level of content. In order to address the problem of a lack of clear development policy objectives, the Commission and the Council issued a 'Statement on Development Policy' in 2000. The reduction and eventual eradication of poverty were highlighted as the core objective, and six areas were identified where the Commission could add particular value (see below).

Under the Barroso Commission and Development Commissioner Louis Michel, no further fundamental institutional reorganisations have taken place. Reform focuses on the content of EU development policy, and on ways to better streamline the 27 + 1 European development policies. Examples are the Africa Strategy, the Policy Coherence for Development (PCD) initiative, and the European Consensus on Development. This last document is particularly remarkable because it was agreed by the Commission, the Member States, and the European Parliament (EP). This Brussels consensus forms the first-ever joint policy on development, and defines a framework of common principles within which the EC and the 27 Member States will each implement their development policies in a spirit of complementarity.

European Competences in Development

Development cooperation is a recent EU competence. While the Community regularly sought to realise development objectives via its long-standing trade competence and the construction of a complicated pyramid of preferences (see Chapter 2), strictly speaking, development cooperation was added to the EC portfolio only 15 years ago. It was not until 1993 that the Community acquired prerogatives in this area with the inclusion of a chapter on development cooperation in the Maastricht Treaty. Even so, and again in contrast with the common commercial policy, development competences are shared between the EC and the Member States. According to the Treaty (Article 177), the Community's development policy has to be 'complementary' to the policies pursued by the Member States. Article 180 states that they

> shall coordinate their policies on development cooperation and shall consult each other on their aid programmes, including in international organizations and during international conferences. They may undertake joint action. Member States shall contribute if necessary to the implementation of Community aid programmes.

Although the principles of complementarity and coordination are enshrined in the Treaty, they have been honoured more in their breach than in their observance.

Lack of coordination has led European development donors to pursue competing objectives, to duplicate programmes, and to overburden recipient countries' administrations with different administrative requirements. Moreover, donors have not systematically engaged in the sharing of expertise, or in carrying out joint programming exercises and joint evaluations of development initiatives.

In addition to sharing responsibility with the Member States, the Commission also faces competition from other international organisations involved in the coordination of development policies, such as UN development agencies, the World Bank, the International Monetary Fund (IMF), the OECD, and the G7. When compared with these forums, the EU's distinctive role is not always clear-cut. The UN and its agencies have a long-standing tradition in Third World issues and, from the developing countries' perspective, they are arguably more legitimate being UN members themselves. Also, some 'Northern' EU Member States (such as the UK, the Scandinavian countries and the Netherlands) tend to give preference to the UN, and do not seem convinced by the EU's added value as an additional layer in the development cooperation process. The IMF and the World Bank have long dominated the debate on aid conditionality and – together with the G7 – the Bretton Woods institutions have been in the driving seat when it comes to debt-relief initiatives. The OECD has a longer track record than the Commission on issues such as the untying of aid and the definition of what constitutes Official Development Assistance (ODA). The Development Assistance Committee (DAC), a subcommittee of the OECD, has been particularly active in soft coordination (standard-setting and peer-review procedures) in the development realm.

Confronted with this internal and external questioning of EU competences, the increasingly proactive DG Development, under Commissioner Michel, has made several suggestions about increasing the 'EU factor' in development aid. While the EU approach is in many respects aligned with the UN, the World Bank, IMF, and so on, the EC is nonetheless also seeking to develop a unique European perspective on development. Louis Michel seems to be keen on enhancing the Commission's clout vis-à-vis other international organisations competent in development. For example, in 2007 a European Trust Fund for infrastructure in Africa was established, financed by grants from the Commission and nine Member States,[3] and loans from the European Investment Bank and the Member States' development financing institutions. This funding initiative for regional infrastructure projects in Africa can be considered as a European variant of initiatives traditionally falling within the scope of the World Bank. However, it is notable that the UK and the Scandinavian Member States do not participate.

Initiatives to increase the EU's role in relation to the Member States include the adoption of a voluntary code of conduct containing ten principles for a better division of labour among European donors (Council 2007, 37-8). The Commission proposal for enhancing the effectiveness of EU aid also suggested the adoption of a common framework amongst all EU donors for the preparation of CSPs. This cooperation between the Community and the Member States would, in turn, from

---

3   Austria, Belgium, France, Germany, Greece, Italy, Luxembourg, the Netherlands and Spain.

the basis for Joint Multi-annual Programming including joint disbursement and reporting mechanisms. In addition, the practice of co-financing was promoted, with the EU hosting structures which, in addition to EC resources, are open to Member States' voluntary contributions (European Commission 2006b/c). The Commissioner (Michel 2006) has amply emphasised that the intention is not to touch upon Member States' development prerogatives:

> Although development is and will remain a competence shared by the Community and the Member States this does not prevent us joining forces, harmonize our procedures and share the job. The EU is the world's biggest aid donor but every single euro we spend will contribute more to the fight against poverty if we share this huge task in an intelligent and coordinated way, as we all promised last year in several international forums.

Despite initial scepticism from countries such as the UK and the Netherlands, joint multi-annual programming with other donors is now being tested in a number of ACP countries, with a view to applying it in the other countries at a later stage.

A further manifestation of Member States' reticence towards 'more Europe' in development aid policy is the eternal debate on the budgetisation of the EDF. This is the main instrument for providing EC development aid to the ACP states. The 1957 Treaty of Rome provided for its creation with a view to granting financial assistance to Member State colonies in Africa. To enable Member States to make contributions in line with their differing levels of commitment to the ACP, the EDF has been funded via national contributions rather than the Community budget. Even though a heading has been reserved for the EDF in the Community budget since 1993, following a request by the EP, the Fund does not yet fall under the Community's general budget. It is funded by the Member States, is subject to its own financial rules, and is managed by a specific committee.

This system has faced criticism from the EP and Northern Member States because it ignores democratic input from the Parliament and perpetuates the 'Africa and the rest' schizophrenia of Europe's external relations. However, the ACP sees this specific fund as a guarantee that European development budgets will not be diverted to other regions and policies. Despite expectations that the EDF would finally be incorporated into the 2007–13 Financial Perspectives, in the end Member States did not want to include the strongly intergovernmental EDF in the regular budget over which they have to share control with the EP.

Although the EC competences in the development policy domain continue to be a sensitive issue, some recent indications suggest that Member States are increasingly willing to accept a degree of integration, albeit non-binding. The 'European Consensus for Development' (EU 2005) underlines the important role of the EC in this area of shared competence. EC development policy, it is argued, has distinct advantages over Member States' national development programmes, as the EC offers a global presence, ensures policy coherence (particularly between trade and development), plays a crucial role in facilitating coordination and harmonisation among donors, promotes best practices in development across the EU, benefits from economies of scale as a deliverer of aid, and possesses particular experience in the areas of good governance, democracy promotion, and the particiation of civil society. Moreover, as will be explained next, the EU has acquired a central role in coordinating Member State ODA levels, as well as other topics such as the untying of aid. In addition, the Union has made additional commitments on top of the Paris Declaration on Aid Effectiveness (EU 2005), and the Council has mandated the Commission to monitor the effectiveness of European aid.

More Aid and More Europe

During the 1990s, a decline in ODA flows from EU Member States (and other donor countries) could be observed.[4] Often-cited explanations for this include donor fatigue because of limited progress in the South, fraudulent use of aid money, the developing countries' decreasing 'commodity power' compared to the 1970s, the emergence of a neoliberal development paradigm in the 1980s which gave priority to structural adjustment, in particular the waning geopolitical importance of developing (especially African) countries since the end of the Cold War. What is remarkable is that *Community* ODA levels remained stable over the same period of time (OECD-DAC 2002, 96). One explanation is the stronger institutional anchoring of EC aid through the EDF and the multi-annual budgeting. Also, at the EU level, pressure to be re-elected is smaller, hence removing the temptation to shift development money to other initiatives which allow for enhanced popularity among the public. EU official aid budgets also include PHARE funding to accession countries, rather than developing countries (see below). Finally, it should be noted that as a 'civilian power' with limited competences in traditional foreign policy the EU has been subjected less to geostrategic considerations driving national aid decisions. After a period of falling ODA levels, since 2000 Member States have been making efforts to step up their aid budgets. As will become clear later, the Commission has played a catalysing role in this respect.

It is common to 'boast' about the fact that the Union provides 55 per cent of development aid worldwide. The statement that 'Europe is the biggest provider of development aid in the world' – the banner at the bottom of each page of DG Development's website – has become a mantra in EU discourse. However, this is somewhat misleading. The Commission and Member States *together* represent around half of the world's ODA, but the Commission itself counts for just 10 per cent. Given continuing problems of coordination, as described above, it is a bit optimistic to suggest that 'Europe' is an international development actor powerfully backed by solid budget resources. Nevertheless, the fact that the EC has at is disposal a substantial budget for development policy – larger than that of any individual EU Member State – is exceptional. Development policy is one of the few policy domains (others are agricultural policy, cohesion policy, humanitarian aid) were the Union can draw on the power of the purse. Because the EU's overall budget is small in comparison to that of its members, it has specialised in regulatory,

---

4 Average Member State budgets evolved from about 0.45 per cent ODA/GNI in the 1980s to 0.32 per cent in 2000.

rather than distributive or redistributive, policies. Most often (for instance, in trade, internal market, competition, and so on), the EU role consists of introducing rules to organise negative integration efficiently. Interestingly, as explained below, the Commission is extending this task to the realm of development policy.

At the 2002 UN Conference in Monterrey (Mexico), the international community gathered to discuss the mobilisation of more financial resources for development. The UN High-level Panel on Financing for Development recommended a doubling of the existing ODA in order to reach the MDGs, and suggested that to address broader development needs 0.7 per cent of donor countries' Gross National Income (GNI) ought to be spent on development.

Two conclusions can be drawn with regard to Europe's position in Monterrey, briefly summarised as 'more aid' and 'more Europe' (Orbie and Versluys 2007). First, EU Member States made a firm commitment to increase European ODA budgets considerably. This is remarkable given the problematic budgetary situation (and low ODA level) of several Member States, and a shift to the right in several governments. At the Barcelona European Summit (15 March 2002), Member States accepted concrete targets in a detailed time schedule. Countries that have already reached the 0.7 per cent target pledged to remain at or above this target, whereas all other members promised to spend a least 0.33 per cent ODA/GNI by 2006. Collectively, this would result in a European average of 0.39 per cent by 2006. The ODA debate at the EU level resulted in tangible commitments by all the Member States, which have managed to keep on track in the subsequent years.

Secondly, both the decision-making process in the run-up to Monterrey as well as the follow-up show signs of an integrationist shift in Europe's development policy – at least as far as the level of ODA is concerned. This is striking too, given traditional national sensitivities in the area of development. It is noteworthy that ODA was discussed at all at the highest levels of EU decision-making: up until then, such debates invariably took place at the national level. Moreover, the Barcelona agreement introduced a form of soft integration by making Member States' ODA budgets part of a broader European strategy rather than a purely national affair. If one Member State fails to reach the minimum of 0.33 per cent, it jeopardises the collective EU average of 0.39 per cent. Even though the Barcelona agreement is of a political rather than a legally binding nature, governments wishing to deviate are likely to feel more constrained in withdrawing their ODA pledges than would be the case without an EU timetable. The Barcelona compromise has set in motion a process of peer pressure among European Member States, making it politically costly for any single government to renege on its ODA promises. Finally, EU involvement did not stop after Monterrey. The Commission was asked by the Council to continue to monitor and report on the progress of Member States in terms of their ODA budgets.

Today, both the 'more Europe' and the 'more aid' observations are still valid (although some qualification should be made – see below). The ODA issue remains firmly anchored at the EU level, with the Commission meticulously monitoring Member States' implementation of the Barcelona agreement. The EU largely reached its ODA targets, and refined its strategy towards the 0.7 per cent objective. In 2005, extended ODA pledges – referred to by the Commission as 'Barcelona II-type commitments' – were accepted (see Table 3.1). Again, a detailed schedule was outlined, this time striving for a collective EU target of 0.56 per cent by 2010 and ultimately the 0.7 per cent aim in 2015. More specifically, all Member States which had not yet reached a level of 0.51 per cent ODA/GNI pledge to do so by 2010, and to further increase this to 0.7 per cent by 2015. The target for new members is 0.17 per cent in 2010 and 0.33 per cent in 2015, as summarised in Table 3.1.

Table 3.1　European development aid commitments

	EU-15		EU-10	
	Baseline MS	**Average EU**	**Baseline**	**Average EU**
Monterrey/Barcelona 2002		0.33%		
2006	0.33%	0.39%	–	–
Millennium+5/Barcelona II				
2010	0.51%	0.56%	(0.17%)	0.17%
2015	0.7%	0.7%	0.33%	0.33%

Source: Based on Eurodad 2006.

The latest Commission report indicates that the EU has reached its first intermediate collective ODA target one year ahead of schedule (2005 instead of 2006), and kept up its good performance in 2006. Collective European ODA levels represented an ODA/GNI ratio of 0.42 per cent, exceeding the 0.39 per cent goal. The Commission adds, however, that the Union's achievement would have been even better if Greece, Italy and Portugal had also lived up to the agreed 0.33 per cent individual target on time (European Commission 2007).

How can this engagement to provide substantially more aid and to grant the Commission a coordinating role be explained? Besides the awareness that renewed aid efforts are necessary to accomplish the MDGs, Santiso (2002) points out that Europe's generous ODA pledges were driven by a sudden realisation that development aid can address the seeds of terrorism. Aid commitments seem to have been stimulated by the events of 11 September 2001, six months prior to Monterrey. With the identification of poverty in the South as one of the roots of terrorism, the obvious policy recommendation was that more aid resources had to be made available to tackle the underlying causes of international terrorism.

Europe's magnanimity also fits in with the EU's civilian power image. The EC has always presented itself as the interlocutor *par excellence* of countries in the South. Sociological institutionalist dynamics such as 'rhetorical entrapment' or 'logic of appropriateness' (see Chapter 1) pushed Member States to accept high ODA targets and a greater role for the EU. Progressive European actors (Member States such as Sweden together with supranational norm entrepreneurs such as the Commission and the Council Presidency) 'shamed' the more reluctant Member States into accepting ambitious ODA benchmarks by drawing on the long-standing, undisputable EU value of solidarity with and sustainable development of the South. EU Member States felt the need to behave appropriately, that is in line with their posture as a benevolent force for the good. In particular, EU discourse has positively contrasted the EU's stance in the ODA debate with the less generous attitude of the US. Norm entrepreneurs highlighted elevated European ODA levels as an expression of Europe's generosity towards the South, explicitly pointing to the recalcitrance of the US, and thereby legitimating a distinctive role for the EU (Orbie 2003). All the elements of the popular Mars-Venus dichotomy were already present in the debates in the run-up to Monterrey concerning Europe's role.

But whereas constructivist accounts may explain Europe's decision to set ambitious ODA targets at the EU level, a look at the *implementation* of the 0.7 per cent target shows a less rosy picture. The discourse on Europe as the world's largest aid provider and on concrete ODA targets seems to follow a '*je dépense donc je suis*' logic – potentially overshadowing the objectives being pursued. In this context, Vogt (2006, 173) uses the image of the Union as a 'bodybuilder': 'the size of his muscles is important in itself; he is not particularly concerned with what the muscles can be used for'.

Development Objectives – Among Other Things

Official Development Objectives

Europe's official development objectives are enumerated in Article 177 of the Treaty: to foster the sustainable economic and social development of developing countries, and more particularly the most disadvantaged among them; the smooth and gradual integration of the developing countries into the world economy; and the campaign against poverty in the developing countries. In addition, the Community's development policy should contribute to the Union's external goals of democracy, the rule of law, human rights and fundamental freedoms.

Various speeches and policy documents (e.g. EU 2005) have highlighted that poverty eradication, including the pursuit of the MDGs,[5] is the primary and overarching objective. But since the end of the Cold War, the Union has also increasingly emphasised political conditionality. Since 1992, all trade and cooperation agreements have an 'essential elements' clause with human rights language. Concerns have been expressed that provisions on human rights, democratic principles, the rule of law and good governance encroach upon the principle of 'equal' partnership – especially in the context of the EU-ACP relationship (cf. Arts and Dickson 2004; Bretherton and Vogler 2006; Vogt 2006).

Furthermore, in 2000, six priority sectors were identified in which the EU benefits from an added value compared to the Member States, and on which EC

---

5   The MDGs were agreed upon by the UN in 2000 and are to be realised by 2015 – as is the deadline for Europe's 0.7 per cent target.

initiatives are to be focused, namely the linkage between trade and development; support for regional integration and cooperation; support for macroeconomic polices and enhancement of equal access to social services; transport; food security and sustainable rural development; and institutional capacity-building, especially to allow for good governance and the rule of law (European Commission 2000, 25–7). The European Consensus on Development reiterates that the EC ought to concentrate upon its (apparently ever-expanding) areas of comparative advantage, with water, energy, agriculture, and social cohesion and employment being added to the original list of activities.

Over the years, a growing number of horizontal issues have been identified which are to be mainstreamed in Community development initiatives, for example: democracy, good governance and human rights; gender equality; the rights of children and indigenous people; environmental sustainability; and HIV/AIDS. Besides the geographical funds (EDF, ALA, MEDA, CARDS, TACIS and PHARE), the creation of new thematic budget lines would provide an innovative approach to these challenges. Through the 1990s, the number of budget lines proliferated, dealing with issues such as poverty diseases, reproductive health, environment, forestry, NGOs, gender integration, food aid, anti-personnel landmines, and so on. This proliferation stems from the EP's proactivity in response to certain issues, and the tendency of each Council Presidency to engage in new areas of activity. The OECD-DAC (2002, 79) mentions difficulties in mainstreaming these issues in European programmes, their disproportionate administrative burden, and the adverse consequences for local ownership. Under the Financial Perspectives 2007–13, the number of horizontal budget lines was reduced, as illustrated in Figure 3.1.

In general, a major added value of the EC in the development realm is its mere existence. As an institution besides and above the Member States, it can present itself as a new and neutral actor without connotations for the colonial era (cf. Vogt 2006, 173). This particular advantage of the European construction links up with its very identity as a civilian power, as described by Duchêne in the 1970s (see Chapter 1).

A final 'objective' is the democratic and transparent *process* of development policy formulation and implementation. The emphasis is on the principles of partnership and ownership of development programmes by the aid-receiving country. For example, they are involved in the establishment of CSPs. Moreover, the Commission has moved from project aid towards an approach comprising budget support. The EU also supports the participation of civil society groups, including trade unions, employers' organisations and the private sector and NGOs. However, European NGO response so far has been one of frustration because of inadequate dialogue, and resistance because of their limited influence (Carbone 2006, 204-5). There may also be a downside to the 'paradigm of dialogue' in the EU's relations with the developing world. Whereas in the 1970s dialogue implied equal partnership, today it is also a means of coercive power. Moreover, it increases European involvement in a country's internal affairs and provides an opportunity to dictate the receiving government (Vogt 2006, 166–7).

Europe's development objectives have also been criticised for not relating to poverty reduction. The debate on the actual spending of development aid has become more intense since Europe's ambitious ODA increases (see e.g. Eurodad 2006; CONCORD 2007), and is likely to become even more salient in the years to come. Below we limit ourselves to an overview of the various facets of the discussion, which basically revolves around the development-orientation of European aid (see also Orbie and Versluys 2007). Each time, we briefly consider Member State and EC policies.

Development Aid for Development Goals?

First, there is the issue of tied aid. This is granted on the condition that the beneficiary country will purchase the goods or services involved in a development project from suppliers in the donor country, as opposed to untied aid for which goods and services can be freely procured in all countries. By tying aid, the donor aims to raise its own exports. However, tied aid increases development project costs by 20 to 30 per cent, and impedes ownership by the recipient country because local production systems are excluded. The question thus rises whether EU aid, if tied, is primarily meant to contribute to the development of the South or rather of European industry. In 2001, the OECD-DAC donors agreed to untie virtually all aid the LDCs. Since then, EU Member States' share of untied aid has substantially increased (EU and OECD 2006, 11). The Commission has played an important role in the implementation of the DAC recommendation, and even going beyond this by proposing to untie *all* aid from the Community and the Member States, without distinguishing between LDCs and other developing countries, and including food aid. In 2005, two regulations[6] were adopted which apply the principle of untying aid to the poorest developing countries to all EC development aid instruments. These regulations also touch upon the EU's position in international competition matters (cf. Chapter 8): third countries, such as the US, have to grant reciprocity in order to be eligible, that is, European actors must benefit from equal access in third countries' public procurement markets for external assistance.

Second, despite rhetorical statements to the contrary,[7] European external aid efforts seem largely focused on middle-income countries (MICs) rather than LDCs and low-income countries (LICs). Research points to the diversion of ODA funds, through the 1990s, from the poorest to other developing countries (Bonaglia et al. 2006, 176–81). In 2000, only 26 per cent of EC aid went to LDCs, and 13 per cent to other LICs, compared to 61 per cent to MICs (OECD-DAC 2002, 98). This trend also reflects a particular focus on the EU's 'near abroad'.

---

6   Regulations EC 2110/2005 and 2112/2005 of 27/12/2005.

7   E.g. the European Consensus states that 'the EU will continue to prioritise support to least-developed and other low-income countries (LIC)'. This statement is qualified, though, by adding that a continuing commitment to the medium-income countries is justified on the ground of their large low-income population, inequalities, weak governance, and important role in political, security and trade issues, and as 'regional anchors' (EU 2006, 6, 20).

The top recipients in 2004 were Serbia and Montenegro, Turkey, Bosnia and Herzegovina, Albania, FYROM Macedonia, Croatia and Moldova.

In contrast, in the 1980s the top 20 recipients were all countries in Africa and Asia (EU and OECD 2006, 22, 45). This concentration of aid on MICs seems even more outspoken in the development spending of the Commission than that of the Member States. This seems to undermine the argument that the EC creates added value as a more objective aid provider allowing for greater equity in development efforts. Perhaps, however, the comparison with the Member States is not entirely fair. Most actions undertaken by Member States in the EU's neighbourhood are taken via the EC channel through programmes like TACIS, PHARE and the new European Neighbourhood and Partnership Instrument (see Chapter 10). However, some improvement might be observed. In 2004, payments to LDCs represented 42 per cent of the Commission's ODA, and about 45 per cent was spent in MICs.[8] However, Member States continue to score higher since 50 per cent of their collective ODA is devoted to LDCs and 32 per cent to MICs (EU and OECD 2006, 30). In the context of the Africa Strategy, the Union also decided that at least 50 per cent of the announced ODA *increase* (not the absolute amount) would be dedicated to Africa. In this respect, we can also point to the growth rate for European humanitarian relief (see Chapter 4) budgets, which has been faster than for development aid. Short-term humanitarian aid in high-profile crises such as the tsunami is not the same as sustained efforts to fight poverty in the LDCs.

Fourth, a substantial part of the European ODA increase is being achieved via 'virtual' aid in the form of debt relief to Iraq and Nigeria. The share of debt relief is especially high in the ODA increases of France, Germany, the UK, Austria and Italy. Without such virtual aid, it is questionable whether Europe would be able to meet its Monterrey pledges. While debt cancellation is included in the current OECD-DAC ODA definition, and highly indebted countries undeniably benefit from this, it does not equal new aid flows for developing countries. It is noteworthy that the EC share of debt relief in the ODA rise is negligible.[9] The Commission and the EP have explicitly opposed this.

Fifth, part of ODA consists of 'domestic' aid. Figures on recent ODA increases might be misleading because they cover money spent on housing refugees and educating students within European countries. Member States such as the Netherlands, Sweden and Denmark – notably those countries which pride themselves on spending 0.7 per cent already – include the first-year cost of accommodating refugees and all repatriation expenses in their ODA. This kind of 'domestic' aid, which never actually leaves the donor country, does not contribute directly to poverty reduction in the South. Together with the share of

---

8   This is, of course, partly attributable to the fact that since the 2004 enlargement a large proportion of aid to the EU's near abroad has become internal aid.

9   If debt cancellation grants are excluded, the 2005 increase in Member States' ODA falls dramatically from 27.9 per cent to 3.8 per cent. For the EC, the ODA increase remains the same (8.7 per cent) (OECD-DAC 2006).

debt relief, this labelling of ODA has provoked fierce criticism from NGOs (e.g. Eurodad 2006; CONCORD 2007).

The sixth concern has also been voiced by development NGOs, and refers to the 'securitisation' of European development policy. Although there is a budgetary dimension to this trend, suggesting that ODA is used to address security objectives rather than fight poverty, it concerns a broader evolution whereby, arguably, security issues are increasingly dominating Europe's approach towards the Third World. Within the EU context, signs of a growing readiness to use development policies to achieve security goals can be found at three levels: budgetary decisions, discourse, and institutional arrangements. In terms of budgetary allocations, a trend can be observed on focusing financial flows towards geostrategically important countries to the detriment of the aid engagement vis-à-vis low-income countries (cf. Bonaglia et al. 2006, 178). According to BOND (a development NGO umbrella organisation), substantial amounts of European ODA were diverted away from the poorest countries to post-conflict support in Afghanistan (2002) and Iraq (2004–05). Another concrete example is EU financing of the African Peace Facility for peacekeeping and peace enforcement with money from the EDF, despite the fact that spending on peace missions does not count as ODA, and without compensating these security-driven expenditures with additional budgets for development (see also Bretherton and Vogler 2006, 123).

At the level of development discourse, one can refer to EU policy documents such as the 2003 European Security Strategy which states that 'security is a first condition for development'. All EU instruments, including the EDF, 'can have an impact on our security and on that of third countries' (European Council 2003, 13). In its Communication on Conflict Prevention, the Commission (2001) indicates that conflict prevention has to be 'mainstreamed' in development assistance. Former Commissioner for Development, Poul Nielson (2001), stated: 'I consider development cooperation as the most important contribution Europe can make to preventing conflicts in developing countries.'

Finally, changes in the institutional architecture seem to confirm the securitisation trend. The most notable modification at the institutional level was the abolition of the Development Council in 2002. Development issues are now discussed in the General Affairs and External Relations Council. Furthermore, the Constitutional Treaty suggests that the new European Minister for Foreign Affairs can resort to EC aid as a tool to achieve the objectives of the CFSP. On the one hand, such institutional reforms might provide opportunities to increase coherence in the Union's international performance. On the other hand, the result might be a marginalisation of development objectives in favour of foreign policy ambitions.

Some OECD-DAC members have argued in favour of admitting support for military training and operational costs of peacekeeping in ODA. This seems to be just one manifestation of a broader 'securitisation' trend since 11 September 2001, which has also influenced the EU. The desirability of a strengthened linkage between aid and security is unclear; and opinions within the Commission and DG Development are divided. On the positive side, it might stimulate increases in development spending, and trigger renewed attention and aid flows for so-called fragile states like Afghanistan which had slipped off the international agenda. It also ties in with the EU's comprehensive approach to international stability, which addresses all dimensions of security – military as well as political, socio-economic, environmental, cultural, and so on – and which resorts to the full spectrum of available instruments. On the other hand, a minority view in the Commission is concerned that security concerns 'may destroy the foundations of a genuine, equality-based dialogue' with the developing world (Vogt 2006, 168). As European development policy becomes more closely intertwined with security concerns, aid allocations might be more attuned to strategic priorities, even if these do not correspond with relative levels of need or contribute to poverty reduction. A fundamental question for the coming years is whether Europe's so-called comprehensive policy is becoming unbalanced, *de facto* prioritising security over development objectives (cf. Manners in Chapter 1 on conflict prevention, and Sterckx in Chapter 5 on migration).

Coherence of Europe's Non-Development Policies

Even if the EU's development policy *as such* was devoted entirely to poverty reduction, the Union's impact may be hampered by its other policies. Inversely, the question then emerges to what extent its *non-development* policies, such as agriculture, fisheries, environment, migration, and trade, contribute to development of the South. Article 178 of the EC Treaty obliges the Community to take account of its development objectives in the policies that it implements which are likely to affect developing countries. But increasing PCD is a challenging task for policy-makers because of incompatibilities between mandates from constituents, on the one hand, and demands from developing countries on the other.

Arguably, coherence for development is even more difficult to achieve in the EU – compared with national states *and* with the above-mentioned goals of development policy as such – given its fragmented institutional structure. Coherence with other policies requires intensive horizontal coordination of various Commission DGs and Council formations, whereas the realisation of autonomous development goals is facilitated if the policy-makers involved are relatively insulated. Despite the 2000 reforms, the relative compartmentalisation of Europe's external policy apparatus continues to exist, making PCD more complicated. A comprehensive evaluation noted that DG Development plays a limited role during inter-service consultations on issues affecting developing countries (CEPS 2006, 19). In their study of PCD and sustainable development, Bretherton and Vogler (2007, 20) also point to unequal power relations in the Commission, suggesting that DG Trade tends to come off best.

Several cases are touched upon in other chapters of this volume, but the common agricultural policy (CAP) is undoubtedly the most obvious example of coherence challenges. The CAP requires the EC to dispose of surplus European products on the world market through the use of export subsidies on agricultural goods. In addition, the EU market is protected from agricultural imports via tariff and non-tariff trade barriers imposed on developing countries trying to increase their exports to the Union. These CAP provisions have been criticised for their adverse impact on local development and the livelihoods of the poor in developing countries. The EU talks about the multifunctionality of agriculture, including non-economic objectives such as food safety, rural development and employment, animal welfare, and nature conservation, which legitimise subsidies. In presenting its interventionist agricultural system as a European model, the Union also appeals to the G33 group of developing countries that are not competitive on the international agricultural markets. However, in practice, and despite reforms, the CAP is still criticised for being trade-distorting and for disrupting local markets.

The EU's Common Fisheries Policy generates similar undesirable external consequences from the point of view of stimulating development in the South. One of the objectives is to protect the activities of the European fishing industry. In this regard, a 1976 Council Resolution agrees 'on the need to ensure, by means of any appropriate Community agreements, that Community fishermen obtain fishing rights in the waters of third countries and that the existing rights are retained'. The EU has concluded 20 such agreements, gaining access for European deep-water fleets to the coastal fishing waters of third (mostly ACP) countries, in return for financial compensations. Such agreements are partly responsible for over-exploitation of the fishing grounds in some developing countries (Hudson 2006; Bretherton and Vogler 2007). Overfishing not only has negative consequences for the marine environment, but it also endangers the livelihood, diet, economic development and social cohesion of coastal communities.[10]

A number of initiatives have been taken to ensure that the objectives and impact of different EC policies do not contradict or undermine one another. All CSPs contain a coherence paragraph, covering linkages between all EC actions in a country and identifying potential incoherence. Yet, a 2002 assessment of the CSP formulation process concluded that addressing policy coherence was a general problem, especially with regard to the EU's agricultural and fisheries policies (European Commission 2002b). The Commission (2005a) issued a Communication including proposals to enhance PCD, covering the following policy areas: trade, environment, security, agriculture, fisheries, social dimension of globalisation, employment and decent work, migration, research and innovation, information society, transport, and energy. The Council (2006, 2) decided that PCD priorities are to be reviewed biannually by each incoming presidency.

'OECD-isation' and Other Scenarios

Development cooperation is a recent EU Community competence. During the past 15 years, the EU has gradually built up its institutional structure and refined its policy objectives in the area of development. Although the shadow of the

---

10   All existing fisheries agreements which involve compensatory payments are being replaced with Fisheries Partnership Agreements. These are meant to meet the needs of both the European fleet and of the fisheries sector in developing countries. For a critical evaluation, see: www.eucoherence.org.

pre-Maastricht era (for example, the focus on the ACP, and the dominance of the Member States) and the teething troubles (lack of coordination, long delays, and fraud) still affect the Union's development initiatives, it is becoming a more 'mature' external policy domain. But it remains difficult to pinpoint the EU's role in this area. This final section will draw some conclusions on recent trends and possible future scenarios.

First, we observed two trends since the 2002 Monterrey Conference: more aid and more Europe. However, this chapter has made it clear that more aid does not necessarily amount to more development. To some extent, the Barcelona-plus commitments boil down to budgetary tricks, rather than development-oriented initiatives. A large share of the European (and especially the EC) aid flows are directed towards middle-income countries in the near abroad and in the South. Another (and partly related) challenge is the extent to which development aid is linked to EU security policy. The debate on appropriate ODA criteria will be high on the international development agenda, and the development-security nexus will occupy a pivotal place in these discussions. The position adopted by the Union on whether flows of government spending to encourage conflict prevention and security in developing countries should be counted as ODA will be indicative of the future focus of EU development – either primarily on poverty reduction or on conflict management. The result of the securitisation trend may well be that the coherence of Europe's relations with developing countries has increased – but not necessarily for development.

Secondly, this patchwork nature of EU development policy (the means-dimension) implies that the Union has acted primarily as a policy-taker rather than a policy-maker (the goals-dimension). Given the fragmentation of both institutional and budgetary power resources, it should not come as a surprise that the EU has faced difficulties in thinking pro-actively on development aid strategies, and has mainly followed international trends (for example, the UN MDGs, the OECD recommendations on untying aid, and so on). The EU seems to be a norm-importer rather than a norm-exporter in development policy, and has only rarely (such as the HIV/AIDS issue) been able to put a distinctive European stamp on the international development agenda. According to the 2002 OECD-DAC evaluation of EC development aid, 'the EC is usually a taker of policy from other sources rather than an institution that sets the international agenda on contemporary problems in development'. One of the reasons cited for this lack of active development thinking by the Community is its limited analytical capacity. The report continues that the EC is 'too often a free rider on other institutions' analysis and more flexible administrative arrangements' (OECD-DAC 2002, 60). This can be contrasted with Europe's role in the 1970s, when a progressive and comprehensive 'aid and trade package' was built under the first Lomé Convention. From this perspective, Arts and Dickson (2004, 2–3) state that EU development policy 'has shifted away from making substantive and innovative attempts to contribute to the North-South dialogue ... to follow global trends much more than before'.

Nevertheless, it has to be added that recently the EU seems to be moving away from merely appropriating development principles introduced by other international development actors to trying to go beyond and do better than the internationally agreed upon benchmarks (see below). It has prepared concrete and ambitious proposals for action on the way towards 2015 in the areas of financing for development (Monterrey), the realisation of the MDGs, and focusing development efforts on Africa. Another example is the establishment of a European code of conduct on complementarity and division of labour in development, which should feed into the OECD-DAC debates on this topic (Council 2007, 38). When asked whether the EU is the competent organisation to deal with this, Commissioner Michel replied:

> I am not one of those who think that Europe should be a one-stop shop, a charitable body. Europe is a political entity founded on values. Why should it not have its own development policy, its own projects? Some would like to see Europe as an NGO, not too involved in the organisation. Myself, I do not want to see a Europe which is reduced to less than the sum of its parts! (Agence Europe 1 March 2007)

This links with the third observation, namely that recent EU documents have put great emphasis on the need to increase the 'visibility' of the Union as a development actor. In the 2000 reform process, the Commission (2000, 17) states aid programmes 'are a vital instrument in ensuring the EU continues to have a strong voice in the world'. This seems to indicate that development policy is considered as a field of action which allows the EU to reinforce both its internal and external legitimacy. It has been suggested that its strong performance on the international scene can constitute a form of 'cement' and legitimisation for the European integration project (Smith 2006, 11). Development cooperation is perfectly suited to this kind of legitimating function, as it offers the Union an opportunity to show itself to the domestic as well as the international public as a 'force for the good' trying to fight poverty in developing countries in a spirit of solidarity. It might also lead to a more cynical conclusion, suggested by Vogt (2006, 169), that the meaningfulness of the EU project itself is becoming more important than bringing about development in the world. In other words, it might be argued that enhancing its international profile has become an objective *an sich* of development policy.

Similarly, Olsen (2004/2005) sees a shift in European interests from the promotion of development to the pursuit of the old ambition to become a significant international actor. He connects this observation with the above-mentioned trend to integrate development aid into the EU's foreign and security policy. The Union's policy towards Africa in particular is increasingly directed towards crisis management and conflict prevention and less focused on development cooperation in the traditional sense. Africa is seen as an easy playground for Europe's ambition to enhance its international profile.

Fourthly, it is interesting to take a closer look at the vision of the various EU actors, both national and supranational ones, on the way forward for Union development. The matrix below (Table 3.2) identifies four *ideal-type* scenarios for European development aid based on two political cleavages (for a similar overview, see Maxwell and Engel 2003). References to EU institutions and Member States are only tentative – for useful overviews of their positions, see Cosgrove-Sacks (1999) and Hoebink and Stokke (2005). The first dimension corresponds to vertical coherence and concerns the distribution of competences. Here, two paths can be walked: renationalising development aid, or full Europeanisation (integration) of development policies. As Rogerson et al. (2004, 28) remark: 'At present, there are some voices in favour of renationalising the EU's aid to its members. Others are arguing, conversely, for denationalising its bilateral aid budgets, and recentralising them in the EU. This stand-off is not likely to change very soon and neither outcome looks probable.'

The second dimension looks at the preferred objectives and corresponds to horizontal coherence between various policy domains. Here, the major question is whether the purpose of development cooperation is the fight against poverty, or whether development assistance is to be used as an instrument to achieve other (mainly foreign policy and security) objectives. Member States seem equally divided over these options. For instance, new Member States tend to focus mainly on regional stability, global security, and cross-cutting themes like human rights rather than poverty reduction *sensu stricto*. Since the first Labour government of 1996, the UK has presented itself as a leading actor in the international fight against poverty, but it sees the UN as the most appropriate forum and, at times, has suggested a re-nationalisation of EC competences in this area.[11]

Table 3.2   **Member State preferences and future scenarios for EU development**

	Poverty eradication	**Subordination to other goals (incl. securitisation)**
Europeanisation	Scandinavian members? European Parliament? DG Development?	France? New Member States?
Renationalisation	United Kingdom?	Italy? Spain?

A potential way out of this deadlock is offered by Holland (2002, 16). He suggests that development policy could become 'an unexpected candidate for the use of enhanced cooperation'. This would enable Member States, such as the Scandinavian countries, which share similar objectives and are willing to move ahead towards fuller European integration in development, to do so faster than others. In the past, a Northern group of 'like-minded countries' has held separate meetings on specific development issues (Arts 2004, 104), for example on the integration of gender in development (Elgström 2000, 465). The participation of

---

11   In 2002, the British Secretary of State for International Development threatened a renationalisation if EU development aid continued to be 'ineffective' (*Guardian* 29 November 2002).

nine Member States in the new European Trust Fund for infrastructure in Africa also constitutes a form of enhanced cooperation.

Finally, there are signs of a growing 'OECD-isation' of the EU as a development actor. The OECD-DAC issues guidelines on the management of development aid. It also publishes a wide range of reports, among them the annual 'OECD Journal on Development'. In addition, the DAC has explored ways to ensure greater coherence in donor policies across sectors that affect developing countries. Furthermore, the Committee provides a setting where donor governments can compare policy experiences, identify good practice, and coordinate domestic and international policies. One condition for acquiring DAC membership is that donors agree to have their development programmes scrutinised by peer members on a regular basis. As such, the DAC is a forum where peer pressure can act as a powerful incentive to adapt policy and implement 'soft' law.

The future role of the EU may well be to focus on tasks similar to those of the OECD-DAC described above, that is, the Union will 'OECD-ise'. While the EU used to be primarily a follower of norms developed by others, more recently it has managed increasingly to set targets and standards for national development policies. It is likely to play an ever more prominent role in the coordination of European development policies (via peer pressure and 'soft' integration, through issuing follow-up reports on the quality of aid and ODA levels, by formulating guidelines on topics such as the untying of aid and enhanced harmonisation of donors' administrative requirements, and so on). Against this, the role of the EU as a funding and implementing body of development programmes in its own right seems to be in decline. Although the Commission continues to manage a substantial amount of aid resources, unlike the OECD, which does not have its own development budget, its budget is declining. Under the Financial Perspectives 2007–13, the share of European aid accounted for by the EC will fall from 20 per cent in 2006 to 13 per cent in 2013 (European Commission 2006a). As such, the representation of the EU as a regulatory rather than distributive actor seems to be confirmed – also in development. The EU's function as a distributor of development assistance is diminishing in importance, while its regulatory role as policy setter is becoming more significant.

References

Arts, K. (2004), 'Changing Interests in EU Development Cooperation', in K. Arts and A.K. Dickson (eds), *EU Development Cooperation: from Model to Symbol* (Manchester: Manchester University Press).

Bonaglia, F., Goldstein, A. and Petito, F. (2006), 'Values in Development Cooperation policy', in S. Lucarelli and I. Manners (eds), *Values and Principles in EU Foreign Policy* (London and New York: Routledge).

Bretherton, C. and Vogler, J. (2006), *The EU as a Global Actor* (London and New York: Routledge).

—— (2007), 'The EU as a Sustainable Development Actor in International Politics', paper presented at the Tenth EUSA Biannual Conference, Montreal, 17-19 May.

British Overseas NGOs for Development (BOND) (n.d.), 'Conflict, Security, and Official Development Assistance (ODA): Issues for NGO Advocacy', http://www.bond.org. uk/pubs/advocacy/gsdpaper.pdf.

Carbone, M. (2006), 'European NGOs and EU Development Policy', in M. Lister and M. Carbone (eds) (2006), *New Pathways in Development: Gender and Civil Society in EU Policy* (Aldershot: Ashgate).

Carbone, M. (2007), *The EU and International Development* (London: Routledge).

CEPS (2006), 'Policy Coherence for Development in the EU Council: Strategies for the Way Forward', Report prepared by the European Centre for Policy Studies, June.

CONCORD (2007), *Hold the Applause! EU Governments Risk Breaking Promises*, Report from the European NGO Confederation for Relief and Development, April 2007.

Cosgrove-Sacks, C. (ed.) (1999) *The EU and Developing Countries* (Houndmills: Macmillan).

Council of the European Union (2006), 'Policy Coherence for Development. Work Programme 2006–07', 8387/06.

Council of the European Union (2007), Press Release, 9471/1/07 REV 1, 14–15 May.

Dearden, S. (2007), 'The Reform Agenda of the EU's Development Policy', *European Development Policy Study Group Discussion Paper* 34.

Elgström, O. (2000), 'Norm Negotiations: The Construction of New Norms Regarding Gender and Development in EU Foreign Aid Policy', *Journal of European Public Policy* 7:3, 457–76.

Eurodad (2006), 'EU Aid: Genuine Leadership or Misleading Figures?', Joint European NGO Briefing, 3 April.

EuropeAid (2004), *European Commission External Assistance Reform: Four Years On* (Brussels: EuropeAid Cooperation Office).

European Commission (2000), 'The European Community's Development Policy', COM(2002)212.

European Commission (2001), 'Conflict Prevention', COM(2001)211.

—— (2002a), 'Untying. Enhancing the Effectiveness of Aid', COM(2002)639.

—— (2002b), 'Progress Report on the Implementation of the Common Framework for CSPs', SEC(2002)1279.

—— (2005a), 'Policy Coherence for Development. Accelerating Progress towards Attaining the MDGs', COM(2005)134.

—— (2005b), 'Qualitative Assessment of the Reform of External Assistance', SEC(2005)963.

—— (2005c), 'Report on the Public Consultation on the Future of EU Development Policy', June.

—— (2006a), 'Financing for Development and Aid Effectiveness', COM(2006)85.

—— (2006b), 'EU Aid: Delivering more, better and faster', COM(2006)87.

—— (2006c), 'Increasing the Impact of EU Aid', COM(2006)88.

—— (2007), 'Keeping Europe's Promises on Financing for Development', COM (2007)164.

European Council (2003), 'A Secure Europe in a Better World', Brussels, 12 December.

EU (2005), 'The European Consensus', 20 December.

EU and OECD (2006), 'EU Donor Atlas 2006'.

Hoebink, P. and Stokke, O. (eds) (2005), *Perspectives on European Development Cooperation* (London and New York: Routledge).

Holland, M. (2002), *The EU and the Third World* (Basingstoke: Palgrave).

Hudson, A. (2006), 'Case Study: The Fisheries Partnership Agreements', in *Policy Coherence for Development in the EU Council: Strategies for the Way Forward* (Brussels: CEPS).

Lister, M. (ed.) (1998), *EU Development Policy* (Houndmills: Macmillan).

Maxwell, S. and Engel, P. (2003), 'European Development Cooperation to 2010', *ODI Working Paper* 219.

Michel, L. (2006), Press Release IP/06/256, 2 March.

Nielson, P. (2001), 'Building Credibility: The Role of European Development Policy in Preventing Conflict', Foreign Policy Centre, London, 8 February.

OECD-DAC (2002), *EC Development Cooperation Review* (Paris: OECD).

—— (2006), 'Aid Flows Top USD 100 billion in 2005', Press Release, 4 April.

Olsen, G.R. (2004), 'Changing European Concerns: Security and Complex Political Emergencies Instead of Development', in K. Arts and A.K. Dickson (eds), *EU Development Cooperation: from Model to Symbol* (Manchester: Manchester University Press).

—— (2005), 'The EU's Development Policy: Shifting Priorities in a Rapidly Changing World', in P. Hoebink and O. Stokke (eds), *Perspectives on European Development Cooperation* (London and New York: Routledge).

Orbie, J. (2003), 'EU Development Policy Integration and the Monterrey Process: A Leading and Benevolent Identity?', *European Foreign Affairs Review* 8:3, 395–415.

—— and Versluys, H. (2007), 'Recent Evolutions in EU Development Aid: More Europe, More Aid, Less Development?', *Studia Diplomatica* LIX:4, 19–40.

Rogerson, A., Hewitt, A. and Waldenberg, D. (2004), *The International Aid System 2005-2010: Forces For and Against Change* (London: ODI).

Santiso, C. (2002), 'Reforming European Foreign Aid: Development Cooperation as an Element of Foreign Policy', *European Foreign Affairs Review* 7:4, 401–22.

Smith, M. (2006), 'The EU and International Order: European and Global Aspects', Paper presented at the EUSA Workshop 'EU Foreign/Security/Defence Policy', Washington DC, 3 April.

Stocker, S. (2000), 'Time to Match EU Rhetoric about the Fight against Poverty with Deeds', *European Voice* 6.

Vogt, H. (2006), 'Coping with Historical Responsibility: Trends and Images of the EU's Development Policy', in H. Mayer and H. Vogt (eds), *A Responsible Europe? Ethical Foundations of EU External Affairs* (Basingstoke: Palgrave Macmillan).

Chapter 4

European Union Humanitarian Aid: Lifesaver or Political Tool?

Helen Versluys

Humanitarian aid is a non-military 'soft' means with which the European Union intervenes in third countries affected by disaster or conflict. The creation of the European Commission Office for Humanitarian Aid (ECHO) in 1992 has to be seen in light of the post-Cold War context which opened a window of opportunity for the Union to assume a more prominent international role with other than strictly military means. European initiatives in the field of humanitarian aid can be seen as 'symbolic politics' (Olsen 2004, 85), allowing the Union to assert its identity – and especially its civilian power image – on the international scene. Through the provision of humanitarian relief the Union shows itself to the (domestic and international) public as a good-hearted international actor addressing human suffering in third countries.

In addition, it has been suggested that a strong performance by the EU on the international stage can constitute a form of 'cement' for the European integration project (Smith 2006, 11). The EU's provision of emergency relief in response to humanitarian disasters such as the December 2004 tsunami can contribute to consolidating the loyalty of European citizens towards European integration. Humanitarian aid operations would seem to be particularly suited to this kind of legitimising function, more so even than traditional development assistance, because of the combined effects of instantly visible results (number of lives saved), strong media focus, and positive popular opinion.

Humanitarian aid entered the realm of Community competences as an instrument for EU development policy towards ACP (Africa, Caribbean, and Pacific) countries in the 1969 Yaoundé II Convention (see Box 4.1). Until 1992, responsibility for humanitarian aid was scattered among different Commission DGs, according to the nature of the aid and the urgency of the situation. As spending on humanitarian activity increased,[1] and confronted with evidence of inadequate preparation for the humanitarian crisis in Iraq after the first Gulf War and by the looming crisis in former Yugoslavia, the Commissioners then in charge of external relations agreed on the need to establish an administrative structure exclusively dedicated to the management of humanitarian assistance – ECHO.

---

1 Humanitarian assistance allocated by the Commission more than doubled between 1986 and 1991 (Randel and German 2002, 25).

The objective was to improve internal coordination and efficiency in delivering EU relief. In addition, the newly created Humanitarian Office had to improve external perceptions of the Union as a major humanitarian aid donor.

In 1996, ECHO's humanitarian work was given a legal basis when EU Member States agreed on a Council Regulation governing humanitarian aid.[2] To date, humanitarian action has not been included in the EU Treaty. For the first time, the Reform Treaty (Article 188) refers to humanitarian assistance as an EU competence shared between the European Commission and the Member States.

Box 4.1   Key moments in EU humanitarian aid policy

1969 Humanitarian aid enters the domain of EC competences in Yaoundé II.

1992 ECHO is established.

1993 – ECHO is placed under the responsibility of Commissioner Manuel Marín (cooperation and development), limiting the potential for explicit instructions from DG Relex on EC humanitarian aid policy.
– First Framework Partnership Agreement with specialised humanitarian organisations.

1995 Emma Bonino is appointed as a separate Commissioner for humanitarian aid, distinct from development policy.

1996 – Council Regulation on EC humanitarian aid.
– The HAC is set up.
– First Commission Communication on LRRD.

1999 – The humanitarian and development aid portfolios are brought together under one Commissioner, Poul Nielson.
– Article 20 Evaluation.

2001 – Second Commission Communication on LRRD.
– ECHO mission statement.

2004 – Louis Michel is nominated Commissioner for humanitarian aid and development.
– ECHO becomes a fully-fledged Directorate-General.
– Humanitarian aid included in the Reform Treaty.

2005 Measures to strengthen the EU's capacity to react to emergencies are announced in the aftermath of the tsunami disaster.

---

2   Council Regulation EC 1257/96 of 20 June 1996.

This chapter starts with an overview of the power resources at the EU's disposal to pursue a humanitarian aid policy. Budgetary resources, decision-making procedures, competences, and institutional architecture are discussed. Then, the goals of EU humanitarian aid policy are examined. Attention is paid to the philosophy of apolitical humanitarian aid. Having explained the rationale behind this interpretation of relief, the question is raised as to whether EU discourse on needs-based humanitarian aid is actually being adhered to. Two issues in particular are addressed. 'Securitisation' refers to the extent to which humanitarian aid is conceived of as a crisis management tool. 'Developmentalisation' denotes the role of humanitarian aid in the promotion of sustainable development. Two periods can be distinguished. Until the end of the 1990s, ECHO sometimes engaged in activities which, strictly speaking, went beyond humanitarian assistance and were more oriented towards conflict resolution or development. From 1999/2000 onwards, a move away from both the securitisation and developmentalisation of humanitarian aid can be noted.

Power Resources for EU Humanitarian Aid Policy

Budgetary Powers

ECHO has three sources of funding: the European Community budget, the European Development Fund (EDF), of which part of the B envelope is used for short-term emergency actions in ACP countries, and the Emergency Aid Reserve which can be called upon to respond rapidly to aid requirements resulting from events which could not have been foreseen when ECHO's budget was drawn up.[3]

In the first half of the 1990s, Member States channelled a growing proportion of their humanitarian aid budget through the Union. By 1994, ECHO had become the world's largest provider of humanitarian assistance. However, because of the rapid growth in the funds being disbursed through the EU, Commission headquarters could not keep up with the increased workload. From the mid-1990s onwards, just like the Union's general development policy (Chapter 3), ECHO began to be criticised for poor management, long delays in the disbursements of funds, insufficient control of its partner organisations, and lack of rigour in analysis, project management and evaluation. Not surprisingly, ECHO's budget gradually declined (see Figure 4.1). However, in 1999, ECHO's budget rose to an exceptional high of €820 million. This was mainly due to the expenditure of almost €400 million on the Kosovo crisis. Since the beginning of the new millennium, ECHO has made efforts towards more professionalism and better management of its aid funds. The increase in ECHO's budget, noticeably since 2000 might be partly attributable to a restored credibility of and enhanced confidence in ECHO.

---

3   In 2005, 75.8 per cent of the total budget came from the general budget, 3.5 per cent came from the EDP, and 20.7 per cent from the emergency reserve.

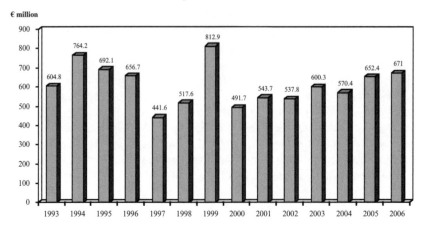

Figure 4.1   ECHO budget 1993–2005

While funding levels vary each year according to assessments of humanitarian need, relief represents about 10 per cent of total EU external aid. ECHO provides around 40 per cent of all European (Commission and Member States together) humanitarian assistance. ECHO's proportion seems to be declining, however. In the course of the 1990s, it still represented more than half of the European total. Currently, the Member States' aggregated humanitarian aid budgets are larger than ECHO's slice of the pie. This can be partly explained by the increase in the number of Member States by 12 since the 2004 and 2007 enlargements. ECHO is still a 'colossus' compared to Member State humanitarian donors. In 2005, ECHO disposed of a budget of €652.5 million, compared to €279 million made available by the UK, €258.5 million allocated by Germany, and €236.9 million disbursed by the Dutch government, the largest donors among the Member States. ECHO is the second largest international donor after the US. These considerable budgetary resources provide the EU with the potential to act as a world-leading humanitarian aid donor achieving a significant impact on international humanitarian action.

Decision-making Procedures

The EU's power as a humanitarian donor is reinforced by the swiftness with which it can respond to sudden disasters. For instance, it was the first international actor to pledge humanitarian aid for the tsunami disaster. Over time, ECHO's authority has expanded in the event that emergency decisions need to be taken, to the benefit of timely and flexible humanitarian aid provision and at the cost of tighter scrutiny by the Member States. The decision-making procedures which ECHO must follow are now less restrictive than those of most other Commission services. The 1996 Council Regulation commented on the need to establish, where necessary, fast decision-making procedures for the financing of humanitarian operations. However, in 1999, a large-scale evaluation pointed out that the Commission's decision-making procedures were ill-suited to acute emergencies. It noted that in this type of situation, the Commission took too long to release funds and adapt to swiftly changing realities in the field (Franklin Advisory Services 1999).

In 2001, a fast-track decision procedure was introduced which grants ECHO's Director-General the power to take primary emergency decisions within 48 hours, on the commitment of a maximum of €3 million, and for a maximum duration of three months, without prior consultation with the Member States or the College of Commissioners. While this fast-track procedure provides ECHO with a large decision autonomy, so far it has only been used in the case of natural disasters, for example in response to the December 2004 Indian Ocean tsunami and the October 2005 earthquake in Pakistan and Northern India. This seems to indicate that with regard to politically sensitive emergencies, Member States are less willing to grant ECHO autonomous budgetary power.

Even since the adoption of the fast-track procedure, both humanitarian NGOs and Commissioner Louis Michel have signalled that the heavy administrative requirements inherent in Commission bureaucracy continue to complicate the rapid release of emergency aid. According to Michel, in an emergency it does not make sense to have an interdepartmental consultation procedure (see Box 4.2) allowing all Commission Cabinets to voice their opinion on humanitarian aid decisions. Mobilising money from the emergency reserve seems to take especially long, because of the required trilateral agreement between the Commission, the Council and the Parliament (*De Standaard* 24 July 2006).

Box 4.2   ECHO's decision-making procedures

Fast-track delegation procedure: to speed up the response to sudden emergencies, the Commission has delegated powers to the Director-General of ECHO for making primary emergency humanitarian decisions within 48 hours, for a maximum of €3 million, and for a maximum duration of three months.

Empowerment procedure: the Commissioner responsible for humanitarian aid is empowered to take decisions relating to emergency operations up to €30 million for a maximum of six months, and non-urgent decisions up to a maximum of €10 million. These decisions are subject to an interdepartmental consultation procedure within the Commission. Emergency decisions exceeding €10 million and non-urgent decisions exceeding €2 million require approval by Member State representatives in the HAC.

Written procedure: for emergency operations exceeding €30 million, and non-emergency programmes amounting to more than €10 million, decisions are taken by the College of Commissioners, and need to be approved by the HAC.

ECHO is allowed to decide autonomously how it wants to spend its annual budget and which specific humanitarian projects it wishes to finance. However, the overall yearly budget for humanitarian aid is determined by the Council and the European Parliament (EP) balancing other priorities, and 'periodically differences between the needs identified that ECHO would like to meet and the budget actually made available have arisen' (Prolog 2004, 15; interview ECHO 24 April 2006).

EU Competences: Competition with Member States and Multilateral Donors

The Union is not the only provider of humanitarian assistance. Its closest 'competitors' are EU Member States – which pursue their own humanitarian policies – and multilateral organisations, notably the United Nations (UN) and, to a lesser extent, the OECD (Organisation for Economic Cooperation and Development). It is quite common to boast about 'Europe' being the largest provider of humanitarian aid. However, as with development policy (see the previous chapter) this is a somewhat misleading representation of a unified donor. Since humanitarian aid is a shared competence,[4] Member States run national humanitarian budgets and policies, the priorities of which are not necessarily compatible with those of the Commission. A lack of coordination and harmonisation among different European donors might be to the detriment of the EU's collective weight in international humanitarian aid policy. For example, Europe's impact on large UN agencies seems limited when compared to the European (Commission and Member States) level of funding and the strong European humanitarian tradition. It has been suggested that the Commission's inability to direct the contributions of Member States is to the detriment of the influence 'Europe' could exert on UN humanitarian organisations (SHER 2005, 41).

The UN system plays a key role not only in the sponsoring, but also in the implementation and coordination of international humanitarian aid. Over the years, the UN's humanitarian role has become a recognised 'fourth pillar' in the organisation's core activities, beyond its three Charter-based responsibilities involving peace and security, economic development, and human rights. In December 1991, the General Assembly gave the UN an unprecedented leadership role in responding to humanitarian crises and coordinating humanitarian aid efforts. Six UN entities – UNHCR, WFP, UNICEF, FAO, WHO and UNDP – play a central role in offering protection and assistance in the event of humanitarian crises. Some EU countries, for example the UK, the Scandinavian countries and the Netherlands, are not entirely convinced that the EU level offers added value compared to the UN as humanitarian actor. The argument is that the UN makes humanitarian coordination more all-encompassing than what ECHO's merely European structure allows for.

Recently, the OECD-DAC (Development Assistance Committee) has assumed a role in the field of humanitarian aid. Traditionally, the DAC focuses on

---

4   Humanitarian aid is not explicitly mentioned in the Treaties. Title XX of the EC Treaty on Development Cooperation served as the legal basis for the 1996 Humanitarian Aid Council Regulation.

development aid. Since 2003, attention has also been devoted to humanitarian assistance. In June 2003, DAC donor governments[5] agreed on the Good Humanitarian Donorship (GHD) declaration. DAC Peer Reviews now evaluate the humanitarian aid policy of DAC donor countries, and their progress towards realising GHD commitments. One possible advantage of the DAC compared to the EU level is that non-EU humanitarian donors – most importantly the US as largest provider of relief assistance – are involved in the GHD. However, new humanitarian donors in Central and Eastern Europe are not DAC members.

The Commission has gone through considerable efforts to translate the GHD principles in its own humanitarian aid policy. However, it has not been in the driving seat if it comes to launching the initiative. GHD was initiated by the Swedish government, and chaired consecutively by Canada and the UK. This confirms earlier observations of the Union as a norm-taker rather than a norm-setter in international thinking on aid policy (see Chapter 3).

Institutional Architecture

The EU's institutional structure provides ECHO with considerable autonomy from the Council of Ministers. Humanitarian aid is a pillar 1 competence, and pillar 2 instructions on how ECHO should dispense funds are not allowed. In addition, it is difficult for the Council to amend the 1996 Council Regulation on Humanitarian Aid, possibly with the aim of curtailing the Commission's competence, since the Commission has a monopoly on initiating new legislation governing pillar 1 issues.

Interference by the EP is also limited. It is not necessary to adopt a new Regulation for every single allocation of humanitarian resources, thereby restricting the Parliament's scope for defining humanitarian aid activities through its legal right to co-decision. Moreover, once a pillar 1 external policy, such as humanitarian aid, has been co-decided by the Parliament, the power of implementation then passes to the Comitology Committee which brings together representatives of the Commission and Member States largely to the exclusion of the EP.[6]

---

5   EU DAC donors are Belgium, Denmark, Finland, Germany, Spain, Portugal, Luxemburg, Greece, the UK, Ireland, Italy, France, Sweden, Austria, the Netherlands, and the European Commission. Australia, New Zealand, Canada, the US, Norway, and Switzerland are the non-EU DAC donors.

6   In July 2006, a new procedure was adopted which, for the first time, confers on the Parliament the formal right to intervene in comitology. The Parliament can block, by an absolute majority, quasi-legislative implementing measures in domains governed by co-decision. ECHO's proposals now have to be sent simultaneously to the HAC and the Parliament. While the Parliament is entitled to examine whether ECHO has not gone beyond the limits of the implementation powers, as stipulated in the 1996 Regulation, it cannot oblige ECHO to finance humanitarian operations, for instance in Kosovo rather than in Rwanda. It remains to be seen whether much will change. The absolute parliamentary majority needed constitutes a significant barrier, and it is unclear whether decisions on humanitarian aid will be considered as quasi-legislative.

Within the Commission, ECHO seems to enjoy a larger degree of autonomy than its counterpart EuropeAid which is responsible for development aid. While EuropeAid is charged with the implementation of development cooperation programmes (see Chapter 3), DG External Relations (for non-ACP countries) and DG Development (for ACP countries) are responsible for formulating policy. ECHO is responsible for the entire project cycle of humanitarian operations, from planning to evaluation. Not only in Brussels but also in the field, ECHO stands somewhat apart from the rest of the Commission. It has established an extensive network of field offices staffed by independent experts and local staff, operating independently from Commission Delegations.

Via the 'comitology' system, Member States can exert some influence over ECHO, albeit mainly indirectly. The Council Regulation on humanitarian aid provided for the creation of a Humanitarian Aid Committee (HAC), giving Member State representatives the opportunity to express their views on those Commission humanitarian aid financial decisions exceeding €2 million. Emergencies are an exception, where ECHO can decide autonomously on interventions costing up to €10 million. The HAC replaces the system in place prior to 1996 whereby Member States were simply informed of the Commission's funding decisions at quarterly meetings (Brusset and Tiberghien 2002, 56; Mowjee and Macrae 2002, 17).

The HAC functions as a management or, for Global Plans,[7] a regulatory committee. The Member States clearly envisaged a committee which had more than a merely advisory role and could exert genuine control over ECHO. A qualified majority of the HAC representatives can block a humanitarian aid programme proposed by the Commission. The HAC has never rejected an ECHO proposal, and in practice seems to function more as a consultative entity than a regulatory body.

However, a zero rejection rate need not necessarily imply that the HAC is no more than a rubber-stamping mechanism, and that Member States are unable to exert influence on ECHO's policy. Principal-Agent theory points to the phenomenon of 'rational anticipation', meaning that an agent (the Commission) tries to anticipate the reactions of the principal (the Member States) and adjusts its behaviour accordingly (Pollack 2001, 203).[8] Member States exercise indirect power, because ECHO tries to anticipate their response and to put forward proposals which are as acceptable as possible to them (Mowjee and Macrae 2002, 17; Macrae et al. 2002, 21). In an attempt to cater for the wishes of all Member States, the plans ECHO proposes to the HAC usually cover the various crises which are of importance to them (interviews with HAC representatives 12 April 2006 and 08 May 2006).

---

7   Global Plans are designed for protracted crisis situations to allow ECHO to establish country- or region-wide strategies usually for 12 (24 if justified) months at a time. They are used for non-emergency situations where ECHO has programmes of over €10 million.

8   For an application of Principal-Agent theory to EU humanitarian policy: see Versluys (2007).

The greatest constraint on ECHO's autonomy seems to be its dependence on others for on-the-ground implementation of EU humanitarian aid operations. ECHO has developed almost no operational capacity of its own, and instead relies on partner organisations specialising in humanitarian aid (NGOs, UN agencies and the International Red Cross) for carrying out humanitarian assistance projects in the field. ECHO is interwoven in a relationship of mutual dependence with humanitarian partner organisations. Its partners are co-responsible for determining the success or failure of EU humanitarian work. ECHO can even become 'paralysed' in the absence of some degree of consensus among partners about the direction of its humanitarian policy. Conversely, humanitarian organisations greatly value sponsoring by a major donor such as ECHO, giving the Humanitarian Office – as holder of the purse strings – a considerable degree of leverage vis-à-vis implementing partners.

A more in-depth evaluation of the Union's role as humanitarian aid donor requires consideration of the goals of EU humanitarian aid policy. The next section examines the kind of humanitarian activities for which the available power resources are used.

The Goals of EU Humanitarian Aid

Humanitarian aid is not intended to mesh with EU foreign policy goals such as conflict prevention, sustainable development or the promotion of human rights. This commitment to apolitical relief is inspired by the so-called humanitarian imperative, and enshrined in EU secondary law. Here, the question is whether from time to time, despite the discourse on needs-based humanitarian aid, in day-to-day practice EU humanitarian aid is nevertheless used as a substitute for political action or development cooperation.

Apolitical Aid: Rationale and Legal Enshrinement

> Political goals such as prevention and long-term development are strictly speaking outside the scope of ECHO's operations. (ECHO 1997, 3)

The 1996 Council Regulation defines EU humanitarian assistance as explicitly apolitical, and legally enshrines the humanitarian principles of humanity (saving human lives and alleviating suffering wherever it is found), impartiality (the implementation of actions solely on the basis of need, without discrimination between or within affected populations), neutrality (humanitarian action must not favour any side in a conflict), and independence (the autonomy of humanitarian objectives from political, economic, or military objectives). The sole aim of EC humanitarian aid 'is to prevent or relieve human suffering'. Humanitarian assistance must not be 'guided by, or subject to, political considerations', and is to be accorded 'without discrimination on the grounds of race, ethnic group, religion, age, sex, nationality or political affiliation'.

The Commission explains the commitment to non-political humanitarian aid by an appeal to the humanitarian imperative, the entitlement of each human being to emergency aid in times of crisis. A nation must ensure that the humanitarian needs of the population within its borders are met. However, when the government of a country is not capable or willing to take on this responsibility, international organisations and third countries with the necessary resources have the duty to support external humanitarian aid operations.

The unconditional entitlement to humanitarian relief is in contrast to EU development aid which has become increasingly subject to political conditionality, namely the recipient country's respect for human rights and democratic principles. For example, while in the spring of 2006 EU foreign ministers decided to suspend aid to the Palestinian Authority controlled by Hamas, this was not to affect humanitarian aid for the Palestinian people.

The Commission argues that the integration of humanitarian aid in a broader political or development-oriented strategy might strain compliance with the humanitarian imperative. If, rather than pursuing the goal of life-saving, humanitarian aid is to contribute to conflict resolution and development, this might allow for the creation of deserving and undeserving victims, based on people's expected contribution to peace-building and development. Such an approach potentially implies withholding aid, which might result in avoidable deaths (De Torrenté 2004, 3; Macrae 2004, 33). For instance, the political imperative to build peace by supporting transitional governments might require marginalising those rebels trying to undermine the transition process, and thus denying humanitarian assistance to those in need who are situated in rebel-controlled areas (Bryer 2003, 5–6).

The apolitical character of humanitarian aid is also fostered because it is considered to be the main vehicle for safeguarding access to crisis victims and the security of humanitarian aid workers. Humanitarians conclude a 'contract' with belligerent parties, based on the understanding that assistance comes with no strings attached. This contract has to guarantee the acceptability of humanitarian operations and the immunity of humanitarian staff from attacks. When humanitarians are seen as part of a politico-military strategy, this might undermine their perceived impartiality, and erode their safety and freedom of movement. For example, it has been argued that during the Iraq war, the perception the local population had of some humanitarian organisations as 'force multipliers' of US foreign policy and military objectives, put all humanitarian workers in a dangerous position and triggered the deadly attacks on both the UN and Red Cross offices in Baghdad (De Torrenté 2004).

By stressing the importance of apolitical humanitarian aid, the Commission supposedly has more than merely the well-being of crisis victims in mind. To an extent it also ensures its own independence. To a large degree, ECHO is free to allocate money to areas facing the most acute humanitarian needs, rather than having to follow the foreign policy-oriented agendas of DG Relex or the Common Foreign and Security Policy (CFSP). If Member States were to decide to abandon the commitment to the non-political nature of humanitarian aid, this could imply a transfer of authority over humanitarian aid decision-making from ECHO to

DG Relex, or even its transformation into a CFSP domain of competence, where responsibility resides with the Council and Commission input is limited.

It is important to deconstruct the Commission's discourse on apolitical humanitarian aid for two reasons. First, a global trend towards an increased politicisation of humanitarian aid has been identified. No longer solely a palliative to address emergency needs in times of crisis, it has come to be considered as a means for intervening in internal conflicts, a tool for peace-building, and the starting point for addressing poverty and promoting human rights and good governance (Barnett 2005; Macrae and Leader 2000). Secondly, coherence in external action has been designated the *sine qua non* for the EU to be able to influence international politics. The European Security Strategy (European Council 2003, 11–13; see also Chapter 3) states:

> The challenge now is to bring together the different instruments and capabilities: European assistance programmes and the EDF, military and civilian capabilities from Member States and other instruments. ... Diplomatic efforts, development, trade and environmental policies, should follow the same agenda.

The following section examines where humanitarian aid can be placed in this policy mix. How does humanitarian action relate to EU crisis management tools (securitisation), and what is its relation to EU instruments for development aid (developmentalisation)?

The 1990s: A Substitute for Political Engagement and Development Cooperation

> Since the Union is not able to have (or rather, since the Member States do not want) a real CFSP, ECHO gives the EU a good conscience: saving the lives of the victims of natural or man-made disasters is an upstanding discharge. (Former ECHO staff quoted in Scappucci 1998, 43)

During the first years of its existence, ECHO engaged in activities transgressing the borders of life-saving humanitarian aid and moving towards conflict management and development, sometimes due to the Office's own desire to extend its turf, and sometimes due to Member State pressure. While the 1992 Treaty officially provided for a CFSP, until at least the end of the 1990s it remained largely declaratory. In the absence of an effective CFSP with proper crisis response mechanisms, humanitarian aid may have been considered as an alternative soft security instrument at the Union's disposal to intervene in third countries and to maintain a more pronounced role on the international stage. In this regard, the chronological concomitance between the creation of ECHO and the Maastricht Treaty seems more than coincidental (Petiteville 2001, 5). Financing under ECHO was less cumbersome and faster than CFSP procedures. Often, ECHO was the only EU entity present in the country facing an outbreak of conflict.

The case of Kosovo (1999) is an example of political pressure by Member States for the allocation of a disproportionate share of ECHO funding to a high-profile crisis in close proximity to the Union. Security concerns rather than humanitarian needs seem to have been the driving factor behind aid allocations to Kosovo. There was a fear that war would spill over into other former Yugoslavia republics and other Balkan countries, and European governments were reluctant to accept large numbers of refugees on a permanent basis (see also Chapter 5). Humanitarian aid was also considered a convenient way of providing assistance to politically sensitive areas, such as Cuba, without imposing human rights conditionality, even in the absence of a humanitarian crisis (Randel and German 2000, 39).

The 1996 Regulation puts forward an interpretation of humanitarian aid that goes beyond life-saving emergency aid and also includes the prevention of disasters, as well as rehabilitation activities designed to bridge the gap between emergency aid and long-term development, such as reconstruction of infrastructure or socio-economic structures (for example, school and hospitals). Because of this relatively broad mandate, combined with the unwillingness or inability to replace ECHO funding with other instruments in protracted crises, during the 1990s ECHO became active in the so-called 'grey zone' between emergency relief and development cooperation.

Since 1999/2000: Strengthened Commitment to Needs-based Humanitarian Aid

> To protect ECHO's budget, freedom of action and core activities, it is necessary to be more careful in drawing a line between what are and what are not core activities. (Nielson 2004, 1)

From 1999 onwards, ECHO began focusing on immediate, life-saving relief in emergencies, maintaining its operational independence from crisis management and withdrawing from activities in the grey zone. What were the factors contributing to this shift in ECHO policy? An important explanation for the decreasing use of humanitarian aid for security purposes can be found in the development of dedicated crisis management tools under the CFSP and the European Security and Defence Policy (ESDP). The Balkan conflict gave rise to the conviction that, while humanitarian aid remained important, more forceful intervention had to be within the Union's reach. Work started on the development of a ESDP. Headline goals were set for the creation of a Rapid Reaction Force (RRF), and more recently EU Battle Groups. A civilian component was also added to crisis management, namely in the domains of policing, strengthening the rule of law, strengthening civilian administration, and civil protection.

In addition to second pillar instruments, the Commission created new emergency response instruments other than ECHO. To avoid using ECHO money for human rights initiatives, media support, police training and election monitoring in (post-)conflict situations, in 2001 the Commission (DG Relex) established a Rapid Reaction Mechanism (RRM). While ECHO's humanitarian action is focused on the individual, interventions under the RRM are aimed at the preservation or re-establishment of the civic structures necessary for political, social and economic stability. While ECHO is politically neutral, the RRM is an explicitly politically oriented emergency instrument aligned with the CFSP, and intended to be operational in the context of crisis management.

Apart from humanitarian aid, the Civil Protection Mechanism (CPM) is the other Commission (DG Environment) instrument for immediate disaster response. Although both civil protection and humanitarian aid aim to relieve human suffering, there are substantial differences in the way civil protection and humanitarian aid resources are mobilised. ECHO concentrates on providing apolitical emergency assistance, particularly in developing countries, through professional aid agencies including UN bodies, the Red Cross and NGOs. The CPM is based on Member States' nationally organised structures, established mainly to tackle internal emergencies, and not bound by traditional humanitarian principles. The use of the CPM outside of the EU is based on a request from the third country affected. On the contrary, ECHO's humanitarian assistance is provided directly to the people in distress regardless of any request from the affected country.

The emergence of the EU as a more politically active international actor has not gone hand in hand with an increased use of ECHO funds for political projects related to conflict management or for military activities. On the contrary, the trend towards a more outspoken European foreign and security policy, with its focus on crisis management and with new means of intervention, has allowed ECHO to focus on core humanitarian tasks and to assume a more neutral role (Brusset and Tiberghien 2002, 59; Randel and German 2003, 80). ECHO has indeed phased out its more political interventions, for instance in Cuba, Bosnia and Kosovo. The recent attention to military and civilian crisis management has not been at the expense of resources devoted to humanitarian action. Since the beginning of the new millennium, there has been a noticeable increase in ECHO's budget, and for the Financial Perspectives 2007–13, a further rise to an annual average of €800 million has been agreed.

However, despite the resistance to overt politicisation, the increasing overlap between exclusively humanitarian operations and more political and even military engagement might blur the distinction between humanitarian aid and other forms of EU crisis response. While previously humanitarian aid was the main instrument at the Union's disposal for responding to crises, the EU has recently emerged as a more diversified and 'robust' emergency actor, undertaking multi-mandated operations in which coherence between diplomatic, military and humanitarian efforts is sought.

EU military forces are charged with the implementation of the Petersberg Tasks (Art. 17 TEU), ranging from humanitarian tasks to full combat operations. The EU supports the UN 1994 Oslo I and 2003 Oslo II Guidelines on the use of military and civil defence assets in disaster relief and humanitarian operations. These stipulate that the use of military means in humanitarian aid operations ought to be a last resort, and that civilian organisations should take the lead in the provision of relief. Even if EU troops have not yet engaged in the direct delivery of humanitarian assistance, the people and governments of recipient countries might not be able to distinguish between the actions and mandates of the various bodies. The fact that military options are now at the EU's disposal when considering crisis management interventions might have negative implications for the perceived impartiality of ECHO-funded humanitarian aid workers, and hence for the EU's 'soft power' as a humanitarian actor. Brusset and Tiberghien (2002, 55) pointedly remark:

> The logistical support of humanitarian interventions by military forces is sometimes necessary, and can be particularly helpful in remote places, or when speed and security are paramount. But there is a risk that a European flag flying over military units involved in such operations could cause confusion. How can a recipient country trust that an RRF operation will keep to humanitarian action if the same institutional framework can be used for peace enforcement?

An EU Civilian-Military Planning Cell was set up in 2005 in order to achieve greater coherence between the civilian and military instruments at the EU's disposal in responding to crises, to identify practical arrangements for the use of military assets in support of Community civilian programmes, and to ensure that humanitarian space is preserved in crisis response operations.

The move away from 'developmentalisation' of humanitarian relief can be linked to the results of the Article 20 Evaluation. Article 20 of the 1996 Council Regulation stipulated that three years after its entry into force, the Commission had to submit to the EP and the Council an overall assessment of the humanitarian operations financed by the EU. The evaluation was crucial for ECHO's survival, which was initially established for a trial period of seven years ending in 1999. The ensuing large-scale evaluation of EU humanitarian work raised concerns about the lack of sustainability of ECHO interventions in the grey zone, and proposed three possible alternatives: limiting ECHO's actions to emergencies only and the return to a stricter definition of humanitarian aid; explicitly extending ECHO's mandate to include operations in the grey zone; creating within the Commission, but outside ECHO, a new service for longer-term operations in grey zone situations (Franklin Advisory Services 1999).

Although the evaluators favoured the second option, Member States were reluctant to extend ECHO's mandate. They were also worried that drastic changes, such as the establishment of a new service charged with transitional aid, might further upset the Prodi Commission, already submerged in substantial reforms after the painful resignation of its predecessor presided over by Jacques Santer. They supported a realignment of ECHO as regards its core functions. The Commissioners themselves also believed that ECHO had strayed too far from its core purpose. As a consequence it was decided to rein in its scope of action (Brusset and Tiberghien 2002, 59; Mowjee and Macrae 2002, 6; ICG 2001, 10).

Recognising the potentially distorting effects of prolonged humanitarian aid – such as the creation of dependency, the undermining of local economic structures, and the fuelling of tension – the Commission (2001a, 9) confirmed that 'humanitarian aid cannot address the structural causes of the problems, and is not an appropriate substitute for sustainable social and economic policies'. Therefore, ECHO should focus on its core mandate, namely life-saving operations in emergencies, and aim for the earliest possible exit. To avoid a gap between the initial emergency phase and the subsequent reconstruction and development phase, the Commission introduced the concept of the 'linkage between relief, rehabilitation and development' (LRRD).[9] In practice, LRRD is often difficult to ensure.

First, this is due to the general difficulty of developing coherent and effective aid strategies for complex or chronic emergencies. The Commission (2001a, 6) has recognised that LRRD is not simply about ECHO handing over to other instruments in a linear 'continuum' or 'conveyor belt' approach, but that relief, rehabilitation, and development must be seen as overlapping activities requiring simultaneous funding from a range of Commission instruments. The Commission increasingly adopts a two-pronged approach to crises. For example, in response to the 2006 humanitarian emergency in the Horn of Africa, ECHO money was allocated for meeting primary humanitarian needs, while simultaneously funds were allocated through the EDF and the food security budget line for supporting long-term solutions for drought-related problems. Sudan provides another example of a country demanding a diversified aid strategy. In January 2005 a peace agreement brought an end to more than 20 years of civil war between the North and the South of Sudan. Following an almost 15-year period of suspension of development cooperation with Sudan during which humanitarian aid was the only channel to help the Sudanese people, the EU agreed on a Country Strategy Paper (CSP) mobilising around €400 million in development funds for the period 2005–07. While the negotiations on peace between the Muslim Arab North and the Christian South gradually advanced, another major conflict erupted in the province of Darfur in February 2003. This led to a large-scale humanitarian crisis, with fighting, internal displacement of civilians, and severe food shortages causing enormous human suffering and loss of life. As such, Sudan constitutes a prime example of a country in which certain zones need emergency humanitarian assistance to cover basic survival needs, while in others the conditions are in place to engage in more structural forms of cooperation. Parallel to the development programme for Sudan, the Commission disburses humanitarian assistance for the victims of the Darfur crisis, including the refugees in Chad.

In addition, there is a growing recognition that even when the acute crisis phase is over, in many 'failed' states traditional development assistance is difficult because there is no legitimate government in place to cooperate with. EU development instruments (such as the EDF, TACIS, and MEDA) are based on the principle of partnership and cannot be used without the involvement of the recipient government. Combined with recent efforts to avoid prolonged humanitarian assistance, this could lead to a situation in which populations trapped in chronic crises are excluded from all external help, both relief and development aid. There is a mounting awareness within the Commission that disengagement from states that fall outside the selectivity criteria for mainstream development is not a viable

---

9   An earlier Commission (1996) Communication on LRRD moved more in the direction of a developmentalisation of humanitarian relief. The implications which this can have for the perceived neutrality of humanitarian aid efforts were overlooked in this earlier text.

option. This trend has been driven partly by security concerns and partly by pressure to reach the UN Millennium Development Goals. The Commission's Humanitarian Plus Programme (now applied in Sudan) is one example of efforts to conceive aid instruments particularly designed for failed states suffering from long-term crises. It is different from traditional humanitarian aid in that it seeks to be more than a 'band aid' and supports sustainable projects intended to contribute to peace and to prepare for development. While financed by the EDF, Humanitarian Plus differs from traditional development aid because programmes are implemented through non-governmental channels rather than based on cooperation with the government in the recipient country.

Secondly, institutional hurdles within the Commission's aid architecture hamper the accomplishment of LRRD. Responsibility for external aid is split between DG Development, DG External Relations, EuropeAid, and ECHO (see Chapter 3). Despite a great deal of debate within the Commission on the link between relief and development, the division separating humanitarian work and development projects remains very clear, and has even become more pronounced since ECHO's decision to direct its energies into its humanitarian assistance mandate rather than incorporating development aspects into its activities. While helpful in maintaining the independent character of humanitarian aid, this compartmentalisation seems disadvantageous in ensuring a smooth transition from relief to development and coherent aid strategies for chronic crises. Funding for transitional projects, which fall between emergency relief and development, is especially limited. It has been reported that the amount of money available for this purpose is insufficient to address two large post-conflict situations at once (ActionAid 2003, 18). The inclusion of humanitarian issues in CSPs and the establishment of an Inter Service Quality Support Group are cautious attempts to work out more coordinated strategies and ensure the overall consistency of Commission action (cf. Chapter 3).

On the one hand, as alternative conflict-management tools (under the CFSP and within the Commission) become operational, the chances that humanitarian assistance is subsumed under EU political objectives decrease, and ECHO is increasingly able to turn to a narrower humanitarian brief. On the other hand, the diversification of crisis response instruments might simultaneously make it more difficult for ECHO to be recognised as neutral and distinct from the political or military dimension of EU external action. The Humanitarian Office is inevitably associated with the Union at large, whose image on the world stage is changing as, to a growing extent, it is both willing and capable of intervening with means other than strictly humanitarian ones.

The greater involvement of DG Development and DG Relex in chronic crises, the use of budget lines such as 'Rehabilitation and reconstruction', 'Food aid' and 'Aid to uprooted people' to finance the transition from emergency to development assistance, and initiatives like the Humanitarian Plus Programme, should allow ECHO to focus on primary emergency tasks and aim for an early exit, while parallel EU aid is available for post-conflict measures and for protracted conflicts. However, while the more restrictive interpretation of ECHO's mandate as emergency aid stricto sensu has indeed led to ECHO's withdrawal from a number of countries, the capacity and willingness of the development side of the Commission to engage in protracted crises remains hesitant (ActionAid 2003, 19). LRRD is a priority embedded in ECHO's yearly strategies and Global Plans. But reportedly, LRRD figures at the bottom of EuropeAid's list of priorities (Mowjee 2004, 12). Also, ECHO's concentration on life-saving assistance might result in artificial compartmentalisation which to date seems insufficiently compensated for by intense coordination among the Commission services responsible for external aid and between the Commission and the second pillar.

Linking Means and Ends: Commitment to the Humanitarian Imperative

This final section links the identified means and ends of EU humanitarian aid in an attempt to assess whether it is fair to speak of a genuine European commitment to the humanitarian imperative. Put differently, are the available power resources used to achieve the goal of apolitical humanitarian aid provision?

Humanitarian Aid Budgets for Alleviating the Most Urgent Humanitarian Needs

> When the cameras are there, we want to wave our flags, but that doesn't stop us being there in regions where there isn't even a radio set. (Emma Bonino quoted in Brusselmans 1995)

Financing patterns indicate that ECHO has strengthened its efforts to provide genuine needs-based aid. Between 1993 and 1999, the former Yugoslavia received over half of ECHO's budget, reflecting a political desire to respond to European security concerns rather than providing humanitarian aid strictly on the basis of need. However, the latest tendency is to focus more on Africa, the continent facing the most severe and enduring humanitarian needs. In 2006, 48 per cent of ECHO's funds went to Africa, up from 27.7 per cent in 1998.[10] In addition, ECHO has devoted particular attention to forgotten crises, high-need areas that have been given little coverage by the media and receive insufficient donor interest. ECHO's support for such crises has been growing steadily, reaching almost 20 per cent of its budget in 2003, and more than 30 per cent in 2005 (Development Initiatives 2006, 184). Examples are, to name but a few, forgotten needs in Nepal and Yemen, hardly countries high on the international political agenda.

Inevitably, deciding where humanitarian needs are highest in itself rests upon a political decision, possibly leading to arbitrariness in humanitarian allocations. Thus, ECHO has developed methodologies for objectively assessing humanitarian needs – the Global Humanitarian Needs Assessment and the Forgotten Crisis Assessment. By scoring crises against a standard set of indicators (such as prevalence of malnutrition, number of natural disasters or conflicts, GNP, mortality rates), complemented by ECHO field assessments, these tools are

---

10   Figures based on ECHO Annual Reviews, published at http://ec.europa.eu/echo/information/publications/annual_reviews_en.htm.

intended to enable the comparative ranking of countries in terms of humanitarian needs, focusing on those with the most urgent needs.

How then can ECHO's neglected emergencies policy be reconciled with its mandate to reinforce the EU's international visibility? Its insistence on making its achievements in the humanitarian aid domain known to EU citizens, host populations and opinion leaders seems to suggest that less disinterested issues are at stake other than purely European solidarity. However, the fact that the provision of humanitarian aid is to play a role in establishing the EU on the international scene need not necessarily mean that the commitment to needs-based humanitarian aid is merely rhetoric.

The forgotten crises policy might even reinforce ECHO's visibility and uniqueness on an overcrowded humanitarian aid scene, as it becomes the Humanitarian Office's 'trademark'. ECHO's added value can be highlighted by focusing on those sectors and/or countries which receive little attention in other donors' humanitarian aid packages. In a sense, ECHO is carving out a niche for itself by clearly limiting its field of action to the delivery of non-political humanitarian aid in emergencies, by defending traditional humanitarian principles, and by focusing on forgotten emergencies where the Commission is almost the only donor.

Institutional Independence as a Guarantee for Apolitical Humanitarian Aid

The European Commission has argued that granting responsibility for humanitarian aid resources to an autonomous office insulated from pillar 2 influence allows relief to preserve its principled character, ensuring that the basic needs of victims of humanitarian emergencies are met equitably, even if this does not correspond to the priorities of political authorities in EU members. The share of European humanitarian resources channelled through ECHO is protected from Member States' narrower interests, which might lead them to devote all humanitarian funds to high-profile crises allowing for donor visibility, or to allocate humanitarian resources on the basis of security considerations or historical ties.

However, ECHO's institutional independence and the protection of humanitarian principles through legislation do not provide an infallible guarantee for the impartial character of humanitarian aid. In the 1990s, ECHO sponsored a broad range of activities, many of which would not usually be regarded as core humanitarian tasks. It seems to be the engagement with explicitly political crisis response instruments which has prevented relief from becoming a crisis management tool.

ECHO's political neutrality also seems related to the general desire on the part of Member States, especially the larger ones, to limit the Commission's role in foreign affairs, which is, after all, still a fortress of sovereignty. Member States in the Council can blow the whistle on ECHO if they feel it attempts to pursue 'real' foreign policy via its humanitarian aid competence. However, somewhat paradoxically, they themselves have on occasion pushed for the use of humanitarian aid for more politically motivated purposes.

In this sense, the temptation to use humanitarian aid as a crisis management tool is never entirely mitigated. While the emergence of new crisis management tools might make it less tempting to use humanitarian aid with the aim of conflict resolution, it must be noted that EU military and civilian crisis management tools are only starting to be developed and are still considered insufficient (Rummel 2004). In addition, decisions on humanitarian interventions under ECHO are less demanding and faster than CFSP decision-making with its unanimity requirement. A situation might occur in which the only thing on which agreement can be reached between the EU members is humanitarian aid, which may then be used as a substitute for a lack of diplomatic and political action. For example, at the outbreak of war in Iraq in March 2003, €100 million in humanitarian funding was pledged, but Member States could not reach a common position on the desirability of any other type of intervention.

Parts of the EU, including the High Representative of the CFSP, see humanitarian assistance as one of the main tools available to the EU in conflict prevention. Other senior officials, including the former Commissioner Nielson and Commissioner Michel, stress that ECHO ought not be associated directly with conflict prevention lest it be overburdened by complex political objectives. Even if some EU policy-makers see humanitarian aid as a crisis management instrument, ECHO has resisted becoming involved in conflict resolution, which it does not regard as part of its core mandate, and has often successfully argued that other Commission services and instruments should be used to support conflict-prevention activities (Mowjee 2004, 22).[11]

Mixed Responsibility for Humanitarian Aid

While Member States decided to keep ECHO within reach as one 'pure', non-political means of intervention, by opting for a shared competence base they simultaneously retained the possibility of attuning their national humanitarian aid policies to foreign policy objectives. This brings us back to the heart of the Civilian Power Europe discussion (see Chapter 1), namely that the absence of a traditional foreign policy gives the Union a comparative advantage in the pursuit of normative goals like the impartial provision of humanitarian aid. The independence of ECHO contrasts with Member States' national humanitarian

---

11   For example: in 2001, fighting broke out between ethnic Albanian insurgents and government forces, as a result of which housing in ethnic Albanian villages was damaged. Solana, wanting to persuade Albanian insurgents that the international community cared for them and that they need not resort to violence, considered that one token measure could be rapid reconstruction of the damaged housing. In the internal EU discussions which followed, Commissioner Nielson reportedly declined to use ECHO funds for this project, which – as it involved provision of permanent housing – was considered to be more a task for providers of development assistance, and too overtly political. Instead, ECHO opted to concentrate on the classic humanitarian mission of caring for the refugees who had fled from the fighting into Kosovo, while Relex Commissioner Patten agreed to undertake the project with the RRM (ICG 2001, 15).

aid agencies which tend to be less shielded from political interference as they are more often than not part and parcel of foreign policy departments.

For example: the Danish humanitarian aid agency is evolving in the direction of a more pronounced integration of humanitarian assistance in 'an overall coordinated framework containing political, conflict-resolving, developmental and humanitarian elements' (Danida 2002, 8). The Swedish agency Sida is moving towards a 'developmentalisation' of its humanitarian aid (Swedish Ministry of Foreign Affairs 2004, 5). The Netherlands provides another illustration of a more integrated approach in which humanitarian, development, and security concerns have been merged, for instance via the use of a joint budget (Randel and German 2003, 64).

Influence of ECHO's Partners on the Apolitical Character of Humanitarian Aid

Whether ECHO-funded humanitarian projects are apolitical or not depends to a certain extent on the humanitarian aid philosophy of the partner organisation carrying out the project on the ground. The International Committee of the Red Cross (ICRC), which receives 10 to 15 per cent of ECHO's funds, has been at the basis of formulating the principles of humanity, impartiality, neutrality, and independence which underscore ECHO's humanitarian aid philosophy. In the ICRC's view, the humanitarian and political spheres are to be separated, and humanitarian organisations ought to remain neutral on political issues (Forsythe 2005, 157–201). UN humanitarian aid is bound by the traditional humanitarian principles which are also defended by ECHO, and UN humanitarian agencies – which receive 30 to 35 per cent of ECHO's resources – try hard to preserve the distinctiveness of their humanitarian activities. Yet, the channelling of ECHO funds through the UN may indirectly weaken the humanitarian neutrality ECHO wants to stand for, since the UN not only fulfils a role as neutral provider of humanitarian assistance, but is first and foremost a political organisation charged with maintaining international peace and stability.[12]

Within the NGO humanitarian community, which receives 55 to 60 per cent of ECHO's funds, council is divided on the relevance of impartial humanitarian aid as promoted by ECHO. Broadly, one can distinguish between those for whom saving lives and preventing suffering always takes priority (e.g. Médecins Sans Frontières), and NGOs (like Oxfam and CARE) whose agendas mix humanitarian, human rights and development work (Stoddard 2003; Minear 2002, 78–81). It is remarkable that ECHO does not only sponsor principle-centred agencies explicitly concentrating on core humanitarian tasks, but also NGOs belonging to the other school of thought. Does this indicate that ECHO lacks clearly defined humanitarian policy preferences and is merely a cash provider for the humanitarian system?

---

12   For example, in Iraq the UN was identified with the occupying power, and had already been the target of much popular resentment for its role in enforcing the 12-year economic sanctions regime. The bombing of the UN offices in Baghdad in August 2003 drove home the precariousness of the UN's position in the country.

Petiteville (2001, 7–10) questions the notion of a genuine EU humanitarian aid policy but speaks rather of a policy of support for humanitarian NGOs. Even those which are strongly dependent on ECHO sponsoring do not feel that they have lost their autonomy in the choice of intervention zones, or in the planning and implementation of humanitarian operations. The Commission (1999, 12) itself has admitted that its direct influence over both the operations it finances and the partners who implement these projects is not always as large as might be desired.

However, being the party holding the purse strings, ECHO might have more impact than Petiteville believes. The way in which ECHO selects the projects it funds might allow it to push NGOs in the direction of its preferred interpretation of humanitarian action. In contrast to private donors, ECHO does not write out blank cheques. Instead, it earmarks funds for particular crises and 'pet' projects which it considers to be important. ECHO makes a selection of the regions to which its humanitarian funds will be allocated, and only funds those NGO proposals covering the selected crisis zones. It only selects those projects which are directed towards core humanitarian tasks, as conceived by ECHO, as such indirectly making its vision of 'back to basics' humanitarian assistance play out in the programmes of partner NGOs. Indeed, NGOs carrying out a broader range of activities have complained that ECHO's focus on primary emergency aid has led to a situation in which there is insufficient money for transition projects. As such, choices regarding the allocation of resources – both in terms of geographical coverage and type of assistance – constitute a source of influence for ECHO which is not to be underestimated in the humanitarian aid world.

In addition, only those NGOs which comply with ECHO's selection criteria can become a party to the Framework Partnership Agreement, and only those which have signed the agreement can submit project proposals to ECHO. The Framework Partnership Agreement provides ECHO with a means of extracting from partners a clear commitment to apolitical humanitarian aid. Article 16 explicitly states that the activities undertaken by organisations which have signed the agreement must be in accordance with the 'fundamental' humanitarian principles of humanity, impartiality, neutrality, and independence. Moreover, in the last couple of years, ECHO has developed tools to help it 'move closer' to its partners who are implementing humanitarian programming and policies. Pressure for compatibility with ECHO-defined priorities and objectives has grown, and ECHO's administrative, financial, and reporting requirements have become 'heavier' (interview MSF Brussels 18 August 2005; Interview Caritas International Belgium 09 August 2005).

However, it would be far from true to depict humanitarian NGOs as mere subcontractors carrying out ECHO priorities. First of all, even under the more stringent control regime, the emphasis is on administrative and financial aspects rather than on the content of specific humanitarian projects, and it is unclear how ECHO concretely evaluates partners in terms of their adherence to humanitarian principles. In addition, the financial dependence of European NGOs should not be exaggerated. NGOs can generally rely on high levels of private funding[13] and enjoy considerable latitude in choosing between various sources of public funding. Apart from ECHO, the various Member State governments provide funding to humanitarian NGOs. Furthermore, the relationship between ECHO and its NGO partners is one of *mutual* dependence, with the former relying on the latter for the implementation of humanitarian assistance operations in the field.

Conclusions

Humanitarian assistance has become an ever-more prominent aspect of EU external action. Yet, the EU's humanitarian aid policy remains under-researched. This chapter has attempted to fill this vacuum. First an overview has been given of the power resources at the EU's disposal to undertake humanitarian activities. The power the Union can exert as a humanitarian donor, on the one hand, is strengthened by the substantial budget and the decisional autonomy it has. On the other hand, the EU's position on the international humanitarian aid scene is constrained by the presence of other – potentially competing – donors, and by its lack of implementing capacity. In terms of goals, the humanitarian concerns of the EU were found to be motivated by an impelling moral obligation to help victims of humanitarian disasters regardless of where and who they are. The EU discourse on apolitical humanitarian assistance was compared to actual practice. Although in the course of the 1990s humanitarian aid was sometimes used as a substitute for political engagement or a gap-filler for development cooperation, the engagement to provide apolitical humanitarian assistance has been complied with more consistently since the beginning of the new millennium.

Financing patterns tend to confirm the presence of a strong European commitment to the provision of needs-based aid. To a certain extent, ECHO is also able to use the power of the purse to push implementing partners in the direction of the impartial humanitarian aid philosophy it defends. Yet, these findings have to be nuanced. While the share of European humanitarian aid resources entrusted to the European Commission is protected from overt securitisation or developmentalisation, EU Member States' own relief efforts are not necessarily strictly guided by the humanitarian imperative.

References

ActionAid (2003), 'Improving European Development Cooperation: The Link Between Relief, Rehabilitation and Development'.

---

13   For example, Médecins Sans Frontières never allows more than 50 per cent of its total funds to come from governments. In the past, MSF has refused funds from donors if it felt its independence and the respect for humanitarian principles it upholds were in danger (interview MSF Brussels 18 August 2005).

Anderson, K. (2004), 'Humanitarian Inviolability in Crisis: The Meaning of Impartiality and Neutrality for UN and NGO Agencies Following the 2003–04 Afghanistan and Iraq Conflicts', *Harvard Human Rights Journal* 17, 41–75.

Aylieff, J. (2004), 'UN-EU Cooperation in the Area of Humanitarian Aid', Speech at the KIIB-VVN-KUL Colloquium, Brussels, 18 May.

Barnettt, M. (2005), 'Humanitarianism Transformed', *Perspectives on Politics* 3:4, 723–40.

Brusselmans, I. (1995), Interview with Emma Bonino, the Commissioner responsible for humanitarian aid, *ECHO News* 6.

Brusset, E. and Tiberghien, C. (2002), 'Trends and Risks in EU Humanitarian Action', in J. Macrae (ed.), *The New Humanitarianisms: A Review of Trends in Global Humanitarian Action* (London: ODI).

Bryer, D. (2003), *Politics and Humanitarianism. Coherence in Crisis?* (Geneva: Henry Dunant Centre for Humanitarian Dialogue).

Danida (2002), *Strategic Priorities in Danish Humanitarian Assistance* (Copenhagen: Ministry of Foreign Affairs).

Development Initiatives (2005), *Global Humanitarian Assistance Update 2004–05*, <http://www.globalhumanitarianassistance.org> (homepage), accessed 1 June 2007.

De Torrenté, N. (2004), 'Humanitarian Action Under Attack: Reflections on the Iraq War', *Harvard Human Rights Journal* 17, 1–29.

Development Initiatives (2006), *Global Humanitarian Assistance 2006* (Development Initiatives: Evercreech).

ECHO (1997), *1997 Strategy Paper* (Brussels: European Commission).

European Commission (1991), Decision to set up a European Office for Humanitarian Aid, P/91/69.

—— (1996), 'Linking Relief, Rehabilitation and Development', COM(1996)153.

—— (1999), 'Assessment and Future of Community Humanitarian Activities', COM(1999)468.

—— (2001a), 'LRRD – An Assessment', COM(2001)153.

—— (2001b), 'Building an Effective Partnership with the UN in the Fields of Development and Humanitarian Affairs', COM(2001)231.

—— (2005), 'Reinforcing EU Disaster and Crisis Response in Third Countries,' COM(2005)153.

European Council (2003), 'A Secure Europe in a Better World – A European Security Strategy', 12 December.

Forsythe, D.P. (2005), *The Humanitarians. The ICRC* (Cambridge: Cambridge University Press).

Franklin Advisory Services (1999), Evaluation of Humanitarian-Aid Actions Stipulated under Article 20 of Council Regulation No. 1257/96 (Brussels: European Commission).

ICG (2001), *ECHO: Crisis Response in the Grey Lane* (Brussels: International Crisis Group).

Kent, R. (2004), 'International Humanitarian Crises: Two Decades Before and Two Decades Beyond', *International Affairs* 80:5, 851–69.

Luck, E.C. (2003), 'Reforming the UN's Humanitarian Machinery: Sisyphus Revisited?', Discussion Paper for the Ground Project of the Stanley Foundation <http://vps.stanleyfoundation.org/programs/hrp/papers/luck.pdf>, accessed 20 June 2007.

Macrae, J. (2004), 'Understanding Integration from Rwanda to Iraq', *Ethics and International Affairs* 18:2, 29–35.

—— and Leader, N. (2000), *Shifting Sands: The Search for 'Coherence' between Political and Humanitarian Responses to Complex Emergencies* (London: ODI).

——, Collinson, S., Buchanan-Smith, M., Reindorp, N., Schmidt, A., Mowjee, T. and Harmer, A. (2002), *Uncertain Power: The Changing Role of Official Donors in Humanitarian Action* (London: ODI).

Minear, L. (2002), *The Humanitarian Enterprise. Dilemmas and Discoveries* (Bloomfield: Kumarian Press).

Mowjee, T. (2004), *EU Policy Approaches in Protracted Crises* (London: ODI).

—— and Macrae, J. (2002), *Accountability and Influence in the EC Humanitarian Aid Office* (London: ODI).

Nielson, P. (2004), Speech at the Annual ECHO Experts' Seminar, Brussels, 27 September.

Olsen, G.R. (2004), 'Changing European Concerns: Security and Complex Political Emergencies Instead of Development', in K. Arts and A. Dickson (eds), *EU Development Cooperation: from Model to Symbol?* (Manchester: Manchester University Press).

Petiteville, F. (2001), 'Les ONG et l'Action Humanitaire dans la Mise en Scène Internationale de l'Union Européenne', paper presented at a colloquium on 'ONG et action humanitaire: entre militantisme transnational et action publique', La Rochelle, 12–13 April.

Pollack, M.A. (2001), 'International Relations Theory and European Integration', *Journal of Common Market Studies* 39:2, 221–44.

Prolog Consult Belgium (2004), 'Evaluation of ECHO's Cooperation with UNICEF and UNICEF Activities Funded by ECHO', January.

Prolog Consult France (2001), 'Evaluation of UNHCR Activities Funded by ECHO in Serbia, Kosovo, Zambia and Guinea', December.

Randel, J. and German, T. (2000), *Global Humanitarian Assistance 2000*; <http://www.globalhumanitarianassistance.org/2000.htm>, accessed 20 June 2007.

—— (2002), 'Trends in the Financing of Humanitarian Assistance', in J. Macrae (ed.), *The New Humanitarianisms: A Review of Trends in Global Humanitarian Action* (London: ODI).

—— (2003), *Global Humanitarian Assistance 2003*; http://www.globalhumanitarian assistance.org/GHA2003/WeblinkPDFs/0p3–4W.pdf, accessed 20 June 2007.

Reindorp, N. and Wiles, P. (2001), *Humanitarian Coordination: Lessons from Recent Field Experience* (London: ODI).

Rummel, R. (2004), 'The EU's Involvement in Conflict Prevention: Strategy and Practice', in V. Kronenberger and J. Wouters (eds), *The EU and Conflict Prevention. Policy and Legal Aspects* (Den Haag: Asser Press).

Scappucci, G. (1998), *The Humanitarian Aid of the EU: 'Alibi', 'Smokescreen' or 'Solidarity in Action'? The Response of the EU to the Humanitarian Disaster in Rwanda* (Brussels: European Interuniversity Press).

SHER (2005), 'Evaluation of the Partnership between ECHO and UNHCR and of UNHCR Activities Funded by ECHO', <http://ec.europa.eu/echo/pdf_files/evaluation/2005/UNHCR_Evaluation_Final_Report.pdf>, accessed 20 June 2007.

Smith, M. (2006), 'The EU and International Order: European and Global Aspects', paper presented at the EUSA Workshop 'EU Foreign/Security/Defence Policy', Washington DC, 3 April.

Stoddard, A. (2003), 'Humanitarian NGOs: Challenges and Trends', in J. Macrae and A. Harmer (eds), *Humanitarian Action and the 'Global War on Terror': A Review of Trends and Issues* (London: ODI).

Swedish Ministry of Foreign Affairs (2004), *The Government's Humanitarian Aid Policy* (Stockholm: Ministry of Foreign Affairs).

Versluys, H. (2007), 'Explaining Patterns of Delegation in EU Humanitarian Policy', *Perspectives*, 28, 63–84.

Chapter 5

The External Dimension of EU Asylum and Migration Policy: Expanding Fortress Europe?

Steven Sterkx

Since 1999, in the aftermath of the Tampere European Council, the external aspects of asylum and migration – situated at the intersection of justice and home affairs and the Union's external relations – have boomed significantly, resulting in the consistent inclusion of a migration dialogue in the Union's cooperation with third countries. In 2001, Lavenex (2001b, 867) had already concluded that the external dimension constitutes one of the most dynamic aspects of European Union (EU) asylum and migration policy. Today, it can be argued strongly that the external dimension has evolved into a fully-fledged policy area.

This chapter will first address the shift from a purely internal to an external policy on asylum and migration. The external aspects of EU asylum and migration policy will be clarified. Secondly, the chapter will draw on critical policy analysis in order to determine whether the policy practice (the power dimension) meets the policy objectives (the normative dimension).

From Internal to External Policy on Asylum and Migration

Arguing that asylum and migration are salient and sensitive policy issues is as obvious as claiming that the hole in the ozone layer constitutes an environmental problem. Deciding on the entry and residence of foreigners has always been a core competence belonging to the full sovereignty of a nation state.[1] Nevertheless, in the context of European integration, asylum and migration matters have gone through a gradual process of communitarisation. Since the beginning of the 1990s, EU Member States have gradually shifted their competencies to the European level.[2]

---

1   EU-wide opinion polls continuously acknowledge the salience of migratory issues. Eurobarometer surveys show that immigration is of concern to citizens of EU Member States (especially the old ones).

2   The following authors give a useful overview of the development of EU asylum and migration policy, in the context of cooperation on JHA: Anderson and Bort 1998; Monar 1998; Geddes 2000; Kostakopoulou 2001; Lavenex 2001a; Marinho 2001; Mitsilegas, Monar et al. 2003; Uçarer 2003.

The entry into force of the Maastricht Treaty (1993) marked the beginning of EU cooperation on asylum and migration issues. Under the heading of 'Cooperation on Justice and Home Affairs' (JHA) – the so-called third pillar – the EU Member States agreed to work together on nine areas of common interest, among which were policies on asylum, external border controls, immigration and third-country nationals (TCNs).[3, 4] Whereas cooperation under the provisions of the Maastricht Treaty took place on a purely intergovernmental basis, the Treaty of Amsterdam (ToA) (1999) introduced the community method in the area of asylum and migration policy. Subject to a five-year window during which intergovernmental decision-making procedures would still be applied, asylum and migration issues were transferred to the first pillar, namely the Community pillar.[5, 6]

It is important to define the context in which EU Member States considered it necessary to cooperate on asylum and migration. Policies on TCNs are being framed as flanking measures, that is as a compensation for the abolishment of internal border controls and, as such, the free movement of persons within the EU (Huysmans 2001, 194; cf. Huysmans 2004; cf. van Munster and Sterkx 2006). The ToA specifies that the Union should evolve towards 'an area of freedom, security and justice, in which the free movement of persons is assured in conjunction with appropriate measures with respect to external border controls, asylum, immigration and the prevention and combating of crime'.[7]

In this framework, asylum and migration policies can be regarded as purely internal or domestic matters, since they concern common legislation on the entry of TCNs – in this case asylum seekers and immigrants – into the Union and their residence in the territory of Member States. The main problem Member States are facing in this regard is as follows: what to do with asylum seekers and immigrants as soon as they enter EU territory.

So, what constitutes the external dimension of EU asylum and migration policy? The Conclusions of the Tampere European Council (1999, para. 11) formulate the answer to this question, introducing the so-called 'comprehensive approach to migration': 'The European Union needs a comprehensive approach to migration addressing political, human rights and development issues in countries and regions of origin and transit.' The Tampere milestones consolidate the idea that asylum and migration policies require a more comprehensive approach,

---

3   Title VI of the EU Treaty, article K1.

4   The concept of TCNs is commonly used as the reference for all different categories of non-EU-citizens, such as asylum seekers, refugees, displaced persons, legal immigrants and irregular immigrants.

5   In principle, the transition period should have been finished on 1 May 2004, but the European Council (2004, 17) decided to postpone the official application of the co-decision procedure until 1 April 2005.

6   Title IV of the EC Treaty (as amended in the ToA), Articles 61–69.

7   Article 2 of the EU Treaty (as amended in the ToA), Title I. Next to the free movement of persons, the establishment of the Internal Market also involves the free movement of goods, capital and services.

involving stronger external action (cf. Sterkx 2004). In Tampere, the heads of state and government acknowledged that cooperation with third countries represents an indispensable element in the Union's efforts to address the phenomenon of migration in a comprehensive manner.

Hence, internal policy is complemented with an external dimension: asylum and migration claim their place in the external relations of the Union, and in particular in the relations with countries of origin and transit. A comprehensive approach to migration gives rise to a broad – and no longer purely internal – perspective on asylum and migration problems. Analogous to the structure of the book, this chapter will look into the congruence between policy practice and policy objectives, or between means and ends. The various means the Union has at its disposal determine policy practice. These means include the instruments for cooperation, the Union's leverage vis-à-vis third countries, the budgets to implement policy, and the competencies and decision-making capacity of EU institutions. The Union's objectives with regard to asylum and migration can be found in its policy discourse. As stated above, the main objective of the EU is to establish a comprehensive approach to migration.

When both practice and objectives have been spelled out, critical analysis is needed to determine whether these policy means and policy goals are pointing in the same direction.[8] This comes down to investigating the implementation of policy discourse, that is, to what extent the comprehensive approach to migration has been put into practice. The outcome of this critical policy analysis will serve as a basis for a reflection on the civilian character of the Union's role and image vis-à-vis the outside world. Can the EU be regarded as a civilian power, or is a different conception of the Union's role more appropriate?[9]

External Cooperation in the Field of Migration

Towards Intensified Cooperation

The first real[10] instruments for asylum and migration cooperation with third countries were the High-Level Working Group action plans. In 1998, the Dutch

8   Diez provides the clarification that critical research attempts to demonstrate the contingency of dominant discourses. 'Critical', according to Diez (2001, 23), 'means to problematise such "secure" but totalising foundations'.

9   The critical investigation builds on the author's doctoral dissertation on the external dimension of EU asylum and migration policy, in which policy documents of the various stakeholders – EU institutions, the Office of the United Nations High Commissioner for Refugees (UNHCR) and non-governmental organisations (NGOs) – as well as interviews with relevant experts, constitute the main data for an advanced discourse analysis (Sterkx 2006).

10   Since 1996, consecutive EU presidencies have drafted programmes on external relations in the field of JHA. These Multi-Presidency programmes – cf. the so-called 'Troika-format', with the aim of ensuring coherence and continuity – provide an overview of external action and relations with third countries in the area of JHA. They set priorities

delegation to the Council proposed the creation of a horizontal task force on asylum and migration in order to establish a common, integrated, cross-pillar approach targeted at the situation in the most important countries of origin of asylum seekers and migrants.[11] The JHA Council of 3–4 December 1998 endorsed the idea and the General Affairs Council (GAC) of 6–7 December 1998 officially established this cross-pillar task force giving it the name High-Level Working Group on Asylum and Migration (HLWG).

In accordance with the tasks proposed by the Dutch delegation in its note, the HLWG drew up a list of the most important countries of origin and transit for which cross-pillar actions plans would be drafted, and prepared its terms of reference during its first two meetings of 17 December 1998 and 11 January 1999. The following countries and regions were selected: Afghanistan/Pakistan, Albania and its neighbouring region, Morocco, Somalia and Sri Lanka. In addition, the HLWG would also take up and assess the already existing action plan on the influx of migrants from Iraq.[12]

According to the terms of reference that were endorsed by the GAC of 25 January 1999,[13] the action plans should comprise the following elements: a joint analysis of the causes of influx, suggestions aimed at strengthening the common strategy for development with the country concerned, identification of humanitarian needs and proposals to this end, proposals for the intensification of political and diplomatic dialogue with the selected countries, indications on readmission[14] clauses and agreements, potential for reception and protection in the region, safe return, repatriation, as well as on the cooperation with intergovernmental, governmental, non-governmental organisations and UNHCR.[15]

---

and policy objectives, suggest a range of instruments and institutional formats for implementation and coordination, and list ongoing activities.

11   Dutch Delegation to the Council, 'Note from the Dutch delegation: Task Force on Asylum and Migration', 13344/98 JAI 37 AG 15, 23 November 1998.

12   'Influx of Migrants from Iraq and the Neighbouring Region: EU Action Plan', 5573/98 ASIM 13 EUROPOL 12 PESC 27 COMEM 4 COSEE 4, adopted by the GAC on 26 January 1998. The UK had taken the initiative for this plan.

13   COREPER, 5264/2/99 rev 2 limite JAI 1 AG 1, 22 January 1999.

14   'Readmission' is defined as the decision by a receiving state on the re-entry of an individual. 'Readmission agreements' regulate the mutual taking back of certain categories of persons: first, the party's own nationals, and secondly, nationals of a third country or stateless persons who have unlawfully entered the territory of one of the contracting parties coming (directly) from the territory of the other party. 'Readmission clauses' intend to commit the contracting parties to readmit their own nationals, TCNs and stateless persons. How this will actually proceed is left to implementing agreements.

15   The ToA conferred powers on the Community in the field of readmission. Article 63(3)(b) determines that the Council can take measures in the area of illegal immigration and residence, including the repatriation of illegal residents. As such, the Council can mandate the Commission to negotiate and conclude a readmission agreement with a third country, under the provisions of Article 300.

The HLWG submitted a final report containing action plans on the selected countries to the European Council in Tampere.[16] The heads of state and government endorsed the validity of the HLWG and extended its mandate. It was also decided that the next task for the Group would be to present an implementation report to the December 2000 European Council meeting in Nice.

The action plans were the first real attempt to establish a cross-pillar approach with respect to the situation in a number of important countries of origin or transit, but they received severe criticism from NGOs (Amnesty International 1999), the European Parliament (EP 2000a/b) and Morocco, one of the target countries. The two main critiques were the following: first, the complete lack of dialogue with the target countries and, as such, of a spirit of partnership, and secondly, the manifest emphasis on security-related measures. This second critical assessment points to an imbalance in the nature of the plans: strong emphasis is given to measures aimed at controlling and preventing migration into the EU territory, especially the conclusion of readmission agreements. The report to the Nice European Council responded to this criticism stressing the need for a long-term comprehensive approach and for genuine partnership based on reciprocity, dialogue, cooperation and co-development (HLWG 2000). It also indicated one of the main obstacles to the implementation of the action plans: the lack of resources to finance the measures proposed.

In 2002, the HLWG's mandate was modified: the Council had asked the Group to investigate the link between migration and development and had broadened its geographical scope.[17] The modification of the Group's terms of reference indicates the transition from the implementation of specific action plans to a more general intensification of the migration dialogue in cooperation with third countries *tout court*. Among others, the new tasks of the HLWG consisted of identifying countries with which to intensify cooperation, the elaboration of a migration management and readmission clause which should be incorporated in cooperation agreements between the Union and third countries, and the development of a mechanism to evaluate the willingness of third countries to cooperate. Consecutive EU presidencies instructed the HLWG to foster 'initiatives aimed at obtaining cooperation with the main countries of origin and transit in the fight against illegal migration'.[18]

The aspiration to intensify cooperation with third countries followed from the European Council meeting in Seville, the closing summit of the Spanish

---

16   HLWG, 30 September 1999; Action Plans for Afghanistan and neighbouring region (11424/99 JAI 73 AG 28), Iraq (11425/99 JAI 74 AG 29), Morocco (11426/99 JAI 75 AG 30), Somalia (11427/99 JAI 76 AG 31), and Sri Lanka (11428/99 JAI 77 AG 32). Due to the crisis in Kosovo, the action plan for Albania and neighbouring region (7886/1/00 JAI 40 AG 41) was submitted with some delay (HLWG, 6 June 2000).

17   COREPER, 9433/02 limite JAI 109 AG 20 ASIM 18, 30 May 2002.

18   See the Multi-Presidency programmes of the Italian Presidency (11091/03 JAI 202 RELEX 269, 38, 2 July 2003), the Irish Presidency (5097/04 JAI 1 RELEX 4, 7 January 2004), and the Dutch Presidency (11044/04 JAI 255 RELEX 317, 30 June 2004) of the Union.

Presidency during the first half of 2002. In the run-up to Seville, and in response to the growing phenomenon of illegal immigration, the prime ministers of Spain and the UK came up with the idea to make development aid dependent on third countries' efforts – which included the signing of a readmission agreement – to combat illegal immigration. Non-cooperative countries would be sanctioned through the suspension of development aid. During this summit, the idea of sanctions met with resistance from France, Sweden and Luxembourg while, at the same time, all Member States shared the concern to step up the fight against illegal immigration. The heads of state and government stressed the importance of the cooperation of third countries as regards the management of migration flows, border controls and readmission. Non-cooperative countries would be evaluated systematically (European Council 2002, para. 64–36).[19]

The Council of Ministers (2002) further specified the required cooperation with third countries in order to manage migration flows, and called for the full integration of the external dimension of JHA in the EU's existing and future relations with third countries. It asserts that the readmission of illegal residents would be the key element of successful relations. Based on the recommendations of the HLWG, nine countries were selected for intensified cooperation: Albania, China, the Federal Republic of Yugoslavia (the State Union of Serbia and Montenegro between 2003 and 2006), Morocco, Russia, Tunisia, Ukraine, Libya and Turkey.

Frameworks and Instruments for Cooperation

Hence, the underlying ambition of intensified cooperation is to mainstream migration in the Union's external relations. Mainstreaming entails the inclusion of a migration dialogue in the cooperation with third countries, and proceeds in particular by means of incorporating a clause on migration management and readmission in all cooperation agreements. The dialogue on migration takes place within various frameworks and is fostered by a range of cooperation instruments. This section will give a brief overview (European Commission 2005).

The first – and probably the most tangible – category of instruments are agreements between the Union and third countries: Association Agreements (AA) and Partnership and Cooperation Agreements with provisions on JHA, specifically asylum and migration; readmission agreements; and visa facilitation agreements (which provide the necessary leverage while negotiating readmission agreements, see below).

Enlargement and pre-accession processes constitute a second area of cooperation in which the Union can assert its influence: both the Enlargement Process with Croatia and Turkey and the Stabilisation and Association Process (SAP) with the Western Balkans include a dialogue and measures on asylum and migration. Likewise, cooperation processes with a regional focus contain asylum

---

19   A negative assessment would not affect the Union's commitments in the field of development cooperation, but it could hamper the establishment of closer cooperation between the Union and the third country in question.

and migration elements: the Action Plans of the European Neighbourhood Policy (ENP; see Chapter 10), the cooperation with Mediterranean countries (Euro-Med), and the inter-regional dialogue of the Asia-Europe Meetings (ASEM, cf. Karatani 2006) all involve components directed towards collaboration on migratory issues. In addition, the external assistance programmes linked to regional cooperation (such as CARDS, TACIS and MEDA) have provisions on asylum, migration and border management.

In addition to regional focus, the EU also concentrates on specific priority countries. The Strategic Partnerships with Russia and with the Ukraine serve as a good example. These partnerships include high-level ministerial meetings to set priorities and evaluate progress, and the issue of readmission seems to come high up on the agenda.

Next to dialogue and the negotiation of agreements, cooperation with third countries also takes place at the operational level. The EU is establishing a network of liaison officers in third countries – mainly at border sites – to assist, monitor and evaluate practices such as asylum procedures, border security, airport checks, document fraud and the issuing of visas. Furthermore, operational cooperation involves capacity- and institution-building in third countries (for example, training of border and security personnel, of migration officers, the setting up of asylum systems, and the transfer of technical equipment), often based on twinning projects between Member State institutions and their counterparts in third countries.

Finally, both the EU and its Member States are key players in international organisations, such as UNHCR and the Council of Europe. The ongoing dialogue in these organisations provides a useful basis for the promotion of common values and priorities. In particular, the EU is actively encouraging third countries to ratify and implement international conventions (such as the 1951 Geneva Convention on Refugees and Stateless Persons) which constitute the cornerstone for international cooperation.

This overview demonstrates that the EU has a range of instruments at its disposal to address migratory issues in its relations with third countries. What is more, such a range should enable the EU to pursue a tailored approach towards target countries and regions, each of which has unique characteristics, faces particular challenges and produces distinct problems. Nevertheless, experience so far has shown that the EU is facing two general obstacles which prevent it from realising its ambitions and putting the possible range of cooperation instruments into practice. One obstacle relates to budgetary constraints and the lack of leverage to ensure the cooperation of third countries. A second problem concerns the need for coherence and coordination of external action – between Community action and bilateral cooperation of individual Member States, and internally between different policy areas and instruments. The following sections will address these issues.

Leverage and Budgets

The amount of leverage the Union has at its disposal determines the power vis-à-vis third countries. Since many elements of the migration dialogue are not in the immediate interest of the countries of origin and transit, leverage is needed to guarantee their willingness to cooperate. The negotiation of readmission agreements illustrates the need for leverage. Readmission concerns two categories of people: first, the nationals of the state with which the Commission is negotiating, and secondly, nationals of third countries, namely people who – on their way to EU territory – have transited through the state concerned.[20] While a state is obligated, under international law, to take back its own nationals, the readmission of transit migrants is more problematic. It is very much in the interest of EU Member States that partner countries also take back transit migrants. However, these countries are very reluctant to do so.

When negotiating provisions on the readmission of transit migrants, the Commission has to provide incentives to guarantee the cooperation of partner countries (European Commission 2002a, 24). Specific accompanying support should be granted on a country-by-country basis. For instance, readmission negotiations with Albania have been facilitated by the parallel negotiation of a Stabilisation and Association Agreement.[21] Here, Albania's aspiration for future EU membership provided the necessary leverage. Concessions in the area of visa policy are another example of leverage. In the case of Hong Kong, negotiations were successfully concluded after the Commission allowed visa-free access for Hong Kong nationals travelling into the EU (European Commission 2002b, 3). In the case of Russia, negotiations centred on visa-facilitation measures, in particular concerning the Kaliningrad issue.

When visa-free entry or visa-facilitation agreements are not an option, the Commission has to come up with other incentives, for example in areas such as development aid, quota for migration labour, and external trade. However, the room for manoeuvre in these areas is very limited: DG Development is rather reluctant to use (the already limited) development funds for migration purposes; the opening up of legal migration channels is a politically sensitive topic; and provisions on improved market access and trade preferences need to be WTO-compatible (cf. European Commission 2002c).

On the other hand, what the EU can do is to provide assistance to third countries that are facing the consequences of readmission. Measures aimed at facilitating sustainable return and reintegration of repatriated people can help third countries while, at the same time, can yield the necessary leverage for the successful conclusion of readmission agreements. Obviously, the provision of financial and technical support raises the issue of Community funding: the realisation of external cooperation in the field of migration depends on the availability of adequate budgets.

---

20   Cf. above. In principle, readmission agreements concern the *mutual* taking back of people, but in practice it is extremely difficult to conceive of a situation in which a third country would force a Member State to readmit a person.

21   The Council has authorised the Commission to negotiate readmission agreements with 11 countries. Agreements with Hong Kong (the first-ever Community readmission agreement), Macao, Sri Lanka and Albania have already entered into force. An agreement with Russia still needs to be ratified. Negotiations are ongoing with Morocco, Turkey, Pakistan and Ukraine, but have not yet started with China and Algeria.

As stated above, the HLWG report to the December 2000 Nice European Council indicated the lack of budgetary means as the main obstacle to implementing the six action plans. This problem was partly solved by the creation of a new budget line (B7-667) to support 'Cooperation with third countries in the area of migration' (European Commission 2001). However, the B7-667 covered only €10 million for preparatory actions in 2001, €12.5 million in 2002, and approximately €20 million in 2003. Furthermore, the nature of the B7-667 budget line was merely temporary, without any legal basis.

In 2004, the budgetary situation changed. The Council and the EP endorsed the establishment of a multi-annual financial framework for the period 2004–08: a Regulation establishing a programme for financial and technical aid to third countries in the area of migration and asylum (AENEAS). In total, €250 million has been made available to support third countries' efforts to improve the management of migratory flows in all their dimensions, in particular to stimulate third countries' readiness to conclude readmission agreements, and to assist them in coping with the consequences of such agreements.[22] This financial instrument – which provides the legal basis for a multi-annual cooperation programme with third countries in the area of migration – acknowledges the priority attached to the external dimension of asylum and migration, and will probably make future cooperation with third countries and the implementation of measures less problematic.

Whereas budget line B7-667 was exclusively programmed for the implementation of the six HLWG action plans, the AENEAS financial framework has a more general purpose, that is, intensification of the migration dialogue with third countries and improved migration management. In principle, expenditures under the new framework are not subject to any geographical limitation, but in practice measures are in particular directed towards countries which are engaged in cooperating on readmission and the negotiation of readmission agreements.

The HLWG is mandated with the implementation of measures under the AENEAS framework. Specific measures include setting up information campaigns on legal migration and the consequences of illegal immigration, development of legislation, exchange of information and know-how, staff training, capacity-building in the areas of border controls and security of travel documents and visas, technical and operational assistance, purchase of equipment and supplies, reintegration of returnees and resettlement programmes, and assistance in the negotiation by third countries of their own readmission agreements with other countries.

However, in 2006, the Commission decided to finish the AENEAS programme prematurely.[23] In line with the Union's new Financial Perspectives for 2007–13, the AENEAS framework will be substituted with a more thematic approach. From 2007, external actions will be financed by means of the 'Thematic programme for the cooperation with third countries in the areas of migration and asylum' (European Commission 2006; see Figure 3.1 in the chapter on development). The

---

22   Regulation EC 491/2004, 18 March 2004.
23   For the period 2004–06, a total €120 million was programmed.

overall objective of the new programme remains the same: 'In continuity with the AENEAS programme, the general objective of the thematic programme in the fields of migration and asylum is to bring specific, complementary assistance to third countries to support them in their efforts to ensure better management of migratory flows in all their dimensions' (European Commission 2006, 7).

Coherence and the Struggle for Policy Ownership

The premise of several European Council Conclusions and Commission Communications is that external actions need to be coherent in order to have any impact. If not, the position of the EU vis-à-vis third countries will be substantially weakened. However, the starting point of external action on asylum and migration is a division of competencies across several policy areas, a varied degree of communitarisation, and different perspectives on how to achieve policy coherence. The paragraphs below show that this reality causes overlap and cultivates a struggle for policy ownership which, in the end, is likely to damage the coherence and firmness of external action.

Coherence has two dimensions: a vertical one (between the European Community and its Member States) and a horizontal one (internally between different policy areas) (cf. Chapter 3). As regards the first dimension, there is a concern that Community action is being duplicated by the bilateral cooperation of Member States. The area of readmission policy illustrates the possible overlap: while the Commission is mandated by the Council to negotiate a Community readmission agreement with a specific third country, Member States are continuing their own bilateral talks. As such, the country teams within DG RELEX are put into an awkward position: the third countries do not understand this situation of parallel negotiations, and take advantage of it, which often results in the deferral of Community negotiations. The reason Member States are not bringing their own efforts to a standstill is that they each have a particular agenda that differs from the Community mandate: each country is facing a distinct influx of TCNs and is inevitably inclined to enter into readmission negotiations with only those countries from which the influx originates. Only when the Community agreement is actually ratified and enters into force does it take precedence over existing bilateral agreements.

The lack of a coherent approach between different policies (that is, the horizontal dimension of coherence) tends to be more problematic. The external aspects of EU asylum and migration policy constitute a new policy area, the ownership of which seems to be at stake: both the Directorate-General on Justice and Home Affairs (DG JAI[24]) and DG RELEX are active at the crossroads of asylum, migration and external relations, but they have competing policy perspectives on how to coordinate (cf. van Selm 2002, 6). The main goal of DG RELEX is to integrate asylum and migration in the relations with third countries, and as such to achieve coherence with the existing cooperation instruments and programming. In particular, DG

---

24   Since 2004 this has become the DG for Justice, Freedom and Security (DG JLS).

RELEX is in favour of discussing migration issues in the framework of the regional and country strategy papers, with the purpose of realising a tailor-made approach towards every single country or region of origin and transit. From a RELEX point of view, the rationale is to accomplish coherent external action. DG JAI, on the other hand, is advocating the addition of an external dimension to asylum and migration policy – and in more general terms to cooperation on JHA. From a JHA perspective, the underlying logic is to use external cooperation as a means of achieving asylum and migration goals, in particular the improved management of migration flows and the fight against illegal immigration.

These diverging perspectives come down to the realisation of different interests: the coherence of external cooperation, on the one hand, and the success of internal asylum and migration policy on the other. Member States, each with their own national agenda on asylum and migration, follow – or actually nurture – the JHA perspective.[25] The competing perspectives and interests become very visible when budgetary allocation and control are at stake: in their pursuit of migration goals, both the Member States and DG JAI would like to make use of budgets for development and external cooperation, whereas DG RELEX (as well as DG Development) is strongly supporting the protection of existing programmes and development funds. Migration problems are a key priority for Member States which try to acquire European budgets in order to undertake measures in third countries,[26] that is, already at the source. DG RELEX is very reluctant vis-à-vis Member States' claims to Community funds because it is worried about the lack of coherence with existing cooperation programmes.

In the past, DG JAI has already successfully taken control of one specific Community budget for external cooperation (namely B7-667). As explained above, this budget line was established with the aim of implementing the HLWG action plans. DG RELEX was not particularly impressed with this: the general B7 budget is intended for 'cooperation with third countries' and is controlled by DG RELEX. Although the action plans set out measures in the field of asylum and migration, the funds for their implementation were deducted from the general budget for external cooperation. DG RELEX functionaries have expressed concerns that DG JAI would finance projects that are not coherent with the general objectives for cooperation with third countries.[27] Despite the reluctance of DG RELEX and DG Development, migration goals – primarily aimed at the management and restriction of migration – are increasingly being incorporated into existing cooperation and development programmes.

---

25   DG JAI is a fairly new DG which, in comparison with DG RELEX, is accustomed to intergovernmental decision-making and Member States' position of power.

26   For examples, see the B7-667 below, on contamination of the cooperation and development agenda, and the repatriation of Afghan asylum seekers and refugees.

27   Cf. Sterkx 2006, interviews at DG RELEX – recording and transcription available. In addition, Member States can propose projects and apply for Community funding (e.g. in the framework of AENEAS). DG RELEX officials fear that these projects will be mainly focused on restrictive goals, such as the (forced) return of asylum seekers and refugees (see below).

The last section will discuss the impact of this evolution on budget allocation. But first we set out the overall objectives the Union wants to achieve in its cooperation with third countries, tracing the origins of external cooperation, and discussing the notion of a comprehensive approach to migration.

A Comprehensive Approach to Migration

The Run-up to Tampere

Back in 1991, the European Commission (1991, para. 47) had already made a plea for a more comprehensive approach to the challenge of migration. It asserted that action was required at three different levels: (i) alleviation of migration pressure at the source; (ii) control of migratory flows, in particular at the Community's external borders; and (iii) integration of legal migrants present on Member State territory. Furthermore, the Commission emphasised that action at the first level could only succeed if migration became part of the Community's external relations. More attention needed to be given to the root causes of migration and the development of countries and regions of origin.

One year later, the European Council meeting in Edinburgh issued a declaration on the external aspects of migration policy. It addressed the causes of growing migration pressure and listed a number of factors that could ease the pressure: '... the preservation of peace and the termination of armed conflicts; full respect for human rights; the creation of democratic societies and adequate social conditions; a liberal trade policy, which should improve economic conditions in the countries of emigration' (European Council 1992, para. ix). Coordination of external relations, economic cooperation, and asylum and migration policy is needed in order to have any impact on these factors. The EU Treaty – enabling Member States to cooperate on JHA and foreign policy matters – should offer the appropriate framework for coordinated action.

In 1994, the Commission presented a second Communication on asylum and migration policies, reiterating its earlier suggestions for action at three different levels. Once more, it stressed the need to tackle the root causes of migration. Much in line with the Edinburgh Conclusions, it contended that the Maastricht Treaty – in particular the introduction of the pillar structure – provided the Union and its Member States with the institutional means to approach migratory problems in a comprehensive way and to coordinate foreign, trade, development, and asylum and migration policies (European Commission 1994, para. 16).

Although these three documents have not sparked any intense debate on the root causes of migration, they should still be seen as the starting points of the evolution towards a comprehensive approach to migration. This is their merit: the Commission Communications and the Edinburgh Declaration are responsible for putting external aspects on the European asylum and migration agenda.

In the more immediate run-up to Tampere, mention should be made of the so-called Austrian strategy paper. On 1 July 1998 – its first day in office – the Austrian Presidency (1998) drafted its notorious strategy paper on asylum and migration policy, which was leaked in early September of the same year.[28] The paper refers to the 1991 and 1994 Communications and the 1992 Edinburgh Declaration. It states that the debate on immigration needs to be picked up again because of the discrepancy between what was claimed at the time and what has actually been implemented. The Presidency argues that this is due to 'the fact that the strategy debate initiated by the Commission was not conducted on a broad basis, no comprehensive political approach was laid down, no operational work programme was derived therefrom and no action plans following a uniform concept were developed and implemented' (para. 6).

The Austrian strategy proposes to link up all migration-related decisions in a cross-pillar approach. Such an approach would not only cover the asylum and migration policy under the JHA pillar, but also 'essential areas of the Union's foreign policy, bilateral relations with third countries particularly in the economic field, AAs, structural dialogues, etc.' (para. 113) However, to a large extent the focus of this cross-pillar approach is directed towards the reduction of migration pressure, the fight against illegal immigration, restricted access to the Union, and the detection and removal of unwanted immigrants through improved control. Controversial measures include, among others: making economic aid dependent on the third country's efforts to reduce push factors; supplementing, amending or replacing the 1951 Geneva Convention; forced repatriation of illegal immigrants to their countries of origin; and military interventions to prevent migratory flows since they can dramatically affect the security interests of the Member States (para. 54, 59, 103 and 133).

Due to the controversy inherent in these proposals, the strategy paper was heavily criticised and rejected by the majority of Member States. Nevertheless, it would remain influential in the years to come: the direction that EU asylum and migration policy would take in the aftermath of the Tampere Summit in many ways reflects the ideas and priorities of the Austrian strategy paper.

The Tampere Agenda

The above-mentioned policy documents, the Austrian strategy paper as well as the creation of the HLWG, bear witness of the increased attention given to external aspects of asylum and migration policy. At the 1999 Tampere Summit, heads of state and government showed the political will and ambition to consolidate this growing awareness: they emphasised the need for external action introducing a comprehensive approach to migration.[29] The following paragraphs will clarify that this approach has an innovative and functional nature, entails a mix of different policy elements, and is labelled with a variety of names.

---

28   After the Austrian paper had been leaked, the Presidency drew up a second draft in which the wording of some controversial statements was watered down. The reading here is based on the first draft.

29   The follow-up of Tampere is ensured by the 2004 Programme of The Hague (also known as 'Tampere II') which basically reaffirms the Tampere milestones and the need for a comprehensive approach.

First of all, the innovative nature of the comprehensive approach essentially comes down to the combination of internal asylum and migration policy and its external dimension. The introduction of a comprehensive approach results from the insight that internal policy on the entry and residence of TCNs needs to be complemented with a strategy for the elimination of the root causes of migration and flight. The understanding that the mere development of internal rules and procedures dealing with the intake of TCNs would never result in a successful European asylum and migration policy, cleared the way for an increased emphasis on the external aspects of asylum and migration issues. For this reason, the Tampere Conclusions call for stronger external action and for coordination of internal and external policy.

In this regard, it is important to highlight the functional character of the external dimension – as part of the comprehensive approach to migration. The Tampere guidelines emphasise that 'all competences and instruments at the disposal of the Union, and in particular, in external relations must be used in an integrated and consistent way to build the area of freedom, security and justice' (European Council 1999, para. 59). Hence, the existence and success of internal asylum and migration policy – and of internal JHA policy *tout court* – are the parameters that justify the need for external action. The bigger picture is the establishment of the so-called Area of Freedom, Security and Justice (AFSJ).

Secondly, the implementation of a comprehensive approach requires versatile action. Intrinsically, a comprehensive approach involves the following elements: eradication of root causes, partnership and dialogue with countries of origin and transit, enhancement of stability, peace and development in the region of origin, enforcement of human rights and international obligations, voluntary return, forced repatriation, the fight against illegal immigration, improvement of reception in the region, and so on. As such, a comprehensive approach comprises both proactive and repressive elements.

Thirdly, the comprehensive approach is labelled in many ways. The aggregate of these labels reveals the philosophy behind a comprehensive approach. Often, policy documents incorporate the following adjectives: holistic, integrated and balanced. When the emphasis lies specifically on the structural and procedural difficulties inherent in a comprehensive approach, the wording cross-pillar or inter-pillar is frequently used. Here, the idea is that comprehensive action requires cross-pillar coordination, between the Community pillar, Common Foreign and Security Policy (CFSP), and JHA. Likewise, when the combination of different policies is stressed, the labels 'horizontal' and 'cross-policy' are sometimes used. However, whatever wording is used, all expressions refer to the same idea: relating internal asylum and migration policy to cooperation with countries of origin and transit as well as to broader questions regarding the political, economic, development and human rights situation in those countries.

Migration Management Through External Action

In this part of the chapter, the congruence between policy practice and policy objectives will be put to the test. The section will first examine how policy goals are being implemented. The aim is to judge whether EU asylum and migration policy practices reflect the discourse of the comprehensive approach. Then, some trends will be singled which share the following priority: migration management through external action.

Implementation of the Tampere Agenda

The comprehensive approach off balance   The ambition and political will at the Tampere Summit to establish a comprehensive approach to migration were of a passing nature.[30] The declarations of intent have been contradicted by policy implementation. In the run-up to Tampere, the German and Finnish EU Presidencies stressed that a comprehensive approach should primarily be a balanced approach. Attention must be given to the root causes of migration and flight, as well as to measures stimulating legal immigration, asylum protection and the integration of TCNs. European asylum and migration policy cannot focus exclusively on the restriction of migration, but should also throw light on the positive aspects of migration into the Union, such as the development of Member State economies and cultural enrichment.

The reality of policy implementation, however, shows a different picture. In the area of migration, priority is given to readmission, return and the fight against illegal immigration. Concrete measures (for instance, conclusion of readmission agreements, insertion of a readmission clause in cooperation agreements, voluntary return as well as forced repatriation of irregular immigrants, visa restrictions, border controls at the Union's external frontiers, improvement of border controls and document checks in countries of origin and transit, training of border and migration personnel in third countries, detachment of liaison officers to third countries, imposition of carrier sanctions, information campaigns on the consequences of illegal immigration) are concerned with dissuasion at the source – in countries of origin and transit – and restriction of access to the Union.

In the field of asylum and refugee policy, the main priority is increased reception in the region of origin. Policy measures and budget allocation should focus on improving the capacity of countries in the region of origin to host and take back persons in need of international protection. However, reality shows that asylum seekers and refugees are still travelling to and reaching Member

---

30   In his doctoral dissertation (Sterkx 2006), the author sketches the circumstances in which both the Tampere Summit and policy implementation took place. He singles out four contextual features that have impacted on the shift from proactive and ambitious policy declarations to restrictive implementation: electoral progress and government participation of conservative and populist parties in several Member States, public fear of EU enlargement, the events of 11 September 2001, and the upsurge of irregular immigration (mainly via the Mediterranean).

State territory. In these cases, the concern is to have better regulated access to the Union, for example by means of setting up resettlement schemes.

Budget allocation illustrates that the comprehensive approach is off balance: for the most part, restrictive measures are being implemented. The Commission's (2002c, 51) report on programming of external assistance in the field of migration gives an overview of the budgetary priorities for the period 2000–06. Table 5.1 indicates that almost half (47.34 per cent) of the total amount is spent on 'Management of migration flows'. The heading of 'Development (sources of emigration)' shows that – in relation to the other expenditures – only a limited budget (13.01 per cent) is allocated to the elimination of root causes.

Furthermore, looking into the details of the Commission (2002c, 52–61) report, it becomes clear that the largest part of the budget is reserved for capacity-building measures, aimed at border management, the fight against illegal immigration, migration management, and JHA matters such as policing, justice, and the fight against organised crime.

Measures in the field of border management account for a considerable share of the total budget. These funds are being invested in border controls in the countries of the Western Balkans, the New Independent States (Russia, Ukraine and Moldova) and Morocco. In practice, this means that substantial parts of the CARDS, TACIS and MEDA programmes are being allocated to strengthening border controls.[31] As stated above, RELEX and DG Development officials within the Commission are critical of such practices: they are very reluctant about incorporating or streamlining migration goals in external and development cooperation, in particular when funds of existing programmes are being used for the restriction of migration. Development NGOs label these practices as contamination of the cooperation and development agenda (cf. Hayes and Bunyan 2003, 77).

Finally, mention should be made of the fact that up to 70 per cent of the resources for relief, rehabilitation and development (see also Chapter 4 on LRRD) has been set aside for the promotion and sustainability of voluntary return to the country of origin. A sizeable amount (€58.4 million) of these funds for voluntary return is programmed for the repatriation of Afghan asylum seekers and refugees, hence disregarding the advice of several organisations which doubt whether Afghanistan is a sufficiently safe country.[32]

Domestic focus of the comprehensive approach   The section above demonstrates that the implementation of the comprehensive approach is biased towards measures restricting access to the Union. The development of the external aspects

---

31 For example, €40 million of the MEDA II budget is reserved for the construction of border-control facilities in the north of Morocco. In principle, the MEDA budget provides assistance for economic and development cooperation within the framework of the Barcelona Process.

32   The EU Amnesty Office was very doubtful about the security situation in Afghanistan, while UNHCR was reluctant to acknowledge the existence of a domestic flight alternative (Sterkx 2006).

Table 5.1   Financial resources for external aid in the area of migration (2000–06)

		BUDGET in €	%
Management of migration flows	Border management	321,971,760	34.5%
	Combating illegal immigration	67,762,256	7.25%
	Management of migration flows	52,617,336	5.63%
Total migration management		*442,351,35,*	*47.34%*
General JHA programmes		*96,500,000*	*10.33%*
Link between relief, rehabilitation and development (LRRD)	Refugees and displaced persons	80,438,000,	8.61%
	Voluntary return of refugees from other third countries	193,609,459	20.72%
Total LRRD		*274,047,459*	*29.33%*
Development (sources of emigration)		*121,569,477*	*13.01%*
GRAND TOTAL		**934,468,288**	**100%**

Source: European Commission 2002c.

of asylum and migration – with due attention being given to the development of countries of origin, poverty eradication and the root causes of migration and flight – is not a goal in itself. Seen from a JHA perspective, the overarching objective is to develop the Area of Freedom, Security and Justice (AFSJ).

Hence, the comprehensive approach has a domestic focus (cf. Hurwitz 2002; Samers 2004). The external aspects of asylum and migration are not of a normative nature. Instead, measures implemented in third countries and at the external borders of the Union have a functional character: they serve the internal objective of strengthening the AFSJ.[33] Both the AENEAS multi-annual framework and external assistance in the area of migration illustrate this: these budgets primarily support capacity-building in the area of border management, the fight against illegal immigration, and the management of migration flows, and are used as leverage to ensure third countries' willingness to cooperate.

From a RELEX and DG Development perspective, the internal focus of the comprehensive approach and the functional character of cooperation with third countries possibly endanger the coherence of external action: the purpose of restricting migration interferes with the general objectives of cooperation programmes and development assistance (cf. Sterkx 2006).

---

33   In this context, Karatani (2006, 142) writes about the *internal responsibility* of the EU towards *its own members*.

Externalisation Trends

Measures aimed at strengthening the AFSJ are intended to manage every step of migration and refugee flows, that is, at the source (in countries and regions of origin), in countries of transit, and at the Union's external borders. By studying the content of these measures, it is obvious that 'management' should be read as 'containment' or 'control'. As policy documents on the external aspects of asylum and migration indicate, 'uncontrolled migration flows' are considered as a worst-case scenario. Migration into the Union needs to proceed in an 'orderly' or 'regulated' fashion.

Practices of migration management reveal certain trends (cf. Zolberg 2003; Guiraudon 2003; Lavenex and Uçarer 2003; van Munster and Sterkx 2006). A first trend has already been dealt with in previous sections: capacity-building in countries of origin and transit as a way of controlling migration in third countries. Capacity-building implies the transfer of know-how, technologies, equipment and legislation, through which third countries are actively being involved in EU efforts to manage migration. The Union is providing technical and financial assistance to third countries in order to provide the necessary leverage to implement control on the ground and to ensure third parties' readiness to cooperate, especially in the area of readmission.

A second trend is the practice of remote control which refers to the transfer of migration control to third countries. By means of screening at the source, the Union and its Member States are in the process of erecting new boundaries in third countries. The ultimate goal is to restrict access to Member State territory and their systems of asylum protection.

Thirdly, the notion of remote protection describes the promotion of extra-territorial ways of providing protection to refugees and displaced persons. Practices of remote protection reflect official EU policy to increase reception in the region of origin. In addition, mention should be made of the idea to set up 'Transit Processing Centres'. During the 2003 Greek Presidency of the Union, the UK government came up with the idea to establish reception and processing centres on transit routes to Europe. At EU level, these proposals to outsource both reception and asylum processing met with resistance from other Member States, and were no longer pursued.[34]

Together, these three trends reveal a strategy of externalisation, which constitutes a non-territorial response to the challenge of migration. It is a deliberate process of exporting both policy and responsibilities through the mobilisation of countries of origin and transit (Guiraudon 2000, 266). With the aim of stemming migration and asylum flows at the source, the EU is implementing its own measures on the territory and at the borders of countries of origin and transit while, at the same time, encouraging these countries to

---

34   The following documents contain the British proposals: 'New vision for refugees. Restricted policy', 7/3/2003, http://www.proasyl.de/texte/europe/union/2003/ UK_NewVision.pdf; 'New international approaches to asylum processing and protection', 10/3/2003, http://www.statewatch.org/news/2003/apr/blair-simitis-asile.pdf.

incorporate elements of EU policy into their own systems of migration control and asylum protection. As such, the strategy of externalisation creates external effects on third countries: capacity-building, remote control and remote protection are shifting the responsibility for migration control and refugee protection to countries of origin and transit.

Conclusion: Fortress Europe?

The EU as a Community of Values

Externalisation is a rather limited and one-sided strategy that narrows down the comprehensive approach. The main concern is the proper management of migration and asylum flows, preferably through the implementation of measures at the source. In contrast with the balanced approach proclaimed at the Tampere Summit, the Union's externalisation strategy does not seem to strive for the development of third countries, poverty alleviation and the consolidation of democracy. Furthermore, externalisation shifts responsibility to countries of origin and transit, while EU budgets for financial and technical cooperation – such as the AENEAS multi-annual framework – only tend to mitigate some of the burden imposed on these countries.

Critical policy analysis shows that the comprehensive approach is no more than empty rhetoric. The comprehensive approach to migration is a broad and soft concept that accommodates the concerns of third countries, and facilitates consensus among the different stakeholders in the policy process, each of them adhering to their own interpretation. However, in the process of implementing policy objectives, the dominant perspective of the most powerful stakeholders in the decision-making process sets the tone (cf. Sterkx 2006). Member States are in a position of power, and their influence on the implementation of the external aspects of asylum and migration policy is substantial. Their main purpose is to control migration and displacement at the source. As shown above, policy measures and budget allocation provide a clear manifestation of this objective.

The other actors in the policy process – European Commission (DG RELEX and DG Development), EP, UNHCR and NGOs – are very critical of Member States' drive for control and containment, and appeal to EU identity. They question the credibility of the Union's role and actions vis-à-vis its external environment. How can the EU uphold its image as a community of values, when within this community the rights of TCNs are being restricted, and when in the cooperation with third countries the restriction of migration takes precedence over the promotion of development, human rights and democracy? On a more fundamental level, do the values which the EU is promoting only apply to its own citizens and Member States?

The EU as a Security Community

Policy discourse seems to function as a means of strengthening the EU's image as a community of values. At the same time, the practices of asylum and migration cooperation with third countries reveal that EU Member States are not truly concerned with projecting these values on to their external environment. On the contrary, they still perceive their external environment in terms of security interests. Since the end of the Cold War, the security agenda has been subject to a vast expansion of security interests and threat perceptions (cf. Buzan et al. 1998). This agenda is no longer exclusively dictated by the traditional conception of military threats to national security, but also includes non-military threats such as migration. Policy practice reveals that EU Member States perceive migration – in the sense of uncontrolled flows of migrants and asylum seekers – as a significant security threat to the AFSJ.[35]

The AFSJ should be read as the Union's contemporary policy version of a security community. The development of the AFSJ results in both exclusion and inclusion (cf. Lavenex 2004). Exclusion is obvious: since migration is perceived as a threat, TCNs are being denied access to the Union. Inclusion takes place at the level of bilateral relations: third countries are increasingly becoming involved in the Union's asylum and migration policy. The EU is in the process of establishing as many partnerships as possible. As stated above, these partnerships are imbalanced and purely functional, their main purpose being to strengthen the internal security of the Union.

Member States' preoccupation with strengthening internal security has led critics – mainly the media and NGOs – to portray the EU as a Fortress Europe. The aim of this chapter was to draw attention to a new characteristic of this so-called fortress: access to the Union is not only being restricted on Member State territory and at the Union's external borders, but also through external action. Migration is being stopped by means of measures taken in countries of origin and transit. Fortress Europe is expanding: the territory and the borders of third countries are new sites for EU governance. They constitute the primary *locus* for the Union to intervene.

References

Amnesty International (1999), 'Comments on the Implementation of the Action Plans Adopted by the HLWG', 23 December.

Anderson, M. and Bort, E. (eds) (1998), *The Frontiers of Europe* (London: Pinter).

Austrian Presidency of the Union (1998), 'Strategy Paper on Immigration and Asylum Policy', 9809/98 limite CK 4 27 ASIM 170, 1 July.

Buzan, B., Wæver, O. and Wilde, J. de (1998), *Security. A New Framework for Analysis* (London: Lynne Rienner).

---

35 In the literature, the process of perceiving and portraying migration as a security threat is described as the securitisation of migration (cf. Huysmans 2000).

Council of the EU (2002), 'Intensified Cooperation on the Management of Migration Flows with Third Countries', 14183/02, 18 November.

Diez, T. (2001), 'Europe as a Discursive Battleground: Discourse Analysis and European Integration Studies', *Cooperation and conflict* 36:1, 5–38.

EP (2000a), 'Report on Asylum Seekers and Migrants – Action Plans for Countries of Origin and Transit', A5-0057/2000, 29 February.

—— (2000b), 'Report on the Draft Action Plan for Albania and Neighbouring Regions', A5-0287/2000, 12 October.

European Commission (1991), 'Communication on Immigration', SEC(1991)1855, 23 October.

—— (1994), 'Communication on Immigration and Asylum Policies', COM(1994)23.

—— (2001), 'Communication from Commissioner Vitorino to the Commission on Framework for Preparatory Actions, Budget line "Cooperation with Third Countries in the Area of Migration (B7-667)"', 28 September.

—— (2002a), 'Green Paper on a Community Return Policy on Illegal Residents', COM(2002)175.

—— (2002b), 'Readmission Agreements', 12625/02 limite migr 91 RELEX 186, 10 October.

—— (2002c), 'Integrating Migration Issues in the EU's Relations with Third Countries', COM(2002)703.

—— (2005), 'A Strategy on the External Dimension of the Area of Freedom, Security and Justice', COM(2005)491.

—— (2006), 'The Thematic Programme for the Cooperation with Third Countries in the Areas of Migration and Asylum', COM(2006)26.

European Council (1992), 'Conclusions of the Presidency, Declaration on Principles Governing External Aspects of Migration Policy', 12 December.

—— (1999), 'Conclusions of the Presidency, Towards a Union of Freedom, Security and Justice: the Tampere Milestones', 15–16 October.

—— (2002), 'Presidency Conclusions, III. Asylum and migration', 21–22 June.

—— (2004), 'Conclusions of the Presidency', 14292/1/04 rev. 1, 4–5 November.

Geddes, A. (2000), *Immigration and European Integration: Towards Fortress Europe?* (Manchester: Manchester University Press).

Guiraudon, V. (2000), 'European Integration and Migration Policy: Vertical Policy-Making as Venue Shopping', *Journal of Common Market Studies* 38:2, 251–71.

—— (2003), *Enlisting Third Parties in Border Control: A Comparative Study of its Causes and Consequences*, <http://www.dcaf.ch/_docs/borders_security_gov/05_paper_Guiraudon. pdf>, accessed 20 June 2007.

Hayes, B. and Bunyan, T. (2003), 'Migration, Development and the EU Security Agenda', in *Europe and the World: Essays on EU Foreign, Security and Development Policies* (London: BOND).

HLWG (2000), 'Report to the European Council in Nice', 13993/00 JAI 152 AG 76, 29 November.

Hurwitz, A. (2002), 'The Externalisation of EU Policies on Migration and Asylum: Readmission Agreements and Comprehensive Approaches', *WIDER Conference on Poverty, International Migration and Asylum*, Helsinki.

Huysmans, J. (2000), 'The EU and the Securitization of Migration', *Journal of Common Market Studies* 38:5, 751–78.

—— (2001), 'European Identity and Migration Policies', in L.-E. Cederman, *Constructing Europe's Identity: The External Dimension* (London: Lynne Rienner).

—— (2004), 'A Foucaultian View on Spill-Over: Freedom and Security in the EU', *Journal of International Relations and Development* 7:3, 294–318.

Karatani, R. (2006), 'Multinational Migration Control and the Case of ASEM', in H. Mayer and H. Vogt (eds), *A Responsible Europe? Ethical Foundations of EU External Affairs* (New York: Palgrave Macmillan).

Kostakopoulou, T. (2001), *Citizenship, Identity and Immigration in the EU* (Manchester: Manchester University Press).

Lavenex, S. (2001a), *The Europeanisation of Refugee Policies: Between Human Rights and Internal Security* (Aldershot: Ashgate).

—— (2001b), 'The Europeanisation of Refugee Policies: Normative Challenges and Institutional Legacies', *Journal of Common Market Studies* 39:5, 851–74.

—— (2004), 'EU External Governance in 'Wider Europe'', *Journal of European Public Policy* 11:4, 680–700.

—— and Uçarer, E.M. (eds) (2003), *Migration and the Externalities of European Integration* (Lanham, MD: Lexington Books).

Marinho, C. (ed.) (2001), *Asylum, Immigration and Schengen Post-Amsterdam: A First Assessment* (Maastricht: EIPA).

Mitsilegas, V., Monar, J. and Rees, W. (2003), *The EU and Internal Security: Guardian of the People?* (Basingstoke: Palgrave Macmillan).

Monar, J. (1998), 'JHA in the Treaty of Amsterdam: Reform at the Price of Fragmentation', *European Law Review* 23: 4, 320–35.

Munster, R. van and Sterkx, S. (2006), 'Governing Mobility: The Externalization of European Migration Policy and the Boundaries of the EU', in R. Holzhacker and M. Haverland (eds), *European Research Reloaded: Cooperation and Integration among Europeanized States* (Dordrecht: Springer).

Samers, M. (2004), 'An Emerging Geopolitics of "Illegal" Immigration in the EU', *European Journal of Migration and Law* 6:1, 27–45.

Selm, J. van (2002), 'The High-Level Working Group: Can Foreign Policy, Development Policy and Asylum and Immigration Policy Really be Mixed?', *WIDER Conference on Poverty, International Migration and Asylum*, Helsinki.

Sterkx, S. (2004), 'The Comprehensive Approach Off Balance: Externalization of EU Asylum and Migration Policy', *PSW Paper* 4, 1–37.

—— (2006), 'De Alomvattende Benadering van Migratie. Een Discourstheoretisch en -Analytisch Onderzoek naar de Externe dimensie van het Asiel- en Migratiebeleid van de Europese Unie', Doctoral dissertation, Faculty of Political and Social Sciences, University of Antwerp.

Uçarer, E.M. (2003), 'Justice and Home Affairs', in M. Cini (ed.), *EU Politics* (Oxford: Oxford University Press).

Zolberg, A.R. (2003), 'The Archeology of 'Remote Control'', in A. Fahrmeir, O. Faron and P. Weil (eds), *Migration Control in the North Atlantic World: The Evolution of State Practices in Europe and the US from the French Revolution to the Inter-War Period* (New York: Berghahn Books).

Chapter 6

Legal Power and Normative Sources in the Field of Social Policy: Normative Power Europe at Work?

Tonia Novitz

This chapter examines the external role of the European Union (EU) in social affairs and, in particular, labour law. Traditionally, due to its restricted competence in the social sphere, EU engagement in this aspect of external relations was extremely limited. Indeed, such matters were understood to lie within the prerogative of individual EU Member States. For example, the European Commission has long had a voice at the International Labour Conference (ILC) of the International Labour Organisation (ILO) and has sought to coordinate the policy positions of EU Member States. Yet the capacity to vote on ILO adoption of Conventions and Recommendations at the ILC lies outside EU competence, and is in the hands not only of representatives of the individual governments of EU Member States, but also employer and worker representatives from those countries. Nonetheless, EU external influence in the social policy domain has gradually been extended as a facet of its competence in trade and development policy. Through these methods, the Union can be considered to be exercising normative power internationally in the field of social policy. The first part of this chapter examines the range of 'means' at the EU's disposal, that is, its legal mechanisms for the exercise of such power.

There is further scope for examination of the normative 'ends' which are served by these means. The Commission (2006, 2) has suggested that the EU's efforts are made in order 'to promote its values and share its experience and its model of integrated economic and social development'. The Council (2006, paras 1 and 4) has endorsed this view, indicating that 'the European Social Policy Agenda' has been extended to an 'external dimension of employment, social policy and equal opportunities', recalling the 'commitment to conduct the EU's internal and external policies in a consistent way'. One might therefore think that the 'end' served by EU external activities in the social policy field is to export a distinctive normative social model, applied internally within the EU, and thereby deemed worthy of application abroad.

It has been asserted that the EU's 'claim to consistency between its internal and external actions is at the heart of its legitimate exercise of power' (Meunier and Nicolaïdes 2006, 919). One difficulty with this claim to legitimacy is that it may seem arrogant to export what works for Europe to the rest of the world. It could be argued that norms for social policy should not be determined within the EU and then disseminated by using trade access or development aid as leverage, but should rather be the subject of multilateral agreement reached within existing international institutions. Another problem is that there are apparent inconsistencies between the terms of EU conditionality in trade and aid agreements and legislative measures taken under European Community (EC) law. This chapter examines two instances in which such inconsistencies would seem to arise, namely collective labour law and gender equality, which provide interesting case studies.

Another possibility, as regards the ends served by EU external relations in the social policy field, is that the EU is oriented not so much to the export of its own social model but towards promotion of the more minimal 'core labour standards' (CLS), norms endorsed by the ILO under its 'Decent Work Agenda'. This aim might be seen as implicit in its selection of social standards for conditionality and would also be consistent with recent political statements. The 'European Consensus on Development', adopted jointly by the Council and the Member States, the European Commission, and the European Parliament in December 2005 (see Chapter 3), indicated that the EU's intentions were to 'promote decent work for all in line with the ILO agenda' (EU 2005, 21). In 2006, the Council reached specific conclusions on 'Decent Work for All', indicating that its aim would be to utilise various facets of its external relations policy to support the Agenda approved multilaterally within the ILO. This shift in orientation has been warmly welcomed by the ILO, as is indicated by a recent statement issued by Friedrich Butler, ILO Regional Director for Europe and Central Asia, who commented that: 'Europe is showing leadership on a crucial issue at a crucial time ... That leadership – and a stronger partnership between the EU and the ILO – is critical to making decent work a global reality ...' (ILO 2006a) Multilateral consensus on ILO CLS seems more likely to lend legitimacy to EU social conditionality, although it is notable that this exercise of normative power has not been endorsed by ILO Member States generally. Moreover, the further development of a special relationship between the EU and ILO may have other consequences, the desirability of which are examined further at the end of this chapter.

The 'Means' of Power by which Social Policy is Promoted Externally

It is possible to identify three primary 'means' through which the EU can pursue the export of social norms through its external relations. The first, and most straightforward, is through exclusive competence in the field of trade, in respect of which express powers are set out in the EC Treaty (see also Chapter 2). This may take the form of EC instruments, such as the EU Generalised System of Preferences (GSP), conclusion of multilateral trade agreements between the EU and other Member States, such as Cotonou, or even EU engagement in bilateral trade agreements. The second is via shared competence in the sphere of development, in respect of which EU political institutions are seeking to promote a new consensus between the actions of the Union and its Member States. Development agreements may again be multilateral or bilateral. Notably, at the time of writing, Cotonou serves as both a trade and aid agreement, although from 2008, it will only be the latter (see Abass 2004; Commission 2007). The third and most controversial is via the exercise of EU influence in international organisations responsible for setting social standards, the most obvious of which is the ILO. The legal competence of the EU to use this means is much less certain and is the subject of complex case law.

Trade Conditionality

Express powers to exercise exclusive competence may arise by virtue of Article 133 of the EC Treaty. This provision applies only to those matters which come within the ambit of the EU's 'Common Commercial Policy' (CCP). It is for this reason that the Union possesses the exclusive competence to represent EU Member States in the World Trade Organisation (WTO), and to operate a GSP. Article 133(1) EC states that 'the common commercial policy shall be based on uniform principles ...', while Article 133(3) provides that 'where agreements with one or more Member States or international organisations need to be negotiated', there is capacity for the Commission to negotiate on behalf of the EU with the Council's authorisation and guidance. In so doing, the Council is to act by qualified majority vote.

It has been established by a series of Opinions issued by the European Court of Justice (ECJ) that CCP is to be given a generous interpretation, such that the EU may still have exclusive competence even where the provisions contained in the agreements negotiated pursue objectives that are not primarily commercial. (See *Opinion 1/78* [1979] ECR 2871, paras 41–46; *Opinion 1/94* [1994] I-5267, paras 28–31; and *Opinion 2/00* [2001] ECR I-9713.) For example, the EU campaign to examine further the linkage of international labour standards and trade through an ILO-WTO Forum (see the discussion in Orbie 2007) seems to have been accepted by Member States on the basis that the exclusive competence relating to trade arose under the CCP. This campaign was abandoned in the Doha Agenda. Nevertheless, the EU continues to make facets of its trade relations conditional on compliance with certain labour standards.

Candidate countries have to seek to abide by the Community *acquis*, including that relating to social policy, so as to be granted accession (cf. Chapter 11). For Member States with which the EU has close trading relations and which could potentially have candidate country status, such as the Ukraine and Russia, current trade agreements reflect the expectation that these States 'shall endeavour to ensure that [their] legislation will be gradually made compatible with that of the Community', including that relating to 'protection of workers at the workplace' (see Article 51 of the EC – Ukraine Partnership and Cooperation Agreement (PCA), and Article 55 of the EC-Russia PCA, respectively).

However, this is not the case in respect of most other countries. Instead, the focus in a range of agreements is on compliance with internationally recognised 'core labour standards' derived from eight 'fundamental' ILO Conventions. These are ILO Convention Nos 87 and 98 on Freedom of Association and Collective Bargaining (1948 and 1949); Conventions Nos 29 and 105 on the Elimination of All Forms of Forced and Compulsory Labour (1930 and 1957); ILO Convention No. 138 on the Minimum Age for Admission to Employment (1973), and Convention No. 182 on the Worst Forms of Child Labour (1999); and ILO Conventions Nos 100 and 111 on the Elimination of Discrimination in Respect of Employment and Occupation (1957 and 1958). The 'fundamental rights' which are the subject of those ILO Conventions are summarised in Article 1(2) of the ILO Declaration of the Fundamental Social Rights of Workers 1998, as follows:

a) freedom of association and the effective recognition of the right to collective bargaining;
b) the elimination of all forms of forced or compulsory labour;
c) the effective abolition of child labour; and
d) the elimination of discrimination in respect of employment and occupation.

Notably, these are also human rights protected under the International Covenant on Civil and Political Rights and the International Covenant on Economic, Social and Cultural Rights, both adopted by the United Nations in 1966.

There remains uncertainty as to whether the content of these rights should be understood to be those set out in full in the ILO Conventions or, rather, a modified entitlement deemed more suitable for application to non-ratifying States. If the latter is ultimately the approach taken, the fear has been expressed that this may undermine the status of the ratified Conventions and is indicative in the declining influence of the ILO (Alston 2004). Indeed, the decision to focus only on these few labour standards and to designate these as 'core' as opposed to other key elements of workers' rights, such as health and safety, has also been questioned (Hepple 2007, 229).

Article 9 of the EU GSP[1] provides for special incentive arrangements in respect of, *inter alia*, compliance with ILO fundamental Conventions, while Article 16 states that preferential arrangements may be withdrawn for 'serious and systematic violations of principles laid down' in such Conventions. This is primarily a trade agreement, but these particular provisions are understood to serve largely ethical as opposed to trade-motivated objectives. It is significant, in this context, that EU reference appears to be to established ILO Conventions rather than the 'core labour standards' in abstract.

We also find reference to ILO standards in other multilateral and bilateral trade agreements. One example is Article 50 of the Cotonou Agreement on 'Trade and Labour Standards', which states that: 'The Parties reaffirm their commitment to the internationally recognised core labour standards, as defined by the relevant International Labour Organisation (ILO) Conventions ...'. Another example is the bilateral South African-EU Free Trade Agreement, Article 86(2) of which

---

1   EC Regulation 980/2005, 27 June 2005.

states that the parties 'recognise the responsibility to guarantee basic social rights …', adding that 'the pertinent standards of the ILO shall be the point of reference for the development of these rights'.

Conditionality in Development Aid Agreements

In relation to 'development agreements', there would seem to be shared competence between the EC and Member States under Title XX of the EC Treaty (cf. Chapter 3). For example, in relation to the Cotonou Agreement, which is also a development agreement, competence is expressly shared between the EU and Member States which are also parties (see Art. 1 of Cotonou; and Kingah 2006).

The 'European Consensus on Development' envisages activity by the EC in nine areas, which will include matters potentially relevant to social policy, including the heads of 'human development', 'social cohesion', and 'employment'. It will also apply a strengthened approach to mainstreaming certain cross-cutting issues such as 'human rights' and 'gender equality'. The mainstreaming programming strategy for human rights is to consider 'the full range of indivisible, interdependent and interrelated rights: civil, cultural, economic, political and social', and the Commission (2006a) is specifically contemplating analysis of compliance with ILO standards. Gender equality has been the subject of particular attention, with the release of a further Commission (2007b, 6) Communication on 'Gender Equality and Women Empowerment in Development Cooperation' which, *inter alia,* contemplates specific measures taken to assist women in the context of employment and economic activities. Budget support in development programmes will now have to 'take into account Gender Equality concerns by linking the disbursement of incentive tranches to gender sensitive indicators and by going hand in hand with a high quality policy dialogue'. However, in this context, there seems to be less obvious linkage between conditions which may be imposed and specific ILO Conventions.

EU Competence to Represent Member States within the ILO

There remains the residual issue of whether additional competence can be claimed for the EU (in respect of CLS) outside incidental inclusion in the CCP or development, but more generally in the field of social policy, on the basis that this is implicit in the internal powers of the EC. Such implied powers are said to arise because 'the system of internal Community measures may not … be separated from that of external relations' (see also Chapter 2 on trade and Chapter 7 on environment).[2] This might include the ability to participate in the setting of international labour standards within the ILO.

Undoubtedly, there is potential for tension between EC law and ILO standards, which might lead the Commission to wish to constrain the ability of EC Member

---

2   Case 22/70 *Commission* v *Council* [1971] ECR 263 (the *AETR case*), para. 19.

States to ratify ILO Conventions, and more generally to play a role in the adoption of ILO standards within the ILC.

The potential for conflict was highlighted by litigation which arose relating to the EC Equal Treatment Directive 76/207/EEC which required equal treatment of the sexes, and the extent to which this would prevail over domestic legislation in those EC Member States implementing ILO Convention No. 89 on Night Work (Women) 1948, which restricted women's ability to work at night.[3] In those circumstances, while EC law could not undermine the established Treaty obligations of Member States, a political solution was found in the denunciation of the ILO Convention.

In *Opinion 2/91* regarding ILO Convention No. 170 on Chemicals at Work [1993] ECR I-1061, the ECJ recognised the importance of future consistency between ILO Conventions and EC Directives, but found that the Commission did not have competence to determine whether Convention No. 170 should be ratified by EC Member States. While the Court accepted that the EC possessed external competence by virtue of its corresponding internal legislative competence in health and safety, such competence was not found to be exclusive. Internal competence in this aspect of social policy, which arose under what was then Article 118a EC, provided only for the adoption of minimum legislative standards, as did certain rules adopted under Article 100 EC (now Article 94 EC). To the extent that EC rules did not seek to harmonise national labour laws, there remained scope for Member States to conclude international standards that lay above this minimum, and there was shared competence with the Commission. This suggests that there are many facets of social policy in which the EU does not have external competence, especially in respect of pay, the right of association, the right to strike and the right to lock-out which are expressly excluded from internal legislative competence by virtue of Article 137(5) of the EC Treaty (see Ryan 1997).

The current position is that the EU has official 'observer' status within the ILO, but is not itself a member capable of voting on the adoption of ILO Conventions or Recommendations; nor is it possible for the EU to ratify an ILO Convention. These matters lie within the competence of each individual EU Member State, both by virtue of the ILO Constitution and EC law. Where the EU exercises exclusive internal competence on a matter of social policy, and thereby acquires implicit external relations competence, or where it is granted explicit external relations competence (for example, in the sphere of trade or development), a joint position will be adopted and can be 'exercised through the medium of the Member States acting jointly in the Community's interest' (Hoffmeister 2007, 52). As regards other aspects of social policy, where there is shared competence or no apparent internal competence, the Member States have greater discretion. They may still seek collectively to formulate a policy position within the IMEC (industrialised market-oriented economy countries) lobby group operating in the ILO, but this is entirely at their discretion.

---

3   See Case C-345/89 *Stoeckel* [1991] ECR I-4047; Case C-158/91 *Levy* [1993] ECR I-4287; and Case C-13/93 *Minne* [1994] ECR I-371; discussed in Kilpatrick (1996).

The Commission seems interested in constraining the exercise of external competence by Member States, as is evident from the 2006 Commission Communication on 'Europe in the World' in which it states that: 'As in national administrations, even when there is sufficient political will, the EU's impact falls short when there are unresolved tensions or a lack of coherence between different policies … Unsatisfactory coordination between different actors and policies means that the EU loses potential leverage internationally, both politically and economically' (European Commission 2006d, 6).

However, it seems highly unlikely that, without further amendment of the EC or EU Treaties, the Commission has competence to exercise greater control over EU Member States within the ILO. As I have suggested earlier, it does not seem that Article 308 EC cannot can be used to fill this lacuna in competence, for this would be inconsistent with the finding of the Court in *Opinion 2/94* [1996] ECR I-2827 (at para. 27) that 'no Treaty provision confers on the Community institutions any general power to enact rules on human rights or to conclude international conventions in this field' (see Novitz 2002, 17–18). Its influence seems to be more likely to arise through high level policy exchanges (see Final Joint Conclusions of the 5th High-Level Meeting between the European Commission and International Labour Officem Geneva, 13 October 2006, and Part IV below) than within the structured setting of the ILO International Labour Conference within which the EU Member States retain their at least nominal sovereign power.

The Normative Ends Served: Export of the EU Social Model or Promotion of the ILO Decent Work Agenda?

The existence of these EU activities poses the obvious question: what end do they serve? One possibility is that the Union is seeking to export what has come to be called an 'EU social model'. The other, which would be consistent both with reference to ILO Conventions and CLS in trade and aid instruments, is that the EU is seeking to promote the ILO agenda of 'Decent Work'.

This section examines two distinctive areas of social policy: collective labour law and gender equality, in an attempt to discern what normative purpose EU conditionality may serve. It is suggested that, while there might at first view appear to be significant discrepancies between social legislation implemented by EU Member States and ways in which social norms are promoted, in particular through EU external relations, they may be capable of being reconciled if the EU is seen primarily as a market-driven entity. An interesting question, however, arises as to whether EU internal and external social policy measures are fully compatible with the ILO Decent Work Agenda. It is arguable that EU external relations reflect both the narrowing ambit of the current policy orientation of the ILO since the end of the Cold War period and the ILO's determination to reconcile labour rights and market objectives (see Alston 2004). To that extent, they may be more compatible than might have been thought previously, but there is an open question as to whether this is a desirable development.

The First Case Study: Collective Labour Law

Two fundamental ILO Conventions, Nos 87 and 98, set out rights to freedom of association and collective bargaining. The interpretation of the rights guaranteed under those instruments has long been delegated to the ILO Governing Body Committee on Freedom of Association (CFA) and the Committee of Experts on the Application of Conventions and Recommendations (CEACR), both of which have concluded that the right to strike is also an essential aspect of freedom of association (ILO CEACR 1994, paras 146–7; and ILO CFA 2006, paras 522–3).

All 27 current EU Member States have ratified Conventions Nos 87 and 98, but they have not all been found to be in full compliance by ILO supervisory bodies. For example, Austria has still to amend its legislation so as to allow foreign workers access to stand for election on works councils; in Belgium there is no official criteria for access of worker and employer representatives to the National Labour Council, such that this is left to the whim of the government; the Czech Republic, Hungary, and the UK have been criticised for their apparent failure to take adequate measures to prevent anti-union discrimination; and in Denmark, the government has yet to respond to the repeated request that it indicates 'measures taken to ensure that Danish trade unions may represent all their members – residents and non-residents employed on ships sailing under the Danish flag – without any interference from the public authorities'. In addition, the adequacy of the protection of the right to strike in Bulgaria, Cyprus, Germany, and the Netherlands has been called into question (ILO CEACR 2006).

Despite these apparent instances of non-compliance, there has been no attempt to implement ILO Conventions Nos 87 and 98 through EC legislation. In fact, as noted above, there is an apparent bar in Article 137(5) of the EC Treaty on the EC institutions doing so. The reason is usually understood to be the principle of subsidiarity, namely that national industrial relations systems should be allowed to operate without unnecessary intervention by EC law (as discussed in Ryan 1997). Rather, there is the potential for these obligations to temper the interpretation of EC instruments, including the EC Treaty. This power currently lies not in the hands of the political institutions, but the ECJ.

There has been a declaratory recognition of rights to association in trade unions, collective bargaining, and industrial action in Points 11–14 of the Community Charter of the Fundamental Rights of Workers 1989, and Articles 12 and 28 of the EU Charter of Fundamental Rights 2000. Each of these instruments makes particular reference to the significance of 'national law and practice', specifically in the context of collective action, but the EU Charter also makes the exercise of rights to collective bargaining and action subject specifically to other facets of 'Community law'.

A recent phenomenon has been the introduction of 'saving' clauses into Directives, designed to protect the rights to engage in collective bargaining and take industrial action where such rights conflict with provision for free movement of goods, and provision for free movement of services and establishment. The latter followed extensive protests in opposition to the first draft of the so-called

'Bolkestein' Services Directive[4] (see Kowalsky 2006, 238). However, confusion may be caused by a potentially significant difference in the wording of the actual clauses. Whereas, it is evident from Article 2 that the 'Monti' Council Regulation EC 2679/98 of 7 December 1998, on the functioning of the internal market in relation to the free movement of goods among the Member States, 'may not be interpreted as affecting in any way the exercise of fundamental rights as recognised in Member States, including the right or freedom to strike', Article 1(7) of the 2006 Services Directive indicates that the latter instrument 'does not affect the exercise of fundamental rights as recognised in the Member States and by Community law. Nor does it affect the right to negotiate, conclude and enforce collective agreements and to take industrial action in accordance with national law and practices which respect Community law'. In other words, while the Services Directive does not prevail over rights of freedom of association, collective bargaining or industrial action, the political message is that other facets of Community law – namely relevant Treaty provisions – may do so. In this respect, the wording is consistent with relevant provisions set out in the EU Charter of Fundamental Rights 2000.

This message may be important because we are currently at a juncture where the scope of any rights to freedom of association, collective bargaining and industrial action are highly uncertain when they come into tension with other facets of the EU market order. The abdication of responsibility by the Members of the Community in the adoption of Article 137(5) leaves this matter to be determined by the ECJ under its fundamental rights jurisprudence. There has been tangential reference to the significance of freedom of association and the right to strike in the context of the staff cases heard by the ECJ, in which limited protection has been given to the activities of staff associations.[5] There has also been a determination that freedom of association can be used as an interpretative tool in the context of determining the scope of free movement of workers,[6] and a decision that some forms of collective agreement may be exempt from competition law provisions.[7]

One curious case is Case C-499/04 *Werhof* v *Freeway Traffic Systems GmbH & Co KG* [2006] IRLR 400, which concerned the extent to which a new employer should be considered to be bound by a collective agreement after the transfer of an undertaking. The ECJ decided that, while terms from the collective agreement should be regarded as being incorporated into each individual worker's contract

---

4   This is now Directive 2006/123/EC on Services in the Internal Market, OJ L 376/36.

5   See, for example, Cases C-193 and C-194/87 *Maurissen and European Public Service Union* v *Court of Auditors* [1990] ECR I-95.

6   Case C-415/93 *Union Royale Belge des Societes de Football Association and Others* v *Bosman and Others* [1995] ECR I-4921, para. 79.

7   Although this was apparently on social policy grounds, rather than that of fundamental rights, in respect of which see the Opinion of AG Jacobs which suggests that there is no right to collective bargaining under the general principles jurisprudence of the Court of Justice: Case C-67/96 *Albany International BV* v *Stichting Bedrijsfonds Textielindustrie* [1999] ECR I-5751, paras 193–4.

of employment for the time being, the employer could not be considered to be bound by a collective agreement without its consent, or to maintain relations with the relevant trade union, citing at para. 33, the principle of negative 'freedom of association' as grounds for the employer's right to disassociate with a union. This is a very individualistic approach to the right to freedom of association, hardly conducive to the promotion of collective bargaining, which the state is obliged to encourage under Article 4 of ILO Convention No. 98. Arguably, it is more consistent with an emphasis on individual contractual freedom otherwise valued within a market order. It is also consistent with the priority which the Court appears to give to civil and political, as opposed to socio-economic rights (Lenaerts 1991, 376; Betten 2001, 157).

Two cases of interest are likely to be Case C-341/05 *Laval un Partneri Ltd v. Svenska Byggnadsarbetareförbundet, Avdelning 1 of the Svenska Byggnadsarbetareförbundet, Svenska Elekrikerförbundet* OJ C291/10, and Case C-438/05 *ITF and the Finnish Seamen's Union v. Viking Line ABP and OU Viking Line Eesti* OJ C60/16-18, which were heard on 10 January 2007. Advocates-General Mengozzi and Poiares Maduro delivered their respective opinions in these cases on 23 May 2007, but at the time of writing the Court's judgment has yet to be delivered. The first issue in these two cases is whether Sweden and Finland, respectively, can be regarded as being in breach of EC Treaty provisions relating to free movement of services and establishment by virtue of their legislative regime governing industrial action. The second is whether private parties, the trade unions organising such action, should be held accountable. In this respect, the Court faces an unpalatable dilemma. Should they secure enlargement through the promotion of market freedoms for enterprises and workers in newer Member States eager to contract their services abroad? Or should the Court be wary of finding that there is any violation, given that this could undermine the industrial relations systems of two highly unionised labour markets in which there is a widespread and effective collective bargaining? It is somewhat astonishing that such a crucial decision should be left to the Court, but the lack of social competence in the EU makes this a necessity.

The failure of EU Member States to comply with their obligations under ILO Conventions Nos 87 and 98, the lack of EU internal competence relating to collective labour law, and the potential for EC law to undermine national systems of industrial relations in which ILO standards are respected, all suggest that collective labour law is not a key aspect of the 'European social model'. One might therefore expect that it would not be regarded as coming within the remit of EU external relations. However, we have recently been reminded that it is, in particular by virtue of EU GSP. The reminder has come in the form of a message sent by the Council to Belarus that it must comply within six months with ILO Conventions Nos 87 and 98 or face the withdrawal of preferences under EU GSP (See EU 2006). There is no doubt that under the EU and EC Treaties, the Union has formal competence to act in this field because this matter comes under the EU's CCP, although questions do arise as to its legitimacy.

It may also be observed that there is some inconsistency not only between internal and external Union social policy, but also as regards the treatment of different third countries under EU GSP. Seven of the 15 states which have gained special incentives under what is currently GSP+ are subject to current criticism by the ILO CEACR. The Trade Commissioner, Peter Mandelson, claimed that they are making 'substantial changes' towards compliance with ILO Conventions Nos 87 and 98, and it is notable that Colombia has at least instigated an investigation into the murder, torture and disappearance of trade unionists.[8] Nevertheless, many of these GSP+ beneficiaries remain in breach of ILO standards by reason of the constraints that they place on trade union organisation, collective bargaining and the right to strike. Most of the ILO CEACR Reports suggest that the Committee is frustrated by the repeated unheeded criticism it has issued in this regard. (See ILO CEACR 2006).

How, then, does the case of Belarus differ from the limited compliance of these States? One explanation may lie in the weight of current international opinion regarding the seriousness of the ongoing recalcitrance of Belarus. The Council's official warning to Belarus comes as a direct response to the findings of the 2004 ILO Commission of Inquiry (ILO 2004), a previous Recommendation from the European Commission (2005), and the adoption of a 'special paragraph' concerning Belarus at the ILO's 95th annual International Labour Conference in 2006, the latter being reserved for the worst violations of international labour standards. Belarus is an international pariah state for its treatment of labour standards, and the Council cannot be accused of acting precipitously or without the weight of international approval in warning of the withdrawal of trade preferences. In this respect, it would seem that EU external relations relating to social policy are more concerned with the promotion of ILO standards and giving force to ILO criticism than pursuing its own social agenda.

Nevertheless, it could also be argued that the criticism of Belarus and consequent withdrawal of trade preferences under EU GSP are not entirely incompatible with Union social policy, if we see the latter as pursuing predominantly a civil liberties, market-led agenda. It has been observed that the situation in Belarus relates significantly to the civil liberty of freedom of association and its role in political resistance to an authoritarian and repressive regime, rather than socio-economic rights to collective bargaining which are compromised within a market order. (See Tortell 2008, and her analysis of the ILO Report of the Commission of Inquiry 2004, at paras 598–634). The government in Belarus was involved in a campaign involving intimidation and harassment of trade unionists, including those who cooperated with the ILO Commission of Inquiry.[9] Such condemnation may be consistent with a liberal view of freedom of association which values 'freedom' of individual choice rather than the strength of collective voice. Indeed, this liberal aspect of ILO jurisprudence has recently been criticised in respect of

---

8   See Orbie 2008, citing the statement by the ETUC relating to violations by the current 15 beneficiaries of the special incentive arrangements, ETUC Press Release, 21 December 2005, and the statement of Trade Commissioner, Peter Mandelson, in the European Parliament H-1052/05, 15 December 2005.

9   ILO CFA, Report No. 339, Vol. LXXXVIII, 2005, Series B, No. 3, para. 89 and 341st Report, 2006, paras 51 and 53(a).

Indonesia and Argentina, on the basis that it promotes fragmented rather than effective collective bargaining (see Caraway 2006). This warning to Belarus is not so much an incursion by the EU into detailed regulation of labour relations within that country, but rather an act of condemnation of its implications for civil liberties and political rights. As such, it may be seen to complement, rather than contradict, the Union's rather *ad hoc* and, thus far, individual rights-based approach to protection of freedom of association within the EU.

The Second Case Study: Gender Equality

ILO Convention No. 100 provides for equal remuneration for men and women workers for work of equal value, while ILO Convention No. 111 prohibits discrimination under Article 1(1) on 'the basis of race, colour, sex, religion, political opinion, national extraction or social origin, which has the effect of nullifying or impairing equality of opportunity or treatment in employment or occupation'. The principle of equal remuneration has foundational importance in the EU by virtue of Article 119 of the Treaty of Rome and now Article 141 of the EC Treaty. It can be understood to be constitutive of the terms of fair competition within the Community's internal market, as well as serving a more general social purpose. In Case C-43/75 *Defrenne (No. 2)* [1976] ECR 455, it was observed that Article 119 'pursues a double aim': first, 'to avoid a situation in which undertakings established in states which have actually implemented the principle of equal pay suffer a competitive disadvantage in intra-Community competition as compared with undertakings established in states which have not yet eliminated discrimination against women workers as regards pay'; and secondly, 'the provision forms part of the social objectives of the Community, which is not merely an economic union, but is at the same time intended by common action to ensure social progress and seek the constant improvement of living and working conditions of their peoples ...'. In the same judgment, the Court explicitly referred to the relevance of ILO Conventions Nos 100 and 111 (at paras 26–27). The ILO concept of equal pay for work of equal value rather than merely equal work), as expressed in ILO Convention No. 100, was also influential in the subsequent interpretation by the ECJ of Council Directive 75/117/EEC.[10] A general principle of 'equality' has emerged as 'a creative tool', the substance of which has yet to be fully determined, but which offers promise, as the extensive jurisprudence on equality indicates (see Costello and Davies 2006, 1615).

There has been extensive legislative activity in this field.[11] Further, 2007 has also been declared the European Year of Equal Opportunities for All, by the European Commissioner for Employment, Social Affairs and Equal Opportunities, Vladimir Spidla.[12]

---

10   See Case 61/81 *Commission* v *UK* [1982] ECR 2601.

11   Such as Council Directives EC 75/117/EEC, 76/207/EEC, 92/85/EEC, 97/80/EC, 2002/73/EC, 269/15; and Consolidated Directive 2006/54.

12   Launch of the European Year of Equal Opportunities for All 2007, Berlin, 30 January 2007.

It is perhaps not so surprising then that the extent of compliance in EU Member States with ILO Convention No. 100 is much more extensive than in respect of ILO Conventions Nos 87 and 98. Of the initial EU-15 Member States, only the UK has been singled out for criticism by the ILO CEACR, due to the remuneration gap which remains in that country between the hourly rates of pay of women and men, particularly women in part-time work. Notably, however, there is no criticism of UK equal pay legislation *per se*, only the delivery of government policy. In 2006, the introduction of equal pay legislation by Poland was 'noted with satisfaction' by the same Committee, which observed, however, that Slovakia had to take further steps towards full compliance. As regards Convention No. 111, recent efforts by the French Government to take proactive action to adopt a 'Diversity Charter' and create a 'High Authority to Combat Discrimination and Promote Equality' were observed with approval by the CEACR. New legislative measures taken in Poland, Romania, Slovakia and Slovenia also received appreciative attention (see ILO CEACR 2006).

Legislative strategies for the achievement of gender equality have been further supplemented by 'gender mainstreaming' – that is, the endeavour to incorporate the promotion of equal opportunities for women and men into all EU policies and activities. This term was created by the UN, but is a longstanding feature of EU social policy (discussed by Kenner 2003, chs 7 and 11). One notable example is engagement with gender-related issues in the context of the European Employment Strategy (EES), which emerged as a key feature of European social policy as part of the EU's Lisbon Strategy for economic, social and environmental renewal. The EES may, however, more accurately be described as serving economic rather than social objectives, an example being the emphasis placed on the active participation of women in the labour market, rather than the social benefits that should come with such participation (Ashiagbor 2005, ch. 6; Ellis 2005, 22). For example, one aspect of the mainstreaming agenda, which Catherine Barnard (2006, 306) stresses in the most recent edition of her impressive text on 'EC Employment Law', is the aim to raise employment of women in the EU, which currently stands at 55.1 per cent (compared to 70.9 per cent for men) to 60 per cent by 2010. She cites this development apparently uncritically, but it might also be observed that such an objective does not allow for positive choices for women to make other decisions about the time they wish to spend raising children or for men to decrease rates of participation in order to take on more childcare responsibilities. Indeed, childcare is clearly not termed 'work' for the purposes of the EU economic agenda, unless it is paid work by someone other than a parent.

Gender equality comes within the remit of the CLS which the Union promotes through the incentive arrangements available under EU GSP, but the EU has yet to act on criticism of any third state for breach of gender equality principles. There are examples of positive change in particular states, such as Moldova, which has not only enacted a new Labour Code prohibiting discrimination on grounds of sex, but has also adopted a national plan for the promotion of gender equality in society. However, concerns remain relating to implementation of equal pay provisions in Honduras, Panama and Peru. Moreover, more significant concerns remain relating to gender equality in beneficiaries under the standard GSP regime, such as Algeria and India. (See ILO CEACR 2006). Thailand, another beneficiary of the standard EU GSP, has yet to ratify ILO Convention No. 111 and therefore its compliance with its provisions must remain doubtful.

In defence of the EU, it could be noted that the Council has withdrawn trade preferences under GSP in relation to other CLS only in the most extraordinary circumstances, where there has been extensive political as well as legal criticism of a state within an ILO context. Belarus is a prime example of the EU's hand being forced in this regard. For some reason, be it the cultural sensitivity of sex equality, or the lack of a flagrant breach, this situation has not arisen in relation to the issue of gender. Common sense would seem to suggest that there has been, and continues to be, a flagrant breach of gender equality in a vast number of EU trading partners, but that the perceived difficulties of and barriers to achieving cultural change leads to evasion of the issue in trade practice. Here, there may be interesting scope for comparison with US trade agreements which exclude gender equality from their remit entirely.[13]

Whatever the reason, the EU's approach has been predominantly concerned with 'soft' development agendas. Gender equality is an explicit objective of the current 'European Consensus on Development', where the economic benefits of equality between men and women are stressed. (EU 2005, 21–2). There is also evidence of cooperation with the ILO in this respect through joint 'pilot projects' in 2005/6 under the ILO's 'Decent Work Agenda' (European Commission 2006e). Indeed, the EU's orientation in this field does seem to be towards 'improvement of the link between GSP and EC external assistance' (Council 2006, 6). Once again, there seems to be a stronger emphasis in EU external relations on the pursuit of objectives determined by the ILO than mere replication of the internal European social model which, in this instance, places strict emphasis on legal compliance with sex equality.

Nevertheless, pursuit of an ILO approach to gender equality may not depart so very significantly from the approach of the EU. Indeed, despite endorsement of the multifaceted nature of ILO programmes by the UN Economic and Social Council in its recent Ministerial Declaration (E/2006/L.8, para. 9), it has been alleged that these are too legalistic and aimed at increasing entry of women into paid work without considering adequately or compensating for the social changes which follow as a consequence (Robinson 2006, 326 and 337).

The desire to build productive labour markets and enhance economic activity seems to have led the EU to promote gender equality internally within the Union as stringently as possible through both hard and soft law mechanisms. The EU would seem to have less incentive to enforce this core labour standard abroad and is therefore likely to be less stringent in its prescriptions for other states. By orienting conditionality towards aid rather than trade, the EU approach seems to be to encourage third states to promote gender equality because this is in their

---

13   Examples include US avoidance of the issue of gender equality in recent free trade agreements with Singapore and Chile, discussed by K. Ewing, 'Bilateral Trade Agreements and Labour Standards: Initiatives from the US', available at <http://www.ictur.labournet.org/Ewing.htm>.

own interests, rather than to demand effective implementation of ILO Conventions Nos 100 and 111. In other words, both case studies tend to indicate that the EU is promoting externally social policy norms tied more closely to ILO standards than its own, but which are certainly not inconsistent with its own market-led agenda.

Future Trends: The Compatibility of EU and ILO Objectives?

The conclusion reached in Part III of this chapter perhaps begs one last question, namely, whether there is any notable distinction to be draw between 'the EU social model' and the ILO 'Decent Work Agenda'. Are these two sets of objectives compatible? Statements to the effect that the ILO and EU are to be regarded as 'partners' suggest that this may be the case. This follows from ongoing 'exchanges of letters', high-level meetings and policy coordination. The last section of this chapter considers the extent to which there may be a unity of approach here, and its implications.

'Decent work' seems to be a potentially malleable term, susceptible to a range of different interpretations. For example, the ILO Director-General Juan Somavia commented in his introduction to his most recent report for the Seventh European Regional Meeting in Budapest, 2005, that his aim was to 'give working women and men a fair chance of a decent job'. The stress on a 'decent' job suggests that entry to employment is not in itself an unqualified good. Nevertheless, in the same preface, he comments on 'the striking similarity between the EU's Lisbon Strategy ... and the ILO's Decent Work Agenda', without apparently recognising the concerns that labour has voiced as to the commercial orientation of the former (ILO 2005, vi-vii).

This ambiguity of approach surfaced again in the Conference on Promoting Decent Work in the World, held by the EU in Brussels in December 2006. There emerged a divergence of opinion between UNICE (now BusinessEurope) and the International Organisation of Employers (IOE), which emphasised the importance of 'employment opportunities' *per se*, and the European Trade Union Confederation (ETUC) which took the view that the Lisbon Agenda Strategy for growth and employment, relaunched in 2005, unduly prioritised 'competitiveness over social cohesion'. John Monks, General Secretary of ETUC, observed that, while its 'strap line' may have been '[a] social Europe in a global economy: jobs and opportunities for all', the EU had failed to examine the 'qualitative objectives that must underpin social policy' – in other words, the decency of the work available.

One concern might be that recent EU initiatives to act in tandem with the ILO through 'partnership' belie the limited competence of the Union as regards the role that it can play within the ILO. The Commission's determination to carve out its own special relationship with the ILO at an operational level seems, at least in part, to be an attempt to tame the potentially divisive exercise of individual Member States' policy preferences. It appears to be using a trade and development agenda to bypass its otherwise limited competence in the external social policy field. In this sense, there seems to be a lack of fit between means and ends.

Secondly, and this is where there may be more reason for concern, while the EU and ILO may be working together collaboratively, gainfully using each other to gain legitimacy and influence respectively, it should be remembered that they have potentially divergent mandates and objectives. The main objectives of the EU, when traced back to its origins as a European Economic Community, are primarily market-oriented. Social policy has played a secondary supplementary role (Davies 1992; Barnard 1999). By way of contrast, since 1919, the ILO Constitution has been aimed primarily at the achievement of social justice (Murray 2001, 35–47). While the two objectives will not always be in conflict, to deny that this might ever be the case seems foolhardy. Indeed, Article II(c) of the ILO Declaration of Philadelphia provides that where the two conflict, the social should prevail. It is less clear that this is the view taken in the judgments delivered by the ECJ or even the EU political institutions.

It does seem that the ends pursued by EU external relations in the social policy field are becoming more closely aligned with ILO standards. This alignment could be applauded insofar as it suggests that the Union is moving away from unilateralism towards the promotion of globally recognised social standards. However, while the standards used as a reference point are derived from the ILO, the Member States within the ILO have not approved the means used by the EU. The use of trade as a means by which to promote labour rights is far from universally approved, as is indicated by the failure to achieve within the WTO multilateral consensus on any such linkage. Moreover, it is possible that in this new partnership it is the ILO rather than the EU which is ultimately more vulnerable and therefore susceptible to policy influence. The Union possesses significant power as a regional trading bloc which is capable of providing effective trade sanctions and incentives for compliance with the norms that it seeks to export. Since the end of the Cold War, the ILO has come under pressure to reform its practices and demonstrate its continuing relevance to its constituency (Novitz 2005). Indeed, the ILO Declaration of 1998 with its narrow focus on a few core labour standards may be indicative of this pressure (Alston 2004).

In the current climate of international relations, it may not be so much that the values of the international community are channelled via the ILO to inform the concrete policies of the EU, but rather that a powerful regional trading bloc, trading on identification with the ILO, can skew the content and relevance of internationally agreed standards. Until the Union changes its mandate, and notably neither constitutional reform nor significant Treaty amendment seem to be on the agenda now, we may need to remain cognisant of the market-orientation of EU internal social policy and its potential influence in external relations.

References

Abass, A. (2004), 'The Cotonou Trade Regime and WTO Law', *European Law Journal* 10:4, 439–62.

Alston, P. (2004), 'Core Labour Standards and the Transformation of the International Labour Rights Regime', *European Journal of International Law* 15:3, 457–522.

Ashiagbor, D. (2005), The European Employment Strategy: Labour Market Regulation and New Governance (Oxford: Oxford University Press).

Barnard, C. (1999), 'EC Social Policy', in P. Craig and G. de Burca (eds), *The Evolution of EU Law* (Oxford: Oxford University Press).

—— (2006), *EC Employment Law*, 3rd edn (Oxford: Oxford University Press).

Betten, L. (2001), 'The EU Charter on Fundamental Rights: A Trojan Horse or a Mouse?', *International Journal of Comparative Labour Law and Industrial Relations* 17:2, 151–64.

Caraway, T. (2006), 'Freedom of Association: Battering Ram or Trojan Horse?', *Review of International Political Economy* 13:2, 210–32.

Clapham, A. and Bourke Martignoni, J. (2006), '"Are We There Yet?" In Search of a Coherent EU Strategy on Labour Rights and External Trade', in V. Leary and D. Warner (eds), *Social Issues, Globalisation and International Institutions: Labour Rights and the EU, ILO, OECD and WTO* (Leiden/Boston: Martinus Nijhoff).

European Commission (2005), 'Commission Decision', 17 August, OJ L213.

—— (2006a), 'Programming Guide for Strategy Papers: Democracy and Human Rights', http://ec.europa.eu/development/How/iqsg/docs/fiches_pdf/F20_human_rights_en.pdf, accessed 20 June 2007.

—— (2006b), Programming Guide for Strategy Papers: Gender Equality', http://ec.europa.eu/development/How/iqsg/docs/fiches_pdf/F43_genderequality_fin.pdf, accessed 20 June 2007.

—— (2006d), 'Europe in the World – Some Practical Proposals for Greater Coherence, Effectiveness and Visibility', COM(2006)278.

—— (2006e), 'Trade and Social Conditions: EU-ILO Pilot Project on Decent Work Indicators', Press Release, 5 December.

—— (2007a), 'Economic Partnership Agreements: Questions and Answers', http://trade.ec.europa.eu/doclib/docs/2007/march/tradoc_133481.pdf, accessed 20 June 2007.

—— (2007b), 'Gender Equality and Women Empowerment in Development Cooperation', COM(2007)100.

Costello, C. and Davies, G. (2006), 'The Case Law of the Court of Justice in the Field of Sex Equality Since 2000', *Common Market Law Review* 43:6, 1567–616.

Council (2006), 'Decent Work for All', 30 November–1 December.

Davies, P. (1992), 'The Emergence of European Labour Law', in W. McCarthy (ed.), *Legal Intervention in Industrial Relations* (Oxford: Blackwell).

Ellis, E. (2005), *EU Anti-discrimination Law* (Oxford: Oxford University Press).

EU (2005), 'The European Consensus on Development', Joint Statement by the Council and the Representatives of the Governments of the Member States Meeting within the Council, the EP and the Commission, 20 December.

—— (2006), 'EU Member States back Commission Recommendation to Withdraw Trade Preferences from Belarus over Labour Standards', Press Release, 20 December.

Hepple, B. (2006), *Labour Laws and Global Trade* (Oxford: Hart Publishing).

—— (2007) 'Does Law Matter? The Future of Binding Norms', in G. Politakis (ed.), *Protecting Labour Rights as Human Rights: Present and Future of International Supervision* (ILO: Geneva).

Hoffmeister, F. (2007), 'Outsider or Frontrunner? Recent Developments under International and European Law on the Status of the EU in International Organizations and Treaty Bodies', *Common Market Law Review* 44:1, 41–68.

ILO (2004), *Report of the Commission of Inquiry: Trade Union Rights in Belarus* (Geneva: ILO).

—— (2005), *Director-General Report: Managing Transitions: Governance for Decent Work* (Budapest: ILO).

—— (2006a), 'ILO Welcomes EU Decision to Promote Decent Work for All', Press Release, 5 December.

ILO CEACR (1994), *General Survey* (ILO: Geneva).

ILO CEACR (2006), *Report, ILC 95th Session* (ILO: Geneva).

ILO CFA (2006), *Digest of Decisions and Principles: Freedom of Association*, 5th rev. edn (ILO: Geneva).

Kenner, J. (2003), *EU Employment Law: From Rome to Amsterdam and Beyond* (Oxford: Hart).

Kilpatrick, C. (1996), 'Production and Circulation of EC Nightwork Jurisprudence', *Industrial Law Journal* 25:3, 169–90.

Kingah, S. (2006), 'The Revised Cotonou Agreement Between the EC and the ACP States', *Journal of African Law* 50:1, 59–71.

Kowalsky, W. (2006), 'The Services Directive: The Legislative Process Clears the First Hurdle', *Transfer* 12:2.

Lenaerts, K. (1991), 'Fundamental Rights to be Included in a Community Catalogue', *European Law Review* 16:5, 367–90.

Meunier, S. and Nicolaïdes, K. (2006), 'The EU as a Conflicted Trade Power', *Journal of European Public Policy* 13:6, 906–25.

Murray, J. (2001), *Transnational Labour Regulation: The ILO and the EC Compared* (The Hague: Kluwer).

Novitz, T. (2002), 'Promoting Core Labour Standards and Improving Global Social Governance: An Assessment of EU Competence to Implement Commission Proposals', *EUI Working Paper Series RSC* 2002/59.

—— (2005), 'The EU and International Labour Standards', in P. Alston (ed.), *Labour Rights as Human Rights* (Oxford: Oxford University Press).

Orbie, J. (2007) 'The Social Dimension of Globalization and EU Development Policy', paper prepared for the EUSA Tenth Biennial International Conference Montreal, Canada, 17–19 May.

—— (2008), 'Core Labour Standards in Trade Policy: The GSP Regime of the EU', in C. Fenwick and T. Novitz (eds) *Legal Protection of Workers' Human Rights: Regulatory Challenges and Innovations* (Oxford: Hart Publishing, forthcoming).

PCA between the EC and their Member States and Ukraine, <http://trade.ec.europa.eu/doclib/docs/2003/october/tradoc_111612.pdf>, accessed 20 June 2007.

PCA between the EC and their Member States and Russia, <http://trade.ec.europa.eu/doclib/docs/2003/november/tradoc_114138.pdf>, accessed 20 June 2007.

Robinson, F. (2006), 'Beyond Labour Rights: The Ethics of Care and Women's Work in the Global Economy', *International Feminist Journal of Politics* 8:3, 321–42.

Ryan, B. (1997), 'Pay, Trade Union Rights and EC Law', *International Journal of Comparative Labour Law and Industrial Relations* 13, 305–25.

Summers, C. (2001), 'The Battle in Seattle: Free Trade, Labor Rights and Societal Values', *University of Pennsylvania Journal of International Economic Law* 22:1, 61–90.

Tortell, L. (2008), 'The ILO, Freedom of Association and Belarus', in C. Fenwick and T. Novitz (eds), *Legal Protection of Workers' Human Rights: Regulatory Challenges and Innovations* (Oxford: Hart Publishing, forthcoming).

Chapter 7

Green Civilian Power Europe?

Edith Vanden Brande

The literature often conceptualises the role of the European Union (EU) in global environmental politics in terms of actorness/presence (Bretherton and Vogler 2006a; Jokela 2002; Vogler 2002; Vogler 1999; Jupille and Caporaso 1998). Presence is granted automatically to the EU, but presence can only be translated into actorness when a number of criteria are fulfilled: authority, autonomy, cohesion and recognition. However, this framework, and research conducted according to it, is inadequate for an analysis of EU environmental policy.

First, it must be observed that the focus is particularly on the European Community (EC), and not on the EU. Secondly, the criteria of actorness are only related to the power dimension of the EC. When the EC fails to meet the actorness test, its power as an international actor diminishes. Actorness/presence ignores the goals for which the power resources are deployed. Both dimensions – the power and the goals – are essential when examining the EU's role in the world (cf. Chapter 1). A third criticism is not of a theoretical nature, but rather of an empiric one. Climate policy is perhaps the only hot topic on which the role of the EU has been examined systematically. Research is mainly limited to the EU's role in a number of 'popular' environmental regimes, while a comparison with Europe's role in several international environmental regimes is lacking. Fourth, the actorness/presence framework fails to explain the EU's aspiration towards global leadership in international environmental politics.

The EU's leadership ambitions can be explained by using the civilian power framework, as described in Chapter 1. Before examining the power resources and objectives of the EU's external environmental policy, the first section takes a closer look at the Union's internal evolution in this domain. Five periods can be discerned on the basis of consecutive changes in the power resources and pursued goals of EU environmental policy. The next section analyses two major internal power resources of EU global environmental policy: economic strength (the growth of Europe's internal market), and the institutional setting (competences and procedures that guide the EU in its role as an international negotiator). Here the question will be addressed as to whether economic power and/or institutional features are decisive in determining Europe's international power in the area of environment. Then three key external power resources are examined: the evolving international context of environmental politics, the transatlantic relationship, and the relationship between the EU and the South. This section concludes that the relationship between a policy's internal and external dimension will determine the power of that policy.

The next part analyses the goals of EU global environmental policy. On the basis that the policy of a civilian power is determined by its values and interests, a differentiation can be made between interest-related economic goals and value-related environmental goals. Yet economic and environmental goals alone cannot explain the EU's leadership in international environmental politics. Therefore, Europe's claim to green leadership is seen as a distinct foreign policy objective, namely the purchase of power in the international system. Although Europe's leadership claim in global environmental politics is rather limited to the level of discourse, and is being challenged, it has some important political functions that could eventually lead to a self-fulfilling prophecy. The conclusions link Europe's leadership aspirations with the power and goals of EU environmental policy.

The History of EU Environmental Policy

Five periods may be distinguished in EU environmental policy. Each passage from one period to another indicates an important institutional or substantive evolution. As summarised in Figure 7.1, this historical overview makes a basic distinction between the power resources and the pursued goals of the intra-EU environmental policies. Building on this distinction, the subsequent sections look more closely at the external dimension of EU environmental policy.

Economic Expansion (1957–1972)

An international consensus regarding economic growth is often used to describe the first period. Environmental policy was only a marginal policy topic; there was hardly any notion of ecological degradation. No reference to environmental policy was made in the Treaty of Rome. The creation of the common market and the free movement of goods were given as the EC's main goals. Anticipating possible market distortions from the first modest national environmental regulations, European environmental legislation originated but without explicit legal authorisation.[1] During this time, European environmental policy was a reactive policy which developed within the framework of the internal market policy. The absence of an independent European environmental policy and minimum involvement at all levels weakened the potential power of EU environmental policy (Jordan 2002; McCormick 2001; Sbragia 1998).

The Environmental Revolution (1972–1987)

Political, social and economic evolutions at the end of the 1960s turned environmental degradation into a hot issue. In Europe, there was a perception that uncontrolled economic expansion could threaten the EC's goals. At a gathering in

---

1   E.g. Directive 70/220 on vehicle emissions, in response to legislative proposals in West Germany and France that would have tightened their national vehicle emission controls, thereby threatening uniform European standards.

| | Power resources | | Pursued goals |
	Competence	Economic	
1957–72 *Economic expansion*	Indirect: common market legislation	Initial phase of market integration CU (1968)	Economic growth *No environmental goals*
1972–87 *Environmental revolution*	Indirect: – ECJ (AETR case 1971) – EAPs	– Consequences of the CU – 1970s: protectionism – Reaction to economic crisis: White Paper on internal market (1985)	*Economic expansion no longer a single goal of the EC*
1987–97 *Sustainable development as a moral responsibility*	Direct: – SEA 1987 – Treaty of Maastricht 1992 Indirect: – EAPs	– Completion of internal market	– End of the 1980s: Environmental goals framed in economic goals – 1990: Moral responsibility *Sustainable development with strong environmental dimension*
1997–? *Sustainable development as 'the next big idea'?*	EU Reform Treaty? Indirect: – EAPs	– Internal market far from complete – New incentives – Climate change	*Sustainable development framed in competitiveness goals* – Consolidation sustainable development as next big idea via climate change hysteria

Figure 7.1 History of EU environmental policy

Paris (1972), European heads of state declared that economic expansion was no longer the EC's single goal. For the first time, it was underlined that Europe needed an environmental policy. The Paris Declaration commissioned the drawing up of an Environmental Action Programme (EAP). In the spirit of the Paris Declaration and the first EAPs, the Member States underlined that they would adopt a common stance at international environmental conferences. Stressing the importance of joint action, this issue appeared as a separate chapter in the first EAP. It gave two main arguments for the importance of international action in the environmental field.

The main reason was an economic one: national engagements in international environmental agreements would have an influence on the common market, so eventually this would influence Community competences (Damro 2006, 177). Second, the first EAP stressed that EU activities responded to the public's growing awareness of environmental issues. In short, Europeans expected joint action in international environmental matters. For the European political elite, this reference to public demands was a way to legitimise the European integration project still further. But while environmental consciousness was growing, it was still framed within economic goals. Although market integration accelerated through the setting up of the Customs Union (CU) (1968), the internal market was far from complete. In a climate of international economic recession, Member States sought ways of promoting their national economic interests. Since, as a result of the CU, national authorities had already lost their control over levying tariffs, they looked for other ways of protecting their markets. Market integration was limited by the use of non-tariff barriers, and national environmental regulations served as a form of protectionism (Young and Wallace 2000, 85–115).

Nonetheless, acceleration in the institutionalisation of European environmental policy can be seen in the period between the first EAP and the formal authorisation of EC environmental competences by the Single European Act (SEA). Between 1972 and 1987 – a period often described as the 'environmental revolution' – there was a proliferation of EC environmental law (Sbragia 1996, 243). In the third EAP (1982–86), the integration of an environmental dimension in other policy areas ('environmental policy integration') became a key objective of the EU. European environmental policy was gaining growing political attention and influence.

Sustainable Development as a Moral Responsibility (1987–1997)

As the European economy entered a new phase – with the SEA marking the beginning of the completion of the internal market – Europe realised once again that environmental protection must complement the principal goal of the integration project, namely economic development. 1987 was also declared the 'European Year of the Environment'. One of the objectives of the campaign was to show the general public the complementarity between economic development and environmental protection.

Environmental protection as the legitimising principle for EU environmental policy would gradually be replaced by 'sustainable development' (Lenschow 2004, 140–57). By that time, the proliferation of environmental law was receiving more criticism than ever before. The traditional command-and-control method no longer seemed desirable. Strict uniform environmental legislation was portrayed as economic assassination for European industry, and in the context of increasing global economic competition this argument gained support from many Member States. Moreover, environmental directives were not being implemented, which justified a more effective and efficient European environmental policy. A far-reaching rationalisation of European environmental policy, and the rise of sustainable development as a paradigm could indicate a weak commitment towards environmental protection. Nevertheless, environmental standards were seen as elementary for European industry both inside and outside the internal market (Lenschow 2004; McCormick 2001; Johnson and Corcelle 1995). According to Baker (2006, 82–4), the fourth EAP (1987–92) introduced the idea that ecological modernisation[2] could offer European industry a competitive advantage. Apparently, there was a perception that the competitive position of the internal market could be maintained globally against external competitors, by internationalising environmental standards.

The ambition to play a leading role in international environmental politics was initially driven by economic objectives. From the 1990s onwards (cf. the Dublin Declaration in 1990), the EU declared itself as economically, politically, but also morally, predestined to exercise global environmental leadership.

The Treaty on the EU allowed the EC to make binding international environmental agreements, and increased the EC's legal competence. Sustainable development was consolidated as the new leading principle (Article 2 of the TEU). Under the mission 'Towards Sustainability' (Fifth EAP 1993–2000), the traditional command-and-control approach was replaced by a more integrated approach. Cost-effective measures and market-based solutions dominated the new European environmental agenda. Sustainable development, with the emphasis on reconciling economic growth with environmental protection, replaced environmental protection as a policy paradigm. Although economic efficiency remained at the heart of this approach, sustainable development had a strong environmental dimension.

Sustainable Development as 'the Next Big Idea' (1997–)

On the one hand, to support its claim as a leader in sustainable development, the EU needed to react collectively and develop a European policy for those themes which dominated the international environmental debate. On the other hand, the integration of the internal market, as a power base for EU environmental policy, was stagnating yet again. The Internal Market Action Plan (1997), Strategy for the Internal Market (1999), Lisbon (2000) and, eventually, a Competitiveness Council (2002) were installed to direct the new political priority of the Union's

---

2   According to ecological modernisation, environmental goals and economic goals are mutually reinforcing (win-win scenario). The traditional command-and-control method does not fit within the logic of ecological modernisation because command and control only enforces badly adapted uniform standards, while ecological modernisation leads to the internalisation of environmental considerations by all stakeholders.

'economic reforms'. It seemed that environmental protection had lost some of its status on the European agenda to the benefit of the promotion of competitiveness (McCormick 2001; Johnson and Corcelle 1995).

Confronted with two contradicting priorities, economic competitiveness and green leadership, EU environmental policy has now reached a crossroads. It will either be consolidated further as a policy sector, alongside other EU policies, or sustainable development will become the next 'big idea', in the same way as economic integration was the main idea in the early years of the European project (Lenschow 2004, 140).

Initially the European agenda was dominated by the 'Lisbon madness' of pursuing high rates of economic growth and short term competitiveness goals. Gradually the Commission and key Member States (UK and Germany) are realising at this strategy failed to make progress. In addition some influential reports, such as the Stern Review (published by the HM Treasury of the UK government) and the Intergovernmental Panel on Climate Change reports, estimate that the costs of environmental problems (in particular climate change) will outweigh the benefits of unconstrained economic growth. Consequently Europe endeavours a low carbon economy to give an incentive for new investments, job creation and competitiveness.

A revival of the ecological modernisation discourse and the belief in a win-win scenario is driven by the climate change hysteria, possibly eventually leading to a consolidation of sustainable development as next big idea (Lenschow 2004, 140).

The EU's Power in Global Environmental Policy

The Union's Economic Power Base

The economic dimension is often described as the EU's core power. Europe's environmental presence on the world stage stems from its internal economic activities. For example, the use of natural resources, and the emission of green house gases (GHG), are creating a considerable ecological footprint. The EU is also the gatekeeper of the internal market (Chapter 2). By granting access to the internal market, Europe can enforce environmental standards on its trading partners, which can eventually lead to a 'race to the top' when similar or even higher environmental standards are adopted in their domestic markets.

This 'trading up' of environmental regulations (Vogel 1995) is a critical argument in the case of REACH – the EU Regulation on the registration, evaluation, and authorisation of chemicals. In light of its intensive trade relations with the European market, US industry feared that trade would eventually force the US authorities to copy REACH-like regulations. Unprepared for a new regulatory system, the US claimed that REACH could spread and set a new global agenda[3] (Kovacs 2006; Logomasini 2006; Schörling and Lind 2004; Ciesla 2002). The European Commission had stated its ambition to spread the principles of REACH. Europe is trying to capture the 'first mover advantage', and hopes to influence the outcome of standards harmonisation. In anticipating of REACH, European industry will be the first to develop new technologies and consequently may develop a competitive advantage when the domestic norm is internationalised (Porter 1998).

Europe also seems to be willing to use this economic power in non-environmental regimes. 'The EU attempts to reconcile, and even exploit, its position as the world's largest trading bloc – with a growing aspiration to exercise environmental leadership' (Bretherton and Vogler 2000, 164). By offering WTO membership to Russia in exchange for Russian ratification of the Kyoto Protocol,[4] the EU made use of its benevolent economic position (Damro 2006, 187–90). Europe also pushed for an equal recognition of the World Trade Organisation's (WTO) authority and Multilateral Environmental Agreements (MEAs) and for the integration of environmental standards in the WTO. It seems that the value of sustainable development has influenced Europe's external policies as a whole – even the trade administrations have attempted to consolidate the position of the EU as a green leader. Given its considerable economic clout, it seems that the EU is more than a 'Scandinavian state' (Chapter 1) in global environmental politics.

The Institutional Setting: Competences and Decision-making

> According to the agenda, the EU can adopt another form, on occasion changing its shape virtually by the hour. (Vogler 1999, 24)

According to the formal competence of both the EC and the Commission, there are three possible gradations; exclusive, shared and competence of the

---

3   It is often stated that the EU is trying to globalise REACH through the Strategic Approach on International Chemicals Management (SAICM) (2006, Dubai). It is creating a non-binding set of declarations, principles and approaches and actions aimed at harmonising international standards, in particular bringing standards in developing countries closer to those in developed nations. A prime objective is to minimise the adverse affects of chemicals by 2020, a goal agreed at the Johannesburg Earth Summit in 2002.

4   The Kyoto agreement enters into force according to two conditions: 55 countries must ratify the agreement and the Protocol has to cover 55 per cent of worldwide greenhouse gas emissions. By 2004, 124 countries had ratified the agreement, which only represented 44 per cent of global greenhouse gas emissions. Considering the definite withdrawal of the US in March 2001, the EU strategy was to persuade Russia to ratify the Protocol. With Russian emissions (17.4 per cent of GHG emissions) the Kyoto Protocol could enter into force before the COP/MOP meeting in Montreal (December 2005). Eventually, the Protocol entered into force on 16 February 2005. The EU had the ambition to lead by forcing an agreement on Kyoto before Montreal; the first meeting of the parties to the protocol (MOP) was of symbolic importance for the EU , while in Montreal the MOPs were obliged to make 'demonstrable progress' (Article 3.2 of the Kyoto Protocol).

Member States. This section analyses the institutional setting of Europe's global environmental policy and examines whether and to what extent this influences the EU's international power in this area.

Under *exclusive competence*, the procedure resembles the formula of the EU's common commercial policy, where the EC, and more specifically the Commission, have a relatively large competence to act (Chapter 2). But in contrast to EU trade policy, the Treaty of Rome did not grant a clear competence in environmental affairs. Initially, the EC's capacity to act in this domain was gained via 'the backdoor', namely the integration of environment into commercial policy (Jokela 2002; Vogler 1999; Jupille and Caporaso 1998). Competence for the external dimension of environmental policy was first recognised by the European Court of Justice (ECJ). The AETR judgement (1971) is seen as an opening for the EU as an international environmental actor. Through the AETR judgement, the ECJ created the doctrine of implied powers, meaning that competence for internal policy automatically leads to EC competence for external action in the same policy field (Sbragia 1998, 287; see also Chapters 2 and 6).

Although the doctrine of implied powers seems clear, a number of problems arose. There is no exhaustive list of EC competences. Moreover, most international environmental agreements include elements that are regulated both by the EC and the Member States. Even in fields where the EC has a clear competence to act, such as trade-, fishery-, or agriculture-related environmental topics, competence is contested internally. One illustration of this concerns the negotiations on the Convention on Artic Marine Living Resources (CAMLR 1980). This treaty was based on an ecosystem approach to protect life in Antarctica. Protection of the fish stock was the Convention's central objective. As a result the Community adapted the Convention on the basis of the exclusive Common Fisheries Policy. Under CAMLR the effect on other species must be considered before a total allowable catch (TAC) for fish can be set. Member States have argued that a TAC which takes the pressure on penguins into account, does not fall under exclusive EC competence. Although the EC Bird Directive could be a precedent for international action, the Member States argued that the directive only includes birds in Europe and not in Antarctica, and refused to accept exclusive competence in those parts of the Convention relating to TAC (Macrory and Hession 1996, 132).

Exclusive competence for external environmental policy seldom exists. Even in regimes that are strongly trade-related, Member States refuse to hand over their power to the EC and the Commission. In fact, the relative power of the Commission and the Member States is dependent on the context of the negotiation.

Given the Member States' reluctance to allocate full sovereignty to the EC, most international environmental themes are of *shared or mixed competence*. Member States prefer shared competence because this means they are not excluded from a seat at the table, and can thus increase their power via the EU. International agreements are then divided by subject according to national or Community competence. There was, and is, a huge political fight over the limits of EC competence.

In fact, the constant quarrelling over competence between the Commission and the Member States is giving the EU a bad reputation. During the ozone negotiations, the US negotiator portrayed the Commission and Member States as more concerned with a rancorous internal struggle over competence than with the substance of saving the ozone layer (Benedick 1991, 35).

The SEA had important consequences for the competence question in general and for EU environmental policy in particular. The SEA made a distinction between national and Community competence. Secondly, the SEA, for the first time and in a separate chapter (Title VII), gave the EC formal authority for environmental policy, which received growing political support (Sbragia 1998, 289–90). Following on from the SEA, the EU vowed to stake out powerful and cohesive positions in a variety of international environmental forums. Since the second half of the 1980s, the EC has gained both formal and informal recognition as an international environmental actor.

Both internally and externally, non-recognition was used as an instrument to limit the EU's power. Non-recognition of EC competence was a Member State strategy to protect their own sovereignty and to counter the competence maximising ambitions of the Commission. Besides the Member States, outsiders – the US in particular – exploited non-recognition to counter EU's power ambitions. Outsiders claimed that the complexity of the EU legitimates any opposition to recognising the EC as a full participant in international agreements (Jokela 2002; Vogler 1999; Jupille en Caporaso 1998). By the end of the 1980s, this fight had been fought, and 'resistance is on the wane' against recognising the EC/EU (Jupille and Caporaso 1998, 215). An important breakthrough was the REIO concept (Regional Economic Integration Organisation) which had become the standard for many international conventions since the Convention on Long Range Transboundary Air Pollution. The EU (de facto the EC) is the only institution which is recognised as a REIO. One of the consequences of this status is the EC's right to be a party of an international convention without the condition that the Member States are party to the same convention.

Although resistance is on the wane, the strategy of non-recognition is still used by the US to counter the EU's power in certain environmental regimes. One example is the ongoing discussion in Convention on International Trade in Endangered Species of Wild Fauna and Flora (CITES Convention, 1973).[5] CITES is trade-related and intuitively it might be assumed that the EC has the competence to act. Uncertainty about the responsibility for compliance and implementation of the Convention prevents the US from recognising the EC as a party to CITES. Despite the fact that the EC is not a member of CITES, there is a common European framework for CITES (Vogler 1999; Jupille and Caporaso 1998). Therefore, the conditions for actorness, competence and recognition are, in fact, not always that significant, as European external environmental policy can exist without competence and recognition.

---

5 CITES aims is to ensure that international trade in specimens of wild animals and plants does not threaten their survival.

Informal rules organise the actions of the EU as an international environmental actor (Sbragia and Damro 1999, 54–8). There is no formal procedure for arranging the pre-negotiation phase (in preparation for an international conference), the negotiation phase (representation and the power to take binding decisions in name of the EU at the conference) and the post-negotiation phase (implementation of the international agreement).

In contrast with areas of exclusive competence, the Council Presidency makes the draft proposal, whereas the Commission has no right of initiative. And although the Commission takes part in Council negotiations, it is the Council, and in most cases the Environment Council, that takes the final decisions about guidelines for the common position.

At the negotiation stage, representation is shared between the Commission and the Presidency. Issues under EC competence are represented by the Commission; the Presidency is the spokesperson regarding issues that come within mixed competence. If the Member States reach an agreement, the representation for mixed competence can be handed over to the Commission (Sbragia 1998, 293). Generally speaking, representation is rather ad hoc, and there is an informal working relationship between the Presidency and the Commission (Vogler 2005; Sbragia and Damro 1999; Jupille and Caporaso 1998). In some cases, the EU is represented by the troika. The troika has no legal foundation for EU environmental policy, but rather the involvement of the Presidency, the next Presidency and the Commission in international environmental negotiations constitutes an informal practice (van Schaik and Egenhofer 2003). However, in general, EU representation remains an intergovernmental process: important political decisions are taken by the ministers, and final conclusions are given in 'the Council meeting at location'. Despite the guidelines on the common position agreed by the ministers, the Union often has to adjust its position during negotiations. But there is no executive authority that can take binding decisions on behalf of the EU. The Presidency or the Commission cannot take binding decisions without consulting the Member States. This explains the widespread criticism that the EU is an inflexible negotiation partner which tries to hold on to the initial common position. Internal coordination demands a lot of energy, and the EU is often blamed for negotiating more internally than internationally.

Another criticism concerns the *technocratic decision-making* and the lack of external influences during the negotiation phase. The EU negotiates behind closed doors: the European Parliament (EP) and NGOs are not allowed in coordination meetings. In fact, the way in which the European position is produced suffers from a huge democratic deficit. The EP only has to be consulted during the pre-negotiation stage, but Europe's point of view can alter during the negotiations. Nevertheless, the EP manages to exert influence by using alternative methods; for example, an EP resolution led to the first control on the export of chemicals, later known as the PIC procedure which was eventually incorporated into the PIC Treaty of Rotterdam (Pallemaerts 1998).[6]

Negotiations during an international conference are mainly conducted by officials and technical experts, while public actors have little influence on the decision-making process. Within the EU, the main decisions are made by Council working parties; internationally, the technical committees and subsidiary agencies prepare and guide the political decisions during the COPs (Conference of the Parties). The technocratic decision-making style relates to the nature of this policy domain: negotiating environmental issues requires the active and essential role of science (Kailis 2006). Technocratic decision-making is crucial in a way for the governance of environmental problems and, as such, the dominance of experts can increase the EU's bargaining capacity. On the other hand, epistemic communities of experts can impose certain perceptions of environmental problems[7] on politicians and the public. In the short run, knowledge is power, but in the long term, a lack of public participation can affect the legitimacy and ultimately the EU's 'soft' power.

The relationship between competence and power is hotly debated in the literature (Jokela 2002; Vogler 2002; Bretherton and Vogler 1999; Vogler 1999; Jupille and Caporaso 1998). The actorness/presence theory assumes a positive correlation between competence and power. Recently this positive relationship has been questioned. The EU can play an essential role and make a difference in conventions that do not fall exclusively under EC competence. The significance of legal competence should indeed be nuanced. Cooperation among Member States, even with an active role for the Commission, can occur and run smoothly in the absence of EC legal competence. Even in international negotiations which involve a complex institutional setting and do not have an intra-European precedent, the EU proves to be a powerful international environmental actor. The climate change dossier is a case in point (Groenleer and van Schaik 2005). Effectiveness of coordination in the pre-negotiation, the negotiation and implementation phases could be a better indicator of the power of EU environmental policy.

The Nature of Environmental Politics: A Window of Opportunity

Europe's international power in environmental issues is obviously influenced by the external context. For example, by the end of the 1960s a notion had developed that there is a limit to economic growth. The oil crisis and the 'Limits to Growth' report led to the first environmental meeting, the United Nations Conference on Human Environment (1972) (Stockholm Convention). This environmental awareness translated into a proliferation of international and

---

6   PIC refers to the Prior Inform Consent Procedure (the Rotterdam Convention 1998). The PIC procedure is a mechanism for formally obtaining and disseminating the decisions of importing Parties as to whether they wish to receive future shipments of certain chemicals and for ensuring compliance with these decisions by exporting Parties.

7   Scientists denying the problem of climate change have a significant influence on the US position in international climate negotiations.

regional environmental agreements. As a result of increased economic competition in the 1980s, the environmental debate underwent a substantive evolution. Ideas such as environmental and nature protection became less attractive, whereas economic competition framed the environmental debate. The end of the Cold War also had a significant influence on environmental politics. More attention was paid to the consequences of international economic activities; as a result, environmental degradation became more visible. Globalisation also had an effect on the nature of environmental problems. Domestic 'behind-the-border' issues came on to the international agenda more and more (cf. Chapter 2).

Previously, the US had acted as a leader in a number of environmental regimes which were mainly linked to trade discussions that stopped at the border. New environmental problems, such as climate change, demand an adaptation of national structures, but the US is more reluctant to accept a sharing of sovereignty in behind-the-border issues. For their part, EU policy-makers accept sharing of sovereignty more readily (Sbragia and Damro 1999).

Another trend is the hype about sustainable development which became the main issue at environmental 'mega-conferences' in the post-Rio process. The predominance of sustainable development in international environmental politics gave the EU an opportunity to present itself as a leader in this field.

Finally, there is no coherent legal framework for international environmental politics. The international environmental regime comprises a variation of international and regional agreements and protocols, international organisations with an environmental component (for example, World Health Organisation, International Labour Organisation, Food and Agriculture Organisation, and more specialised institutions, such as the United Nations Environment Programme (UNEP) and the Commission on Sustainable Development. Even in the limited case of the international regulation of chemicals, there are different relevant conventions depending on the specific substance in question. More power for UNEP could enhance coherence in international environmental politics. The EU supports the idea of granting more political and financial power to UNEP. Strengthening the current structures of environmental regimes could eventually lead to the foundation of a World Environmental Organisation. The question remains whether the EU has enough power to take advantage of this 'window of opportunity' which the international context offers.

The Transatlantic Relationship: Role Switching and Sharing Leadership

Although the US is usually ascribed the role of 'environmental laggard', and the EU is often seen as a 'leader', their respective positions used to be completely opposite. In the 1970s and the first half of the 1980s, the US was one of the most progressive countries. Confronted with increased competition, the US gradually defined its interests in a different way, which resulted in a role metamorphose. The negotiations concerning the Ozone Treaty (1985) (Vienna Convention) symbolise this transformation of the US, as well as its concomitant role switch with the EU. At first, the US appeared as a proponent of a can ban, but was opposed by the EU which showed little commitment for regulating CFCs (chlorofluocarbons).

By the time the negotiations on the Montreal Protocol (1987) of the Ozone Treaty had started, Europe changed its position from laggard to leader. It even went to the point where the German Presidency (in the first half of 1988) had the ambition to push the Community to go beyond the terms of the Protocol (Rowlands 1998, 34–59). Sbragia and Damro (1999, 53) describe this role switch: 'The US had gone from being the Vienna leader to the Kyoto laggard. The EU had moved from being the Vienna laggard to the Kyoto leader.'

By the end of the 1980s, the increasing internal power resources of the EU – formal environmental competence in the SEA, growing economic power relevance with the internal market – partly explain the European role switch. Policy entrepreneurs within the Council (for example, green leadership by Germany) and the Commission also played a part. Externally, the relative decline of the US provided an opportunity for the EU to present itself as an international leader. Discussions with the US on the formal recognition of the EC were on the wane which gave more opportunity for substantive conflict. This shift to a more substantive EU-US debate on environmental topics was further encouraged by the evolution to behind-the-border issues.

Substantive discussion emerged as a result of the economic dimension in many environmental agreements. For this reason, shared leadership is a more likely scenario for the future than a green European hegemony. At first sight, there is too much disagreement between the US and the EU to reach a consensus in the field of environmental policy. On the other hand, however, there is more agreement than might be expected. Ethical arguments, which are dominant in the environmental discourse, are often an alibi to hide real policy priorities. Economic priorities guide environmental policy in both the EU and US (Baker, 2006).[8] Nonetheless, the gap between the US and the EU is smaller than it seems. The EU copies the US' technological approach and use of regional agreements which, in the long term, could threaten multilateralism and binding regimes such as Kyoto.[9] The rise of a number of new economies, especially in Asia, with little experience of environmental policy, is creating a new challenge. In that sense, the tension between North and South is a greater potential conflict than the EU-US relationship.

---

8   Yet in the US the relative weight of economic values over environmental ones is larger than in the EU. According to Baker, there is still a difference between US and EU environmental policy, which can be explained by the relative priorities given to values and principles (Baker 2006).

9   EU-Asia regional agreements can be seen as a reaction on the Asia-Pacific Partnership on Clean Development and Climate, also known as AP6. This is a non-treaty agreement between Australia, India, Japan, China, South Korea, and the US. Unlike the Kyoto Protocol (currently unratified by both the US), which imposes mandatory limits on greenhouse gas emissions, this agreement allows member countries to set their goals for reducing emissions individually, with no mandatory enforcement mechanism.

Convincing Developing Countries

In reaction to the new assertiveness of developing countries since the 1970s, the EU has gradually embraced sustainable development as a goal. During the 1972 Stockholm Conference (see above), developing countries demanded equal recognition of environmental protection and economic development. The EU reacted by promoting a compromise between environment and development – sustainable development *avant la lettre*.

After the Cold War, and in the run-up to the Rio conference, the sustainable development debate dominated the international agenda. The United Nations Conference on Environment and Development (Rio 1992) was perceived as the ultimate opportunity to demonstrate the relevance and potential power of the EU. The integration of financial assistance in environmental agreements for developing countries is an instrument either to win, or to buy, their souls.[10] But environmental regulation is often perceived as a form of green protectionism that only serves the interests of the EU. On the other hand, developing countries expect Europe to bear its historical responsibility. As regards climate change, the argument of historical responsibility is used (abused) by China and India to escape their duties. In the meantime, the EU is supposed to support the Kyoto regime, in the worst case unilaterally.

The Clean Development Mechanism (CDM) serves as an example of this debate. CDM allows Europe to invest in developing countries in exchange for emission rights. These investments demand a certain infrastructure and climate for investment. Only the South-east Asian region and Central and South America attract CDM projects, since African countries often lack the necessary basic requirements for such investments. Funds for adaptations to climate change are the main concern of the poorest developing countries. They expect Western countries, especially the EU, to fund these compensating financial mechanisms. External expectations confirm the Union's role as a green leader, and thus confer power on it. It is in Europe's interest to sustain its identity as a leader in sustainable development, although the question is whether the EU is able and willing to maintain this role.

Interaction between Internal and External Dimensions

Two contradicting hypotheses are currently circulating regarding the relationship between the policy's internal and external dimensions. Europe's internal activities may function as a precedent for external action. In this scenario, the EU tries to *externalise* its own policy. As the EU's internal environmental regulation develops further, its international power in this area will also gradually increase. The above-mentioned REACH initiative, which is described as the model for a new global

---

10   Inversely, the EU established a budget line on the integration of environment in development policy in 1997. Since 2007 'Environment and sustainable management of natural resources including energy' is a thematic programme under the Union's development cooperation instrument (see Figure 3.1 in Chapter 3).

strategy on chemicals regulation, may be a case in point. REACH could serve as an empowering factor for the EU in international negotiations on chemicals management (Schörling and Lind 2004).

In contrast, EU participation in international environmental issues could stimulate action within the Union. By *internalising* certain principles and approaches (for example, sustainable development) and policy measures (emissions trading) the EU is attempting to respond to the international debate. Climate policy can serve as an example where the link between internal and external dimensions is obvious. In analysing the rapid decision-making process on the emission trading Directive, Wettestad (2005) argues that the ambition to 'lead by example' on the international front was the main argument for the need for an intra-European climate policy and a European Union Emissions Trading Scheme (EUETS).

Irrespective of the origin and early motivation of the EU policy – whether the Union tries to externalise its own policy or internalise certain principles and policies – the power of the EU will increase if the relationship between the internal and external dimension is a close one. A strong internal policy will empower the EU to externalise its own policy preferences and, in return, externalisation can boost the Union's internal policy (for example, SAICM, a REACH-like deal on global chemicals management, can boost the EU's own regulation). By internalising certain principles and policies, initially to respond to the international debate, the EU can act as a policy entrepreneur at a later stage. At first, the EU copied the design of its climate policy from the US (emissions trading). After a while, the US and Kyoto-style climate policy design became internalised in the EU. In fact, European climate policy is based almost entirely on the implementation of an international agreement. In a sense, Kyoto-style regulations are integrated in the EU machine, and the costs of dismissal are often larger than the costs of consolidation. In fact, the Union copied the design of the climate regime (internalisation) and is now trying to externalise the rules on the content of the regime (externalisation of the content of emissions trading). The distinction between internalisation and externalisation is often blurred, but a strong connection between both dimensions will enhance the power of EU environmental policy.

EU Goals in Global Environmental Policy

Economic versus Environmental Goals: Squaring the Circle

> Progress on environmental quality has become a kind of arm-wrestling match. One side pushes for tougher standards; the other tries to roll them back. The balance of power shifts one way or the other depending on the prevailing political winds. (Porter and van der Linde 1999, 1)

Analyses of the goals that the EU pursues in its (external) environmental policy typically distinguish between interest-related economic and normative environmental objectives. The prevailing belief is that there is an inherent *trade-off* between competitiveness and environmental protection. The historical overview given at the beginning of this chapter showed that changes in Europe's economic project interact with evolutions in environmental policy.

Periods in which the impression was that the internal market programme was advancing correlate with a high level of environmental awareness. Conversely, there is resistance to environmental regulation when a perception of competition loss exists. Nevertheless, it is hard to generalise over these conclusions – environmental regulations can even be used to protect economic interests in an attempt to compensate for competition losses, even in periods of stagnation in the internal market programme (for example, the environmental revolution in 1970s coincided with the period of 'Eurosclerose').

The perception of competition loss is often used by industry in opposing environmental regulation (Golub 1998, 1–33). During the ozone negotiations, the predominance of economic goals even went as far as industry taking a seat at the negotiation table. Economic considerations clarify the role of the EU as the Vienna laggard. However, economic goals can also serve as an explanation for its later role as leader in the ozone regime negotiations concerning the Montreal Protocol (1987). Environmental regulation was perceived by industry and by certain European countries, such as the UK and Germany, as an instrument to advance their economic interests (Rowlands 1998, 34–59).[11] It is in the interest of the EU that the Kyoto Protocol becomes operational; a global emissions market could extend the economic advantages of the EUETS. Environmental protection has to compete with economic goals, and trade interests often prevail. In the tuna-dolphin dispute, the US restricted the import of tuna that was not dolphin-friendly; the EU reacted by making a complaint to the GATT panel because the ban was perceived as unilateral and extra-territorial. This dispute serves as an example of the tensions that arise between the EU's different roles. In this case, the Union decided to act as a Trading State (see Chapter 1). It would appear that there is a growing conflict between the different faces of 'civilian' or 'normative' power Europe, where free trade often receives a higher ranking than environmental protection. The EU has a normative commitment to sustainable development but when this interferes with trade issues, the commitment to sustainable development will diminish in favour of a more market-oriented approach (Lightfoot and Burchell 2005, 76–90).

In contrast to the classical trade-off between ecology and economy, strategic environmental policy (see ecological modernisation above) claims to exceed this unavoidable tension. In this setting, environmental policy is portrayed as a *win-win scenario*. Environmental regulation can lead to optimal efficiency, given the scarcity of natural resources (for example, energy). Even industry could favour

---

11   At the end of the 1980s there was a perception that the end of the CFC era was near. British industrials, especially the chemical company ICI, also had interest in the substitutes market. By controlling CFCs, through the Montreal Protocol, the potential market for substitutes would grow much faster than it would without regulation. Developing countries in particular were perceived as lucrative potential importers (Rowlands 1998).

this argument because it could lead to increased resource productivity (Golub 1998, 1–33; Porter and van der Linde 1999). The idea of a win-win scenario is integrated into the sustainable development concept, as well.

Although sustainable development should avoid the tension between economic and environmental goals, in practice it is evident that decision-making in EU environmental policy remains a trade-off between ecology and economy. Jordan even claims that this balancing of environmental versus economic goals is the *new conflict* in EU environmental policy. Whereas in the 1980s there was a heated debate about competence, recent environmental discussions are played out among different interests across the European institutions, governments and advocacy groups, rather than between institutions at different governance levels (Jordan 2005, 12). Depending on the issue and phase in the decision-making process, the advocacy coalition in favour of environmental protection can be strong. In the case of REACH, leading Member States (such as Sweden, Denmark, the Netherlands, Germany and the UK), DG Environment, the EP and NGOs initially managed to control the preparation of the White Paper and pre-draft on REACH. Later in the decision-making procedure, the industry built a coalition that favoured a less environmentally progressive REACH, and it succeeded. REACH was handed over from DG Environment and the Environment Council to DG Enterprise and the Competitiveness Council (Selin 2005, 1–12).

Sustainable development should represent a win-win solution, but in practice environmental demands are often undermined by the economic dimension of sustainable development.

Foreign Policy Objective: Global Leadership

> In some cases the ambition of leadership is only a declared value, highly visible in declaratory political statements, but absent in actual practice. (Baker 2006, 78–9)

The Union's green mission is not only motivated by economic and environmental goals, but also as a foreign policy objective where leadership is used to legitimise its actions. Grubb and Gupta (2000, 79) defined it as the 'hegemonic ambitions' of the EU. Growing internal and external expectations towards Union action and the increasing complexity of the international context created pressure on the EU at the end of the Cold War. Assertive participation in international environmental negotiations – particularly in the climate debate – was an answer to those demands. Step by step the EU realised that its power was being recognised more rapidly thanks to this assertive role (Sbragia and Damro 1999). Furthermore, the EU expected to achieve emission reductions without considerable economic costs – the restructuring of the energy system in both East Germany and the UK should allow the Union to achieve its commitments without additional policies. In a sense, this was an easy way to gain political influence internationally.

Indeed, climate policy was used to demonstrate the power of the EU. It acted as a front-runner in international commitments. Yet its leadership ambition was rather 'symbolic politics' and many questioned its capacity to implement internally. In fact, when it comes to implementation the results are far behind the rhetoric.

Green Leadership: The Next Big Idea?

There is a limit on how far words can take you in global politics. (Smith 2006, 20)

Earlier it was stated that EU environmental policy is at a new crossroads: either it will become a 'normal' policy domain alongside other areas, or sustainable development will be the next 'big idea' (Lenschow 2004, 140). In a mission such as global green leader or the consolidation of environmental policy as the 'next big European idea', there is often no direct link between environmental goals and interests (economic goals). Europe does not contribute any more to climate change than other international actors, and the principal victims of climate change will be the developing countries, not the Europeans. Even the economic advantages from emissions trading can be reduced by the burden of binding targets.

It seems that this economic logic dominated the EU's agenda in 2005. At the climate negotiations in Montreal (December 2005 COP11/MOP 1) the predominance of economic objectives sent the EU's point of view in the American direction. Kyoto was even questioned by the European representatives (Vanden Brande 2006, 79). Moreover, the Commission (2005, 8) shared the opinion that Europe can no longer allow itself to be dogmatic from now on the EU would let its efforts depend on the efforts of others [read the US].

Another tendency is the securitisation of the climate debate. There is a growing recognition that climate change is a new potential security threat for the twenty-first century. Moreover, the link between climate change and energy is the new hot topic in the climate debate (Chapter 9).[12] As a result, other actors – and even the US – are becoming interested in the climate debate, and are trying to frame the discussion in line with their priorities. This is creating an external context that lessens the opportunity for the EU to maintain and develop its identity, and threatens the capacity to sustain its leadership ambitions (Bretherton and Vogler 2006b, 9).

An additional criticism is that the EU is the leading actor in the international negotiations but when it comes to possible solutions for climate change, it is failing to deliver. Emissions trading can realise the goals of Kyoto's first commitment period (2008–12) but it is doing little to force a direct reduction of emission levels in the Member States (Damro 2006, 94–5). And when the Union tries to develop policy solutions for the climate problem, effective implementation is often unsuccessful.

---

12   This link was made during the Gleneagles G8 summit; one of the goals was to provide a sustainable energy future. This creates the potential danger that powerful states take the lead in a small forum, like the G8, without consulting the world community. Securitising the climate change debate can transform it into power politics, where the climate policy now is often perceived as soft politics within a multilateral context, the UN.

There are a lot of arguments against the role as global green leader. Nevertheless, the Union claims a leadership role in the Euro-discourse. Constantly repeating that message can eventually lead to a self-fulfilling prophecy; the self-perception is created that the EU must play the role of green leader. This self-image is embedded in the Union's formal goals, but is also cognitively anchored. Green leadership is not only an ambition of the political elite. There is a broad popular basis for this mission in the EU as a whole. In the case of biodiversity, European representatives defended the regulation of genetically modified organisms (GMOs) to counter the criticism from the European public. In this way, the European institutions hope to solve the broader legitimacy crisis in the EU by taking a strong and proactive stance in certain environmental regimes (Tiberghien and Starrs 2004). It appears that foreign policy is least affected by the controversy, and external policy could be a possible answer to the EU crisis (Smith 2006, 1). The leadership discourse on environmental issues has to give a new impetus to the European project when direction is lost. Several natural events in 2006–07, notably the warm winter and natural disasters, and Al Gore's documentary on global warming 'An inconvenient truth', have led to a new sense of climate change urgency. This creates a momentum for the EU to defend its leadership in the 'hot war on climate change.

According to Baker (2006, 77–8) normative power Europe is mainly restricted to a discourse but nonetheless serves certain *functions* in the integration process. Values and principles forge a sense of group identity, can mobilise support for European integration, and distinguish the EU on the international stage. The articulation of shared values and principles in international politics has an important legitimising function. Its seems as though, according to the opinion of Europeans, unregulated globalisation has reached its limit, and they are willing to support and even demand a role for the EU as global and green civilian power.[13]

---

13   Eurobarometer surveys show that Europeans have a greater trust in the EU to regulate globalisation than in the US (European Commission 2003). 83 per cent of Europeans (EU-15) say that environment should be an EU policy priority (European Commission 2000). According to another survey, environment worries Europeans most, even more than employment (European Commission 2001; this high level of worry was measured in 1997, the same year as the Kyoto Protocol). One could expect that, given the economic context, the greatest concern of Europeans now is employment. Eurobarometer 65 of Spring 2006 confirms this: environment is not even mentioned as a major concern; employment, crime and economic situation are the major European concerns (European Commission 2006). However; a majority of the EU citizens is concerned about climate change and looks at the EU rather than at the national level for measures (Special Eurobarometer 2006a). A FT/Harris poll (19 March 2007) shows that in the five largest European countries (UK, France, Italy, Spain and Germany) 82 per cent are of the opinion that the EU should do more in the area of environment. Furthermore environment and energy turned out to be one of three topics answering the question 'what Europe do we want?' in the agenda-setting event of the European citizens consultations (European Citizens Agenda 2006). Thus an assertive climate strategy could be the next big idea to rally support for the EU project.

A Green Civilian Power?

By conceptualising the EU as a civilian power, this chapter explains the aspirations of leadership by linking the power resources with the goals of EU environmental policy. Europe's economic power stemming from the internal market determines the EU's aspirations and capacity to carry out a role as an environmental leader. Even outside international environmental politics, such as in the trade regime, the EU uses its economic clout to empower European environmental policy. But it is also in the strategic interest of the Union that the model of sustainable development does not damage its competitiveness (or economic power). Through the idea of sustainable development, the EU has tried to reconcile environmental protection and competitiveness. Yet competitiveness is still an important and even dominant argument in environmental policy-making. Sustainable development and environmental policy are relatively subtle ways to advance a (neoliberal) economic agenda. The informal rules that guide the institutional setting of the EU as an international environmental actor increase the power of the Member States. Most decisions need the consent of each Member State. Consequently, low-common-denominator EU options resemble the position of the Member State with clear interests – which are often economic objectives (see Ozone above). Technocratic decision-making in the EU and in international negotiations is another argument why it is unlikely that the Union's quest is a normative environmental policy. Decisions are inspired by knowledge about optimal eco-efficiency. In contrast with national ministers – who often see environmental regulation as an economic constraint – environmental experts perceive environmental regulation more as economic enabling; but in the end, environmental protection as a normative objective remains subordinate to economic objectives.

Even though the leadership objective of green civilian power is rather discursive, it seems that the aspiration of green civilian power serves certain non-economic objectives. Green leadership has two important political functions: gaining power in the international system and legitimising European integration. At first, the aspiration of green leadership served certain functions – economic or political objectives – but after a while the idea of green civilian power was embedded formally and cognitively in the heads of the political elite, academics and the European public. Green leadership has become rather path-dependent; the cost of non-leadership has become too costly. Moreover, the idea of green civilian power Europe is entrenched in the feeling of European identity.

Although the aspiration of green leadership is locked-in in the Union and seems appropriate, the EU is now at a new crossroads. It appears that green leadership in the context of increasing globalisation is perceived as too costly. On the one hand, it seems that the EU is reversing its initial option to act as a green civilian power. On the other hand, the objective of green leadership is a crucial element of EU identity. In the international negotiations on a post-2012 deal on climate change it appeared that the EU was originally not prepared to take up its responsibility as a leader. The atmosphere changed in 2007 when the European political elite realised that a progressive stance in the debate could solve other EU-related problems. The EU heads of state committed themselves to an independent pledge to achieve at least 20 per cent greenhouse gas emissions reductions by 2020 and 30 per cent when other international actors follow the EU's lead. Various factors explain why there was hardly any resistance against these ambitious proposals: economic reorientations in Europe (greening of the Lisbon agenda) and geopolitical considerations (energy crisis) forged an intra-European consensus; a progressive EU stance answers the climate change anxiety among the public opinion and replies to the anti-EU backlash among EU citizens; and the EU was losing its international credibility and power as climate change leader. European policy-makers have recently rediscovered the functions of the green civilian power role via the climate change policy debate. Climate change can be seen as an attempt to consolidate the green civilian power identity and could eventually trigger the embedding of sustainable development as next big idea.

References

Baker, S. (2006), 'Environmental Values and Climate Change Policy. Contrasting the EU and the US', in S. Lucarelli and I. Manners (eds), *Values and Principles in European Foreign Policy* (London: Routledge).

Benedick, R.E. (1991), *Ozone Diplomacy: New Directions in Safeguarding the Planet* (Cambridge, MA: Harvard University Press).

Bretherton, C. and Vogler, J. (1999), *The EU as a Global Actor* (London: Routledge).

—— (2000), 'The EU as Trade Actor and Environmental Activist: Contradictory Roles?', *Journal of Economic Integration* 15:2, 163–94.

—— (2006a), *The EU as a Global Actor* (London: Routledge).

—— (2006b), 'The EU as a Protagonist to the US on Climate Change', *International Studies Perspectives* 7, 1–22.

Ciesla, E. (2002), 'Will the US let the EU Regulate our Chemicals Industry through OECD?', Competitive Enterprise Institute, *On Point*, 15 April.

Damro, C. (2006), 'EU-UN Environmental Relations: Shared Competence and Effective Multilateralism', in K. Laatikainen and K.E. Smith (eds), *The EU at the UN: Intersecting Multilateralisms* (Houndmills: Palgrave Macmillan).

European Commission (2000), 'Standard Eurobarometer 52', April (Fieldwork October–November 1999).

—— (2001), 'How Europeans see Themselves. Looking Through the Mirror with Public Opinion Surveys'.

—— (2003), 'Flash Eurobarometer. Globalisation', November (Fieldwork October 2003).

—— (2005), 'Winning the Battle against Global Climate Change', COM(2005)35.

—— (2006), 'Standard Eurobarometer 65', July (Fieldwork March–April 2006).

—— (2006), 'Special Eurobarometer 247 Attitudes towards Energy', January (Fieldwork October–November 2005).

European Citizens' Agenda (2006), 'Agenda Setting Event Outcomes', October.

Golub, J. (ed.) (1998), *Global Competition and EU Environmental Policy* (London: Routledge).

Groenleer, M.L.P and van Schaik, L.D. (2005), 'The EU as an 'Intergovernmental Actor in Foreign Affairs': Case Studies of the International Criminal Court and the Kyoto Protocol', *CEPS Working document 228*.

Grubb, M. and Gupta, J. (2000), *Climate Change and European Leadership: A Sustainable Role for Europe?* (Dordrecht: Kluwer Academic).

Johnson, S.P and Corcelle, G. (1995), *The Environmental Policy of the European Communities* (London: Kluwer Law International).

Jokela, M. (2002) 'EU as a Global Policy Actor: The Case of Desertification', in F. Biermann, Campe, S. and Jacob, K. (eds), *Proceedings of the 2001 Berlin Conference on the Human Dimensions of Global Environmental Change 'Global Environmental Change and the Nation State'* (Potsdam: Institute for Climate Impact Research).

Jordan, A. (ed.) (2002), *Environmental Policy in the EU: Actors, Institutions and Processes* (London: Earthscan).

—— (2005), 'Introduction', in A. Jordan (ed.), *Environmental Policy in the EU: Actors, Institutions, and Processes* (London: Earthscan).

Jupille, J. and Caporaso, J. (1998), 'States, Agency and Rules: the EU in Global Environmental Politics', in C. Rhodes (ed.) *The EU in the World Community* (Boulder, CO: Lynne Rienner).

Kailis, A. (2006), 'Management and Integration of Scientific-Technical Issues at the Negotiation Stage of International Environmental Negotiation', paper presented at the *ECPR Summer School on Environmental Politics and Policy*, Keele University, 25 June–7 July.

Kovacs, W. (2006), 'New EU, UN Chemicals Rules to Affect US', The Heartland Institute, *Environment News*, 1 July.

Lenschow, A. (2004), 'Environmental Policy: at a Crossroads?', in M.G. Cowles and D. Dinan (eds), *Developments in the EU 2* (Basingstoke: Palgrave Macmillan).

Lightfoot, S. and Burchell, J. (2005), 'The EU and the World Summit on Sustainable Development: Normative Power Europe in Action?', *Journal of Common Market Studies* 43:1, 75–95.

Logomasini, A. (2006), 'The UN's Strategic Approach to International Chemicals Management Program, Stealth attempt at Global Regulation', Competitive Enterprise Institute, *On Point*, 29 March.

Macrory, R. and Hession, M. (1996), 'The EC and Climate Change: The Role of Law and Legal Competence', in T. O'Riordan and J. Jäger (eds), *Politics of Climate Change: A European Perspective* (London: Routledge).

McCormick, J. (2001), *Environmental Policy in the EU* (Basingstoke: Palgrave).

Pallemaerts, M. (1998), 'Regulating Exports of Hazardous Chemicals: The EU's External Chemical Safety Policy', in J. Golub (ed.), *Global Competition and EU Environmental Policy* (London: Routledge).

Porter, M. (1998), *Competitive Advantage of Nations* (Basingstoke: Macmillan).

—— and Linde, C. van der (1999), 'Green and Competitive: Ending the Stalemate', *Journal of Business Administration and Policy Analysis* 28, 1–16.

Rowlands, I. (1998), 'EU Policy for Ozone Layer Protection', in J. Golub (ed.), *Global Competition and EU Environmental Policy* (London: Routledge).

Sbragia, A. (1996), 'Environmental Policy, the Push-Pull of Policy-Making', in H. Wallace and W. Wallace (eds), *Policy Making in the EU* (Oxford: Oxford University Press).

—— (1998), 'Institution-building from Below and Above: The EC in Global Environmental Politics', in W. Sandholtz and A. Stone Sweet (eds), *European Integration and Supranational Governance* (Oxford: Oxford University Press).

—— and Damro, C. (1999), 'The Changing Role of the EU in International Environmental Politics: Institution Building and the Politics of Climate Change', *Government and Policy* 17:1, 53–68.

Schörling, I. and Lind, G. (2004), *REACH – The Only Planet Guide to the Secrets of Chemicals Policy in the EU. What Happened and Why?* (Brussels: The Greens/European Free Alliance in the EP).

Selin, H. (2005), 'European Over-REACH? Efforts to Revise European Chemical Legislation and Regulation', *Conference on Human Dimensions of Global Environmental Change*, Berlin, 2–3 December.

Smith, M. (2006), 'The EU and International Order: European and Global Aspects', paper presented at the EUSA Workshop 'EU Foreign/Security/Defence Policy', Washington DC, 3 April.

Tibergien, Y. and Starrs, S. (2004), 'The EU as a Global Trouble Maker in Chief: A Political Analysis of EU Regulations and EU Global Leadership in the Field of GMOs', *2004 Conference of Europeanists*, CES, Chicago, 11–13 March.

Vanden Brande, E. (2006), 'Europa, Klimaatleider ook na Kyoto?', *Internationale Spectator* 60:2, 78–81.

Van Schaik, L.D. and Egenhofer, C. (2003), 'Reform of the EU Institutions: Implications for the EU's Performance in Climate Negotiations', *CEPS Policy Brief* 40.

Vogel, D. (1995), *Trading-Up: Consumer and Environmental Regulation in a Global Economy* (Cambridge, MA: Harvard University Press).

Vogler, J. (1999), 'The EU as an Actor in International Environmental Politics', *Environmental Politics* 8:3, 65–71.

—— (2005), 'The European Contribution to Global Environmental Governance', *International Affairs* 81:4, 835–50.

Wettestad, J. (2005), 'The Making of the 2003 EU Emissions Trading Directive. An Ultra-Quick Process due to Entrepreneurial Proficiency?', *Global Environmental Politics* 5:1, 1–23.

Young, A.R. and Wallace, H. (2000), 'The Single Market', in H. Wallace and W. Wallace (eds), *Policy-Making in the EU* (Oxford: Oxford University Press).

Chapter 8

The External Dimension of EU Competition Policy: Exporting Europe's Core Business?

Angela Wigger

The inclusion of competition policy in the founding Treaty of Rome in 1957 was pivotal for setting European economic integration in motion. Competition is the engine of market capitalism. It gives rise to a relationship of contention and rivalry between undertakings that strive for market supremacy and economic survival. Market players frequently try to evade the vicissitudes of the competitive process. Monopolisation, collusion and cartelisation in the form of fixing prices, prorating geographical markets and distribution channels are examples thereof. Traditionally, the proclivity of market players to abuse their market position brought competition policy into existence. Situated at the interface of both enabling and constraining private market power, within the setting of European integration, competition policy constituted a focal point for opening up national markets and providing market access for newcomers. It regulates the conditions of commercial agreements and determines the degree of market concentration.

Competition policy constitutes a unique field of EU power. There is no comparable first pillar policy in which the European Commission enjoys similar wide-ranging competences. Over time, these competences have expanded considerably and created an important source of EU standing power. From the mid-1980s onwards, with the accelerated pace of the creation of the Common Market and the advent of neoliberal ideas, competition policy achieved heightened importance. Together with the establishment of four freedoms of movement, competition policy was declared the backbone of economic growth, ensuring that the means of production and capital were allocated in the most efficient and profitable way. Strengthened by a boost in deeper integration, the Commission's DG Competition conquered additional decision-making powers, such as the right to vet transnational large-scale mergers, which considerably increased the EU's visibility to the outside world.

Competition policy reached political momentum when it achieved global agenda status. The Commission pushed hard for levelling the road towards formalising a binding multilateral agreement on competition within the institutional setting of the World Trade Organisation (WTO), which demonstrated once more that EU competition policy is not limited to Brussels and the subsequent governance levels below, but marked by an external dimension that exceeds the Union's geographical boundaries. As the result of fierce opposition from the US authorities and a number of developing countries, albeit for different reasons, the Commission's initiative suffered an embarrassing downfall at the Cancún Ministerial Meeting in 2003. At that time, WTO members abandoned the idea of a binding multilateral competition agreement.

This chapter explains why the EU proposal arrived at the WTO and who drove this process. It demonstrates that the impetus for the EU to become an important actor in 'crafting' a common understanding on competition principles is based on the interests of transnationally operating companies (TNCs) that seek to institutionalise free competition as a means of ensuring market access for goods, services and capital on a global scale. On the basis of the historical embedding of the Commission's subsequent struggles for expanding its competence into new areas of competition control, the next section introduces the conditions for structural scope that enabled the EU to become a vanguard in bringing cross-border competition control into the remit of the WTO. Going back in history illustrates that the Commission's role in advocating global competition rules bears witness to a fundamental shift in its field of activities. During the first three decades after the Treaty of Rome, competition policy had a strong intra-Community orientation. The expansionary drifts were 'timid' and focused primarily on safeguarding the status quo of its competences. Departing from the notion that 'thought is the point of access to an understanding of the continuing interaction of mind and material conditions in the making of history' (Cox and Schlechter 2002, 169), the subsequent section argues that the shift within competition policy from a solely intra-Community towards an extra-Community dimension parallels the shift in the prevalent ideological thinking. Well into the 1980s, competition policy formed part of a broader macroeconomic welfare vision inspired by ordoliberalism and exemplifying significant neo-mercantilist traits. With the enactment of the Single Market project, neoliberal thinking became the dominant organising concept of European integration more generally, and competition policy in particular.

With the subsequent expansion of the WTO's regulatory reach into ever-more 'trade and ... issues' in the 1990s, the Commission was given the opportunity to maximise the spectrum of the external negotiation mandate it enjoyed in trade affairs and to extrapolate its role in orchestrating the neoliberal free market ideology worldwide. Together with the progressive reduction of conventional barriers to trade, the conclusion of a multilateral competition agreement should further consolidate the logic of free markets on a global scale. The chapter proceeds by unravelling the conflicting positions of the EU and the US – the major regulatory protagonists in the formation of a common understanding on how to address cross-border competition questions. Structural intra-EU developments allowed the Commission to cohabit the realm of antitrust matters in duopoly with the US, which long used to be a hegemonic player in combating anticompetitive conduct on a global scale. This time, the EU, not the US, emerged as a proactive Western power in promoting multilateralism to regulate the global political economy. As a countermove, the US authorities introduced the International

Competition Network (ICN) – an informal and voluntary framework to deal with global competition questions. The chapter concludes that despite the fact that both the US and the EU share a common interest in the creation of global free markets, the transatlantic 'cohabitation' does not have the shape of an organic unity but rather a friendly rivalry.

EU Power in Competition Policy: From a Regional to a Global Policy

Going Back in History: The Origins of EU Competition Policy Revisited

It is generally assumed that vested US influence in post-war Europe has given shape to competition laws at EU level. Going back in the history of EU competition policy reveals that strong US influence can indeed be held responsible for competition laws becoming one of the core constitutional principles of the founding Treaty of Rome in 1957. Nevertheless, the institutional design for the enforcement mechanisms, as well as the competences attributed to the European Commission, eventually appeared very distinct from those of the US Federal antitrust agencies.

After the Second World War, West Germany was the first country to establish competition rules which can be ascribed to the heritage of the denazification and decartelisation programmes of the US Occupation Forces, which intended to restructure the West German economy and channel it towards market capitalism (Djelic and Kleiner 2003, 3). Cartels played a pivotal role in the rise of the Third Reich, in particular with regard to the production of military equipment. The imposition of competition laws aimed at dismantling their economic and political power. Yet, this seemed insufficient. Bearing in mind the experience of Nazi Germany, European governments were concerned by the rapid resurgence of German steel and coal industries' dominant position. The establishment of the European Coal and Steel Community (ECSC) in 1951 was intended to encapsulate the German economy in a framework of political control, and to safeguard free access to the key production sectors of coal and steel. On the verge of the Cold War and of a hostile political climate towards the imperatives of free market liberalism in Western Europe, the US government feared that the ECSC would evolve as a clever cover for 'a gigantic European cartel' for coal and steel producers (Dinan 1999, 22). With a stake in channelling the decision for market capitalism not only in Germany but all over Europe, competition laws were considered vital for guaranteeing US corporations free access to the European market. The same US antitrust specialists that had already helped Germany draft competition laws drew up the ECSC provisions that outlawed cartels and other discriminatory practices. Eventually, they served as a template for the subsequent Treaty of Rome as the rules for the coal and steel industries would also apply to other economic sectors. Consequently, EC competition laws came to look very similar to those of the US – at least on the surface. Nonetheless, the EC provisions on competition ended up being 'a much watered-down version' of those of the ECSC (Cini and McGowan 1998, 17). Initially, rules on transactions leading to a concentration, such as mergers and acquisitions, were excluded. For more than 30 years, European industry successfully lobbied against supranational merger control, which it saw as a legal constraint on the economic freedom to grow in size and power.

As one of the first truly supranational policy areas, controlled competition would become the primary structuring device for a rule-based capitalist market economy. The idea of 'free competition in an open market economy' was given a strong constitutional character in Article 2 which stated that the Community task was to ensure 'a high degree of competitiveness', and in Article 3 (TEC), which required a system 'ensuring that competition in the Internal Market is not distorted'. No secondary legislation or political intervention by the Member States should overrule the idea of competition. EC competition laws rest on three central pillars: cartel law, monopoly law and a law on state aid – stipulated in what became Articles 81, 82 and 86 to 89 (TEU) following the renumbering of the Treaty of Amsterdam (ToA). As a result of their constitutional framework characteristics, they were phrased in rather vague terms, including notions such as 'the intention to monopolise' or 'if trade between Member States is affected'. As further specifications were necessary, in 1962 the Community adopted the renowned Regulation 17 (now Regulation 1/2003), which for more than 40 years provided the procedural and interpretative framework for the application of Articles 81 and 82.

Because of its statuary provisions, the Commission can act as a supranational competition authority, which is investigator, prosecutor, judge, jury, and executioner in one. Entrusted with far-reaching executive powers, it can patrol the Common Market and investigate competition cases with a Community-dimension either its own initiative or following a third-party request. It can access all relevant documentation on the companies under investigation – both announced and unannounced, interrogate employees, and fine anticompetitive conduct with up to 10 per cent of the company's annual turnover. Moreover, under Regulation 17, it could issue so-called exemption regulations specifying entire categories of inter-company agreements that were not considered anticompetitive. Thereby, the Commission enjoys considerable leeway in setting the tone for the future direction of competition control and formulating its content without the Council or the European Parliament (EP) having a say. Compared to other first pillar areas where the Commission sets the agenda on what the Council and the EP will decide, in the field of competition policy it does not have to accommodate the other Community institutions. In addition, over time the EC competition regime has been enriched with an abundance of jurisprudence by the European Court of Justice (ECJ), and from 1989 onwards, the Court of First Instance, too.

The Single Market Project: New Competences for the Commission in Merger Control

With the adoption of the Single European Act (SEA) in 1986, the political goal of 'an ever-closer Union', which had already been incorporated in a preamble to the Treaty of Rome, received a new impetus. 'Rationalised production and stronger competition' were declared the Common Market's trump card (European

Commission 1982, 9; 1988, 14). In the spirit of the SEA and confident about the use of its own powers, the Commission articulated more ambitious policies – one example of which was the adoption of the EC Merger Regulation in 1989.

Attempts to supranationalise merger control date back to 1973, 1982, 1984, and 1986. However, due to the enduring opposition of industry and Member State governments, which fits into the overall landscape of the integration deadlock of the 1970s and early 1980s, none of the proposals proved successful. In 1988, Commissioner Peter Sutherland revised the 1973 proposal. In order to gain political support for a fully-fledged pan-European Merger Regulation, he used the Single Market project as a proxy: 'Those who favour the completion of the Internal Market must logically favour a Community-wide regime' (*Financial Times* 27 March 1985). Initially, the Member States remained reluctant to delegate more competences to the Commission in a policy area where it already enjoyed unparalleled powers. Industry feared that an EC-wide Merger Regulation would significantly curb their freedom to expand – most notably in a time when their US competitors sought ever-larger mergers in Europe (*Financial Times* 5 August 1987). The attempts to introduce the Merger Regulation in the 1980s evoked the picture of an EC moving in the opposite direction of US where, under President Reagan, competition law enforcement had moved towards a 'hands-off approach', especially with regard to mergers (Motta 2004, 8). There was also fierce resistance from the UK's Prime Minister Margaret Thatcher who promoted neoliberal free market philosophies, privatisation, and deregulation, rather than more public market intervention. As Council unanimity was required, each Member State could theoretically insist on its own amendments. Sutherland, however, 'warned' the Council that if it did not come up with an 'adequate agreement' by the autumn, the Commission would simply start to review mergers under existing competition law (*Financial Times* 5 August 1987).

The Commission demonstrated its seriousness by starting to investigate planned mergers, such as that between *BAT* and *Philip Morris*, whose appeal at the ECJ against this practice became an important landmark case. The ECJ ruled that Article 81 prohibiting cartels and other anti-competitive business practices could also be applied to 'agreements between two or more companies that allowed one of the companies to obtain legal or *de facto* control over the other'. Thereby, the Commission could use an existing competition law as a 'backdoor means' to control mergers (Pollack 1998, 233–4). When it applied Article 81 to a range of high-profile mergers, companies voluntarily began to notify their planned mergers to the Commission. In a climate of legal uncertainty for companies intending to merge, European business organisations began to see the potential rewards of a pan-European merger control and started to lobby the Member States to equip the Commission with autonomous powers in the field of merger control (Pollack 1998, 232).

As a result, the Commission acquired exclusive competence over deals involving companies with a combined worldwide turnover of €5 billion, or those with more than €250 million in sales each in Europe, unless individually they realised more than two-thirds of their European turnover in one and the same country. Mergers below these thresholds remained subject to the Member States.

The Commission's regulatory reach was not limited to companies operating in the Common Market – those generating their turnover elsewhere also became subject to the Commission's jurisdiction, which significantly strengthened the EU's authority and visibility worldwide.

The Consolidation and 'Globalisation' of the Internal Market Project

With the accomplishment of the Maastricht Treaty of 1991 and the immersion of the free movement of capital, goods, services and people, as well as prospects of a common currency, major institutional hurdles were overcome in the consolidation of economic integration. As a pivotal political actor in coordinating the Single Market endeavour, the salience of the Commission protruded alongside the increase in its workload. This was even more so the case with the fourth enlargement involving Austria, Finland and Sweden, as well as the creation of the European Economic Area which considerably expanded the geographical scope of the Common Market. Moreover, as a part of the larger geopolitical transformation that resulted from collapsing socialist regimes, the Commission's focus shifted to the Central and Eastern European Countries (CEECs).

Convergence of Competition Laws and Practices through Enlargement

The Commission was given the mission to guide the new aspirant Member States through the transition period of institutional restructuring towards market capitalism, and to institutionalise market freedoms and ownership rights. The establishment of competition regimes formed part of Interim Agreements with the CEECs in the early 1990s. Competition laws served as a key instrument for introducing the logic of open competition into economies, where previously large government-controlled monopolies and centralised price-fixing were the norm. The Commission helped the CEECs dismantle the state from economic activities through privatisation and de-monopolisation. It controlled 'progress' on the basis of regular compliance reports. In the 1997 enlargement package, the 'approximation of competition legislation and the implementation of competition laws' were made a precondition for accession – together with the entire *acquis communautaire* which the candidate countries had to incorporate into their legal systems (cf. Chapter 11). As a result, the enlargement on 1 May 2004 was a significant 'convergence' leap in the intra-EU situation of national competition regimes. The imposition of look-alike competition regimes was achieved through bilateral agreements – a Commission instrument that was also successful in other countries.

Convergence of Competition Laws and Practices through Bilateralism

The world of bilateralism in competition matters has long been reserved for industrialised states alone. During the 1990s, a number of competition authorities engaged in bilateral cooperation activities with their major trading partners in order to deal with the cross-border aspects of competition control. This resulted in a dense web of cooperative activities. Similarly to the US, the EU concluded bilateral agreements with other industrialised states, including the US, Canada, Japan, Israel, Brazil, Switzerland, and Australia. Meanwhile, the agreements negotiated by the EU outnumbered those by the US. The EU's span of competition agreements has taken in the Newly Independent States and Russia, the Baltic and the Mediterranean counties (namely Turkey, Tunisia, Morocco, Algeria, Jordan, the Palestinian Authority and Lebanon), as well as China, South Africa, and Latin and Central American countries (namely Chile, Mexico, including Mercosur and Caricom countries).

The agreements differed significantly in scope and content, and the purposes were far from compatible. Those concluded with the developed OECD (Organisation for Economic Cooperation and Development) world, where mature competition regimes are in place, were very detailed in nature, focusing on inter-agency coordination and cooperation activities for competition cases of mutual interest. In marked contrast, those concluded with economically less developed or transition countries with either no or weak competition regimes were formulated in less meticulous terms. They were shaped in the language of development aid, including notions such as 'technical assistance' in building up competition authorities, 'policy-learning' and 'competition advocacy', as well as 'the recommendation of best practices' (European Commission 1999, 20). Marked by a profound power imbalance, these agreements illustrate a mature donor agency giving a young, inexperienced recipient agency a hand in imposing institutional structures to control competition. Examples include the cases of the Mediterranean Association Agreements – also called the MED Agreements (cf. Szepesi 2004). Similar to the bilateral agreements with the CEECs, they provided the Commission with a window of opportunity to compel the signatories to impose competition rules that mirror those of the EU. Likewise, the implementation of competition legislation was supervised by the Commission's monitoring mechanisms.

In the case of Turkey, the EU made the establishment of competition laws compatible with the EU system a precondition for concluding the Customs Union in March 1995. Article 39 of the Decision of the Association Council No 1/95 reads: '… with a view to achieving the economic integration sought by the Customs Union, Turkey shall ensure that its legislation in the field of competition rules is made compatible with that of the European Community, and is applied effectively' (European Commission 1995). The subsequent provisions defining anticompetitive practices (Article 4) and the prohibition on the abuse of dominant position (Article 6), which were adopted on 7 December 1994, are almost identical to the EU's Article 81 and 82 (Devellennos 1998, 5). The rules on their implementation are equivalent to Regulation 17/62, and the Turkish merger control regime closely matches the EC Merger Regulation. Thus, the EU's bilateral trajectory in competition matters shows that it has become an important actor in 'crafting' a common understanding of competition principles abroad.

EU Competition Policy is Going Global

In the optimism of the late 1980s and early 1990s, the Commission set out on its most ambitious endeavour, namely, advocating a multilateral competition agreement in the WTO setting. It was at the Berlin Cartel Conference on 19 June 1990 that Competition Commissioner Sir Leon Brittan announced that 'the time was ripe to address international antitrust convergence' (Calvani 2004, 7). As convergence does not occur automatically, only two years later at the World Economic Forum in Switzerland Brittan put forward the WTO as the appropriate forum. His successors, Karel van Miert and Mario Monti further developed the idea and dedicated their office to establishing a WTO competition agreement. The initiative took shape at the Singapore Ministerial Meeting in 1996 when competition policy was declared one of the Singapore Issues – next to trade and investment, transparency in government procurement, and trade facilitation (cf. Chapter 2). With the subsequent proliferation of non-tariff-related issue linkages, so-called 'trade and ... issues' (such as TRIMS and TRIPS) an agreement on competition rules seemed within striking distance. The Working Group on the Interaction between Trade and Competition Policy was established and given the mandate to 'study issues raised by members relating to the interaction between trade and competition policy, including anti-competitive practices, in order to identify any areas that may merit further consideration in the WTO framework' (WTO 1996).

In the absence of a clear commitment to future negotiations after Singapore, the Commission pushed hard for the inclusion of competition policy in the WTO's regulatory realm. It argued that the WTO framework should not only focus on the elimination of the conventional tariff and non-tariff barriers to free trade imposed by governments, but also on private market barriers that hinder market access for foreign competitors (Monti 2002, 81). The WTO's Dispute Settlement Mechanism (DSM) – so the proposal – should address WTO members whose national competition authorities fail to cure harmful business conducts. As a result of far-reaching disagreements, the Working Group's report in 1998 lacked the necessary vigour to substantiate serious negotiations (WTO 1998). In order to avoid a stalemate, the Commission tempered its proposal considerably. Whereas it initially envisaged a detailed and binding competition agreement subject to the DSM, the emphasis shifted to concluding a voluntary WTO agreement on core principles that national competition authorities could adopt. At the subsequent Ministerial in Doha, Qatar, in November 2001, the competition agreement was declared a long-term objective, according to which negotiations on the Singapore Issues were postponed until the Cancún Summit in September 2003. Furthermore, officials from developing countries insisted that 'explicit' consensus was necessary for the launch of future negotiations. On the negotiating table were loosely defined core principles, including stipulations, such as transparency, procedural fairness, and non-discrimination, as well as provisions on hard-core cartels, modalities for voluntary cooperation, technical assistance and institutional capacity building to support competition regimes in developing countries (WTO 2003). At the Cancún Meeting there was fierce resistance of the US and a number of developing countries led by Brazil and India, albeit for different reasons, which brought the negotiations to a halt. With the adoption of the 'July 2004 Package', the Singapore Issues, and with it the idea of a binding multilateral competition agreement, were dropped from the WTO agenda for the time being.

The Opposition of the Developing World

The stance of the developing world represented a critical turning point at the preparations for the Punta Del Este Declaration launching the GATT (General Agreement on Tariffs and Trade) Uruguay Round in 1986, when they demanded a multilateral competition regime and when industrialised countries – among the EC – blocked the initiative (Carl 2001, 2). Whereas in the 1980s, developing countries saw an agreement on competition policy as a means to empower government institutions vis-à-vis TNCs, the Singapore project was perceived as a 'Trojan Horse' designed for TNCs by industrialised countries to access their markets (Lee and Morand 2003). In particular, the suggestion to include a principle of non-discrimination prohibiting nationality-based discrimination between corporations, and inspired by the most-favoured-nation treatment, evoked opposition. In fact, the Cancún draft text epitomised free access for industrial goods to new product markets, as well as unconditional access for TNCs to valuable natural resources, and henceforth, access to corporate expansion. Arguably, such access might extinguish competition by ousting smaller indigenous competitors from the market, thereby worsening the prospects for sustainable economic development – let alone the prospect of being able to compete in global markets. As the developed world blocked the same market access to developing countries in the field of agriculture, officials from net exporters in agricultural products, such as Brazil, were not ready to compromise and resolutely insisted on making market access compatible with the directions set in the Doha Declaration, which identifies agricultural trade distortions caused by the developed countries.

The Commission and its delegation to the Singapore Working Group tried to convince the opponents of the beneficial aspects of a WTO competition agreement, on the basis of a 'competition for economic development' discourse. Next to 'integrating developing countries into a rules-based world economy' and enhancing the capacity of domestic competition authorities to enforce competition rules against large (foreign) companies (Monti 2003), it would help to prevent consumers in developing economies falling victim of cartels, monopoly abuses and the creation of new monopolies through mergers (Anderson and Jenny 2005, 2). Underlying the project to establish a multilateral competition agreement, however, is a much broader political rationale, notably to foster market-capitalist regimes in countries with high entry barriers for foreign corporations, and so-called 'intrusive governments' interfering with the private market processes. As Monti (2003) argued, competition authorities would be strengthened 'with regard to other governmental institutions that might form a hostile attitude, such as industrial planning institutions'.

The Opposition of the US Authorities

Even though the US authorities welcome the idea of greater consistency among competition laws and enforcement practices, their resistance to a treaty-based solution in competition matters remains constant. The long-standing hegemonic approach of applying its competition laws on an extraterritorial basis did not create a straightforward necessity to accommodate other competition authorities. The idea that global competition laws should be defined in Washington, and in Washington alone, is widespread among US antitrust hawks, especially as the US competition regime was for a long time 'the only show in town' (Jenny 1998, 7). As Joel Klein, US Assistant Attorney General for Antitrust, put it: 'If you want a perfect solution, there is only one perfect solution … and that is to let the United States Department of Justice do global enforcement! … (I)t would be terribly efficient' (Klein 2002, 338). Following Robert Pitofsky, Chairman of the Federal Trade Commission in the US, the answer to multilateral initiatives seems quite definitive: '… convergence by law is an aspiration … it is just not going to happen' (Pitofsky 2002, 58).

   Much of the US reluctance towards a global competition regime temporarily waned under the Clinton Administration, which explains why competition policy could reach WTO agenda status in Singapore and Doha. However, when the negotiations started, US officials under the Bush Administration were far from enthusiastic about making the WTO the principal coordinating body of cross-border competition issues. The US delegations watered down the whole idea of establishing detailed competition rules that would be subject to the DSM. Alternatively, establishing a minimum set of core principles was considered as legitimising fallible and ineffective competition rules (Hwang 2004, 123). The US authorities did not want to come to terms with 132 WTO members, the overwhelming majority of which were developing countries with different socio-economic interests. Convinced they had in place the most advanced competition regime, they were not ready to compromise and impose an international body that could rule against decisions by the US competition authorities.

Shifting Objectives of EU Competition Policy: From Ordoliberalism to Neoliberalism

The Ordoliberal Imprint on EC Competition Policy

During the formative phase of the European competition regime, most notably the early institution-building process, and the subsequent development of procedural principles and enforcement practices, the ideas and theoretical concepts of the Ordoliberal School of the Freiburg University in Germany were influential (Gerber 1998, 8). The core of *Ordnungspolitik* entailed that capitalism should be organised according to an economic constitution which, like a political constitution, protects citizens from the abuse of economic power. The dynamics of competition were considered the centrepiece for economic welfare and democracy. Building on the premise that markets are not self-regulatory, or guided by Adam Smith's (1776) 'invisible hand', the ordoliberal intelligentsia foresaw a strong role for the state in guaranteeing a continuously 'policed competition order' (Budzinski 2003, 15). The interventionist arm of the state should take the form of an independent, proactive and strong, quasi-judicial competition authority, free from partisan influence. This authority should seek to establish a balanced market structure in which more or less equally matched market players are safeguarded from the anarchy of unconstrained market forces. In order to guarantee free and fair competition, it should prosecute abusive market behaviour and excessive market concentration, such as monopolies and oligopolies – the epitome of private market power. Thus, as a part of a long-term macroeconomic orientation, competition control should serve a broader, multi-goal purpose.

Ordoliberals played a significant role in assisting the US Occupation Force in restructuring Germany's oligopolistic and cartel-dense post-war economy. Their political colour and predisposition towards a free market economy perfectly matched with the US' outspoken liberal goals. Only a few years later, the lack of experience regarding competition laws among the founding EC members provided ordoliberals with a window of opportunity to bring their visions on the constitutional outlook of European integration to the fore. Outspoken ordoliberals, such as Hans von der Gröben, the first Competition Commissioner, developed the regulatory procedures for implementing EC competition laws. Even though ordoliberal influence on economic regulatory policies have waned since the 1960s, its maxims had a remarkable stronghold in the Commission's competition division until the mid-1980s.

The ordoliberal legacy of embedding competition laws into a broader socio-political view (cf. Chapter 2 on 'embedded liberalism') explains their strong constitutional character within the EU, and concomitantly, the important role of the Commission. The 'system ensuring that competition in the Common Market is not distorted', as outlined in Article 3, should help to create a 'harmonious, balanced and sustainable development of economic activities' and 'a high level of employment and of social protection' (Article 2).

Competition Law Enforcement in the 1960s and 1970s: Ordoliberalism and Neo-mercantilism

During the first three decades, EC competition law enforcement had a strong intra-Community orientation, and served the purpose of breaking up national market barriers in order to provide market access for newcomers from other Member States. During much of the 1960s and 1970s, the ordoliberal notion of an ideal-typical market structure manifested itself in streamlining competition policy with the active pursuit of industrial policy and the special privileges given to small and medium-sized enterprises. As the 'common market' was still rather fragmented and limited in terms of economies of scale, cross-border inter-company cooperation was considered beneficial to economic integration and even actively stimulated by the Commission (Gröben 1966). The pro-industrial cooperation stance in the 1960s led to enduring corporate alliances with the government-sponsored Concorde and Airbus as illustrative examples (Dinan 1999, 392).

The underlying political rationale was to create so-called Eurochampions, which should be able to defy what J.J. Servan-Schreiber (1967) termed *Le défi américain* (the American challenge) – the invasion of US capital that subcontracted parts of the European industry to larger US subsidiaries. Although the overarching purpose of competition policy was still 'the creation and proper operation of the Common Market' (European Commission 1980, 9), competition law enforcement was not reversed against European companies confronted with fierce US competition. The goal of 'ensuring a high degree of competitiveness' was specified by the Commission in the terms of enhancing the competitiveness of EC firms on both world and domestic markets (European Commission 1987). It temporarily tolerated so-called 'structural crisis cartels' in order to maintain the competitiveness of European industries against the presumed technological challenge from across the Atlantic and increasingly from Japan, too. It allowed industries in despair to deal with chronic excess production capacities, decreases in demand, and to maintain prices that did not cover production costs (European Commission 1981, 13). Rather than competing each other to 'death', declining industries, such as steel, shipbuilding, chemistry, textiles, sugar, as well as car manufacturing, gratefully took advantage of this option.

In addition, the Commission exempted countless other types of commercial inter-company agreements by referring to their propensity to 'promote technological or economic progress' (that is a legal condition justifying exemption). It also adopted a passive attitude towards Member State practices, such as subsidised loans, state aid, tax concessions, guaranteed procurement, financial guarantees and exports assistance, and other measures aimed at rescuing what have come to be known as 'sunset industries'. Overall, the Commission's rather lenient stance denoted a neo-mercantilist approach aimed at fencing off indigenous companies from harsh competition from abroad. Across the Atlantic, this approach gave raise to the famous adage: 'We protect competition, you protect competitors' (Fox 2003).

Competition Law Enforcement in the 1980s: Towards a Neoliberal Shift

With the advent of neoliberal ideas in Europe in the 1980s, echoing the Reagan Revolution or Thatcherism in the UK, old-style ordoliberal-inspired competition policy, selective public market intervention and industrial policy waned increasingly at the expense of deregulation, privatisation and less state intervention. The Internal Market was considered nowhere near as open as that of the US, and thus regarded as a severe handicap for prospering economic development. With SEA, market integration was put back on track and competition policy declared paramount to breaking down intra-European market barriers inhibiting the completion of the Internal Market. Competition policy was tuned in terms of a staunch neoliberal tenet framed in terms of a 'competition for competitiveness strategy', according to which fierce inter-company competition was presumed to lead to improved market performance (European Commission 1982, 9).

The process of market liberalisation in the EC would not take shape in isolation, but would be fortified by energetically committing 'the rest of the world' to a free market environment. The Commission evolved as a powerful pro-market-orientated force in the promotion of liberalisation. It extrapolated the spirit of eliminating the barriers to intra-Community trade to the GATT Ministerial Meeting in 1982, and the launching of a new round of multilateral trade negotiations in Punta Del Este in Uruguay in 1986. The new trade round would halt protective behaviour by national governments and proclaim a progressive removal of tariff and non-tariff barriers to trade – with the exception of agriculture – the issue that brought the negotiations to the verge of collapsing after almost eight years of difficult negotiations.

The subsequent abolition of government-imposed barriers to free trade boosted a spirit in which the removal of the remaining barriers seemed tangible, including barriers to competition. The finalisation of the Uruguay Round and the context of the larger geopolitical transformations caused by the breakdown of the Soviet Regime in the early 1990s fostered the belief in neoliberal economic principles – a historical turning point that even academic pundits like Francis Fukuyama (1992, xiii) came to celebrate as the 'end point of mankind's ideological evolution'. Thus, the subsequent subordination of EC competition policy to neoliberal ideas became constitutive to the spread of neoliberal ideas elsewhere in the world. The next section explains the driving motives of the interest coalition behind this project.

The shift from an ordoliberal, neo-mercantilist towards a neoliberal competition enforcement philosophy closely ties in with the shift from an intra-EU- towards an extra-EU-orientated competition focus. Both shifts are inherently interlocked and can be explained on the basis of the structural changes induced by the progressive market integration, and the dominant interests of TNCs seeking an ever-wider level playing field.

Structural changes in the political economy of the EU   The progressive reduction of trade barriers and the fundamental structural reconfiguration of several national markets into one giant Common Market made it easier for companies to compete on a global scale. The sweeping liberalisation and privatisation process significantly increased the range of companies available in the European takeover market or, 'the market for corporate control' – an expression that refers to the phenomenon of companies bought and sold on a market as if they were commodities (cf. Apeldoorn and Horn 2007). Changes in corporate governance regulations and the increased presence of foreign investors significantly facilitated a greater shareholder and capital market orientation in Europe (Höpner and Jackson 2001). With the decision on the euro, which eliminated exchange-rate fluctuations, the transaction costs of cross-border business deals have been significantly reduced. Alongside with the progress of communication technology, improved and cheaper transport opportunities, the level of cross-border trade and market interdependence arrived at an unprecedented scale.

Together, this resulted in an accelerated pace of cross-border merger activity, acquisitions, and other forms of market concentration in the 1990s. Enhanced competitive pressures forced many industries to pool their production activities to achieve synergy effects, such as economies of scale and scope. Intensified merger activity often prompts a self-perpetuating mechanism: the greater the concentration of economic power, the more onerous it becomes for smaller competitors to keep up, and the more further concentrations are the only viable solution for economic survival. Jumping on the merger bandwagon became a necessity for many industries in order to avoid so-called 'fire sales' (that is, cheap acquisitions of companies in dire straights).

With the consolidation of the Internal Market, ever-more companies from the US tried to gain a foothold through mergers and acquisitions. In 1994, more than a third of all mergers in the EU involved a company from across the Atlantic (Martinez Torre-Enciso and Bilbao Garcia 1996, 7). Most of the assets acquired by US companies were concentrated in the UK. In fact, FDI flows from the US into the UK equalled that invested in Asian, Latin American, and Middle Eastern countries combined (ibid). In 1999, for the first time in history, the number of concentrations in the EU exceeded that in the US, which shows that large-scale M&As were no longer confined to the US market, but had become a fact of economic life in Europe.

The influence of the transnational business community   The structural changes in the political economy of the EU are the reason why industry eventually actively supported the introduction of the pan-European Merger Regulation after many years of staunch opposition. With the revitalisation of the economic integration project, the resulting cross-border concentration activity evoked so-called 'negative externalities' in the form of multiple merger reviews by different Member State jurisdictions. In the absence of a harmonised EU-wide merger regime, the phenomenon of 'multi-jurisdictional overlap' was not only time consuming, but also produced high costs. As each jurisdiction handled different notification procedures, timetables, fees and information requests, the risk of inconsistent rulings became prominent, as did the judicial conflicts between the companies involved and the respective competition authorities. Business representatives successfully lobbied for the inclusion of a 'one-stop-shop'-principle into the Merger Regulation, which entailed that companies meeting a certain turnover threshold only had to notify cross-border transactions to the Commission, rather than to five or six different EC competition authorities.

In addition, a fairly tight timetable committing the Commission to a fast review procedure provided corporations with the wished-for legal certainty and the creation of 'a level playing field' – an expression that entered Eurojargon in the late 1980s to denote enhanced neoliberal free-market thinking and reduced transaction costs for transnationally operating businesses. Finally, when Competition Commissioner Peter Sutherland assured European business organisations 'We're not taking the line that bringing the big together is bad' (*Financial Times* 27 March 1985), transnationally operating business eventually assured its support for a supranational merger regime at the EU level.

Similar to the quest to create a level playing field within the Common Market, transnational business interests constituted the driving force behind the idea of more consistency in the application of competition laws globally. At first sight, business interests lobbying for a global competition regime may sound counter-intuitive, as one would assume that they prefer free havens of public market intervention in which they can fully exploit a dominant position. Yet, as the option of abandoning competition rules on a worldwide scale was not feasible, competition regimes should, at the very least, not inhibit competition nor impose negative policy externalities, nor discriminate between domestic and foreign corporate interests.

The problem of the negative externalities of cross-border business transactions gained heightened prominence during the 1990s. One example was the planned merger of MCI WorldCom and Sprint, which was notified to 37 different jurisdictions before the two companies finally abandoned the deal in 2000 (Bannerman 2002, 55–6). The transnational business community repeatedly complained about high transaction costs, legal uncertainty and complexity when having to comply with 15 to 30 different merger regimes. The risk of jurisdictional conflicts was exacerbated, particularly with the vast proliferation of competition regimes around the globe which have more than doubled in the past ten years. Of the 100 competition regimes worldwide, 80 established some form of merger control. Many developing countries set up competition regimes. In particular, South American countries even went as far as incorporating agreements on competition into their regional cooperation organisations of the Mercosur, the Andean Community, and Caricom (cf. Lee and Morand 2003).

The choir of transnational corporate interests that lobbied in favour of global competition rules comprised the Transatlantic Business Dialogue (TABD), the European Round Table of Industrialists (ERT), the Union of Industrial and Employers' Confederation of Europe (UNICE), and AmCham, the EU Committee of American Chambers of Commerce. With the bulk of the cross-border merger activity in Europe having a significantly transatlantic dimension, large US corporations sought ever-stronger representation of their interests at the EU institutions. It has even been argued that AmCham became the most effective lobbying organisation in Brussels (Wilks and McGowan 1996, 242). It solidified its influence by providing a major source of inspiration for European corporate lobby groups such as UNICE and ERT.

The priority agenda point was the harmonisation of the different national procedures in the clearance of mergers and acquisitions. Transnational business deliberately kept other potential issues dealing with competition off the agenda, such as the prosecution of cartel activities and restrictive business practices. Moreover, the elite business networks TABD and ERT, comprising leading business representatives at the top-executive level, attached great importance to the fact that a multilateral agreement on competition policy should be 'able to address structural impediments to market access which foreign investors might come across' (ERT 1996; TABD 1996). As these high-level business organisations enjoyed an exceptionally privileged relationship with the Commission, they could exert significant political power in the political agenda setting. Free market access to new product and labour markets geographically, as well as natural resources, is essential for the long-term survival of TNCs. The desire for corporate expansion, and henceforth, capital accumulation, lies at the heart of companies striving for a competitive market position and eventually market dominance.

The role of the European Commission   Rather than problematise concentrated economic power, the Commission adopted a rather lenient stance towards companies' expansionary interests. Between 1990 and 2004, it gave a decision in more than 2,000 merger cases, of which 95 per cent were directly approved, 5 per cent were further investigated, and only 1 per cent was blocked (Resch 2005, 19). Consequently, many CEOs in large transnational corporations came to prefer a Commission ruling to that of other competition authorities. Company lawyers even presented so-called borderline mergers in a way that the deal would pass the required turnover threshold that effects a Commission ruling (*Financial Times* 15 June 1993). The Commission's overall permissive stance is one reason why representatives of the transnational business elite – seeking a level playing field that encompasses the whole globe – encouraged the Commission to conclude a multilateral competition agreement within the WTO.

The origins of the TABD can be traced back to a joint initiative of the US Commerce Department and the Commission, from which the former Competition Commissioner Sir Leon Brittan emerged as a crucial and powerful political force (cf. Green-Cowles 2001). The institutionalised access of the TABD to EU and US decision-makers provided it with an exclusive channel to promote detailed policy recommendations and to influence the WTO agenda. As a quasi-policy-making organisation bringing together CEOs from both sides of the Atlantic, the TABD urged the EU and the US to make joint efforts in establishing WTO competition rules that give priority to free market access. Rather than prohibitions on the abuse of monopolistic positions, the TABD sought 'unimpaired market access on a worldwide scale for foreign goods, services, ideas, investments and business people' (TABD 1995, Sections II.13 and II.14).

This time it was not the founding fathers of the Bretton Woods institutions who took the lead in configuring the free-market system, but an EU institution. The Commission evolved as the major protagonist in advocating a global competition regime. Its proactivity constitutes an attempt to consolidate the idea of global free markets, the liberalisation of trade, and worldwide economic integration. As a net industrial exporter, the EU depends strongly on unhindered access for its companies which are seeking ever-larger and ever-more open product, labour and investment markets. Protectionist behaviour elsewhere negatively affects export-oriented TNCs. From this point of view, economic freedom within the Internal Market implies *a fortiori* economic freedom at world level. The next section illustrates why the US authorities – in spite of their similar interests – resigned as active proponents of international economic institutions – at least in the domain of global competition rules.

The Future Role of the EU: Towards a Duopoly with the United States

Challenging US Hegemony

The deeply engrained US distrust as regards the competition cultures practised elsewhere also includes the OECD countries which, in the past, tended to apply competition laws as part of a broader neo-mercantilist project. Against the backdrop of looming trade wars on bananas, beef, and biotechnological products which overshadowed the transatlantic trade relation in the 1990s, disputes in merger cases between the US and EU authorities seemed likely. Commissioner Brittan declared in a speech that the transatlantic relationship was doomed: 'With the best will in the world ... the US and the Community may well one day soon take different views of a competition case. ... The problem cases may be rare now, but they will increase in number and complexity' (Blumenthal 2005, 1) When the EU started to control mergers between non-EU companies outside its territorial boundaries, this prospect became even more likely. Although the EU's level of extraterritoriality in competition matters long remained relatively harmless compared to that of the US, the number has steadily increased since the 1990s. An example is the planned takeover of the US computer manufacturer AST Research Incorporated in 1998 by the South Korean electronics manufacturer Samsung. The companies failed to notify to the Commission in advance and, for the first time, it imposed a fine on an extraterritorial case (*European Voice* 19 February 1998). The sanctioning was an act of power demonstration not only to the corporate world, but also to the US competition authorities. Against the background of the longstanding US economic and political hegemony, it signalled that the Commission carries comparable global weight in the area of competition law enforcement, in particular in the area of merger control, which no longer could be ignored by the US authorities. As Competition Commissioner Monti once joked in one of his speeches 'today Henry Kissinger would know who to phone if you want to speak to Europe about competition policy' (Monti 2004).

The EU was not only successful in exporting its competition regime to the new Member States in Central and Eastern Europe and other nearby European countries, but also to some extent in South American countries. When building up competition regimes, Argentina, Brazil, Chile, Colombia, and Venezuela combined aspects of both US and EU competition law (Slaughter 2004, 175), which indicates that the US authorities were losing ground to the EU in countries within their traditional sphere of influence.

Towards a Friendly Rivalry: Transatlantic Cooperation and Convergence

As tensions were becoming raised, the Commission formalised a range of bilateral cooperation agreements with the US government which have evolved into an intensive working relationship over the past decade. Cooperation encompasses the whole spectrum of competition control, but is most advanced in the field of mergers. The bilateral trajectory of the EU and the US received considerable intellectual support from the private business sector, most notably from TNCs represented at the TABD. The genuine promptness by public actors to take seriously regulatory recommendations by high-level industry representatives resulted in an agreement on 'positive comity'. The signatories decided mutually to notify competition cases and to keep the other party informed about the proceedings, as well as only to act unilaterally when all other means provided by comity had been exhausted. In other words, the purpose of bilateral cooperation was to prevent regulatory conflicts that emerge with the extraterritorial application of competition law.

In practice, the competition authorities participate in each other's staff meetings and final hearings during the investigation phase, provided that the companies give their permission – which they usually do as a smooth review procedure eliminates the risk of negative externalities in the form of a multi-jurisdictional overlap.

The broader context of transformed transatlantic power (in)balance explains why transatlantic cooperation in competition matters evolved into the intensive working relationship we witness today. Cooperation goes largely unnoticed by the wider public, with the exception of major disputes, such as the Boeing-McDonnell-Douglas and the GE-Honeywell mergers which almost caused a trade war. The Commission's initial ban on the deals, which had been granted permission by the US authorities, reinforced the conviction among US officials to block a WTO agreement on competition.

The Post-Cancún Agenda: The Convergence Discourse

Following the downfall of the EU's multilateral competition project, the alternative route came to be labelled with the catchword 'convergence'. EU and US competition officials alike were captivated by the convergence discourse, which led to the establishment of the ICN in 2001. Other global fora addressing questions of convergence in competition matters include the OECD and the UNCTAD, which are generally referred to as supporting institutions. US officials launched the ICN as an alternative to the Commission's WTO endeavour. Informal and non-binding in nature, it came to encompass almost all national and regional competition authorities worldwide. By identifying 'best practices', it aims to produce recommendations and promote a worldwide competition 'policy-learning' (see more: www.internationalcompetitionnetwork.org). As those sitting in the driver's seat determine the course to be followed, the ICN offers a perfect means for the diffusion of norms, and eventually a way to coerce competition authorities to move towards a certain reference point. The voluntary and non-binding character of ICN's network structure is no surprise given the high commitment by the US. It seems to remedy the US's 'tie anxiety' to a more constraining global rule system for competition questions.

Conclusions

During the 1990s, the Commission, and hence the EU, attempted to establish a binding multilateral regime on competition within the WTO framework. After the successful orchestration of the Single Market project and the subsequent increase in the Commission's competition competences, it concentrated its efforts on smoothing the path of market integration on a worldwide scale. Thereby, first and foremost it responded to the requests of a transnational business community that sought to increase its level playing field in the global realm. With the enhanced prominence of 'business going global', the opening of national markets, and the liberalisation of trade and financial services forging ahead, in particular the right to compete on a 'non-discriminatory' basis, came high up the WTO agenda. Thus, the principal rationale behind introducing the initiative for a multilateral competition agreement was given by transnational companies seeking to enter new product and cheap labour markets, to take over domestic players, and to further consolidate their position on the world market.

The effort to reach a WTO agreement on global competition rules was not successful because of fierce resistance from the US and a number of developing countries. US competition officials displayed a deeply ingrained mistrust on how competition control is enforced elsewhere. After their long-standing hegemonic position, US competition officials were not willing to compromise with different visions on what accounts for 'appropriate' competition control. Instead, they declared the ICN's voluntary framework as the only viable strategy left to reach convergence of competition laws and practices – alongside the conclusion of bilateral competition agreements. The ICN provides a platform for the two major protagonists, the EU and the US, to formulate in duopoly the parameters of a common understanding on how cross-border competition questions should be addressed. Thereby, regulatory convergence in competition matters is not an automatic process driven by anonymous market forces, but a political project of competition authorities. They set the parameters for an open and free global competition culture which is to the benefit of unconstrained market access for transnationally operating companies.

References

Anderson, R. and Jenny, F. (2005), 'Competition Policy, Economic Development and the Role of a Possible Multilateral Framework on Competition Policy: Insights from the WTO Working Group on Trade and Competition Policy', in E. Medalla (ed.), *Competition Policy in East Asia* (London: Routledge).

Apeldoorn, B. van and Horn, L. (2007), 'The Transformation of Corporate Governance Regulation in the EU: From Harmonization to Marketization', in H. Overbeek, B. van Apeldoorn and A. Nölke (eds), *The Transnational Politics of Corporate Governance Regulation* (London and New York: Routledge).

Bannerman, E. (2002), *The Future of EU Competition Policy* (London: Centre for European Reform).

Blumenthal, W. (2005), 'The Status Of Convergence On Transatlantic Merger Policy. Remarks Before the ABA Section of International Law', paper for Program on 'Cross-Atlantic Perspectives on Antitrust Enforcement', Brussels, 27 October.

Budzinski, O. (2003), 'Pluralism of Competition Policy Paradigms and the Call for Regulatory Diversity', *Volkswirtschaftliche Beiträge Universität Marburg* 14, 1–51.

Calvani, T. (2004), 'Conflict, Cooperation & Convergence in International Competition', *Antitrust Law Journal* 72:3, 1127–46.

Carl, M.P. (2001), 'Towards Basic Rules on Trade Related Competition Policy', speech, DG Trade, 2 March.

Cini, M. and McGowan, F. (1998), *Competition Policy in the EU* (New York: St Martins Press).

Cox, R.W. and Schlechter, M.G. (2002), *The Political Economy of a Plural World: Critical Reflections on Power, Morals and Civilization* (London: Routledge).

Devellennos, Y. (1998), 'An European View on the Implementation of the Competition Policy in the Republic of Turkey', paper for Turkish Competition Board Conference, Ankara, 5 March.

Dinan, D. (1999), *Ever Closer Union* (London: Lynne Rienner Publishers).

Djelic, M.L. and Kleiner, T. (2003), 'The ICN – Illustrating the Evolution of Transnational Governance', paper presented at the Workshop *The Multiplicity of Regulatory Actors in the Transnational Space*, Uppsala University, 23–24 May.

ERT (1996), 'Investment in the Developing World: New Openings and Challenges for European Industry', Brussels: ERT.

European Commission (1980/1981/1982/1987/1988), Various Annual Reports on Competition Policy.

—— (1995), 'Decision No. 1/95 of the EC-Turkey Association Council on Implementing the Final Phase of the Customs Union (96/142/EC)'.

—— (1999), 'The EU Approach to the Millennium Round', COM(1999)331.

Fox, E.M. (2003), 'We Protect Competition, You Protect Competitors', *World Competition* 26:2, 149–65.

Fukuyama, F. (1992), *The End of History and the Last Man* (London: Hamish Hamilton).

Gerber, D.J. (1998), *Law and Competition in Twentieth Century Europe: Protecting Prometheus* (Oxford: Oxford University Press).

Green-Cowles, M. (2001), 'The Transatlantic Business Dialogue: Transforming the New Transatlantic Dialogue', in M.A. Pollack and G.C. Shaffer (eds), *Transatlantic Governance in a Global Economy* (Lanham, MD: Rowman and Littlefield).

Gröben, von der H. (1966), 'Aufgaben und Ergebnisse der deutschen Europa-Politik', Vortrag auf einer gemeinsamen Veranstaltung der Europa-Union Deutschlands der Handwerkskammer Köln und der Industrie- und Handelskammer zu Köln, 6 June, Brussels: Historical Archives of the European Commission.

Höpner, M. and Jackson, G. (2001), 'An Emerging Market for Corporate Control? The Mannesmann Takeover and German Corporate Governance', *MPIfG Discussion Paper* 1:4.

Hwang, L. (2004), 'Influencing A Global Agenda: Implications of the Modernization of the European Competition Law for the WTO', *Erasmus Law and Economics Review* 1:22, 111–41.

Jenny, A. (1998), 'Proposed Answers to Professor Jenny's Questions', paper for Antitrust and Trade Policy – Round Table, Fordham Corporate Law Institute, New York, 22–23 October.

Klein, J. (2002), 'Expanding Our Web of Bilateral Agreements', in C.A. Jones and M. Matsushita (eds), *Competition in the Global Trading System* (The Hague: Kluwer Law International).

Lee, M. and Morand, C. (2003), 'Competition Policy in the WTO and FTAA: A Trojan Horse for International Trade Negotiations?', <http://www.policyalternatives.ca/publications/competition-policy.pdf>, accessed 25 February 2004.

Martinez Torre-Enciso, I. and Bilbao Garcia, J. (1996), 'Mergers and Acquisition Trends in Europe', *International Advances in Economic Research* 2:3, 279–86.

Monti, M. (2002), 'Cooperation Between Competition Authorities: A Vision for the Future', in C. Jones and M. Matsushita (eds), *Competition Policy in the Global Trading System* (The Hague: Kluwer Law International).

—— (2003), 'Introductory Remarks for the ICN Capacity Building and Competition Policy Implementation Working GrOxford University Press', Speech 03/323, paper for Second ICN Annual Conference, Merida, Mexico, 23–25 June.

—— (2004), 'Convergence in EU-US Antitrust Policy Regarding Mergers and Acquisitions: An EU Perspective', Speech 04/107, Los Angeles, 28 February.

Motta, M. (2004), *Competition Policy: Theory and Practice* (Cambridge: Cambridge University Press).

Pitofsky, R. (2002), 'Antitrust Cooperation, Global Trade, and US Competition Policy', in C.A. Jones and M. Matsushita (eds), *Competition Policy in the Global Trading System* (The Hague: Kluwer Law International).

Pollack, M. A. (1998), 'The Engines of Integration? Supranational Autonomy and Influence in the EU', in W. Sandholtz and A. Stone Sweet (eds), *European Integration and Supranational Governance* (Oxford: Oxford University Press).

Resch, A. (2005), 'Phases of Competition Policy in Europe', *Paper of the Institute of European Studies* (050401).

Slaughter, A.M. (2004), *New World Order* (Princeton, NJ: Princeton University Press).

Szepesi, S. (2004), 'Comparing EU Free Trade Agreements. Competition Policy and State Aid', *In Brief. European Centre For Development Policy Management* 6:E.

TABD (1996), 'The Chicago Declaration', 9 November, <http://static.tabd.com/manila Gems/1996ChicagoCEOReport.pdf>, accessed 14 March 2007.

Wilks, S. and McGowan, F. (1996), 'Competition Policy in the EU: Creating a Federal Agency?', in G.B. Doern and S. Wilks (eds), *Comparative Competition Policy* (Oxford: Oxford University Press).

WTO (1996), 'The Singapore Ministerial Declaration', WT/MIN(96)/DEC, 13 December.

—— (1998), 'Annual Report of the Working GrOxford University Press on the Interaction between Trade and Competition Policy to the General Council', WT/WGTCP/2, 8 December.

—— (2003), 'Report of the Working GrOxford University Press on the Interaction between Trade and Competition Policy to the General Council', WT/WGTCP/7, 17 July.

Chapter 9

EU External Energy Policies: A Paradox of Integration

Andrei V. Belyi

The energy sector represents one of the most paradoxical areas of the European Union (EU). On the one hand, energy had been the main cause of European integration: indeed, the first two European Communities covered coal and nuclear energy policies. On the other hand, neither the energy security policy nor the energy market regulation have ever become the subject of the supranational policy. The trend is confirmed by the European Commission's recently published Green Paper on energy security which also outlines the need for a Community energy policy at both internal and external levels (Bahgad 2006). Nevertheless, the active involvement of the supranational authorities in the energy security does not reallocate this strategic sphere away from national competences.

The complexity of EU external energy policy stems from the complex and hybrid nature of European integration, which can be defined by three different dimensions (Caporaso 1996). First, the EU is defined in realist terms, where states form a geopolitical union, but keep political control over crucial security issues (for example, nuclear weapons, representation at the Security Council). Second, the EU is seen as a functionalist economic integration, which implies a single European market and a subsequent economic block at the international level. Third, the EU is a post-modern empire which exerts a new kind of influence over the external world by exporting its integration model, its support towards free market values, and liberal democracy.

Therefore, its external policy can be defined as a combination of an international organisation and international actor. We can observe that external energy security as well as energy market regulation is still dominated by the intergovernmental logic of an international organisation, whereas the discourse of the European Commission attempts to represent the economic union as a very coherent entity. This creates a problematic relationship between the EU and other international economic organisations in terms of coherence between the external legitimacy of the organisations and the internal non-implementation of their provisions. This duality leads to the special position which the EU reserved for itself within the Energy Charter process and its transit provisions. Likewise, the EU avoided applying the WTO principles on quantitative restrictions and subsidies for the energy sector.

The present chapter considers the complexity of the EU's actorness in international relations in energy policy. Indeed, the complex nature of the Union's external energy policy stems from the three dimensions of European integration. In order to analyse the complexity of EU external energy policy, the chapter is divided into two parts. The first part examines the internal dimension of EU energy policy, simultaneously focusing on the European goals in energy policy as well as the extent of EU integration in this area. Here, an uneven pattern of integration emerges: whereas the geopolitical objective to guarantee supply has typically been dominated by EU Member States, the European Community plays a more powerful (yet still restricted) role in the liberalisation of the European energy markets.[1]

The second part looks at the consequences of the EU's incomplete integration for the realisation of its energy goals on the international scene. First, it analyses the EU's value-related conception of economic cooperation with third countries. Secondly, it involves an analysis of the EU influence on the Southern Mediterranean and South Eastern European region. Thirdly, the EU's position in both the WTO and ECT is examined – with a particular focus on the relationship with Russia.

EU Power and Goals in Energy: Uneven Patterns of Integration

The first part overviews the goals and powers of the EU in defining energy security policy. It is mainly defined by intergovernmental cooperation, where Member States keep control over the most important security agendas. However, this chapter also notes increasing involvement at the supranational level – with the development of the internal market for gas and electricity, the European Community is taking greater responsibility in energy policy.

Security of Supply: Member States in the Driving Seat

The foundations of EU energy policy are located directly in its very integration process, which the creation of the European Community for Steel and Coal (ECSC). It takes its roots from the European Coal Organisation (ECO) of 1947, an ad hoc intergovernmental institution dealing with the dissemination of information on the production and supply of coal among the Member States. Created a few years later, in 1952, the ECSC regrouped only a few members of the ECO with some supranational powers allocated to the High Authority. The ECSC remained a purely European organisation, regrouping both producing and consumer countries. Therefore, it never became an internationally acting organisation until the expiry of the Treaty in 2002.

European joint support for civil nuclear energy was synchronous with the European Economic Community. Indeed, in 1957, both Treaties were signed by

---

1   The third and increasingly important objective in international energy politics, namely sustainable development, is analysed in Chapter 7 of this book.

the same initial Member States. The idea of nuclear energy being a substitute for oil in electricity generation was born after the Suez crisis in 1956 – the Canal had long served as a way of transporting oil. Nuclear energy appeared to be a strategic instrument for the security of supply. The strategic importance of the Euratom Treaty diminished later when, because of its capital-intensive construction costs, and the nuclear accident in Chernobyl, nuclear energy lost its primary political support.

The events of 1973–74 and 1979–80 associated with the crisis in the oil sector helped Europeans to understand the level of dependency on oil imports. Subsequently, after the crisis the oil sector came to be considered as one of the most strategic political areas. The scale of its economic and political implications was much greater than that of the Suez Canal oil transport disruptions and hence constituted a real fear as regards energy supply cuts. The political effect of the crisis was translated into the nationalisation of energy policies. Each Member State attempted to avoid infrastructural dependency on other states. For instance, sea-bordering states built their own oil terminals on the coastline. The oil pipeline interconnections between west European countries were actually developed to supply specific refineries. Electricity and gas supply were both considered as being a question of national sovereignty.[2]

In fact, since the oil crises, European energy policy as regards the questions of supply and market regulation has been removed from the political agenda of the European Treaties establishing and reinforcing the EU. Likewise, in the Reform Treaty of Lisbon, energy supply security does not appear in the text.

A similar trend is observed in the security of gas supplies. For instance, the recent Security of Gas Supply Directive (2004/67/EC) reiterates the role of Member States in the energy security mechanisms. In particular, in its Article 3, the Directive outlines, 'in establishing their general policies with respect to ensuring adequate levels of security of gas supply, Member States shall define the roles and responsibilities of different gas market players in achieving these policies …'. Prior to its adoption, the Council had insisted that gas supply be considered as an intergovernmental security issue rather than the initial proposal from the European Commission to integrate the Directive into the Internal Market regime.

The approach to energy security remains nationally oriented and defined within each Member State. Spain and Hungary have institutionalised energy import restrictions. The former imposes a 60 per cent quota on the share of the biggest gas supplier.[3] The latter requires an improvement in energy diversification and restricts extra-EU electricity imports.[4] Other countries, such as Italy, are rather implicit about the diversification issue. Sweden represents the most extreme

---

2   The situation is different in the new EU Member States which were included in the USSR-lead economic block COMECON and have been interconnected by the Druzhba oil and gas pipeline networks.

3   Hydrocarbon Law, Bulletin Official del Estado, 34, 5, October 1998.

4   Gas Supply Law, No.112/2003 amended 49/2006.

example of a country which integrates its security of supply policy into its national defence policy.

Consequently, EU Member States create a geopolitical entity, dominated by the members' interests. They keep the traditional Waltzian international system, which assumes states struggle for survival within an international structure characterised by the absence of any 'worldwide' authority. The rise of power features in interstate relations, including those relating to access to resources.

The European Commission is trying to establish a common framework for energy policy. Publication of the 2006 Green Paper (European Commission 2006) and the energy package in January 2007 represents an important initiative in European energy policy. However, these documents focus on the internal energy markets, while external energy policy remains dominated by EU Member States. The best recent examples are:

- German support towards the North European Gas Pipeline, in spite of the denunciation of the project by Poland and the Baltic States;
- unilateral Polish veto on the EU-Russia agreement in November 2006 laying down the conditions of the agreement for the ratification of the Energy Charter Treaty (see below), which was not supported by other Member States;
- conclusion of bilateral agreements at the end of 2006 between Italy and France, on the one hand and Russia on the other, where both countries committed to importing Russian gas on a long-term basis and to allowing Gazprom partial access to their distribution markets, in spite of the European Commission's objective to decrease the importance of long-term contracts.

Competitiveness in the Internal Market: Europeanisation through Liberalisation

In spite of the strong national orientation of energy security, energy policy has been getting the European Community's attention. Its role emerged in the mid-1990s, with the Licensing Directive (94/22/EC) of 1994 which regulates the licensing procedures for exploration, taking into account safety and environmental issues. Among the largest oil producers, the UK adopted the Petroleum Act of 1998 in order to implement the aforementioned Directive. Likewise, the Community's competences expanded to the promotion of Trans-European Networks for Energy. Investments in network capacities will reduce short-term risks associated with decreasing disturbances of the grid, and a better distribution of the latter will enhance the diversification of supply (Belyi 2003, 359).

In addition, a number of Community-financed projects were launched during the 1990s to enhance energy security: (a) promotion of new technologies (Thermie), of energy efficiency (Save), and renewables (Altener); (b) promotion of infrastructural energy links with the candidate countries (Phare); (c) promotion of energy cooperation with non-EU suppliers (Synergy).

In the mid-1990s, the European Commission undertook a number of initiatives in order to consolidate the internal energy market. In 1995, the 'White Paper on energy policy' outlined three major dimensions of Community common energy policy: (1) security of supply; (2) competitiveness; and (3) environmental protection (European Commission 1995). This document established the main EU ideology in developing energy policy. Indeed, the impact of the White Paper does not emerge at the legal level of EU Community law, but represents a major influence on policy-makers.

The White Paper initiated the 'Europeanization' of energy policy, which can be defined as a progressive 'relocation of decision-making to the supranational level, and allows an understanding of the dynamics of the European energy security policy' (Fuerst et al. 2002, 3). It implies that not all national policies can become a European competence, although there is a strong influence of the supra-national level on Member States, their positions and their policies. To that extent, the process of Europeanisation introduces contradictions among the Member States but tends to create political and economic coherence at the EU level. Institutionally, the process is associated with the principle of subsidiarity, which is the framework for Community energy policy used when a 'proposed action cannot be sufficiently achieved by the Member States' and can 'therefore be better achieved by action on behalf of the Community' (TEU Art. 5). A definition of subsidiarity underlines the importance of Member States in decision-making: they remain dominant in the allocation of subsidiarity status, and can decide either to stop or to accelerate the process.

Furthermore, the principle of subsidiarity created a political and legal framework for the development of the liberalised internal energy market. In 1996, after seven years of intergovernmental negotiation (Eising 2002), the EU established a Directive on electricity sector liberalisation. Two years later, a similar gas Directive was adopted. Both Directives introduce a competitive retail model within the electricity and gas sectors that requires the unbundling of transmission and distribution, which remain exempt from the competitive model, and from generation and distribution, which are subject to competition. The unbundling is coupled with rules on non-discriminatory and transparent third-party access (Green 2000).

In 2003, two renewed Directives were adopted, with a more precise time schedule as regards the market opening. EU targets reflect the state of the art within the decentralisation process which already exists among the Member States. Indeed, energy industries proceeded with unbundling and third-party access rules independently of the European normative targets. Liberalisation provides new opportunities for energy companies: cross-border trade, investments in emerging markets, and the possibility to acquire shares in other energy and non-energy sectors. EU Directives on opening up the gas market introduces a different conception of the international gas trade (Belyi 2004). More specifically, the traditional concept of long-term gas supply is being replaced progressively by the concept of gas and electricity markets.

The EU framework aims to reduce imbalances between those Member States where markets are fully operational (Germany, UK, Scandinavian states), those where vertical monopolies still dominate (France, Greece), or where the liberalisation process has taken place but market fragmentation is too weak (Spain, Italy). The absence of an EU-level regulator is the main obstacle for Union-wide regulatory reforms. Subsequent developments have shown the need for such a body to – at the very least – to resolve cross-border regulatory issues. However, there is still no political or industry support for this – rather a huge amount of opposition. Interestingly, even the UK – the most proactive regulatory state as regards liberalisation and competition – strongly opposes such a development on the grounds of unnecessary bureaucracy. These arguments hide the real political reason: the allocation of a regulatory authority to the EU level would mean the loss of control over markets and hence over security of supply.

However, the Union has pushed for centralisation in the regulatory approaches of its Member States. At the EU level, national regulators coordinate their approaches to: promoting competition; taking explicit responsibility for the security of electricity and gas supply; and, in terms of price/cost adequacy, incentives for new entrants and new investments. The Council of European Energy Regulators tends to coordinate tariff policies (especially cross-border tariffs) and the transparency rules for access to transport capacity (Council of European Energy Regulators 2005, 25–6).

Therefore, the EU internal energy market is becoming a feature of a continuous integration process. One of the main objectives of the internal market is the creation of positive conditions for the diversification of energy supplies per source and per country.[5] Indeed, an integrated market allows creating better cross-border exchanges in case of the supply shortages in one of the countries. Nevertheless, the liberalisation pushes towards a gas use in the European energy portfolio. It might complicate the issue of the gas import dependency (Belyi 2003).

The International Role of the EU in Energy

The second part of this chapter aims to respond to the following issue: how powerful is the EU in realising energy security and the internal energy market externally? Basically, it involves an analysis of EU capability at the international level as well as its representation as a coherent actor vis-à-vis the third actors. As previously mentioned, the overview comprises three parts: the Union's value-related conception of external economic and political relations; exporting its model of energy markets to the outside world; and the EU's role within international organisations.

Values in the Union's External Relations

The EU's conception of external economic relations is strongly linked to the political values of the Union itself. This means, in its external economic policy, the EU sets an objective to export not only its own economic success story, but also to defend the values of liberal democracy (see Chapter 1). The EU Treaty, Article 181 on economic cooperation with the third countries, states: 'Community policy in this area shall contribute to the general objective of developing and

---

5   See for example the Commission's 'Energy for a Changing Global World' website at <http://ec.europa.eu/energy/energy_policy/index_en.htm>.

consolidating democracy and the rule of law, and to the objective of respecting human rights and fundamental freedoms.'

This feature of the EU corresponds to Caporaso's definition of a 'post-modern' actor which expands its influence upon third countries. It is interesting to note that energy security is somehow making an exception to this rule, and we should rather consider a realist approach from the European Union.

The most interesting example is EU cooperation with the Gulf states which have set up political systems very different from liberal democracies. In the Gulf region, the EU has a more limited involvement, mainly due to the US political and military presence and influence. For instance, relations with Iran and Iraq are mainly influenced by the US' external policy towards these countries which, in addition, does not create a consensus among the EU Member States. Likewise, the EU does not have an energy dialogue or any other institutionalised relations with the Gulf Cooperation Council (the GCC countries are Bahrain, Kuwait, Oman, Qatar, Saudi Arabia and United Arab Emirates). With a lack of any common security policy in the region, the EU it unable to wield any influence comparable to that of the US.

The EU has attempted to institutionalise its relations with the GCC. In 1989 the European Community signed a cooperation agreement with it, aiming at establishing a free trade area. Article 6 of the Agreement provides: 'In the field of energy, the Contracting Parties shall strive to encourage and facilitate, *inter alia*: cooperation in the two regions by energy undertakings of the Community and the GCC countries, joint analyses of trade between the two regions in crude oil, gas and petroleum products and its industrial aspects with a view to considering ways and means of improving their trade exchanges, exchanges of views and information on matters relating to energy in general and respective energy policies, without prejudice to the parties' international obligations, training, studies, notably on new and renewable sources of energy.' This mainly demonstrates that there are no concrete objectives or measures for energy cooperation (Salem Haghighi 2006, 334). It also demonstrates that the EU is concerned by the security of supply in the first place.

The situation is unlike other regions and countries which share, at least via discourse, the values of liberal democracies. However, a discrepancy in political values is emerging between the EU and energy-producing countries like Russia and Venezuela. Indeed, the latter prefer to set stronger national control over resources. In turn, the EU has often appeared cautious about respect of the rule of law (especially investors' rights[6]), such as non-discriminative and transparent behaviour towards the nationalisation of resources.

---

6   In the case of Russia, the European Commission expressed concern about environmental control over Royal Dutch Shell in September 2006, where there was some concern about respect of the non-discrimination principle towards Shell; cf. European Commission, Newsletter 195, 22 September 2006.

Exporting the EU's Unfinished Model in the Neighbourhood

The EU internal market is a process which encounters a number of barriers related to the new experience of market liberalisation. Indeed, the two sectors have generally remained exempt from competition. The new EU system provides a legal and political framework for cross-border markets in both gas and electricity.

The European Commission has been following the UK model for liberalisation: spot markets, unbundling of production and supply from transmission and distribution, and short-term auctions for the capacity entry. The recent Regulation EC 1775/2005 requires secondary markets for the available capacity in order to avoid hoarding in the networks. Secondary markets are the auctions for capacity allocation in order to diminish congestion in the networks. Paradoxically, since the beginning of the twenty-first century, the UK model has evolved towards more long-term contracts. For instance, 80 per cent of capacity trading is done for long-term contracts. Moreover, critics of the UK model point out its difficulties in attracting new investments in a law price environment. In contrast, market players tend to sell gas more profitably to continental Europe, which creates a market deficit in the UK. In addition, the EU/UK model is weakened by non-implementation of Union Directives by the new EU Member States, as well as by France. Southern EU members did implement the Directives, but the market fragmentation remains too low for retail competition.

The idea of market liberalisation has emerged from within the EU Mediterranean Energy Forum. Since 1995, the focus has been on the energy dialogue with non-EU Mediterranean countries. It was then that the Declaration of Barcelona was adopted during the Euro-Mediterranean Conference, which aimed to promote cooperation in the field of energy. Subsequently, a permenant Euro-Mediterranean Forum was officially established in 1997. The Euro-Mediterranean process is aiming to create a free trade area. The Energy Forum is attempting to regulate energy trade practices while reducing uncertainties. For instance, the EU is pushing for a market-based approach to gas supplies. Indeed, removal of long-term contracts with non-EU suppliers, which contain restrictions on the onward sales and use of gas to a contractually specified geographic area – the so-called 'destination clause' – would give a non-EU gas producer direct access to European gas consumers. This situation is permitted with a reciprocity clause: non-EU states must liberalise their retail markets to access the Union's retail markets.

For the electricity sector, the Energy Forum also integrates the idea of a common liberalised electricity market between the EU and the Maghreb countries.[7] Hence, the EU is attempting to exert its economic and financial influence in the Mediterranean region by promoting liberalisation and integration of the Internal Market.

A step forward towards the EU export model has been also outlined by the Energy Community Treaty of South-eastern Europe, signed in 2005, introduces a qualitatively new relationship with the EU, on the one hand, and non-EU

---

7   'Ministerial Declaration of the Euro-Mediterranean Energy Forum', Athens, 21 May 2003.

countries of South-eastern Europe on the other. Later, in 2006, accession to the Treaty was enlarged to the new observer countries: Moldova, Norway and Ukraine. The Treaty aims to establish a common regulatory space and to improve energy security within a single regulatory space. For both the EU Member States and those countries which recognise Union legislation, the EU regime has an important impact on the centralisation of their regulatory policies.

In political terms, the Treaty integrates South-east Europe into the EU regime of practices. For instance, it requires all the contracting parties to apply the *acquis communautaire*. Indeed, the countries in the region are economies in transition, changing from a planned economy to the market model. The EU presents itself as the perfect model of regulatory issues, and requires countries to introduce major Union practices such as energy liberalisation, integration of the Kyoto targets, and integration of energy security measures. The Treaty demonstrates that the influence of the EU regime goes beyond its political borders. Alternatively, the South-eastern European countries do not participate in decision-making at the EU level. Thus, the Treaty reiterates the relation of centre-periphery within the EU regulatory regime.

Energy in the EU's Relationship with International Organisations: WTO and ECT

The WTO is the centerpiece of world trade norms. However, traditionally it has avoided treating energy matters. The WTO mechanisms do not concern energy matters specifically, but removal of barriers to trade in goods and agricultural products in general. One component of the WTO system is the subsidy regime. The agreement on Subsidies and Countervailing Measures (SCM), concluded at the final decision of the Uruguay Round, addresses the legacy of subsidies. The subsidies concerned are those which might affect exports. Since many energy-exporting countries use different tariff mechanisms for their energy use inland and for export, those actions would be considered as a subsidy influencing exports (Salem Haghighi 2006, 210).

Using these arguments based on SCM principles, the EU attempted to remove the dual-pricing system used by the exporting countries. For instance, the question of dual pricing has arisen during negotiations with Russia on its accession to the WTO because of its dual pricing for gas, which creates a discrepancy between tariffs within the Former Soviet Union (FSU) and the EU. Indeed, by keeping internal gas prices low, FSU has maintained Russia's ability to keep a political influence over its direct neighbours. In turn, the double pricing of gas is the main stumbling block in Russia's ability to be accessed and regulated by WTO procedures. In particular, EU countries perceive the discrepancy between internal Russian prices and export prices to the EU as unfair competition.

The issue was resolved by a bilateral agreement on 21 May 2004 between Russia and the EU on the former's accession to the WTO, which would also involve the tariff reforms in Russia. Nevertheless, the tariff discrepancy still persists due to the unclear nature of gas market reforms in Russia. A similar concern was raised during negotiations between the EU and Saudi Arabia for the latter's accession to the WTO. However, in 2005, the EU decided to abandon its requirements on dual pricing with the Kingdom, and Saudi Arabia became a WTO member (Salem Haghighi 2006, 240).

The EU's position against dual pricing is based on its own political and economic concerns. However, the question of dual pricing has never been subject to any particular condemnation on behalf of the WTO. The reason for this is also related to the abstract definition of subsidies by the SCM Agreement, which only provides a general definition of subsidies. In turn, it does not provide any adequate information on how and against what benchmark the price difference should be compared (Salem Haghighi 2006, 246). Due to its abstract feature, the producing countries have argued that dual pricing should not be included in the definition of a subsidy. Consequently, the WTO framework has become a limited instrument used by the EU to influence the internal policies of the producing countries.

The second major treaty is the ECT – the first and unique multilateral treaty for energy trade and investments. Unlike the WTO, the ECT is an issue-specific regime. The overarching objective of the ECT, which includes all the FSU countries, is to create an international legal framework. It represents a major attempt to regulate energy trade and transit rules and practices. The treaty covers all cross-border energy markets, although its main focus is on covering the oil, gas and electricity sectors (Wälde 1996).

For its trade provisions, the ECT integrates the values established within the GATT/WTO framework. It presents an additional set of practices for international arbitration, and favours conciliation between states and provides clear conciliation procedures. In the field of energy investments, investors prefer to use the Energy Charter Treaty framework when claiming their rights from the host states.

The ECT has a particular focus – it attempts to constitute a legal framework for the freedom of energy transit. The treaty outlines two major aspects of freedom of transit, stipulated in Article 7: (1) Non-discrimination in access to the transit onshore pipeline network; (2) Non-discrimination when according rights to construct new onshore transit capacities.

The institutional framework presented by the Energy Charter Treaty is an ever-evolving set of initiatives related to facilitating the energy trade. In addition to the text of the treaty itself, contracting parties are in the process of negotiating a Transit Protocol.

As regards transit, particular arbitration procedures are foreseen by Article 7(7) of the ECT which addresses transit disputes involving a conciliation mechanism and no interruption or reduction in the flow of energy materials and products. The conciliator seeks to secure the existing agreement and recommends a resolution or procedure to resolve the dispute. The treaty iterates that a conciliator for transit issues must establish tariffs for transit to ensure non-disruption of the transit before a dispute is settled. Those provisions could have been used during the supply-transit crises between Russia, on the one hand, and Ukraine (in 2006) and Belarus (in 2007) on the other.[8] Therefore, the EU views the ECT transit provisions as the main elements in regulating relations with Russia.

---

    8   During both crises, the Energy Charter Secretariat sent a letter to the parties in dispute proposing the mediation procedures foreseen by the ECT Article 7(7).

However, the creation of the internal market for energy creates additional difficulties. The European Commission has remained reluctant to apply the ECT regime over the *acquis communautaire*. For instance, during the negotiations on the Transit Protocol, the EU claimed the particularity of its own regime compared to that of the ECT, and proposed that the Regional Economic Integration Organisation (REIO) clause applied within the Transit Protocol (Article 20). Hence, the provisions foreseen by the ECT became outdated in light of EU Internal Market development, especially as regards third-party access. In spite of its more advanced stage of cross-border regulation, there are Internal Market Directive provisions which might contradict the principles of the freedom of transit, such as Article 22 authorising exemptions from third-party access to the newly built pipelines. The exemptions are allocated at EU Member State level by regulators who are supervised by the European Commission. An uneven allocation of exemptions can then emerge from the different regulatory frameworks of each country. For instance, more exemptions have been allocated in northern-western Europe in contrast to the east and south where hardly any have been made. The allocation of exemptions can influence the access of non-EU suppliers to Union retail markets. Indeed, if an exemption is allocated to a new pipeline, third-party access for non-EU suppliers is limited.

This complex position towards the ECT creates an additional difficulty in political understanding with Russia. The latter, in particular its gas producer Gazprom, is worried about possible market losses in Europe. Under the EU regime, long-term capacity booking in the pipelines has become illegitimate. In this context, Gazprom needs to diversify its demand structure by getting shares directly in the distribution markets. In this situation, if the Transit Protocol is exempted from EU law, the ECT does not help Russia to use it as an instrument to get non-discriminatory third-party access. If, however, the instruments used to acquire distribution markets are based on EU law, Russia expresses concern at having to comply with a regime in which the country does not participate.

The complexity of the situation is coupled with Russia's political attitude to the freedom of transit. Indeed, Russia is not keen to apply the principle of freedom of transit through its own country. Gazprom ruled out any possibility of demonopolising its export pipeline which, in practice, limits the application of the Transit Protocol within the former Soviet Union. Gazprom claimed the right of first refusal for the pipeline capacity if it already has a long-term contract for gas supply. It created the situation of 'exchange of positions' (Konoplyanik 2003) between Russia and the EU: the former claimed the removal of the REIO clause and the EU insisted on the illegitimacy of the right of first refusal. Therefore, the political support towards the Transit Protocol has been weakened by the deadlock in negotiations between the two largest actors involved.

One of the major contradictions between the EU and the ECT is that the former started its own process of market integration, which went beyond the ECT provisions. Russia has linked ECT ratification to the successful negotiations on the Transit Protocol. So far, the EU has been unable to convince Russia to conclude the Transit Protocol, mainly due to the lack of compromise over the REIO clause. Nevertheless, it is still uncertain that, even without the REIO clause,

Gazprom would be willing to leave the export and transit monopoly within former Soviet Union. Subsequently, the ECT remains an unsuccessful political device for the EU.

Conclusions

EU external energy policy is indistinguishable from the nature of European integration which can be defined under three different dimensions: (1) The realist dimension, which considers a state-centered definition of security, and also shapes energy security; (2) The functionalist dimension, which views the EU as a single economic block for its Member States and for third parties, too; in this context, the emerging role of the internal energy market occupies a crucial place in EU external energy policy; (3) The post-modernist dimension which considers the Union as an exporting political and economic model, in particular principles of the free market and liberal democracy; here, external energy policy is linked to the set of values, although not always coherent, of the EU and its Member States.

The overview of the three dimensions demonstrates the triangular complexity of EU external energy policy:

1) energy security remains a high national priority for many Member States which are unwilling to allocate energy security at the EU level; in spite of attempts to coordinate this, the energy security policy is defined and implemented mainly by the Member States. Moreover, Member States differ in their definition of regional strategies – or the different positions of the old and new EU members as regards their relations with Russia;

2) EU energy policy emerges from economic integration and the liberalisation of markets within the Union. However, the liberalisation process remains incomplete and a regulatory harmonisation is only embryonic. It creates a problem in the EU approach to the ECT's multilateral legal framework: the EU has positioned itself as a particular single market (REIO clause) before the EU single energy market has been built;

3) the EU emerges as an international actor which is exporting its liberalisation model beyond its own borders. Hence, the EU becomes a generator of new norms in energy markets which, regardless of their implementation inside the Union, become models for non-EU members to follow. This postmodern cross-border influence is combined with a particular status of the EU regime within other international legal regimes of energy trade, such as the WTO and ECT. We should note, however, that the regional energy security strategy is not always supported by values of liberal democracy, apart from the investors' right to access such resources.

The success of the EU's external energy policy can be evaluated through its impact on other countries, where the liberalisation and regulatory regime at EU level is considered to be a success. At the same time, a vulnerable point within EU external energy policy is the gap between the discourse on the 'coherent energy market' and of a coherent energy security block, on the one hand, and the actual role of Member States on the other.

References

Bahgad, G. (2006), 'Europe's Energy Security: Challenges and Opportunities', *International Affairs* 82:5, 961–75.

Belyi, A. (2003), 'New dimensions of Energy Security of the Enlarging EU and their Impact on Relations with Russia', *Journal for European Integration* 25:4, 351–69.

Belyi, A. (2004), 'Le Marché Unique Européen d'Energie face aux Conceptions Traditionnelles de la Sécurité d'Approvisionnement', *Revue de l'Energie* 558, 368–75.

Caporaso, J. (1996), 'The EU and Forms of State: Westphalian, Regulatory or Post-Modern?', *Journal of Common Market Studies*, 34:1, 29–53.

Council of European Energy Regulators (2005), 'Roadmap for a Competitive Single Market in Europe', November.

Eising, R. (2002), 'Policy Learning in Embedded Negotiation: Explaining EU Electricity Liberalization', *International Organization*, 56:1, 85–120.

European Commission (1995), 'White Paper. An Energy Policy for the EU', COM(1995)682.

—— (2006), 'Green Paper. A European Strategy for Sustainable, Competitive and Secure Energy', COM(2006)105.

Fuerst, V., Prange, H. and Wolf, D. (2002), 'Globalisation, Europeanisation and All That: Sorting out the issues', presentation at the 5th conference of the Association d'Etudes sur la Communauté européenne – 'The EU, Enlargement and Reform', Toronto, 31 May–1 June.

Green, R. (2000), 'Energy Liberalisation in Europe', Department of Applied Economics, University of Cambridge.

Konoplyanik, A. (2004), 'Energy Charter Protocol: On the Way to Agreement', *Oil, Gas, Energy Law Intelligence* 2:1.

Salem Haghighi, S. (2006), 'Energy Security: The External Legal Relations of the EU with Energy Producing Countries', PhD thesis, European University Institute.

Wälde T. (ed.) (1996), *The Energy Charter Treaty: An East-West Gateway for Investment and Trade* (London: Kluwer Law International).

Chapter 10

'Everybody Needs Good Neighbours': The EU and its Neighbourhood

Viktoriya Khasson, Syuzanna Vasilyan and Hendrik Vos

Building a Distinct European Neighbourhood Policy

'Since the 2004 enlargement, relations with our neighbours have become the EU's main external priority', it says on the EU's Europa website. Although relations with its neighbours have always represented a challenge for the European Community (EC), the idea of a distinct European Neighbourhood Policy (ENP) is rather new. It builds on the existing relationship with Mediterranean states, but is also inextricably linked with the enlargement towards Central and Eastern Europe. Basically, ENP is a framework for the Union's relations with those neighbouring countries that do not have an immediate or medium-term perspective of EU membership. The Union aims to develop a 'ring of friends' (European Commission 2003, 4).

The initiative did not come all of a sudden. Relations with the Mediterranean region had already been given a boost in 1995 with the Euro-Mediterranean Partnership, launched at the Barcelona Conference. The aim of this partnership was the reinforcement of political and security dialogue, the gradual establishment of a free-trade area, and construction of a social, cultural and human partnership. The EU negotiated Association Agreements (AAs) with the Mediterranean Partners individually – eight have entered into force.[1] One of the most notable features of the AAs was an incentive for the partners to approximate their legislation to that of the internal market in order to facilitate free trade.

Eastern enlargement of the EU created an immediate need to deal with the insecurities of proximity to the post-Soviet area: the physical exposure of the newly acquired Eastern border and the risks of instability spilling over into the EU. In the second half of the 1990s, bilateral negotiations started with the prospective new neighbours. These resulted in Partnership and Cooperation Agreements (PCAs) between the EU and a number of Eastern European and Central Asian countries. PCAs set out the political, economic and trade relationship between the EU and

---

1   More specifically: Egypt, Israel, Jordan, Lebanon, Morocco, Palestinian Authority, and Tunisia. With the other Mediterranean partner, Turkey, the EC concluded first-generation AAs in the 1960s.

its partner countries but, compared to the AAs, they did not envisage the same preferential treatment for trade, or a timetable for regulatory approximation.

Given the different starting points and objectives, it was difficult to establish a coherent framework under the ENP. At the 2002 Copenhagen Summit, which dealt with enlargement, the European leaders addressed the neighbourhood challenge in general: 'The enlargement will bring about new dynamics in the European integration. This presents an important opportunity to take forward relations with neighbouring countries based on shared political and economic values. The Union remains determined to avoid new dividing lines in Europe and to promote stability and prosperity within and beyond the new border of the Union' (European Council 2002, 6). The ENP was subsequently outlined in a Commission Communication on Wider Europe, in March 2003, followed by a more developed Strategy Paper in May 2004 (European Commission 2003; 2004).

Until now there is no explicit Treaty basis for this policy. The Reform Treaty, however, would give the ENP a legal basis. Article 7a reads 'the Union and its neighbours'. Article I-57 reads: '1. The Union shall develop a special relationship with neighbouring countries, aiming to establish an area of prosperity and good neighbourliness, founded on the values of the Union and characterised by close and peaceful relations based on cooperation. 2. For the purposes of paragraph 1, the Union may conclude specific agreements with the countries concerned. These agreements may contain reciprocal rights and obligations as well as the possibility of undertaking activities jointly. Their implementation shall be the subject of periodic consultation.'

The neighbouring countries constitute a heterogeneous group, with different levels of economic and political development. The ENP covers 16 of the EU's neighbours to the East and along the southern and eastern shores of the Mediterranean, namely Algeria, Armenia, Azerbaijan, Belarus, Egypt, Georgia, Israel, Jordan, Lebanon, Libya, Moldova, Morocco, the Palestinian Authority, Syria, Tunisia and Ukraine. ENP has yet to be 'activated' for Belarus, Libya and Syria since currently there are no AAs or PCAs with these countries.[2]

Indeed, the ENP builds on the existing contractual relationships between the partner country and the EU (see Table 10.1). The ENP Action Plans form its backbone. By defining the way ahead over the next three to five years, these Action Plans set out an agenda of political and economic reforms with short- and medium-term priorities. The Action Plans must be endorsed by the relevant Association and Cooperation Councils, set up under the AAs and PCAs. The chapters are the same for each country,[3] but the content is different, according

---

2   For a history of the ENP and alternative concepts for dealing with the neighbours, see Smith (2005, 761–2).

3   Political dialogue and reform; economic and social cooperation and development; trade-related issues, market and regulatory reform; Cooperation in Justice, Freedom and Security issues; sectoral issues, for example transport, energy, information society, environment, research and development; human dimension: people-to-people contacts, civil society, education, public health.

Table 10.1   EU contractual relations with ENP partners

ENP partner countries	Entry into force of contractual relations with EC	ENP Country Report	ENP Action Plan	Joint adoption EU and partner country
Eastern Europe				
Belarus	–	–	–	–
Moldova	PCA – July 1998	May 2004	Agreed end 2004	22.02.2005
Ukraine	PCA – March 1998	May 2004	Agreed end 2004	21.02.2005
Caucasus				
Armenia	PCA – 1999	March 2005	Agreed autumn 2006	14.11.2006
Azerbaijan	PCA – 1999	March 2005	Agreed autumn 2006	14.11.2006
Georgia	PCA – 1999	March 2005	Agreed autumn 2006	14.11.2006
Mediterranean				
Algeria	AA – September 2005	–	–	–
Egypt	AA – June 2004	March 2005	Agreed end 2006	–
Israel	AA – June 2000	May 2004	Agreed end 2004	11.04.2005
Jordan	AA – May 2002	May 2004	Agreed end 2004	02.06.2005
Lebanon	AA – April 2006	March 2005	Agreed autumn 2006	19.01.2007
Libya	–	–	–	–
Morocco	AA – Mar 2000	May 2004	Agreed end 2004	27.07.2005
Palestinian Authority	Interim AA – July 1997	May 2004	Agreed end 2004	04.05.2005
Syria	–	–	–	–
Tunisia	AA – March 1998	May 2004	Agreed end 2004	04.07.2005

Source: http://ec.europa.eu/world/enp/faq_en.htm (4 June 2007).

to the specific situation. In 2004, ENP Action Plans were proposed and agreed with the seven neighbourhood countries whose Agreements were in force at that time. Since then, Action Plans are being developed with countries whose AAs have come into effect (Egypt and Lebanon) and with the three countries which already had PCAs in operation but which were only included in the ENP in 2004 (Armenia, Azerbaijan and Georgia).

The implementation of the ENP Action Plans is jointly promoted and monitored through (sub)committees already set up under the AAs and PCAs. Since the beginning of the budget cycle 2007–13, there has been a new instrument to provide assistance to the partner countries in support of the objectives agreed in the plans. In its 2004 Strategy Paper, the Commission (2004, 3) promised to report periodically on the progress accomplished: a mid-term review within two years after the Action Plans have been approved and a further report within three years. In December 2006, progress reports were presented on the implementation of the ENP (a sectoral progress report, seven country reports and an overall assessment) (European Commission 2006).

The next step could entail the negotiation of European Neighbourhood Agreements, to replace the present generation of bilateral agreements, once Action Plan priorities have been met (European Commission 2004, 5, 28). These new agreements will be equally comprehensive in scope. In March 2007, negotiations started on a new Enhanced Agreement between EU and Ukraine.

It could easily be argued that ENP is the example *par excellence* of Civilian Power Europe. The spread of democratic values in the neighbourhood, and the strengthening of stability and well-being are often cited as the main objectives of the policy. Security issues are discussed, but they are put in a broader framework, clearly devoid of the military component. The instruments that are used to pursue these goals include a 'carrot' rather than 'stick' approach, offering financial assistance and political dialogue under certain conditions. Compared with EU enlargement policy, one of the most striking differences is, of course, the absence of the membership carrot. The ambiguity regarding future relations between the EU and its neighbours might result in the latter becoming more motivated to perform well and to manifest their eligibility for membership. However, the open-ended nature of the ENP might also be discouraging for the neighbours, making them reluctant to take their commitments seriously.

This contribution will address these questions. It first looks at the objectives envisaged by the ENP, before moving to the means: which instruments does the EU use to endorse its objectives. In the final part, we make an evaluation.

Goals through ENP: Everything but Enlargement?

'The objective of the ENP is to share the benefits of the EU's 2004 enlargement with neighbouring countries in strengthening stability, security and well-being for all concerned. It is designed to prevent the emergence of new dividing lines between the enlarged EU and its neighbours, and to offer them the chance to participate in various EU activities, through greater political, security, economic

---

Box 10.1   What about Russia in the ENP?

Russia is the EU's largest neighbour, brought even closer by the 2004 enlargement. The bilateral basis for EU relations with Russia is a PCA which came into force on 1 December 1997 for an initial duration of ten years. This will be extended automatically beyond 2007 on an annual basis – unless either side withdraws from the agreement. It sets the principal common objectives, establishes the institutional framework for bilateral contacts, and calls for activities and dialogue in a number of areas.

Contrary to the other countries with which EU has concluded a PCA, Russia was sceptical about being included in the ENP, and has subsequently refused to be part of it. Compared with other ENP countries, Russia holds a special position in wanting to deal with the EU as an equal. The Union recognises that Russia is a 'strategic partner' and both sides have agreed to develop four common spaces. Road maps on the four common spaces – the common economic space, the common space of freedom, security and justice, the common space on external security and the common space on research, education and culture – were endorsed by the two sides at the EU-Russia Summit in May 2005. Differences of opinion between EU Member States (not least between 'old' and 'new' members), conflicting views with Russia on a number of politically sensitive issues (status of Kosovo, human rights issues, etc.), and concrete incidents (problems in energy supply, possible government involvement in political murders, etc.) make the development of mutual relations an issue of permanent disagreement, albeit in diplomatic language most of the time.

---

and cultural co-operation' (European Commission 2004, 3). The following paragraphs will summarise the main objectives – the explicit goals as well as the more implicit ones.

Security in a New Context

Geographical proximity creates a situation in which threats to mutual security, whether from the trans-border dimension of environmental and nuclear hazards, communicable diseases, illegal immigration, trafficking, organised crime or terrorist networks, require joint approaches in order to be addressed comprehensively, according to the Wider Europe Communication (European Commission 2003, 6).

It must be borne in mind, however, that the EU presence in the new neighbouring countries to the East during the last decade was not significant. With the exception of Russia, the EU's direct neighbour since Finland's accession in 1995, the Union had demonstrated a certain degree of reluctance to engage in the western CIS countries. There was ambiguity and decisions were mainly reactive. This is particularly true as regards the conflict-resolution procedures in Moldova, Georgia, Armenia and Azerbaijan, where the EU had left the efforts to be taken by the Organisation for Security and Cooperation in Europe (OSCE). These countries in Russia's 'near abroad', where the latter has special interests, have often been 'naturally' considered as Russia's legitimate sphere of influence which confirms the existing historical East-West divide within Europe.

In 2003, the EU adopted its Security Strategy, drafted under the responsibility of EU High Representative Javier Solana. This Strategy can be seen as Europe's answer to the US-led approach towards the new security threats, but also as a response to the challenge of Eastern enlargement. It refers to the challenges the EU is facing globally, which demand proportional security responses on its part. 'Building security in our neighbourhood' is one of the three strategic objectives of EU security policy: 'Our task is to promote a ring of well-governed countries to the East of the European Union and on the borders of the Mediterranean with whom we can enjoy close and co-operative relations' (European Council 2003, 8).

In this context, ENP explicitly addresses a number of issues set out in the Security Strategy. This is an important objective since internal conflicts in the neighbourhood have negative effects on economic and political development, including the danger of spillover. The Strategy states that 'neighbours who are engaged in violent conflict, weak states where organised crime flourishes, dysfunctional societies or exploding population growth on its borders all pose problems for Europe' (European Council 2003, 7). In its Wider Europe Communication, the Commission gives a concrete example: 'unrecognised statelets such as Transdniestria are a magnet for organised crime and can destabilise or throw off course the process of state-building, political consolidation and sustainable development' (European Council 2003, 9).

Conflict settlement is an important issue in the Action Plans: the ENP should reinforce the EU's contribution to promoting the settlement of regional conflicts. It is also in this context that regional cooperation is promoted amongst the partners (see below), a tricky issue in some areas, for example the Southern Caucasus or the Middle East. But generally speaking, the ENP is a conflict-prevention policy in a rather indirect way. For example, the ENP attaches importance to people-to-people contacts and socialisation, to confidence-building measures and regional cooperation. By emphasising bilateral relations and differentiation, as well as dialogue and sub-regional cooperation, the EU contributes to a climate in which security threats might be resolved. ENP serves to support more specific actions carried out in the context of the Common Foreign and Security Policy (CFSP), but the EU tries (especially in the East) to avoid any direct involvement in frozen or open conflicts.

The Commission (2004, 6) adds that 'the ENP can also help the Union's objectives in the area of Justice and Home Affairs, in particular in the fight against organised crime and corruption, money laundering and all forms of trafficking, as well as with regard to issues related to migration'. These issues are indeed discussed in the Action Plans. They deal with cooperation in fighting terrorism and cross-border crime, such as trafficking in drugs and human beings, and some of them even reflect the Union's interest in concluding readmission agreements with partner countries.

The EU has a clear interest in ensuring that these common security challenges are addressed. Neighbouring countries play a crucial role in the maintenance of security and stability in Europe (Lavenex 2004, 681), so ENP could be considered as an instrument for managing vulnerabilities in the EU's security. When referring to the sphere of security, the wording in the ENP Communications and Action Plans carries a civilian charge, being clearly devoid of the military component. For example, the EU re-emphasises the role of other multilateral institutions, such as the OSCE, UN, NATO, as if complacently delegating the hard security tasks to them. This largely corresponds with the Union's image as a civilian power, as outlined in Chapter 1.

Energy

However, looking at the place of energy in the ENP Action Plans, the 'normativity' of the EU as a power can be contested (cf. Chapter 9). The ENP Action Plans, as well as concrete funding programmes, refer to cooperation in the context of energy and the transportation of energy. The EU has a clear interest in these energy-related projects. After all, the creation of a ring between the Union and its neighbours, among which are the oil-rich Algeria in the South and Azerbaijan in the East, with the latter also securing access to the hydrocarbon resources of Kazakhstan and the Middle Eastern Iraq and Iran, cast a rational veil over the ENP. According to Dannreuther (2006, 197) 'the EU's energy dependence with its neighbours is set to grow over the coming decades'. The author refers to projections from the International Energy Agency that by 2030 the EU's oil imports will rise from the current 52 to 85 per cent, and gas imports from 36 to 63 per cent. It is also remarkable that the Commission Green Paper on a European Strategy for the Security of Energy Supply suggests that 45 per cent of the EU's oil imports originate from the Middle East, while 40 per cent of gas is imported from Russia and 30 per cent from Algeria (Dannreuther 2006, 197).

In this respect, the ENP must have been a strategic step not only to secure fossil-fuel supply, but also to diversify the EU's imports. The Baku-Ceyhan oil and the Baku-Erzrum gas pipelines, in the meantime, indicate the geo-strategic importance not only of Turkey but also of the neighbouring Georgia as a transit state, and Azerbaijan as a reservoir, based on the EU's growing energy needs. Oil and gas resources within the above-mentioned non-neighbours can be transported across the neighbours' territory. In this sense, stabilisation of the neighbourhood would ensure the security of energy supply. Inclusion of Russia and Central Asia, via the cross-regional and inter-regional strata of the ENP, can also be seen as markers of opportunism. After all, given the current situation in the Middle East, both Russia and Central Asia are essential for the EU, given its energy demands.

Market Integration: Exporting the EU Model

The EU is the neighbouring countries' main trade partner. Further trade facilitation and deeper economic integration are key objectives of the ENP. All of the Action Plans contain a range of priorities including harmonisation of standards, aligning regulation, improving customs procedures, and addressing existing trade barriers. Non-tariff barriers ('behind the border' issues) are also included. This comes down to the EU's desire to export its internal *acquis communautaire*, that is, Europeanisation of the partner's policy. Using the argument of creating a level playing field, EU norms on health, consumer and environment protection need to be respected. As Lavenex (2004, 683) says, the EU is expanding its legal boundary, without moving the institutional boundary.

However, a difference can be noted between the Southern neighbours and the Eastern partners. Through the Euro Mediterranean Partnership, the gradual establishment of a free trade area with the countries of the Mediterranean, long-standing market economies, is already foreseen. For Eastern ENP countries, such as Ukraine and Moldova, a perspective of free trade has also been established, but there is no timetable. The PCAs with the South Caucasian countries do not embrace an immediate medium-term free trade perspective at all (see also Gstöhl 2007, 4). The priorities are first full implementation of the trade-related provisions of the existing PCAs and accession to the WTO, or full implementation of the WTO accession agreement. Only then can deeper integration of trade and economic relations be considered. In the long run, the implementation of the ENP Action Plans will prepare the ground for the conclusion of a new generation of 'deep and comprehensive free trade agreements' with all ENP partners (also mentioned in European Commission 2006, 3).

The ENP thus holds out the prospect of a significant degree of integration, including a stake for the partner states in the EU's internal market. The process will be gradual, but whether free movement of agricultural products or persons is also envisaged is not so clear. In its 2006 evaluation, the Commission (2006, 3–4) makes a vague promise that trade in goods and services will include 'products of particular importance for our partners'. A timetable for this is not foreseen.

Why are preferential trade relations and market access important objectives? It must be taken into account that most of the EU's neighbours have a nominal GDP per capita of less than €2,000. The Union talks about avoiding 'new dividing lines', and thus reducing poverty, which is considered a moral challenge. In its vision, investment and growth should follow when barriers to trade and investment are reduced in these countries, when there is further liberalisation and convergence of economic legislation and the opening of partner economies to each other, as well as the promotion of regional and network integration between them and with the EU. In other words, the export of its own model and legal *acquis* will establish a better macroeconomic environment. This will create investment opportunities and will have a stabilising effect on the region as a whole. This is, of course, beneficial for the Union as well. Economic deprivation is a source of conflict and leads to security risks. But there is more: the EU has a clear interest in exporting its high standards (and thus protecting its own market). Moreover, by gradually introducing the perspectives, the EU is making sure that the process is not going against its own interests.

Exporting the EU's Political Values and Multilateralism

Under the ENP, the EU also seeks to encourage human rights, the rule of law, good governance and the development of a flourishing civil society. Even cultural cooperation is envisaged. The parts of the ENP Action Plans dealing with political reform and human rights are based on the principles of international and human rights law to which the EU and partners countries have subscribed under existing universal (core UN conventions) and regional conventions (Council of Europe, OSCE), with specific reference to country's international obligations in these areas. Democracy, pluralism, respect for human rights, civil liberties, the rule of law and core labour standards are all essential prerequisites for political stability, as well as for peaceful and sustained social and economic development, it reads in the 2003 Commission Communication. It is too soon to make an evaluation of this thesis, but at least in the Mediterranean countries Freedom House ratings do not suggest an increase in the level of democratic consolidation since the introduction of the Barcelona Process. Moreover, the EU has never sanctioned this poor record.

In line with its civilian power role, a distinctive feature fostered by the ENP is multilateralism (cf. Telò 2006). The above-mentioned political values are preferably promoted through multilateral institutions. The ENP Action Plans mention almost all the UN agencies, as well as other organisations, such as NATO, the OSCE, the Council of Europe, and so on. In this way, while normativity is preserved and confirmed by the ENP, one should also acknowledge that the EU is acting intelligently by trying not to be redundant and, above all, by benefiting from the work already done by others. By reinvigorating the neighbours to take another look at their commitments to other international organisations, the EU is making its task easier while continuing to foster the desired reforms within its vicinity.

Regionalisation

Regionalisation is another objective that the EU is fostering in the neighbourhood. In fact, regionalisation can be seen as an all-embracing goal, since the Union claims that regional integration helps to achieve security, welfare, and democracy. A distinction can be made between micro and macro levels of regionalisation. On the micro level, while the Action Plans explicitly refer to 'regional cooperation' (for example, between Armenia, Azerbaijan and Georgia), the concept seems to convey all the possible forms of regionalisation that have ever taken shape: ranging from intra-regional through introducing a Euro-region model to cross-regional to inter-regional and, finally, to trans-regional layers. On the macro level, the Action Plans are complemented with the ENPI Regional Programme for the Mediterranean, the ENPI Eastern Regional Programme, the ENPI Interregional Programme, the ENPI Cross-Border Cooperation Programme and the Black Sea Synergy – a New Regional Cooperation Initiative. The latter also encompass Russia (Vasilyan 2007a).

Both comprise a Strategy Paper 2007–13 and an Indicative Programme 2007–10. It is noteworthy that the Eastern Regional Programme also makes the five Central Asian states of Kazakhstan, Kyrgyzstan, Uzbekistan, Tajikistan and Turkmenistan eligible for the ENPI funding, in addition to the assistance foreseen through the Development Cooperation Instrument (DCI). These regional programmes top up the bilaterally negotiated Action Plans and, in this respect, re-emphasise the importance for the EU of (various forms of) regionalism.

Don't Mention Enlargement!

Finally, ENP seems to serve a more hidden agenda: avoiding further enlargement. It is no coincidence that the neighbouring countries, which are partners under the ENP, do not include those countries with an explicitly recognised prospect of membership, such as the Balkan countries or Turkey. The EU suffers from 'enlargement fatigue'. The European public, as well as several EU leaders, are sceptical about any immediate further enlargement of the Union. Debates are being held on absorption capacity or integration capacity. The rejection of the Constitutional Treaty in France and The Netherlands of the Constitutional Treaty has enforced the scepticism towards enlargement.

Consequently, ENP can be seen as a way of avoiding further enlargement by offering the neighbours less than membership but more than partnership. In the words of former Commission President Romano Prodi: 'sharing with the neighbours everything but institutions'. The Commission (2004, 3) Strategy Paper uses a more diplomatic wording: 'The EU has emphasised that it offers a means to reinforce relations between the EU and partner countries, which is distinct from the possibilities available to European countries under Article 49 of the Treaty on European Union.' In 2003, the Council (2003a, 6) had already taken a similar stance: 'The initiative should be seen as separate from the question of EU membership'. This view was repeated one month later: 'the Wider Europe initiative should not prejudge the question of future EU membership' (Council 2003b, 8).

The UK House of Lords Standing Committee on EU sees the ENP as a 'membership neutral' policy (House of Lords 2006, para. 245). However, we must keep in mind that, in the past, all attempts to create a neighbourhood policy were regarded as mere stepping stones to accession, rather than permanent alternatives to membership (Vahl 2006, 9, 17–18). It is clear that at least some of the Eastern partner countries, such as Georgia, Ukraine or Moldova, still foster the hope of full membership. They have some allies among current Member States and major political parties in Europe.

For its part, the EU has also contributed to an atmosphere of ambiguity from time to time. In May 2006, Enlargement Commissioner Olli Rehn admitted that it would be a strategic mistake to definitely say 'no' to Ukraine (*De Standaard* 24 May 2006). Gstöhl (2007) comes to a similar conclusion: 'the Eastern neighbours cherish a hidden "membership carrot"'. The issue is not under discussion all the time the EU's internal institutional problems remain unsolved, but it is not settled either. Compared to the CEECs in the 1990s, there is no clear commitment.

The 'rhetorical entrapment' that could be seen in the case of the CEECs (see next chapter) is thus less likely to happen in the case of the other neighbouring countries, at least in the short term.

The Function of Fuzziness

Needing a stable environment while dealing with the internal consequences of enlargement, the EU recognises its vulnerability towards its neighbours and considers that it is in its own self-interest to invest in stability and cooperation around its borders. For their part, all of the highly diverse countries around the Union have the EU as their main trade partner, and depend to a large extent on access to the EU single market for their economic development.

The ENP is a new policy, but it builds on a previous partnership with the Mediterranean countries and on cooperation with Eastern neighbours following EU enlargement towards the CEECs. It aims to achieve a considerable number of objectives and could be considered as a cross-pillar policy *par excellence*. Trade-related objectives are in almost every case part of EU external policy. By exporting its internal *acquis communautaire* and, in return, offering a stake in the internal market, the EU goes further. The ENP also builds on the Security Strategy and underpins CFSP issues. It envisages the export of the EU model, promoting general principles such as regional and subregional cooperation, multilateralism, democracy, fundamental values, human rights, the rule of law, and market economy. Items of 'soft' security, such as migration, nuclear risks, and so on, which are becoming part of the internal *acquis*, have spilled over in the EU's relations with its neighbours.

Each of the Action Plans contains a (long) list of priorities, differentiated according to the specific circumstances. A general trend of protecting the EU border can be observed; with the difference that, in the Eastern part, the focus is on issues of border controls and trafficking over the newly acquired EU border, while in the South, the objectives traditionally concern mainly migration issues. We can also confirm the thesis of Gstöhl (2007, 3–6), who notes that while trade-related objectives are central when dealing with the Southern partners, the spread of democratic values and political reform is more crucial in contacts with the Eastern neighbours which seem to be more open to political reform.

Some of the ENP objectives are clearly related to EU material goals and its interpretation of security threats. Energy and migration are obvious examples. Others correspond to the EU's own conception of its role on the international scene (promoting multilateralism, spreading democracy, combating poverty and social divisions) and thus relate to the notion of civilian power.

But more fundamentally, it is difficult to identify the main ENP priorities. The fact that the several priorities identified in the Action Plans are placed on an equal footing gives the EU the flexibility to manoeuvre if it wants to show more favouritism towards one neighbour rather than another. This could result in subjective evaluations and the establishment of patronage by the EU towards the neighbours. Moreover, one might ask whether the absence of clear guidelines and priorities might not confuse or annoy the neighbours, and even lead to alienation towards the EU. This could be the case especially because they are denied the top prize-membership.

Lack of prioratisation could also have been unintended, namely an EU-specific way of handling affairs. In a Union of 25 Member States (at the time the Action Plans were being negotiated) it could be considered quite normal that the ENP is not as specific as many would like to see. Negotiation on what to prioritise could lead to endless discussions and delay the possibility for the EU to engage in the neighbourhood now. In the next section we turn to the means deployed to reach these ambitious and comprehensive goals.

The Instruments of EU Power in the Neighbourhood

Generally speaking, we can say that the EU is relatively powerful towards its ENP partners. As it turns out, the relations between the Union and its partners are developing bilaterally, and the former makes an agreement with each of the countries separately. According to the EU, this hub-and-spoke model has the advantage of offering the partners more involvement, thereby promoting 'joint ownership'. Tailor-made, or not, Smith (2005, 766) argues that the Action Plans are rather commanding from the EU side (with the exception of Israel). Research points to the fact that the agenda of the ENP Action Plans is overwhelmingly EU-led (International Crisis Group 2006, 9).

The bilateral approach also offers possibilities for the EU to prioritise specific countries. One such example is that while Armenia and Georgia requested inclusion in the ENP, oil-rich Azerbaijan received a draft Action Plan developed by the Commission. This not only testifies to the fact that the ENP is driven (at least partially) by rational interests, but also that the concepts of 'joint ownership', as well as 'partnership', are exaggerations (cf. Chapter 3 on development). Moreover, when considering the actors included in the negotiations on the Action Plan, we see that on the side of the neighbours, neither the opposition, nor civil society representatives nor other non-state entities were properly informed about the ENP (ibid., 9, 13).

Although the relationship between the EU and the partner countries is highly asymmetrical, it tries to achieve the ENP objectives by using several instruments which at first sight could be considered as rather 'soft'. As External Relations Commissioner Ferrero-Waldner (2006, 139–40) says: 'The question is how to use our soft power to leverage the kinds of reforms that would make it possible to expand the zone of prosperity, stability and security beyond our borders'. She puts emphasis on the soft character of the tools by stressing that 'it is about helping our neighbours towards their own prosperity, security and stability, not by imposing reforms, but by supporting and encouraging reformers'. We can distinguish several instruments: political dialogue, the carrot of the internal market, and financial support. One more aspect is crucial in assessing the instruments: conditionality.

Political Dialogue

The ENP foresees a strengthened political dialogue between the EU and its neighbours, managed by the bodies set up under the PCAs and AAs. These bodies bring together representatives of partner countries, Member States, the European Commission and the Council Secretariat. ENP Action Plans and progress in achieving the objectives are discussed in these fora.

In all the Action Plans a (rather small) section is devoted to political dialogue. The EU puts issues of democracy and human rights on the table, although it is difficult to assess the importance attached to them. Closer political cooperation should also cover foreign and security policy issues, including discussions on regional and international issues, conflict prevention, crisis management and common security threats. The Eastern partners are offered the possibility of aligning, on a case-by-case basis, with CFSP declarations. In a later stage, this could also include the Mediterranean partners. In addition, ENP partners could be invited on a case-by-case basis to briefing and coordination meetings organised by the EU in international fora such as the UN, the Council of Europe and OSCE. This might also lead to the eventual involvement of partner countries in aspects of the European Security and Defence Policy (ESDP), such as possible participation in EU-led crisis-management operations. It is too soon to make an assessment of the political dialogue, thus it is difficult to distinguish obvious results of the dialogue until now. The case of Belarus (see Box 10.2) shows, however, that certain basic conditions have to be met before starting a political dialogue.

Internal Market Carrot

The EU offers the partner countries a stake in the internal market and involvement in its programmes and networks. Integration in the internal market is a goal, but offering the prospect is a carrot and thus a means as well. It is comparable to the 'membership carrot' (Chapter 11), although obviously it does not go that far. The option of full membership was offered to most CEECs in the 1990s and is considered an effective instrument in influencing policy. Whether the prospect of a stake in the single market is as good an incentive for the neighbours to cooperate with the EU remains unclear. Because the Union is the neighbouring countries' main trading partner it has some leverage. Several market-economy-oriented reforms are clearly stimulated by the Action Plans. When this concerns the free movement of people we see that talks on visa facilitation and the establishment of local border traffic regimes are more complicated.

Money, Money!

Neighbouring countries are offered technical and financial assistance under the ENP. The most obvious channel of EU assistance is the new European Neighbourhood and Partnership Instrument (ENPI). It was introduced within the budgetary cycle 2007–13, and replaces the existing TACIS and MEDA

Box 10.2   EU policy vis-à-vis Belarus

The reluctance of Belarus to cooperate with the EU is noteworthy because it testifies to both the weaknesses and the strengths of the ENP. The advantage is that hereby the reference in the Action Plans to 'joint ownership' is confirmed: it is up to the respective government (and the will of the latter) to sit down at the table with the Commission and negotiate possible cooperation. In the case of Belarus, President Lukashenko seems disinclined to formalise a relationship with the EU. Unwilling to accept 'no' as the answer, the EU has resorted to informal measures to influence the Belorussian political climate. This has been done by the European Commission which initiated awareness-raising TV and radio programmes via a two-year project amounting to €2 million, and the European Parliament, notably the Party of European Socialists, taking particular interest in the democratic reform of the country. The EU has also buttressed the creation of an opposition-backing Office for Democratic Belarus in Brussels with the aim of mobilising civil society in the country. At the same time, the EU has decided on a visa ban and asset freeze of Belorussian officials and it has withdrawn trade preferences for imports into the European market (see Chapter 6).

But because of the position of the Belorussian government – and this is a weakness of the ENP – the congruity of the ENP can be questioned as a 'policy' and objections raised to the generalised belief in the EU as a magnetic force. After all, the current world order set-up around the notion of state sovereignty makes it clear that if there is lack of internal will on the part of a particular government, external efforts are unlikely to be successful – no matter how benevolent.

programmes (see Figure 3.1). Total funding (nearly €12 billion) is 32 per cent greater, in real terms, than the amount available for the budget cycle 2000–06.[4]

The ENPI is called a 'policy-driven' instrument which operates within the framework of the bilateral agreements and regional programmes between the EU and its neighbours. It is used to implement the Action Plans: support is given for poverty-reduction programmes and tackling environmental problems, for fighting corruption and strengthening the rule of law, and also for measures leading to progressive participation in the internal market. For the 2007–10 period, 73 per cent of the amount will be used for 'country programmes' (ranging from €8 million for Israel to €654 million for Morocco). It must be noted that ENPI funding is also used for the implementation of the strategic partnership with Russia (previously covered by the TACIS programme): €120 million has been allocated to the Russian Federation for the 2007–10 period.

---

4   It must be noted, however, that only a part of the €8.5 billion for the 2000–06 period was actually used by the neighbouring countries because of administrative obstacles and problems of absorption capacity (see, for example, Dannreuther 2006, 192).

In the same period, a total of €827 million is available for regional cooperation activities: €277 million for cross-border cooperation, involving that between local and regional authorities on both sides of the EU's external border. These programmes are co-financed by the European Regional Development Fund, aiming, for example, at infrastructure connection or the establishment of business-to-business dialogue.

The Technical Assistance and Information Exchange Instrument and twinning instruments that have already been used in the enlargement process, and which envisage technical assistance by EU experts in the partner countries, could be used under the ENP Action Plans.

The ENP partners can also obtain funding from other thematic EU instruments, for example the European Initiative for Democracy and Human Rights. Individual Member States provide additional bilateral assistance to these countries as well. A Governance Facility and a Neighbourhood Investment Fund (€400 million during the 2007–10 period) will provide additional support for governments to strengthen democratic reforms and to promote investments.

A new lending mandate by the European Investment Bank (up to a total of €12.4 billion in the period 2007–13) will make it possible to get further access to loans and risk capital. The ENP also offers partners the possibility to participate in other EU programmes, such as the European Research Area (under the Commission's Seventh Framework Programme for Research – FP7) and other educational, environmental and cultural initiatives.

Conditionality

Political conditionality is an important external governance tool. Closer political cooperation, increased economic integration and access to funding depend on the realisation of the objectives by the partner countries. The Commission (2003, 16) states that 'the extension of the benefits ... including increased financial assistance, should be conducted so as to encourage and reward reform ... Engagement should therefore be introduced progressively, and be conditional on meeting agreed targets for reform. New benefits should only be offered to reflect the progress made by the partner countries in political and economic reform. In the absence of progress, partners will not be offered these opportunities'.

All agreements contain a suspension clause but, generally speaking, the EU stresses that it is a carrot approach, rather than threatening to use the stick. The Action Plans contain targets, reflecting political and economic objectives and expectations (such as the ratification and implementation of international commitments which are supposed to demonstrate respect for democratic values). Smith (2005, 765), however, is very critical: 'Clear benchmarks these are not'. Priorities related to democratic reforms, are sometimes described in vague wording and it is not clear how progress will be judged. In this respect, there is a radical difference in approach between the ENP's approach and the Millennium Challenge Account (MCA) of the US[5] (Vasilyan, 2007b).

Vahl argues, moreover, that the interpretation of conditionality depends on the phase of the relationship. He argues that it is not applied consistently. While it is frequently applied during negotiations and in the ratification process, with temporary suspensions and delays before entry into force, the EU has been very reluctant to interrupt the smooth functioning of agreements already entered into force in order to comply with the principle of conditionality also in practice. For instance, the Union has never made use of the human rights provisions, in spite of numerous obvious breaches of the political commitments made by its neighbours (Vahl 2006, 10–11).

This may either reinforce the argument in favour of the EU as a soft power or it may also introduce doubts about the extent to which the neighbours will commit themselves to their obligations. Thus, on the one hand, the benchmarks might be valuable to employ but, on the other hand, introduction of quantitative criteria might estrange the neighbours given the lacking membership carrot.

Issues to Keep an Eye On

It is too early for an in-depth evaluation of the ENP. Many agreements have been concluded or ratified recently. The ENPI, as the main budgetary instrument, has only been operating since 2007. In this part of our contribution we try to detect the points of particular interest that will be crucial in a later assessment of ENP in general and the bilateral agreements in particular. Initially, these have to do with the added value of the policy and the question concerning who benefits from it. Secondly, it remains to be seen whether the ENP instruments are sufficient to encourage reform, without the membership carrot. Thirdly, the importance of geopolitics, energy concerns and security threats cannot be overestimated. Finally, we must ask in what sense the ENP will acquire a multi-speed character.

What is the Added Value? And Who Benefits?

ENP builds on previous cooperation between the EU and its Southern and Eastern neighbours. It is thus not a radically new policy, but it seeks to accelerate the

---

5   This US Government development fund, administered by the Millennium Challenge Corporation (MCC) established in 2004 aims to tie aid to good governance, economic freedom and investing in people. Among the EU's neighbours, Armenia, Georgia, Jordan, Moldova, Morocco and Ukraine are beneficiaries of the MCA. While also stressing 'partnership' with the areas of development being identified by the country and the latter preparing its own proposal, the MCC uses quantitative indicators from the Freedom House, the World Bank and other institutions. The three categories mentioned are made operational through specific criteria which enable progress to be monitored more precisely and closely. Moreover, the assessments are made on an annual basis through the publication of reports.

process towards economic and political reform. The trade component is more advanced (especially in the case of the Mediterranean partners) and the political dialogue is upgraded (especially with some former Soviet states) (Vahl 2006, 9). ENP also includes the perspective of a stake in the internal market and a projection of governance beyond EU borders: by expanding its legal boundary outside external borders the Union influences policy developments in neighbouring countries (Lavenex 2004, 685). We can conclude that ENP has the intention of reinforcing previous cooperation policies, giving them a new impetus following the 2004 EU enlargement.

We also have the 'why question'. The EU does not hide its long-term interest in political and economic stability in the region. External Relations Commissioner Ferrero-Waldner (2006, 140–42) is very explicit: 'ENP has enabled us to tackle some of our citizens' most pressing concerns, like energy supplies, migration, security, and stability. ENP also promotes economic and social reform, both for reasons of solidarity, but also because we want stability in our neighbourhood and thus added security for ourselves.'

At the same time, it is stressed that more benevolent motivations are at the heart of the policy, too. For example, the 2004 Strategy Paper talks about preventing the emergence of new dividing lines (p. 3), about a contribution to conflict resolution (p. 4), and about addressing poverty and inequality, improving working conditions and enhancing social assistance (p. 14). But when looking at the Action Plans and the central issues in the discussion, there is obviously a strong emphasis on border management, migration issues and even readmission agreements. The energy dialogue is important for some partners, just like transport networks or illegal arms exports. Progress in discussions on free movement of people and agricultural products, which could be harmful for the EU, is considerably more difficult. Somewhat exaggerated, it could be concluded that the agenda is overwhelmed by issues with clear short-term EU interest.

Geopolitics and Other Considerations

When making an evaluation of the ENP, we must also take into account that the ENP agenda could be thwarted by other considerations, such as security and strategic factors. What happens if the EU considers it more important to work with existing governments, even if they have a poor record on human rights, rather than waiting for a longer-term internal transformation within these states (see also Dannreuther 2004, 198)? As mentioned previously, the instrument of conditionality has not been used in a consistent way in the past (see also Smith 2005, 770).

More specifically, the energy issue makes the EU vulnerable and dependent on its neighbours (in the East as well as in the South) (see also Dannreuther 2004, 197). The situation is further complicated by the fact that other major powers also play a role in the region: there is continual competition with Russia in the post-Soviet space, and US strategic interests in the Arab world and the former Soviet terrain. These issues are important, but it is not clear to what degree they will have an influence on ENP objectives and instruments. Another challenge concerns the serious conflicts in and between the neighbours, both in the South and East. The question is whether the EU, with its present tools, will be able to deal with these challenges.

The EU as a rising global power – even if defined as a civilian or normative one – cannot avoid competition with other global powers, such as the US and Russia. The EU's Eastern neighbourhood coincides with that of Russia, although the Russian Foreign Security Concept of the Near Abroad, formulated in 1993, also covers the former Soviet Central Asian states. However, there is a complete overlap between Russia's near abroad and the EU's Eastern neighbourhood if the ENPI Eastern Regional Programme is taken into consideration.

As far as the US is concerned, what the EU has started by launching the ENP has already been done by the US through respective separate policies and projects, some of which the EU seems to have copied (Vasilyan, 2007b). While additional support to the neighbours would not be exigent given their disparity with the EU's level of development, the interests and the work of the US should not be ignored by the Union. The US is a vital player in the neighbourhood, especially as seen through the neighbours' eyes. In other words, to be successful in its neighbourhood the EU would have to find a common language of communication with Russia and the US. The will of the neighbours and, thus, the EU's magnetism, even if necessary, would not be sufficient for the transformation of the neighbourhood if there were no agreement on the terms of the game between the major global players. Realpolitik is played by the US and Russia, even though the EU wished it no longer existed. Thus, if the normative aspirations of the EU could be seen as commensurate with those of the US, competition over the import of fossil fuel resources might trigger rivalry between the two. This is more likely to happen with Russia since the EU's active engagement with Central Asian states would not only deprive Russia of the revenues but would also eradicate Moscow's 'revenue-draining monopoly' (purchase of Central Asian oil and gas and high selling prices). These are the points of conflict the EU could confront when asserting itself in the neighbourhood.

A Multi-Speed Neighbourhood Policy?

When looking at the future development of the ENP, we must take into account that very different countries are lumped together in one policy. While Gstöhl (2007) refers to a South-East divide, this could be considered as an overgeneralisation. On the one hand, if looked at from the inside, the neighbouring countries – both in the South and the East – are too different to be boxed in the two-dimensional manner. Their aspirations towards the EU are also on different levels: Ukraine, Georgia, Moldova and Morocco seem to be more willing to join the club than the rest. Furthermore, there are specificities behind their motives alongside different levels of ambition. On the other hand, seen from the EU's perspective, if overemphasised by the EU, dimensionalisation may either undermine the ENP or give more credibility to it as a policy. The alternative way of grouping the eager and the reluctant neighbours and offering membership to the former and nothing to the latter would disrupt the geographical logic of gradual spillover, the political logic of the policy and the neighbourhood, and the normative power-related logic of regionalisation.

Another feasible scenario is that the relations between the EU and the neighbours might primarily become bilateral. After all, by launching the Action Plans for Ukraine, Moldova in the East, and Morocco, Tunisia, Jordan, Israel and the Palestinian Authority in the South in February 2005, the ENP predetermined the likelihood of having a multi-speed neighbourhood. The EU states that given the success made in accordance with the Action Plans, 'deeper' Agreements might be offered to the partners. If this were to happen, the policy might become void, giving way to the emergence of a multiplicity of bilateral frameworks on cooperation.

Magnetic Force Without the Carrot of Accession?

By using the 'enlargement carrot' the EU has proven it has 'transformative power'. Dannreuther (2006, 184) introduces this concept as specifically applicable to the neighbourhood where the EU acts by 'gaining influence through encouraging the internal transformation of societies rather than through physical or military coercion'. It is widely accepted that this makes enlargement the EU's most powerful foreign policy tool. The basic question is whether an 'internal market carrot', combined with subsidies and access to Union programmes, is sufficient to trigger the political, institutional, economic and social transformations envisaged by the ENP.

It is difficult to assess the effect of the absence of membership prospects. The conclusion by Vahl (2006, 59–62) that over the last couple of years most progress towards economic and political freedom can be seen in countries with a prospect of membership (such as the Balkan countries or Turkey), is hardly surprising. It remains to be seen whether the alternative carrot provides sufficient incentives for radical domestic economic and political transformation. One complicating factor is that a certain degree of market access is also foreseen under other commitments made by the EU in other institutions, such as the WTO (see also Vahl 2006, 30).

At least as important is the fact that the EU is ambiguous about the membership issue. The Commission (2003, 5) states that 'the aim of the new Neighbourhood Policy is therefore to provide a framework for the development of a new relationship which would not, in the medium term, include a perspective of membership or a role in the Union's institutions'. With the explicit reference to 'medium term', the door remains open and the Union will continue to experience pressure to admit new members. Formal acceptance of Turkey's candidate status had 'lifted a taboo' on the eligibility of other Muslim states. Some of the newly acquired European neighbours have also expressed repeatedly their wish to join the EU (most explicitly Ukraine, and also Moldova, although neither Belarus nor Russia). Clearly, the ambivalence of current policies regarding the question of membership offer great potential for awkward misunderstandings in future and, as noted by Wallace (2003, 11), have presented a strong argument for a coherent strategy towards all of the EU's Southern and Eastern neighbours.

It must be said that in the past the EU has not been so successful in developing alternatives to full membership: it seems difficult to offer incentives for economic and political transformation without the membership carrot.

Conclusion: ENP and the Many Unanswered Questions

ENP is not only seen as the EU's main external priority, but its instruments and objectives are also very comprehensive. Security objectives, economic goals and the spread of democratic values and good governance are envisaged. ENP is cross-pillar in nature: it covers trade, environmental and development issues, but also migration and cross-border control, CFSP and even ESDP. The EU's toolbox contains an internal market carrot, political dialogue and financial and technical assistance. The ENP Action Plans are tailor-made and the conditionality instrument allows the EU to steer the process in the desired direction.

But the absence of the membership carrot and ambiguity on future membership prospects constitute a major difference between ENP and enlargement policy. This poses questions about the strength of the EU's 'magnetic force' or 'transformative power'. Moreover, it is not so easy to determine what the EU really wants: the ENP objectives are manifold, reflecting ideational as well as material goals. ENP could illustrate the EU's ambitions to play a more prominent role on the world stage beyond traditional power politics. But one could also argue that the Union is becoming more introvert and basically limiting its world role to its direct neighbourhood: the creation of a buffering zone, a protective ring around the EU, in an attempt to prevent further accessions. Perhaps a more detailed analysis of the Action Plans, in particular, of the implementation of the ENP in the coming years (also in budgetary terms) will reveal the true priorities.

This chapter cautiously suggested that self-serving interests, especially in the areas of security and migration, might have taken priority in the ENP. Apart from the more specific objectives, it can be said that the EU tries to project its own model beyond its borders: regionalisation is encouraged, actions promoting good governance and market economic reforms are stimulated, and the neighbouring countries are even invited to implement the *acquis communautaire*.

These conclusions largely correspond with the thesis of Hettne and Soderbaum (2005, 538-9), who argue that the EU is acting in line with 'soft imperialism'. Thereby they refer to 'soft power in the hard way, that is an asymmetric form of dialogue or even the imposition or strategic use of norms and conditionalities in the self-interest rather than for the creation of a genuine (inter-regional) dialogue'. The asymmetrical relationship in the negotiations does not guarantee that the interests and the diversity of the neighbouring countries are adequately taken into account. This is, however, an essential prerequisite if good neighbours are to become good friends. And it is vital for the policy to succeed.

References

European Commission (2000), 'Green Paper: Towards a European Strategy for the Security of Energy Supply', COM(2000)769.

—— (2003), 'Wider Europe – Neighbourhood: A New Framework for Relations with our Eastern and Southern Neighbourhood', COM(2003)104.

—— (2004), 'European Neighbourhood Policy – Strategy Paper', COM(2004)373.

—— (2006), 'Strengthening the European Neighbourhood Policy', COM(2006)726.

Council of the EU (2003a), Press Release, 6941/03 Presse 63, 18 March.

—— (2003b), Press Release, 8220/03 Presse 105, 14 April.

Dannreuther, R. (2006), 'Developing the Alternative to Enlargement: The European Neighbourhood Policy', *European Foreign Affairs Review* 11:2, 183–201.

—— (ed.) (2004), *EU Foreign and Security Policy – Towards a Neighbourhood Strategy* (London: Routledge).

Emerson, M. (2004), 'European Neighbourhood Policy: Strategy or Placebo', *CEPS Working Document* 215, November.

European Council (2002), 'Copenhagen European Council – Presidency Conclusions', 12–13 December.

—— (2003), 'A Secure Europe in a Better World – A European Security Strategy', 12 December.

Ferrero-Waldner, B. (2006), 'The ENP: The EU's Newest Foreign Policy Instrument', *European Foreign Affairs Review* 11:2, 139–42.

Gstöhl, S. (2007), 'EU External Action: European Neighbourhood Policy', paper presented at the colloquium *Working for Europe: Perspectives on the EU 50 Years after the Treaty of Rome*, Brussels, 9 March.

Hettne, B. and Söderbaum, F. (2005), 'Civilian Power or Soft Imperialism? The EU as a Global Actor and the Role of Interregionalism', *European Foreign Affairs Review*, 10:4, 535–52

House of Lords (2006), 'European Union – Fifty Third Report', London.

International Crisis Group (2006), 'Conflict Resolution in the South Caucasus', *Europe Report 173*.

Lavenex, S. (2004), 'EU External Governance in "Wider Europe"', *Journal of European Public Policy* 11:4, 680–700.

Schimmelfennig, F. and Wagner, W. (2004), 'Preface: External Governance in the EU', *Journal of European Public Policy* 11:4, 657–60.

Smith, K. (2005), 'The Outsiders: The European Neighbourhood Policy', *International Affairs* 81:4, 752–73.

Telò, M. (2006), *Europe: A Civilian Power? EU, Global Governance, World Order* (Basingstoke: Palgrave).

Vahl, M. (2006), 'International Agreements in EU Neighbourhood Policy', *SIEPS Report* 10, November.

Vasilyan, S. (2007a), 'EU Regionalising the South Caucasus', in P. De Lomaerde and M. Schulz (eds), *The 'Makability' of Regions: An Evaluation of EU Monitoring and Support to Regional Integration Worldwide* (Aldershot: Ashgate, forthcoming).

—— (2007b), 'The EU as a "Civilian" and "Normative" Power: Connotational Meanings from Outside', paper presented at the EUSA Tenth Biennial International Conference, Montreal, 17–19 May.

Wallace, W. (2003), 'Looking After the Neighbourhood: Responsibility for the EU-25', *Notre Europe Policy Papers* 4, July.

Chapter 11

Civilian Power Europe and Eastern Enlargement: The More the Merrier?

Eline De Ridder, An Schrijvers and Hendrik Vos

Enlargement is often seen as the Union's most successful foreign policy tool. In particular, enlargement towards the Central and Eastern European Countries (CEECs) seems to prove the thesis that the European Union (EU) has transformative power. This chapter presents an evaluation of EU policy towards its immediate neighbours: by offering full membership, did the EU use its civilian power to expand its region of prosperity, democracy and good governance? First, the chapter develops the reasons behind the enlargement and exposes the different motives behind the policy. In the second part, the focus lies on the tools: which instruments and procedures have been used to stimulate the candidate countries (CCs) towards more democracy, better governance and other reforms? In the third part, we make a cautious assessment of the EU's impact on the CEECs, and turn our attention to the unintended consequences. Some illustrations, based on the 'Europeanisation' of Poland, are also developed. The analysis puts the idea of enlargement as a civilian power policy *par excellence* into perspective.

Why Enlarge? Bridging Values and Interests

After the regime changes of 1989 in Central and Eastern Europe (CEE), there was discussion among EU Member States about what to do with this part of Europe. Did the EU have to offer the CEECs full membership or would mere association and economic cooperation suffice in order to stabilise the region? In parallel with the political debate and the opinions aired during EU negotiations, a discussion began among academic scholars about the arguments behind enlargement. Compared to previous enlargement processes, this debate attracted a lot of attention because of the scope and size of the upcoming enlargement to include at least five, eight or ten former communist countries,[1] which were largely lagging in

---

1   The European Council of Luxembourg (1997) accepted, besides Cyprus, five CEECs (Poland, Czech Republic, Hungary, Slovenia and Estonia) as CCs. The European Council of Helsinki (1999) accepted Lithuania, Latvia, Bulgaria, Romania and Slovakia besides Malta as CCs. Eight CEECs (the Czech Republic, Estonia, Hungary, Latvia, Lithuania, Poland, Slovakia and Slovenia), Malta and Cyprus entered the EU on 1 May 2004. Bulgaria and Romania entered on 1 January 2007.

political and economic terms. A lively debate arose which involved two theoretical schools: the rationalist approach and the social constructivist approach.

A Rationalist View: The CEECs' and EU's Perspective

The starting point of the rationalist school is the assumption that states act as self-interested actors in the international environment. They try to accumulate their political and economic power in order to safeguard their national interests. In the enlargement context, this implies that countries will apply for membership if the political, economic and institutional benefits turn out to be higher than the expected costs.

The reasons for the CEECs to join the EU were quite straightforward. Considering their political and, in particular, their economic leeway, joining the Union would bring them substantial benefits. As full EU members they would benefit from the common agricultural policy (CAP) and Structural Funds. In addition, they would have unrestricted access to the European single market. Membership would also help them to stabilise their domestic economy, to modernise it, and to attract foreign direct investment. Moreover, during a considerable period, they would receive financial and technical assistance to help them with adaptation problems.

EU assistance would help these countries during the transformation to a liberal, market-based democracy. By the beginning of the 1990s, they had successfully implemented a first series of reforms, including a cautious opening of the market and the first administrative and judicial reforms. Nevertheless, the situation in the region remained delicate. The number of reforms waiting to be implemented was still huge, and the possibilities of a relapse were real. Therefore, many of the countries turned to the EU in search of support in this critical process.

On the other hand, the benefits for the EU of enlarging towards CEE were less clear-cut. Rationalist theories postulate that an international organisation will admit new members when the latter will enrich the community economically and/or politically. If this is not the case, the organisation can take the decision to admit them as long as the risks of leaving them outside are greater than the cost of admitting them.

At the plus side, we could discern security and economic reasons and the EU's influence in world affairs. First, following the end of the Cold War, Central and Eastern Europe remained a very unstable and sensitive region, which was proven by the conflict in Former Yugoslavia. Economic mismanagement, political instability or social unrest could arise and hamper the transformation. A population disillusioned with the harsh reforms could choose to go back to authoritarian or nationalist regimes. This would create a threat to the Union's stability and security. Second, by including the CEECs, the EU would enlarge its single market and create new possibilities for trade and investment, and hence for economic growth. Furthermore, access to primary resources and labour at low cost in the countries would benefit the EU's competitiveness on a global scale. Third, by expanding, the EU would enhance and strengthen its position in the world. It would be able to have greater influence on international and global politics.

Looking at the costs, however, we could distinguish several motives for any reluctance towards enlargement. The process would entail an institutional cost: decision-making would become more difficult, possibly resulting in a watering down of the integration project. But the economic costs, in particular, attracted attention: a possible loss of competitiveness in the EU-15 Member States and the financial consequences for the CAP and the Structural Funds.

Several authors argue that the costs and benefits of enlargement were unequally distributed between the Member States (Baldwin et al. 1997). Within the rationalist framework of liberal intergovernmentalism, scholars discern two major variables defining the different state preferences of the EU-15 vis-à-vis the enlargement project – the geographical position and the socio-economic situation of each Member State (Moravcsik 1998, 26–9). A Member State's geographical situation plays an important role because the proximity to the CEECs determines its interdependence and opportunities for economic involvement. The closer a Member State is situated, the greater its international interdependence with the Eastern countries and the higher the material benefits it may expect from EU enlargement. At the same time, problems such as conflicts and wars or ecological deterioration can spread across the borders easily. Firm institutional ties with the neighbouring countries in question would help to block any possible negative developments. This explains why most of the countries bordering CEE – with Germany in first place – were in favour of enlargement, while the more remote countries were generally against it.

A second explanatory factor is the socio-economic structure of the countries. The financial assistance from CAP and the Structural Funds, normally at the disposition of 15 Member States, would have to be divided among 25. As a logical consequence, the poorer countries would be harmed more fundamentally by this evolution than the richer countries. The latter were the net beneficiaries before an Eastern enlargement and would see their share of financial support diminish considerably when the CEECs joined the Union. This evolution explains the opposition of countries like Greece, Portugal, Spain and Ireland towards further EU enlargement.

Last but not least, some Member States had their own specific reasons, based on a cost-benefit calculation, either to be enthusiastic about or reluctant towards an Eastern enlargement (Friis and Murphy 1999, 221; Schimmelfennig 2001, 52–3). France, for example, feared that Germany would have significant influence over the future Member States of CEE, through which it would increase its power in the EU. The United Kingdom, for its part, has always been an ardent supporter of EU enlargement. As a traditional opponent of far-reaching European integration, it hoped that enlargement and the institutional costs accompanying the process, would hamper the process to an ever-closer Union.

In the rationalist logic, a process of interstate bargaining began, determined by the preferences and relative bargaining power of the Member States. Disagreement on enlarging the EU to the CEECs was solved with side payments and concessions on the part of the winners of the process to the so-called losers. Germany, for example, succeeded in convincing France by making concessions concerning the Structural Funds, and the CAP in particular. With the so-called Konrad deal

(October 2002) France was assured of a stable income from agricultural payments, at least until 2013.

Social Constructivist Contributions and the Strategic Use of Arguments

Gradually, in the course of the process, social constructivist theories started to challenge the rationalist explanations, claiming that mere material costs and benefits were not able to explain the decision to enlarge (Fierke and Wiener 1999; Sjursen 2002; Sedelmeier 2000). The authors argue that the decision was based on, and motivated by somewhat immaterial concepts such as identity, norms, values and ideas. For them, Eastern enlargement has to be understood as an expansion of the European international community. They argue that an international organisation like the EU represents a community with its own values and norms, defining its goals and working methods. States that share these values and norms will try to be part of the organisation that represents them. As the EU is a liberal community guided by democratic norms and values, the CEECs, supporting these ideas of liberal democracy and social pluralism, naturally wanted to join this Union.

For its part, the EU will admit new members only when these countries share its Community values and norms. According to social constructivists, this explains why the Union regarded the CEECs' application as legitimate after their turnover in 1989. As explained in Chapter 1, the Union's enlargement policy practice has, in turn, stimulated the formation of Europe's global role as a promoter of democracy and human rights.

Following this line of thought, a lot of attention is paid to the discourse and the arguments that were heard during the process. The concepts of a European identity and a common history were stressed. It was repeated that the EU had a strong political imperative and even a moral obligation to enlarge in order to overcome the Cold War division. By joining the EU, the CEECs would finally return to the European community, to which they naturally belonged. According to social constructivist theories, this reunion of two parts with one European identity, with the same social and cultural tradition and historic heritage, played an important role in the EU's decision to enlarge Eastwards.

While rationalist authors see the enlargement as the result of a utilitarian analysis, social constructivists emphasise the importance of discourse and the intention to create a community of values and norms. Frank Schimmelfennig (2001) has successfully combined the best of both the rationalist as the social constructivist explanation. He agrees with the rationalists that a self-interested cost-benefit analysis shaped the EU Member States' preferences on the question of Eastern enlargement. He listed the different preferences but, according to him, rationalism cannot account for the Union's decision to move from association with the CEECs to their full membership. In an overview of the different reasons at play in the process, which he published together with Ulrich Sedelmeier (Schimmelfennig and Sedelmeier 2002), a similar conclusion is made. Both rational and normative arguments account for the decision to enlarge.

If self-serving economic and security concerns were the only reasons why the EU decided to enlarge Eastwards, its aims could have been met by offering these countries economic cooperation agreements or an association status. To explain the Union's move to full membership, Schimmelfennig and Sedelmeier propose the mechanism of 'rhetorical action' or the strategic use of norm-based arguments (see also Chapter 1). By referring to the Community's pan-European orientation and liberal constitutive values and norms, the 'drivers' of enlargement (those Member States with a clear interest in it) were able to shame the 'brakemen' (the reluctant Member States) and argumentatively 'entrap' them into a firm EU commitment to Eastern enlargement. Consequently, the kind of 'negative consensus' resulting from this meant that, in practice, the process could not be blocked (Sedelmeier 2000, 188).

It was not only those Member States in favour of Eastern enlargement which used the European norms and values to push towards EU membership. The CEECs themselves also did this. They referred in particular to the pan-European rhetorical commitments the EU had made in its successive treaties to support their claim for membership. The preamble of the Treaty of Rome notes that the participating states are 'determined to lay the foundations of an ever-closer union among the peoples of Europe', and are 'resolved to ensure the economic and social progress of their countries by common action to eliminate the barriers which divide Europe.' The preamble to the Treaty of Maastricht recalls 'the historic importance of the ending of the division of the European continent and the need to create firm bases for the construction of the future Europe'. The CEECs interpreted these statements as the promise of membership and urged the EU Member States to live up to their commitments. Or, as Fierke and Wiener (1999, 725) put it, they turned the 'promises' made by the EU into 'threats'.

To sum up, the distinct theoretical schools substantiate the reasons behind the enlargement process differently. Both visions can be found in the political discourse. Some speeches put an emphasis on the material interests, while others stress the moral obligations. The latter, in particular, coincides with an image of the EU as a civilian power, offering more to the neighbours than could be traced back to its narrow self-interest.

Enlargement Policy: Instruments for Creating an Area of Democracy and Prosperity

It is widely accepted that the EU disposed of a great potential for spreading its liberal democratic norms to the CEECs. First, the Union is so attractive that some authors talk about its 'magnetic force' (see Chapter 1): without enforcing reforms, the EU's model became inspiring for the CEECs. Once these countries turned to the Union and explicitly asked for full membership, the EU's leverage to contribute to the reform process increased. The EU tried to influence developments in the Eastern CCs mainly by using the 'carrot' of membership and by providing considerable financial support. The most crucial tool for influencing the CEECs is the conditionality instrument.

The EU as a Magnetic Force and Holder of the Membership Carrot

During the Cold War, contacts between the EU and the CEECs were limited. Nevertheless, the general idea in the Soviet countries about the European Community (EC) was a very positive one. This idea was mainly based on the awareness of its economic strength (Bretherton and Vogler 2006a, 139). Most countries in the region looked to the West and the EC as the promised land of security and prosperity. For this reason, they were eager to join the EC immediately after 1989. 'Returning to Europe' became the number-one priority of their foreign policy. As both concepts of Europe and the EC were often conflated (Grabbe 2006, 40), 'returning to Europe' often became synonymous with joining the EC. In order to achieve this goal they began to undertake the necessary reforms, hereby using the EC and its Member States as 'role models' (Friss and Murphy 1999, 220). In this first phase of reforms the EC served as a 'pool of attraction' (so-called by Konrad Adenauer, cited in Rupnik 2000, 116) and exerted a rather passive influence (EC as a presence rather than a player). Without any explicit pressure or direct instruments, it was able to put its stamp on the early transformation processes in the CEECs.

Most Member States, however, were rather 'reluctant' to discuss an enlargement policy (Torreblanca 2001, 1). This explains why the EC initially limited itself to opening up association negotiations (Europe Agreements) in December 1990 with Hungary, Poland and Czechoslovakia. The prospect of membership, however, was left vague: in the preamble to these agreements the Union refused to share in the CEECs' ultimate goal of accession. Due to disagreement among the then 12 (and later 15) Member States, it eventually took the EC/EU four years before it could officially answer the CEECs' membership aspirations. Finally, at the 1993 meeting of the European Council in Copenhagen, it was decided to offer them an accession perspective. By promising ever-closer institutional ties leading eventually to membership, the Union was from then on able to interfere in the domestic situation of the CEECs in a more determined way (Smith 2005a, 271; Grabbe 2006, 53). The basic instrument it used for this purpose was conditionality. The active use of conditionality and financial assistance complement the magnetic force effect, providing a more tangible explanation for the EU's influence in the CCs.

Conditionality

The ultimate prospect of membership was based on the fulfilment of criteria, as stated by the European Council in Copenhagen. These criteria reflected not only the economic concerns of the Union (a functioning market economy) and the duty to take on the obligations of membership (the *acquis communautaire*), but also its political goals. The civilian aspect of the EU is most prominent in these political criteria. Membership requires that the given country 'has achieved stability of institutions guaranteeing democracy, the rule of law, human rights and respect for and protection of minorities' (European Council 1993, 14). For the first time in its enlargement history, the EU officially formulated the political criteria to be fulfilled by a CC. In the enlargement towards the former communist countries, the political criteria became substantially important. Accession negotiations with a CC were not formally opened until most of the political conditions had been met. In this regard, the start of talks with Slovakia was postponed as its democratic record under the Meciar regime was considered insufficient. This is the principle of gatekeeping: as long as the postulated conditions are not met, the EU's 'gate' to the next phase towards membership remains closed.

Over the years, the policy of democratic conditionality was fleshed out to include criteria of substantive democracy, such as independence of the judiciaries, the pursuit of anti-corruption measures, the pluralism of the media, the importance of local government, an involved civil society, and the protection of rights relating to gender equality. Moreover, it has been noticed that the EU became more demanding towards Romania and Bulgaria, which joined the Union in 2007 (Phinnemore 2004). Issues concerning corruption, the penal system, treatment of mentally disabled people, and protection of the child welfare system were raised more than before (Jora 2006, 6–10; Pridham 2006, 383ff.). When looking at future prospects (Balkan, Turkey), it seems that the EU is setting more rigorous standards and that the political criteria are becoming even more important.

By including criteria of substantive democracy in the Eastern enlargement process, the EU touched upon areas which, strictly speaking, are not part of its competences. The Union meddled in affairs which are formally not covered by the *acquis* (Pridham 2002, 960). With particular reference to the protection of minority rights, the Union has imposed strict requirements on the CEECs which it could not make internally. Respect for minority rights was explicitly stated in the Copenhagen criteria. This minority condition was not part of the *acquis*, either as a formal right or as a shared norm. 'In fact, minority rights were not identified by common EU principles (rules) or shared expectations (norms)' (Wiener and Wobbe 2002, 5). By demanding more from the new members than the old ones, the EU gave the impression of applying double standards.

The policy of conditionality mainly follows a 'strategy of reinforcement by reward', not by punishment (Schimmelfennig et al. 2003, 496–7). According to this strategy, the EU pays the reward (membership and additional funding) if the candidate state complies with the conditions. If the target government fails to do this, it withholds the reward although it does not punish the state by inflicting extra costs. The conditionality policy was meant to redirect the CEECs and to stimulate them into making reforms. For this purpose, the EU used various direct instruments of conditionality on the CEECs. Grabbe (2001, 1020ff.) has listed the five most important: gatekeeping; benchmarking and monitoring in successive Commission reports; providing models and templates of good governance and best practice; providing financial and technical assistance, and giving advice and developing twinning projects. These tools were used by the Commission to keep the CCs on the reform track. Its regular progress reports listed the achievements made, and indicated for each candidate state separately where further progress was needed. These reports were made public, increasing the effect of the naming and blaming strategy.

The principle of conditionality is highly interconnected with the principles of bilateralism and differentiation (Smith 2005b, 352). In this regard, the EU's accession governance differs greatly from its commonly used multi-level governance model (Dimitrova 2002, 174–5). Only a limited number of actors are directly involved in accession governance: the Commission, the Council (Member State ministries of foreign affairs) and the government of the candidate state. The European Parliament and non-governmental organisations, affecting the EU's daily decision-making procedures, are barely present in the process. The same is true for the parliament of the given CC.

Accession consists predominantly of bilateral intergovernmental negotiations between the applicant state and the EU, in which the Commission plays the role of mediator. In the 2004/2007 enlargements, this bilateral character rendered it difficult for the CEECs to present a common front to the EU (Smith 2005b, 352). However, on the other hand, the EU maintained the principle that each country was treated separately and on its own merits. This is called the principle of differentiation. By handling accession in this way, in theory the Union passes all the responsibility for becoming a member to the CC. 'The path to accession is one taken by individual countries, not groups of them' (Smith 2005b, 357). The faster and better a given country implements the EU rules, the quicker it becomes a member. In the previous enlargements, this generated strong competition among the candidate states. All the CEECs tried to close as many of the 31 negotiation chapters as quickly as possible, which resulted in a kind of 'regatta'.

Accession negotiations on the *acquis* do not comprise genuine negotiations. Newcomers simply have to comply with the EU system, 95 per cent of which is untouchable. In the past, and before accession, the *acquis* was defined without any contribution from the CC, which is why Wiener (2002, 14) speaks of the 'static and past-focused rationale' of the Union's enlargement policy. The reason why the EU was able to force the CEECs to the adoption of, and adaptation to the *acquis* lies in its superior power. As explained above, the Union did not need the Eastern enlargement as much as the CEECs wanted it. This 'asymmetrical interdependence' determined to a significant degree the relative bargaining power of the actors (Moravcsik and Vachudová 2003, 44). As the CEECs had more to gain from the EU than vice versa, the Union had superior bargaining power as a result of which it had at its disposal greater leverage to determine the conditions of the process. The CEECs, on the other hand, found themselves in a weak position, making them concede to EU requirements.

The effectiveness of accession conditionality depends not only on the strong desire of the candidate states to become EU members and the asymmetrical relationship inherent in the process, but also on the degree of clarity that exists about what is required. Research has pointed to the often contradictory and diffuse nature of EU conditionality (Hughes et al. 2004; Smith 2003). Membership criteria are not laid down in the Treaties and their interpretation and relative importance may differ over time (see below), depending on the Commission DGs involved.

Financial Assistance

Another tool applied by the EU to enforce and stimulate reform in the CEECs is financial and technical assistance. From the start of the enlargement process, Union aid to the CEECs was based on the fulfilment of political and economic criteria. Already in 1989, 24 OECD countries decided that financial aid would become an instrument of Western policy towards the CEECs. In the first place, support would be provided to Poland and Hungary. With reference to these initial beneficiaries of financial aid, the support resulted in the Phare programme. The coordination of this programme would lie in the European Commission's hands. Considering the amount of financial aid, it had great potential for influencing the CEECs (Smith 2004, 70ff.).

The programme's first aim was to support economic restructuring in the region, although the objectives were also political: the eventual aim was to support the establishment of liberal democracies, starting from the creation of market-based economies. To be eligible for Phare support, several civilian conditions had to be met: commitment to the rule of law, respect for human rights, the establishment of multi-party systems, the holding of free elections, and the implementation of economic liberalisation. This conditionality formed the basis on which financial support was provided, at least on paper.

Following the 1993 Copenhagen Council's invitation to the CEECs to apply for membership, Phare support was reoriented towards this aim, including greater support for infrastructure investment. Phare's total pre-accession focus was put in place in 1997, in response to the launch of the enlargement process by the Luxembourg Council. From then on, Phare funds focused entirely on pre-accession priorities and the implementation of the *acquis communautaire*.

Economic and social cohesion was promoted by measures similar to those supported in the Member States through the European Regional Development Fund and the European Social Fund. Phare helped to build capacity to ensure that the enterprises and infrastructure in the CEECs complied with Community standards, as well as to establish an appropriate institutional and regulatory context. Funds were intended to support democratisation efforts, too. In 1993, a Phare democratic programme was launched with the aim of helping to develop parliamentary practices, promote human and minority rights, establish an independent media, and encourage local democracy and education. However, funding for this programme was minimal compared to the financial help for economic development or implementation of the *acquis*. It also lost importance during the process. In a later phase (the accession negotiations, see below) the Phare programme was redirected to address two top priorities, being institution building and enhancing administrative capacity to comply with the *acquis*.

In 1999, two more funding instruments were created to take over some of the objectives of the Phare programme: Sapard (Support for Agriculture and Rural Development) and Ispa (Instrument for Structural Policies for Pre-Accession Assistance). The latter was oriented to infrastructure projects in the environmental and transport fields. This allowed Phare to focus on its key priorities that were not covered by these fields.

Besides the Phare programme and its successors, the EU also provided financial help in the form of massive loans from the European Investment Bank and the European Bank for Reconstruction and Development (EBRD). The latter was established in 1991 with the explicit purpose of financially supporting the CEECs in their transition to a market economy. Its primary aim was helping to create a stable private sector in the post-communist countries. EBRD's mandate stipulated that only those countries committed to democratic principles were eligible for loans.

Enlargement as a Civilian Power Policy *Par Excellence*?

Looking at what has happened in the CEECs since the fall of the Berlin Wall, it must be acknowledged that important changes have occurred. After the collapse of the communist regimes, the countries became market economies. They moved towards liberal democracies, and debates on their future policy included issues of human rights, minorities, gender equality, social and environmental protection, anti-corruption measures, and so on. During the 1990s, the EU played a prominent part in the region. As we have seen, the EU was a role model and a force of attraction for most CEECs. By offering conditional financial assistance and, in particular, by holding out the membership carrot, the EU's impact has grown substantially. The offers were subject to tough conditions, some of them reflecting objectives which could obviously be described as civilian.

In this part of our contribution a cautious assessment is made as to whether these civilian objectives also resulted in civilian results, and to what degree effects in the CEE can be attributed to the EU. As the Union's influence ran parallel with other factors, it is difficult to assess its precise impact. First, the international context in the 1990s and the importance of the domestic context on the democratisation process in the region are analysed. Then we give attention to the unintended consequences of the Europeanisation of the CEECs. Finally, some illustrations, based on the Polish experience, will be developed further.

The International Context: A Window of Opportunity

The situation in the former communist countries in CEE in the early 1990s was influenced by rapid changes on the international scene. This makes it difficult to define the precise impact made by the EU. Especially in a context of transformation – as was the context in the CEECs – it is a 'tricky game to determine which force is at work' (Lippert et al. 2001, 985). Many international organisations, from the North Atlantic Treaty Organisation (NATO) through to the Organisation for Economic Cooperation and Development (OECD) and the International Monetary Fund (IMF), intervened during the transformation period, especially as regards promoting market-oriented reforms, but also for endorsing good governance and disseminating democratic standards.

These Western international actors had great potential for influencing the CEE's transition processes. With the collapse of communism, the Western liberal and democratic order appeared to be the sole winner of the ideological battle between capitalism and communism. As it stood for the 'the only internationally recognised principles of legitimate statehood and state conduct in Europe' (Schimmelfennig 2000, 123) the CEECs were very open to influence and pressure from the Western international community. As Grabbe (2001, 1014) argues, the Eastern accession countries were in the process of throwing off communist-era legislative frameworks and creating new ones for a liberal, market-based democracy. This process has made them more receptive to regulatory paradigms from the West. An argument underlining this thesis lies in the institutional lacunae the CEECs inherited from the communist period. In some policy areas, such as competition, migration, asylum, and the protection of minorities, the CEECs had to start from scratch, which made them susceptible to Western models. Although it remains difficult to discern the EU's influence over other external influencing agents, there is no doubt that the Union became the most influential actor in the CEE during the 1990s. While CEE policy-makers were seeking new models to implement, these were offered by the EU and put forward as membership conditions. In this regard, transition reforms went hand in hand with the process of Europeanisation, which explains why the EU had much more influence in the Central European candidate countries than it had in previous accession processes.

The National Context

Nevertheless, the EU's influence should not be overstated, as the domestic situation in the different CEECs must be taken into account too. Vachudová (2001, 15–16) distinguishes between the two kinds of countries which emerged in CEE after 1989: those supporting liberal democracy, and those choosing a more nationalistic path. In those countries striving for liberal democracy, former dissidents took over power following the collapse of communism. They made 'returning to Europe' the principal aim of their country's foreign policy. The domestic incentives for joining the EU were extremely high, and support for the European values of liberal democracy legitimised the power of the leading politicians. Society in these countries was strongly oriented towards the liberal West, and extreme nationalists and communists were sidelined. Classic examples of such countries are the Czech Republic, Poland, Hungary, Slovenia and the Baltic states. Immediately after the fall of communist power, these states decided to become liberal democracies, independently of the EU. At a later stage, the prospect of Union membership created an additional motivation to reform. It helped them to speed up the process. Thus it might be suggested that in the absence of any interference by the EU, these countries would have found their own way to liberal democracy. Some have claimed that the Union's influence on making this choice was close to zero (Schimmelfennig 2000, 111), without denying the influence it has exerted on the way democratisation took place in these countries.

Other countries in the region, however, chose to walk a different path. In these countries, power was seized by nationalists who were usually unreformed communists. The new class of politicians based their power on communist ideologies and/or programmes of ethnic nationalism. They won power in democratic elections by playing on the fear of economic reform and the mistrust of ethnic minorities (Vachudová 2001, 16). In these countries, the political leaders considered the costs of adapting to the EC's liberal norms too high. More than likely, adopting democratic norms would bring an end to their political power.

It is often suggested that the EU had a positive influence on the democratisation process even in these countries. By providing membership prospects as a convincing electoral platform for the more moderate parties (Vachudová 2001, 25) and by supporting the existing opposition groups, the Union tried to remove the nationalist and communist politicians from power. Classic examples of countries where this policy was successful include Slovakia, Romania and Bulgaria. However, it must be acknowledged that it is equally important to have a clear and united opposition to the government. Moreover, if the government is capable of continually suppressing the opposition groups, there is very little the Union can do to democratise these countries. Without the presence of moderate parties and a strong opposition to the authoritarian government, EU influence might remain rather limited.

The Reality of Conditionality

From democratic to acquis conditionality   Once the CEECs turned to the EU and the latter offered financial assistance and, ultimately, full membership, we have seen that conditionality was a major instrument in further influencing the reforms. The Commission was engaged in monitoring the implementation of the conditions and intervened in the enlargement process by publishing its annual progress reports for each CC.

However, as regards the political conditionality, there was no clear and conceptual framework for the democratic requirements. Issues – such as independence of the judiciaries, pluralism of the media, the involvement of regional and local government or civil society – were raised on a rather ad hoc basis and it was often unclear to the accession governments what had to be implemented in order to meet the political standards.

In this context, a distinction can be made between the phase prior to the negotiations (until 1997 or 1999, depending on the country) and the actual negotiations (Pridham 2002, 958; Schimmelfennig and Sedelmeier 2004, 669–71). During the first phase, it was important to meet the political criteria: negotiations would only start if political reforms were implemented to a substantial degree. Schimmelfennig and Sedelmeier (2004, 671ff.) speak of the period of democratic conditionality preceding the period of *acquis* conditionality, which started with the accession negotiations. By moving on to the phase of *acquis* negotiations, differences can be noted with respect to political conditionality. First, once negotiations start, the priorities of the CCs change, whereby the balance shifts from democratisation to administrative and bureaucratic considerations. The CCs' governments now focus their attention on taking over the *acquis communautaire*, which is described in more than 30 rather technical and juridical chapters. As Geoffrey Pridham (2005, 110) argues, 'high-political perspectives as evident at times in the first period become subordinated ... to micro-political and administrative concerns'.

Secondly, the political conditionality is less directly linked to accession prospects now that the EU has decided to start membership negotiations. It is still covered by the Commission Progress Reports, but development of the political conditions is to a lesser extent related to an immediate and drastic decision on their membership perspective – as was the decision to start negotiations. After all, breaking off membership negotiations with a CC is a complicated procedure for the EU and one that has never been enforced. EU focus in the actual negotiations is on implementation of the *acquis*, even if this requires reforms in the opposite direction compared to the conditions that were formulated prior to the start of these negotiations. The devolution process in Poland (see below) illustrates this case. The decentralisation of the Polish state was stimulated in a first phase but, due to ambivalent recommendations, it was relegated to the back-burner, especially once the actual accession negotiations had begun.

Unexpected consequences for democracy   The political conditionality received less attention as time went by. But there is more: the accession process tended to produce unexpected consequences. The Europeanisation (for a definition, see Börzel and Risse 2003, 60) of the CEECs has mainly consisted of downloading European policy into the national policies, polity and politics. Having received the invitation to start entry negotiations, the Central and Eastern European CCs faced the huge task of accommodating the 80,000 pages of the *acquis communautaire*. This created immense pressure on and a work overload for the acceding governments. In order to maintain the dynamic of integration, the job had to be finished at relatively high speed and the number of actors involved was limited. In practice, the whole negotiating process was handled by the executive, at the expense of the national legislatives. The regulations were implemented under great pressure with insufficient time or effort to consult where necessary. Local and regional governments were sidelined (see below), as were civil society organisations. In this way, according to some scholars (Korkut 2002; Hughes et al. 2004; Lewis 2004, 162) integration into the EU even counteracted democratisation of the CEE accession countries.

By focusing on *acquis* conditionality, the legislative power was weakened to the benefit of the executive structures (Grabbe 2001, 1017). Particularly in the first years of negotiations, the process was an elite and executive-driven undertaking, which often widened the gap between the state and citizenry. The Polish case illustrates this unintended effect of accession to the EU. It demonstrates how centres of technocratic excellence weakened the legislative structures during the accession process (see below).

These effects on the polity of the CEECs entailed unforeseen consequences for the politics and party system in the CEE. During the negotiations, the European Commission favoured and underlined more than once in its reports the need for an inter-party consensus on accession. The compelled implementation of the *acquis* and the need for consensus hindered any genuine debate and undermined the basic function of the political parties. Parliamentarians were reduced to puppets who had to pass the necessary bills and legislation at breakneck speed in order to fulfil the EU criteria (Grabbe 2001, 1016). This left little room for them to create a distinct profile. As most centre parties in the CEECs were united behind the goal of accession and had little opportunity for party competition, they tended to develop catch-all-strategies (Grzymała-Busse and Innes 2003). Thereby, a vacuum was left from which extreme rightist or leftist parties of a populist nature, in particular, could benefit by adopting an anti-EU position. These parties were less constrained, tapped the sceptical views among the population and quickly gained support in some of the CEECs. Depending on the domestic political situation in the different CEECs, these tendencies had the potential to shake up the party system and make it even more unpredictable than before, as was the case in Poland (see below).

The Polish Case

This case illustrates the three above-mentioned tendencies. The unforeseen Europeanisation in the polity and politics stem from both domestic Polish as well as 'external' European factors. As regards the latter, the Commission's advice was not always consistent. This was especially true in Poland's devolution procedure. Immediately after 1989, the Polish government began with – albeit minimal – reforms to decentralise the country in order to empower sub-national levels and inverse the communist centralised past. In the first phase, the EU supported the decentralisation movement and asked for greater involvement by local and regional governments in policy formulation, thereby using such tools as the Phare programme (see above). Later, faced with the Polish regions' insufficient administrative capacities, the Union reversed this process (Hughes et al. 2004). The correct implementation of the regional *acquis* and the efficient distribution of the pre-accession and post-accession funds urged the EU to slow down and ultimately inverse the devolution process, which had already evolved substantially. Due to the U-turn by Commission officials, the accession ultimately led to a re-centralisation of the Polish state structures. In this regard, Hughes et al. (2002, 337) speak of a 'regional deficit'. This result demonstrates how *acquis* conditionality (of the second phase) can come at the cost of democratic conditionality (of the first phase), and contradicts the regionalisation model the Union is committed to stimulate.

Another tendency reversed by EU accession is the development in Poland towards a strong parliamentary and participative democracy. In order to wipe out the communist past, in the early 1990s the new Polish democratic republic introduced very powerful parliamentary structures. These have played a significant role in defining the transition policies, as the post-communist executive was weak at that time (Olson 1997). During accession negotiations, the Commission preferred to deal with one central Polish coordination unit for EU policy, as this would make the highly technical process easier to manage. That is why the accession negotiations became 'the hour of the executive' (Lippert et al. 2001, 994–5).

Due to time pressure, work overload and the highly technical nature of *acquis* implementation, the EU accession process led to a strengthening of the

Polish executive to the disadvantage of the legislative and the emergence of a 'core executive' (Zubek 2001). Although the administration in general remained largely incompetent during the negotiations, centres of technocratic excellence and professionalism did emerge in the administrations of the main executive departments, which Goetz and Wollmann (2001, 882) call 'islands of excellence'. These islands had (and still have) an almost absolute monopoly on coordinating and defining Polish EU policy, thereby outstripping the Polish parliament. In this respect, Lippert et al. (2001, 1004) speak of the 'technocratisation of governance' which happens at the expense of political actors who are accountable to the electorate. In the rush for EU membership, the link with civil society was also often lacking (Korkut 2002).

As the Polish parliament was sidelined in the accession process, political parties started to revolt against the prospect of EU membership, which resulted in growing party-based and popular Euro-scepticism. This happened more easily in Poland than in other CEEC countries, as the communist legacy had left the country with a very weak party system, high levels of party fragmentation, fluidity and volatility among the voters, and a lack of firm party structures. The vulnerability of the system, with its subsequent party splits and mergers, was the ideal breeding ground for new anti-EU populist parties. Basically, these parties gained support in three sectors of society. First, they could easily convince the quarter of the population who are farmers or live in the countryside, because they feared competition with Union farmers. Second, the conservative nationalistic Roman-Catholic segment, accounting for almost another fifth of the population, was also conducive to Euro-scepticism. They feared a loss of national sovereignty and culture. A third segment, susceptible to a populist anti-EU vote, not only in Poland but also throughout the whole CEE region, was to be found in the group of transition losers. Because of what Pridham (2001, 55) calls an 'exaggerated policy inter-linkage', EU accession became synonymous with and responsible for all the socially painful reforms of the previous decade, at least in the public's perception.

The breeding ground for catch-all parties, for growing popular Euro-scepticism, for the emergence of populist anti-EU parties in parliament, and for the destabilisation of the government as a result, was already present in Poland during the transition period which was characterised by weak party structures and a reform imperative excluding any debate. But, undeniably, the accession process strengthened these tendencies. Rather than leading to greater consolidation of the political scene, it had the unintended effect of shaking it. So, it was not that surprising that three anti-European Polish populist and nationalist parties came to power after accession (parliamentary elections of autumn 2005).

Conclusion: The Paradox of Accession

By offering the prospect of membership, the EU disposes of power vis-à-vis the CCs. In the case of Eastern enlargement, the relationship was rather asymmetrical: from a rationalist point of view, the candidate states had much more to gain from enlargement than the incumbent Member States. The latter used their leverage to impose substantial reforms. These reforms were of an economic nature (market-oriented), although in social constructivist literature it has been stressed that the decision to enlarge the Union was also based on identity and ideas. Countries adhering to democratic norms and values, thus sharing the foundations on which the EU has been built, have a legitimate right to join the Union. From this perspective, enlargement has even been perceived as a moral duty.

In any case, the membership criteria, as defined in Copenhagen in 1993, included political requirements that could be interpreted as civilian goals. In the following years, criteria regarding substantive democracy were raised, such as the protection of human rights, good governance, independence of the judiciaries, gender equality, pluralism of the media, the importance of regional and local government or civil society involvement, and so on. Some of the EU demands even went beyond Union competences *strictu sensu*, which resulted in a feeling of double standards in the CEECs. This was the case, for example, with issues related to minority rights.

Serving as a role model, and by making financial assistance and the ultimate prospect of membership conditional on substantial reforms within the candidate states, the Union seemed to prove its 'transformative power'. By offering the carrot, rather than using the stick, the EU made use of the tools that are associated with a civilian power. The CEECs have indeed undergone a serious process of democratic transformation in just over a decade. However, the fact that, following the collapse of communism, several transformation processes were taking place in this region makes it difficult to strictly define the role played by the EU. We have seen that the domestic situation cannot be underestimated.

More important in this contribution, however, is the conclusion that, as time passed, there was a shift in EU policy from democratic conditionality to *acquis* conditionality. The start of the actual negotiations was a turning point and democratisation issues were relegated to the background. In addition, the EU accession process did not necessarily lead to better governance, more democracy, more involvement and the decentralisation or stabilisation of the party system. The interaction of domestic factors and deficiencies in the EU's conditionality produced unintended consequences, inversing some of the initial democratic requirements.

These unintended effects on the polity and the politics of the CCs go back to the paradox of accession. On the one hand, the EU has tried to promote a model of multi-level governance providing incentives to empower the legislative, the regions and civil society. On the other hand, the accession procedure – based on bilateralism, differentiation, asymmetry and conditionality – left little space for development towards a participative democratic model. The dilemma between quantity and quality, between centralisation/co-ordination and participation/deliberation, was nearly always settled to the disadvantage of the latter, due to considerations of work overload, time pressure and efficiency. *Acquis* conditionality came at the expense of democratic conditionality or, put in another way, the phase of accession negotiations tended to reverse some of the accomplishments of the first phase of democratic conditionality.

The paradox/discrepancy between democratic and *acquis* conditionality, or between civilian goals and results, raises the question whether the accession procedure, as developed by the EU, answered the main challenges of transition in the post-communist states. Are both processes (transition/democratisation and EU accession) compatible? According to Heather Grabbe (2002, 253) there are sufficient reasons for doubt. The EU models and regulations are developed to fit the advanced west European Member States. The *acquis*, as presented to the CEECs, is based solely on west European experiences and traditions which the CEECs do not share. The *acquis* solutions, often suboptimal and inconsistent in character for the old Member States – being the result of a compromise – definitely did not fit the CEECs. They required complex institutional structures for implementation, lacking in these countries. Neither did they answer the primary needs of the countries in transition.

That is why a European 'development agency' role may be preferable to the 'regulatory agency' role the EU took on during the accession process. As explained by McGowan and Wallace, the requirement that new Member States align themselves with the Union's regulatory model implied a belief that they could 'leapfrog the experience of west European countries', including the history of market interventionism and protection that had characterised the post-war period of economic modernisation in western Europe. In particular, the Union insisted on the implementation of the core *acquis* of the single market, namely regulations which allowed products to move freely, and competition rules (cf. Chapter 8), whereas the adoption of high social and environmental process standards was delayed. The accession process has prevented the CEECs from benefiting from a type of 'East Asian experimentation', involving a more interventionist and developmental state (McGowan and Wallace 1996, 571–2).

It is too early to make a final assessment of the Eastern enlargement process and to determine to what extent the EU has influenced their democratic consolidation. Indeed, the third stage in the process, namely actual membership, has only recently started, either in 2004 or 2007. The indirect effects of 'outsiders' becoming 'insiders', introducing a process of socialisation and an intensification of networking, remains to be seen. Although, generally speaking, the democratic balance might be considered as a positive one, we must be cautious not to overestimate the EU's success. This analysis of the enlargement policy towards the CEECs has demonstrated that 'the more' does not simply mean 'the merrier'.

References

Baldwin, R., Francois, J. and Portes, R. (1997), 'The Costs and Benefits of Eastern Enlargement', *Economic Policy* 12:24, 125–76.

Börzel, T. and Risse, T. (2003), 'Conceptualizing the Domestic Impact of Europe', in K. Featherstone and C. Radaelli (eds), *The Politics of Europeanization* (Oxford: Oxford University Press).

Bretherton, C. and Vogler, J. (2006a), 'Candidates and Neighbours. The Union as a Regional actor', in C. Bretherton and J. Vogler (eds), *The EU as a Global Actor* (London: Routledge).

Cremona, M. (ed.) (2003), *The Enlargement of the EU* (New York: Oxford University Press).

Dimitrova, A. (2002), 'Enlargement, Institution-building and the EU's Administrative Capacity Requirement', *West European Politics* 25:4, 171–90.

European Council (1993), *Conclusions of the Presidency*, Copenhagen, 21–22 June.

Featherstone, K. and Radaelli, C. (eds) (2003), *The Politics of Europeanization* (Oxford: Oxford University Press).

Fierke, K. and Wiener, A. (1999), 'Constructing Institutional Interests: EU and NATO Enlargement', *Journal of European Public Policy* 6:5, 721–42.

Friis, L. and Murphy, A. (1999), 'The EU and Central and Eastern Europe: Governance and Boundaries', *Journal of Common Market Studies* 37:2, 211–32.

Goetz, K. and Wollmann, H. (2001), 'Governmentalizing Central Executives in Post-Communist Europe: A Four-Country Comparison', *Journal of European Public Policy* 8:6, 864–87.

Grabbe, H. (2001), 'How does Europeanization Affect CEE Governance? Conditionality, Diffusion and Diversity', *Journal of European Public Policy* 8:6, 1013–31.

—— (2002), 'EU Conditionality and the *Acquis Communautaire*', *International Political Science Review* 23:3, 249–68.

—— (2006), *The EU's Transformative Power. Europeanization through Conditionality in CEE* (Basingstoke: Palgrave Macmillan).

Grzymała-Busse, A. and Innes, A. (2003), 'Great Expectations: The EU and Domestic Political Competition in East Central Europe', *East European Politics and Societies* 17:1, 64–73.

Hughes, J., Sasse, G. and Gordon, C. (2002), 'Saying "Maybe" to the "Return To Europe". Elites and the Political Space for Euro-scepticism in CEE', *European Union Politics* 3:3, 327–55.

—— (2004), 'Conditionality and Compliance in the EU's Eastward Enlargement: Regional Policy and the Reform of Sub-national Government', *Journal of Common Market Studies* 42:3, 523–51.

Jora, S. (2006), 'International Organizations and Democratization Models: The Case of EU Accession of Romania', *CDAMS Discussion Paper* 06/10E.

Korkut, U. (2002), 'The EU and the Accession Process in Hungary, Poland and Romania: Is There a Place for Social Dialogue?', *Perspectives on European Politics and Society* 3:2, 297–324.

Lewis, P. (2004), 'Democracy in Post-Communist Europe, Fifteen Years On: A Concluding Note', *Journal of Communist Studies and Transition Politics* 20:1, 162–5.

—— (2005), 'EU Enlargement and Party Systems in Central Europe', *Journal of Communist Studies and Transition Politics* 21:2, 171–99.

Lippert, B., Umbach, G. and Wessels, W. (2001), 'Europeanization of CEE Executives: EU Membership Negotiations as a Shaping Power', *Journal of European Public Policy* 8:6, 980–1012.

McGowan, F. and Wallace, H. (1996), 'Towards a European Regulatory State', *Journal of European Public Policy* 3:4, 560–76.

Moravcsik, A. (1998), *The Choice for Europe: Social Purpose and State Power from Messina to Maastricht* (Ithaca, NY: Cornell University Press).

—— and Vachudová, M. (2003), 'National Interests, State Power, and EU Enlargement', *East European Politics and Societies* 17:1, 42–57.

Olson, D. (1997), 'Paradoxes of Institutional Development: The New Democratic Parliaments of Central Europe', *International Political Science Review* 18:4, 401–16.

Phinnemore, D. (2004), '"And not Forgetting the Rest ...". EU (25) and the Changing Dynamics of EU Enlargement', Paper for the Second Pan-European Conference, ECPR Standing Group on EU Politics, Bologna, 24–26 June.

Pridham, G. (2001), 'EU Accession and Domestic Politics: Policy Consensus and Interactive Dynamics in Central and Eastern Europe', *Perspectives on European Politics and Society* 1:1, 49–74.

—— (2002), 'EU Enlargement and Consolidating Democracy in Post-Communist States – Formality and Reality', *Journal of Common Market Studies* 40:3, 953–73.

—— (2005), *Designing Democracy: EU Enlargement and Regime Change in Post-Communist Europe* (Basingstoke: Palgrave Macmillan).

—— (2006), 'EU Accession Dynamics and Democratisation in Central and Eastern Europe: Past and Future Perspectives', *Government and Opposition* 41:3, 373–400.

Rupnik, J. (2000), 'Eastern Europe: The International Context', *Journal of Democracy* 11:2, 115–29.

Schimmelfennig, F. (2000), 'International Socialization in the New Europe: Rational Action in an Institutional Environment', *European Journal of International Relations* 6:1, 109–39.

—— (2001), 'The Community Trap: Liberal Norms, Rhetorical Action, and the Eastern Enlargement of the EU', *International Organization* 55:1, 47–80.

—— (2004), 'Governance by Conditionality: EU Rule Transfer to the Candidate Countries of Central and Eastern Europe', *Journal of European Public Policy* 11:4, 661–79.

Schimmelfennig, F., Engert, S. and Knobel, H. (2003), 'Costs, Commitment, and Compliance: The Impact of EU Democratic Conditionality on Latvia, Slovakia, and Turkey', *Journal of Common Market Studies* 41:3, 495–517.

Schimmelfennig, F. and Sedelmeier, U. (2002), 'Theorizing EU Enlargement: Research Focus, Hypotheses, and the State of Research', *Journal of European Public Policy* 9:4, 500–28.

Sedelmeier, U. (2000), 'Eastern Enlargement: Risk, Rationality, and Role-Compliance', in M. Green Cowles and M. Smith (eds), *Risk, Reforms, Resistance, and Revival: The State of the EU* (Oxford: Oxford University Press).

Sjursen, H. (2002), 'Why Expand? The Question of Legitimacy and Justification in the EU's Enlargement Policy', *Journal of Common Market Studies* 40:3, 491–513.

Smith, K. (2003), 'The Evolution and Application of EU Membership conditionality', in M. Cremona (ed.), *The Enlargement of the EU* (New York: Oxford University Press).

—— (2004), *The Making of EU Foreign Policy: The Case of Eastern Europe* (Basingstoke: Palgrave Macmillan).

—— (2005a), 'Enlargement and European Order', in C. Hill and M. Smith (eds), *International Relations and the EU* (Oxford: Oxford University Press).

—— (2005b), 'The EU and Central and Eastern Europe: The Absence of Interregionalism', *European Integration* 27:3, 347–64.

Torreblanca, J. (2001), *The Reuniting of Europe: Promises, Negotiations and Compromises* (Aldershot: Ashgate).

Vachudová, M. (2001), 'The Leverage of International Institutions on Democratizing States: Eastern Europe and the EU', *EUI Working Papers* 33.

Wiener, A. (2002), 'Finality vs. Enlargement: Constitutive Practices and Opposing Rationales in the Reconstruction of Europe', *Jean Monnet Working Paper* 8/02.

—— and Wobbe, T. (2002), 'Norm Resonance in Global Governance: Contested Norms in the Process of EU enlargement', paper for the Annual Meeting of the ISA, New Orleans, 24–27 March.

Zubek, R. (2001), 'A Core in Check: The Transformation of the Polish Core Executive', *Journal of European Public Policy* 8:6, 911–32.

Index